# The
# Adult
# Learner
## at Work

First published by Allen & Unwin in 2002
First published in May 2002

Allen & Unwin
83 Alexander Street,
Crows Nest NSW 2065 Australia
Phone:   (61 2) 8425 0100
Fax:      (61 2) 9906 2218
E-mail:   info@allenandunwin.com
Web:     www.allenandunwin.com

National Library of Australia
Cataloguing-in-Publication entry:

Burns, Robert, 1958
The adult learner at work: the challenges of lifelong education in the new millenium.

2nd ed.
Bibliography.
Includes index.

ISBN 1 86508 989 3

1. Adult learning. 2. Educational psychology. 3. Employees—
Training of. 4. Learning, Psychology of. I. Title.

331.2592

Publisher: Tim Edwards
Copy Editor: Megan Maniscalco
Text design: Peta Nugent
Printed by McPherson's Printing Group

10 9 8 7 6 5 4 3 2 1

# The Adult Learner at Work

The challenges of lifelong education
in the new millennium

**2nd Edition**

## Robert Burns

ALLEN&UNWIN

# table of contents

# chapter 9: implications for teaching, training and the organisation ■ 306

# preface

> **Whether we will acquire the understanding and wisdom necessary to come to grips with the scientific revelations and progress of the twentieth century will be the most important challenge of the twenty-first century.**
> Karl Sagan

**This book is aimed at a wide audience** of managers, human resource practitioners, trainers and teachers in industry, commerce, government and TAFE. It should provide them with a greater understanding of the role of workplace training and lifelong education in the contemporary context of technological, economic and industrial change. It also provides broad coverage of the psychology of the adult learner and general strategies of teaching and instruction that are consistent with that psychological information. It is now six years since the first edition of this text was published. Since then there have been considerable changes in many areas with which the book was concerned. I am grateful to the publishers for giving me the opportunity to bring the text up to date.

Since the first edition of this text appeared in 1995, global competition, the use of interactive communication technologies and the application of technology in production, distribution and services have been on the increase, all of which is creating new challenges for employers, managers, employees, those seeking work and those wishing to improve existing skills, develop new ones and expand their knowledge for the twenty-first century. Success requires high-performance workplaces that allow employees to operate with greater autonomy and accountability. These new forms of organisation and management cannot succeed without additional investments in the skills of employees. The workplace of the twenty-first century will require better educated and better skilled people, capable of flexibly filling new jobs and roles to meet changing knowledge and skill requirements.

For those teaching in the post-compulsory years of vocational training and adult education or training in the workplace, one of the challenges of the changing world in which we live is to adapt to the emerging policies, practices and philosophy of this area of education. Lifelong learning, rather than training or education, is becoming the key organising concept. A greater range of settings are now acceptable sites for learning, whether for work or personal development and whether informal or formal — leading to debate about the purposes and forms of learning that should characterise adult learning and consequent policy initiatives that should flow from such deliberations.

While there is an obvious emphasis on the psycho-educational aspects of teaching adults in a lifelong education context, the text is not written solely for current and trainee TAFE educators and workplace trainers. It is also aimed at an audience of human resource and other departmental managers of enterprises great and small who really need to understand that the bottom line may well depend on how they respond to, encourage and deliver appropriate training and lifelong education. They should also understand that to do this well requires changes to the structures and internal organisation of their endeavours so that the folly of imposing training and education, however relevant and vital, on the unwilling is avoided and a recognisable degree of ownership and participation in what is offered is in the hands of employees.

While the economic, technical and structural changes impacting on all societies imperiously demand increasing technical and personal development by each employee — an imperative that is well recognised — real, valid, individual human development involves a commitment from the person too: willingness, interest and intrinsic motivation to seek skills and knowledge. Education and development can never be imposed from the top down with a given, already-decided content, determined by global concerns and 'political' considerations. Lifelong learning can flourish for the benefit of all elements of society only if the learner is also actively involved in deciding what, how and when to learn. The learning organisation concept may go some way to facilitating a partnership between management and employee in promoting lifelong learning that is not driven just by fear of unemployment or bankruptcy but by genuine participation that satisfies both organisational and human needs.

So to meet the challenge of new forms of employment, training and even living, new forms of collaboration between government, employers, unions, educators, communities and individuals must develop. Lifelong education involving all aspects of skills and adult education will be the basis of the twenty-first century economy and society. Many developing countries are moving forward rapidly along these lines. Australia, too, is now getting beyond the simplistic approach of behaviourist competency-based training (CBT) in terms of which skills training was solely in the interests of the economy — the situation that existed in the early 1990s when the first edition of this text was prepared. Australia is now moving ahead with the impetus of the Australian National Training Authority (ANTA) and Chris Robinson at the National Centre for Vocational Educational Research

(NCVER) towards a more holistic notion of lifelong learning that benefits not only the economy in a narrow sense but also the individual, enterprise and nation in the broadest sense. There may also be an audience of politicians who could benefit from an awareness of the issues, policies and psycho-educational bases involved in lifelong education as applied to adult workers and citizens, as they legislate for overarching blueprints and policies to shape the future not only for business but for all adults in the lifelong education era ahead.

Lifelong learning is not a fad or intellectual fashion but an observable and essential part of the world in which we live. It offers an attractive vision of sustainable prosperity, a knowledgeable citizenry and a civilized society in which access and equity no longer figure as constraints. Internationally, there has been a torrent of official reports promoting lifelong education, including three Green Papers in the UK, similar papers in Norway, Germany and Ireland, legislation in Spain, the USA and Japan, as well as a UNESCO world conference, a series of statements from the OECD and a White Paper from the European Commission. Lifelong education is therefore being taken very seriously and has overtaken the more limited approach subsumed under the various concepts of vocational education and training, adult education, community education and recurrent education.

Lifelong education has a range and universality that should be mirrored in diversity of provision: through formal and informal courses at institutions, the workplace, professional associations, adult education organisations, community organisations, etc. The proportion of adults engaging in learning that may or may not be related to their working lives is growing and will continue to grow. This provides a much broader perspective than mere vocational education, confined to specific career preparation and training. From now on one-off front-end education will never be sufficient in an internationally competitive, ever-changing business world.

This second edition therefore takes the story of adult learning further within the context of lifelong learning as this approach propels Australia into a new paradigm of education for employability, personal development and social equity, considering not only the more recent policy background but also the psychological and pedagogical features that underlie this shift. The second edition contains new and more critical material on andragogy, CBT and on the concept of lifelong education itself, as well as introducing new material on intellectual abilities, reconceptualising workplace training, and locating developments in Australia in a historical context of developments overseas. Overall, the text tries to present a picture of where Australia is going relative to trends in other major developed countries and to the relationships between lifelong education policy and the characteristics of adult learners.

Australia is on the verge of a promising but challenging new set of opportunities, which will come to fruition only if tied closely to lifelong education and training. Enabling as many as possible to acquire skills for the twenty-first century will ensure the economic, social and political health of the nation as a whole and of all communities, groups and individuals within it. The overriding theme is that education and learning, particularly in the post-compulsory years, are about inclusiveness, an imperative for improving lives and enhancing economic prosperity. In the long term, this will help reduce disadvantage, ignorance and exclusion among the diverse Australian society, leading to a better society for tomorrow.

Education in the workplace is not just about teaching specific job skills, it is concerned centrally with the evolution of an ethos in which staff self-development at all levels is encouraged and permitted to feed back into processes and practices and thus maximise the success of the organisation in a business sense. The focus is on learning new roles as much as on gaining new skills. Traditional skill learning is often too removed from the big-picture requirements of the world of work. Obviously, there is contact at the margins, but learning and work are not well coordinated. Formal education may provide little that is useful for developing human potential, while specific skill learning may have scant application in the outside world. This book presents a vision of workplaces as learning environments in the broadest sense and will open up the debate on how to achieve this, particularly at management level since the support, drive and understanding of managers are key elements in ensuring that learning environments flourish. The essential theme is that workplace training and lifelong education are vital to increasing Australia's competitiveness internationally and the personal and community sense of inclusiveness and life satisfaction.

*R. Burns*
*February 2002*

# about the author

**Dr Robert Burns, BA, MA, Med, PhD, FBpsS, CPsychol,** started out as a school teacher. This was followed by 28 years' experience in career counselling, training management and research. His special focus was on career education, counselling theory and practice, and psychological testing and evaluation.

Dr Burns has held academic positions in British, South African and Australian universities, including Curtin, Bradford and Cape Town Universities. At the last-mentioned, he established and ran a psychological clinic where educational psychologists and career counsellors were trained.

He has written many successful books in the areas of psychology, health education, career guidance and child development, and has written numerous journal articles. These previous books include Introduction to Research in Education, Psychology for Effective Managers, 10 Skills for Working with Stress, The Secrets of Finding and Keeping a Job and Making Meetings Happen.

Currently, Dr Burns works at the University of Brunei designing and implementing courses to train counselling and careers teachers and special education teachers.

As an educator, he has always been concerned with the development of people's potential. While this focus is usually on the years of childhood and adolescence, he believes more emphasis and resources should be applied to the working years to enable adults to derive job satisfaction and self-esteem and develop the necessary skills to cope with an indeterminate future in the workplace and in society in general.

# part one

# the context — national and international

**Part 1 of this book** examines the national and international context in which new approaches to workplace learning are being promoted. Teachers, trainers, human resource practitioners and managers all need to understand the changes that are taking place and why education, training and personal development for members of the workforce and the community at all levels must be integrated in a comprehensive strategy that directs the activities of the nation and individual enterprises towards lifelong education. A future learning society should be concerned not only with broadening its knowledge and innovation base but with improving access and equity, facilitating the resolution of problems a complex future will bring in the economic, social, environmental and political arenas.

# chapter 1

# the changing context of work

If you give a man a fish, he will have a single meal.
If you teach him to fish, he will eat all his life.
Kuan Tzu

It is important to remember that there is no one predetermined
future but a range of potential futures depending on which
purposeful decisions and actions we take. There is a past that
is gone forever but there is a future that is still ours to determine.
R. Burns 1991

As we enter the twenty-first century, the context in which individuals, organisations and the national productive endeavour are jointly engaged is changing at an
exponential and disruptive rate. Ellyard (2000) argues that we are midway through
a transition from a Cowboy Culture to a Spaceship Earth Culture or Planetism.
The journey involves moving from an individualistic, unsustainable consumption-
directed and confrontational world to one of interdependence, sustainable living
and equity, supported by innovative technologies. The changes might be global,
but they are creating greater divides between the 'haves' and the 'have nots'. The
gap between 'amazon.com' and the Amazon is growing. Even in industrialised
countries, there is a disturbing growth in inequality.

The Australian Bureau of Statistics (ABS) in its Survey of Household Expenditure
(2000a) on behalf of the Australian Council of Trade Unions (ACTU) reveals a sizeable body of 'working poor': two million people battling to survive. In the USA, the
ratio of CEO pay to that of the average company worker rose from 42:1 in 1980 to
419:1 in 1998 (Evans, 2000). Recent census data from Singapore (*Straights Times*,
10 Feb. 2001), a very wealthy country using the intellectual capital of as many citizens as possible, reveals that the gap between rich and poor has widened, with the
monthly income of the latter actually declining by nearly $100 a month from 1999.

The upper 20 per cent income bracket earned 21 times more than the bottom 20 per cent, up from 17.9 times in 1999. The International Labour Office's (ILO) report World Employment 2001 emphasises a widening global digital divide, with an increasing number of workers unable to gain access to emerging technological resources to ensure productivity in an increasingly digitalised world. For example, the report notes that 90 per cent of all Internet users are in industrialised countries, whereas Africa and the Middle East contribute only one per cent. The speed of diffusion between wealthy and poor countries is increasing. Unless this is addressed as a matter of urgency, human and national aspirations, whether in occupational, social, educational or moral terms, cannot be realised.

Ensuring access to technologies and ensuring that employees possess the constantly emerging specific and personal portable skills to use them are fundamental policy areas that all countries need to consider. There is a bewildering mix of uncertainty, risk, insecurity, division and massive opportunity in all of this. Even in OECD countries, the challenge is to try to remove the digital divide, along with the growing insecurity it brings, and enhance the wellbeing that emanates from new ways of working and living out one's life. The most successful countries will be those that can balance market pressures of adaptation and dynamism with social concerns of equity, access, security and involvement. This means broadening access to post-school education and introducing a general entitlement to lifelong learning similar to the entitlement established in the past to retirement pensions. This chapter will consider in brief the context of change and the specialised and general skills needed by individuals and enterprises that promote lifelong learning during the adult years to satisfy the economic and social imperative to create learning societies, cultures and organisations — themes taken up again in Chapters 2 and 3. In the areas of education, training and work, the changes governments, organisations and individuals must respond to can be grouped in categories, including globalisation, technological, economic and structural change and job/career redefinition.


## ■■■ GLOBALISATION

Globalisation is changing the way enterprises are managed and work is performed. The focus on productivity, quality, efficiency and competitiveness, derived from innovation, skills and quality improvement, has made the quality of the workforce — and consequently training — critical components of competitiveness. Australia is facing increased pressure to be responsive and competitive in a global market. New enlarged markets like the EU, ASEAN and APEC provide considerable competition, while the removal of protective tariffs opens up local industry to imports from lower-cost emerging economies. In Australia this has been devastating for the textile, footwear and clothing industries.

It is clear that many futurists, such as Toffler (1980) and Ellyard (2000), see us moving into the twenty-first century as a post-industrial society. What we are experiencing is a world-wide transformation in production and processing methods, a move from heavy industry to professional services and a move from local economies to massive regional and world economies controlled by multinationals and non-elected bodies like the WTO (Greider, 1997). (Of the top 100 economies 51 are corporations.) Whether or not this should be the case and how we as a society should cope with these issues and transformations is for debate elsewhere. However, what is apparent already is that the impact of the technological future combined with a global economy underpinned by an ill-balanced so-called free trade system has already changed the employment outlook for the generation at present in schools and colleges and for future generations, particularly in less developed countries beset by depredation of their natural non-renewable resources, unfair free trade, other environmental issues and deskilling. Many big brand corporations employ no factory workers at all, outsourcing their goods to create a corporate weightlessness, making nothing, but selling a brand that they morph into a lifestyle of logoed shirts, reverse caps and polychromatic rubber footwear.

An awareness is dawning that the global economy is a subsystem of the global ecosystem; growth is not gain but in reality decline, with the destruction of assets. Production and consumption can no longer be conceived as separate from the total environment — the source of the inputs and the waste heap for the outputs. The balance sheet of local, national and global economics must include the losses — those costs derived from air and water pollution, ozone depletion, wetland and forest destruction, clean-up costs, the consumption of non-renewable resources, etc. This makes future prosperity and developmental possibilities look less healthy. It should redirect thoughts about jobs in an unsustainable-development 'Cowboy Culture' context towards portable life skills that enable people to live at a reasonable level in self-renewing communities that permit both development and environmentally virtuous behaviour through human-scale activities.

The global economy is not so much global in operation but global in its ability to move freely to wherever it perceives a more profitable production base or market to be (Barnet & Cavanah, 1994). These socioeconomic and ultimately political issues raise questions about the style, content and aims of education and training provision in all parts of the world, but most pressingly in developing countries where many young people are destined to be mere window shoppers while the rest of us buy through e-commerce. The contrast between the 'haves' and 'have nots' will become more stark rather than diminishing in the contemporary global systems. Barnet and Cavanah (1994) and Greider (1997) all critically review the negative impact so-called globalisation is having on work availability and the ability of individuals, groups and nations to benefit from global economics and migratory multinationals.

Market reform in the region has created a new future for Australia. External trade barrier removal is opening up Australia to competition. Nonetheless, Australia's ability to compete in world markets is eroding. The prosperous Dreamtime of the lucky country has turned into a nightmare of harsh reality. The productivity growth of competitors outdistances our own. The capability of our economy to provide a high standard of living for all Australians is increasingly in doubt. As jobs requiring little skill are automated or go offshore, the demands for a highly skilled talented pool of employees grows and the backwater of unemployable rises. The dilemma that Australia faces is that without technology the country will not be competitive in world markets and unemployment will soar even higher. New technology does, however, help to maintain competitiveness and prevent countless others from joining the ranks of the jobless. Protection for manufactured goods has until recently prevented Australian manufacturers from being efficient and in so doing kept them incapable of selling abroad to offset the decline in the export of primary products. Removal of tariffs in a phased program from 1988 now forces Australian manufacturers to face international competition. In addition, in 1983 the exchange rate was floated and controls on foreign capital flows by Australian companies removed. All this has induced the Australian economy, historically inward looking apart from primary products, to become increasingly open and internationalised. The Government required organisations to stand on their own feet, become more self-reliant and efficient and perform at world best practice standards.

At the same time over the past decade, the pace of Asian development has moved up a few gears, stuttering somewhat in the late 1990s but picking up again, not only through the application of technological progress but with billions of potential customers in Asia, the old USSR, India and Latin America who have all joined the global market economy. The increased international mobility of capital is driving productive capacity to new low-cost industrial countries particularly in Asia. The opening up of trade with developing Asian nations has major implications for unemployment and real wage levels for unskilled employees in Australia's workforce. Large numbers of unskilled workers in Asia are concentrating on labour-intensive manufactured goods. The prices of these goods are therefore falling and this has implications for all old, industrial countries of an increasing emphasis on services instead of manufacturing.

Despite this downside, improvements in transport and communications and the reduction in protection will ensure that international trade will continue to grow. It will provide Australia with greater market opportunities for the agricultural, mining and manufacturing industries. The growing economies in South-East Asia will provide substantial market opportunities. Citizens of these economies will also travel more and will require services in Australia, such as accommodation, recreation, restaurant and retail. These areas will experience very strong employment growth.

While the provision of services has always been important, this sector took off in the 1980s and is a typical phenomenon throughout the world as GDP per capita increases. Developments in developing countries place formerly strong manufacturing countries under strain with regard to wages relative to production costs. This means the Western World must move over to selling expertise, being problem solvers and continually refining and developing products in order to stay ahead of the pack. There is a premium on intelligent manufacturing and provision of services, particularly value added services. Organisations in these circumstances must be flexible, innovative and possess quality management. The old approach that called for an unintelligent workforce mass-producing specialist items is past. The real hope to sustain income in the future is not just numeracy, literacy and technological skills, it is also 'operacy' — the ability to make things happen. A key strategy Australia could use to take advantage of globalism is improving and developing its workforce skills.

## ■■■ TECHNOLOGICAL CHANGE

Many terms have been used to denote the current technological revolution, many linked with the word 'age' such as 'computer age', 'robot age', 'microelectronic age' and 'knowledge age'. Other terms describe new versions of society such as 'information society' and 'post-industrial society'. We have other labels like 'the third wave', 'the global village' and 'Planetism'. But whatever the name we prefer, it signifies a major discontinuity with the past. No matter what label future generations give this period it will be remembered as an era of social, economic and industrial transformation that impacted on every aspect of life.

Change is an inevitable part of life and has been a feature of every era, impacting on social, economic and political life. The Agricultural and Industrial Revolutions — previous major changes in the way life was organised — both had massive effects on how and where people lived and how they earned their livelihood. The technology of steam gave way to the technology of electricity, which, in its turn, is gradually being replaced by newer technologies. Each innovation brought with it consequent changes to production methods, skill requirements, organisational structures and the social and economic infrastructure needed to support the change. The latest change, the Technological Revolution, with its microelectronics, communication super-highways, nano-technology and biotechnology is no different in its impact on the way work and life itself will need to be reorganised. The shift will bring new values, new pressures, new products, new services, new relationships, new ways of living out one's life, new sources of identity and esteem, new career structures, new demands for coping with change and new opportunities.

This kind of change is rapid, widespread and penetrating, influencing the structure and thinking of whole societies. People need to learn very different skills from those of previous ages – how to use different equipment, how to use different materials to make products that were unknown a decade before. Mankind is no longer the labour force, it is now the developer and controller of energising machines that are far more powerful, involved in increasingly complex situations in a game that is increasingly abstract. Words and symbols replace action and direct personal links. For example, money as a form of exchange now exists in the form of credit systems, plastic cards and electronic transfer, while purchases can be made in the virtual world in which knowledge is keystrokes away on the Internet and messages can be instantly relayed around the world. Computing power is doubling every 18 months, while the cost of computing power drops by 25 per cent each year. A modern Ford family car now has more computing power than the Apollo 11 that went to the moon. Technological development has redrawn the everyday routines of life and work.

A first step in understanding the impact of technology is to understand what is meant by the term. Often 'technology' is used to refer broadly to machines, but it is more than that. It also relates to systems and methods. It is really the way we organise ourselves in productive enterprises. A useful general definition is that technology is the means and processes through which we as a society produce the substance of our existence. This definition sees technology as a human process with human choices and decision making at its centre. It comprises tools, materials, energy forms, techniques and the organisation of work. The organisation of work is as significant as the tools and is concerned with how we are organised to produce the goods and services we need.

The only area where Marx got it right was in his understanding that there is a relationship between the means of production and the social structure of society. Means of production can for our purposes be read as technology. The factory was created to house and run machines with an employee structure to suit the way in which the machines were operated. The industrial revolution changed class structure, social life and power relations. The nineteenth-century technology of the assembly line restricted workers, and continues to do so for some today. Individual workers repeat the same task all day every day, locked into a position on a bench or shop floor, with complex operations split into many discrete steps. This type of work was closely monitored, supervised, timed and measured. The approach has often been termed 'scientific management', 'Taylorism' (after Frederick Taylor) or 'Fordism' (after Henry Ford). This approach to work organisation was the basis for mass production. This conveyor-belt approach, epitomised in the Charlie Chaplin film Modern Times, was amenable to the scientific management techniques of Taylorism. Specialisation lead to the dominance of experts and hierarchical bureaucracies and to the downplaying of the importance of the individual worker, who felt ineffective, powerless and unskilled. This sets the scene for us of large pyramidal industrial and public service organisations with centralised planning producing goods and services for the masses — the factory and the welfare state. This was the case in both capitalist and socialist economies.

In the same way, the technological revolution is effecting dynamic changes and rendering traditional concepts of industrial practices obsolete. Industrial democracy, team work, participation, performance indicators and competency are now the buzz words. Technology is a strongly value-laden force. It determines social relationships, often reducing them to the technical level, for example banking via an automatic teller, the layout of modern, computerised offices and chat rooms and telecommuting.

The danger is that the new microchip technology might reproduce the old Fordist strict division of labour. Many technologies are designed to be 'idiot-proof'. This is hardly a formula for technology as a liberating force. Much technology is designed with a bias that entrenches workers as mere components in the production process rather than increasing workers' knowledge, involvement and participation in the workplace.

The implications of technological change are often hard to predict and, therefore, plan for. A striking instance is how much the period between the development of an idea and its first commercial use has shrunk. Photography, for instance, was first developed in 1738 but not used commercially until 1850. With radio that period of time was reduced to 28 years, with television 12 years, nuclear fission six years, the integrated circuit three years and the microchip one year. Now instantaneous implementation is routine.

There is no doubt that technology has transformed jobs, skills and organisational structure, including the location of work and the way it is organised. There has been an explosion of knowledge that is requiring continuing education if one is to keep abreast of developments. The new technologies are opening up new delivery possibilities in education and training so that those in rural and even remote areas can get access to training. Technological change has brought with it both an expansion of and broader access to information that formerly was known only to the higher realms of management. This will necessitate a redirection of management philosophy towards more democratic and participative organisations, coupled with an acknowledgment of the vital importance of a workforce that has job satisfaction, that is encouraged to be responsible and involved and that uses initiative and self-direction.

Education will be also be freed from geographical boundaries as distance learning expands, particularly via Internet- and web-based courses. Skilled instructors or knowledge entrepreneurs will sell their knowledge to the highest bidder as they sell their courses to knowledge packagers and virtual universities. With education becoming a critical personal investment, adult learners will expect quality, availability and convenient delivery. Students will gain power by choice as they access courses from around the world. Technology shatters geographical educational boundaries and shifts power over educational content away from local policy makers.

There are, in fact, two technological revolutions that are impacting on the workplace. One is manufacturing through computer-integrated systems. This involves such elements as computer-aided design, automatic materials transfer and robotics. The other is new office technology. It includes not only the ubiquitous word processing but also electronic mail and a host of message storing, retrieval and transferral facilities. This has been referred to as the 'paperless office' — a misnomer in view of the amount of printed matter generated to maintain filing systems, especially in bureaucratic government departments. New office technology is revolutionising communication processes in offices and in and between organisations as a whole. Both revolutions have enormous implications for our lives.

## ■■■ ECONOMIC AND STRUCTURAL CHANGE

Advances in technology and structural changes in the economy have shifted the emphasis away from the mass market to services and consumer choice for segments of the population. Information technology enables 'just in time' ordering systems to meet specific market needs. Services can respond quickly to changing demand, products have a shorter life span and there is a premium on innovation and improved, customised design to capture volatile and fickle niche markets. Mass production lines and standardised products are no longer appropriate. Organisations contract out many aspects of peripheral activities. Like birds on the rhino's back, they can be shaken off if need be without damage to the rhino. Greater flexibility and innovation will be the organisational requirements of the future, with multiskilled workers dropping old tasks and taking up new ones as demands change. This implies continuous training and the development of lifelong learning mostly in the workplace or organised through the workplace.

There has also been a sophistication of demand for goods and services. Quality, service, flexibility and customisation are as important as price. These changes and their impact on Australia are fundamental and irrevocable. The market place has become the world and competition has intensified sharply. Unfortunately, Australia entered this new arena with what Garnaut (1991, p. 1) called a 'huge baggage of anti-productive work, and management practices, uncompetitive public enterprises and productivity restricting regulation'. So, in order to cope with these changed circumstances, organisations must alter their internal structures and organisation and ensure their employees are developing and using a wide range of job and personal skills in more sophisticated ways.

Clearly, in these conditions Australia's capacity to expand in the Asian and other markets depends first on its capacity to produce sophisticated high value added products and services using creative, flexible and innovative management and employees and second on labour market reform. Both these imply that for organisations and workforces to remain in business there must be a mutually supportive approach and willingness to develop skills at all levels that promote the characteristics of a successful organisation of the future. The danger is that decisions such as that recently of the Industrial Relations Court regarding broadening the entitlements of casual employees will impact on small employers who need flexibility and cause a drop in the employability of casuals.

Over the past two decades Australia has been making a classic progression through the traditional paradigms of wealth creation, beginning at primary production, moving on to manufacturing and finally into an era of services. This process has been accelerated by technological change. Two thirds of the civil workforce of Australia are already in the service sector and this figure will continue to grow. In the service sector people are both product and process and they are the key to adding value to a greater extent than in other industries. Human capital is the most important resource of the organisation as it is the only route by which access can be gained to the valuable commodities of knowledge, information and creativity.

The old paradigm was producer driven, emphasising raw physical resources and materials using mass production techniques that limited the need for the training of employees. The new paradigm is customer driven, relies on human capital and flexible technology, with workplaces organised to customise products and to capture the creativity of staff. Australia still has 65 per cent of its manufacturing workforce in low technology jobs. However, in the near future most jobs will require less memorising of facts, fewer physical skills and more conceptual ability.

However vital for the health of Australia's industrial and business sectors, such restructuring has its costs for staff managers and employees alike. They must be capable of learning new skills, returning to learning if necessary, be willing to adopt and operate within new work practices and, for some, learn to adapt to redundancy, relocation and temporary unemployment. For example, decentralisation and enterprise bargaining will put a premium on communication skills at all management levels.

The labour force move out of manufacturing does not mean manufacturing is in decline. In fact, we are manufacturing more rather than less owing to the application of new technology. The nexus between production and employment has been broken. Yet the skills and know-how of those left are of greater value than before and they are required to be more self-managing, multiskilled and flexible. As simple tasks can be done by machines the remaining work can increase in complexity, requiring a high degree of interdependence between levels and units of employees, with teams formed for specific purposes and then disbanded. These teams cut across established lines of authority. Hierarchies and power relations are no longer appropriate.

## ■■■ RAPID KNOWLEDGE OBSOLESCENCE

The exponential growth of knowledge and the rapid changes in science and technology are another global trend. Knowledge is doubling every seven to ten years. The resultant relatively rapid obsolescence of knowledge and skills has implications for HRD. *The Week-End Australian* contacted education experts in a range of fields to estimate the shelf-life of Australian undergraduate degrees (*The Week-End Australian*, May 11-12, 1996, p. 11). The shelf-life of the degrees was estimated as follows:

1 year for computer science
2 years for electrical engineering
3 years for accounting and general medical practice

4 years for business
5 years for civil engineering and biotechnology
6 years for dentistry and surgery
10 years for architecture.

All the education experts asked agreed that the undergraduate degree provided the essential 'intellectual capital' on which to build future learning. But the rapid rate at which new knowledge is accumulated and the fast pace of technological change create a need for regular knowledge updating and skills upgrading. More frequent job changes will become the norm. Schools and other education and training institutions will have to teach the ability to learn and inculcate an acceptance of lifelong education and training. Continuing education and training programs will have to be developed not only by education and training institutions but also by professional bodies and employers. Today's and tomorrow's workers must never stop learning: learning is not just for children and young adults — it is lifelong. Only lifelong learning can guarantee that individual Australians will be prepared for change. Lifelong education must be seen as an investment on the part of government, industry and individuals.

In fact, because of the growing redundancy of what most adults learnt earlier in life and the new knowledge and skills required now for the mere act of living, most people are, though they might not admit it, permanently learning. Much, of course, is done at home where a sort of inverse socialisation has taken place, with younger family members inducting older ones into such activities as using the Internet and other mysteries of modern existence. Many people buy books and videos that are educative in an effort to develop leisure activities and interests or go on working vacations to learning about archeology and the like, tagging nocturnal animals, etc. This informal learning is a silent explosion that signifies a tremendous amount of latent knowledge and skill in the community.

## ■■■ CHANGING ORGANISATIONAL STRUCTURES AND WORK PATTERNS

Technological changes, especially information technology and telecommunications, and competition in the fast-moving, competitive global marketplace have changed work organisations and working patterns. The production of goods and services has become flexible and customised instead of being mass produced in long production lines. Online quality control has replaced end-of-line checking. Instead of fragmentation of tasks, increasing use is made of teams and multiskilled workers. Decision making is being decentralised to points of production and sale. The organisational hierarchy is flatter, with management structures delayered (often middle management) and this, in turn, places greater emphasis on participatory models of management. The gap between those in positions of institutional leadership and those responsible for the production and delivery of products or services is narrowed. Table 1.1 provides a comparison of some old and new workplace characteristics.

TABLE 1.1 COMPARISON OF SOME OLD AND NEW WORKPLACE CHARACTERISTICS

| ELEMENT | OLD SYSTEM | NEW SYSTEM |
|---|---|---|
| Workplace organisation | Rigid, hierarchical, specialised | Flat, flexible, networked with cross-functional teams |
| Job design | Narrow, single job, standardised and repetitive | Broad, many jobs, multiple responsibilities |
| Skills | Specialised | Multiskilled |
| Management | Command and control | Self-management and team work |
| Communications | Top down, need to know | Diffused, big picture |
| Decision making | Chain of command | Decentralised |
| Direction | Standard and fixed | Procedures under constant revision as required |
| Autonomy | Low | High |
| Knowledge of organisation | Narrow | Broad |

As a result of these changes in working patterns, the role of workers has broadened, with a consequent need for a wider range of skills. Thus we find many workers are expected not only to perform their own jobs but also to understand a range of additional functions. The ABS (1998) has collected information on changes in work level by employee. The most commonly reported change was more responsibility (38%) and new or different or extra duties (36%). Only 5 per cent reported no change at all. This is to maximise the flexibility of the teams. Furthermore, employees must be largely self-supervising, working together in informal teams responsible for planning their work, controlling quality and devising new ways to improve work processes, reduce defects and shorten cycle time. In banking, for example, the role of a customer service person has been broadened beyond a series of repetitive tasks of approving cheques, answering routine questions and helping customers reconcile account balances. Included in their role can be making recommendations to customers on appropriate mixes of products and services offered by the bank (e.g. mutual funds and annuities). Employees now need a much broader complement of skills than was the case in the previous traditional slower-moving hierarchical organisation, with its clear chains of command and 'thinkers' at the top and 'doers' at the bottom.

Workforces themselves have become more distinct segments. One distinction common now is between core and peripheral workers, many of whom are casual, part-time, agency-leased or on contract. Distinctions are also drawn between high and low knowledge workers. Work arrangement options include differential performance incentives, self-managed work teams, telecommuting, flexi-time, compressed work weeks, outsourcing and subcontracting. On the supply side, there is the growth in female employment, reduced male full-time employment and the demographic changes leading to an ageing workforce. Where workforces were once organised for mass production, they are now organised for flexibility and innovation to satisfy the needs of the moment. All the changing workplace practices are aimed at a number of benefits, including:

- enhanced capacity to respond and adapt to change and uncertainty
- retention of key employees
- improved productivity
- access to specific skilled employees, when necessary.

As a result, most companies of the future are likely to be shamrock organisations. Shamrock organisations are characterised by the following three elements:

1. A small and essential core group of professionals, knowledge makers/users, technicians and managers.
2. A group of outsourced subcontractors who produce specialist goods and services so that the core group does not have to, for example IT, legal and accountancy experts.
3. A growing group of casual and part-time workers (contingent workers) who are hired to provide basic services or to help at peak workloads. What one might term 'just-in-time workers'. Placement companies are a large growth area as companies seek specific skills for contract work. Thus more and more people become self-employed and lose the economic and welfare benefits associated with full-time employment.

Companies in the industrialised countries are increasingly becoming shamrock organisations and shamrock organisations are emerging in developing Asian countries too. For example, the Singapore National Trade Unions Congress (NTUC,1996) in a study on employment structure and its impact on union membership has pointed out that the shamrock organisation has already taken shape in Singapore. Even government departments are heading that way in Australia, with, for example, the Department of Agriculture, Fisheries and Forestry being 'fined' $7 million of its 2000 annual budget for not outsourcing its IT network and corporate service functions, while the Quarantine Inspection Service has been pressured to outsource many of its functions or face budget cuts.

A chasm is opening up between permanently employed core employees who owe allegiance to the company and those on a variety of contract, part-time, contingency and agency-leased conditions who owe no allegiance. This can easily lead to a perception of second-class employment from which the employee benefits little; the risks are borne by the employee and the employer bears the minimal cost.

However, it could be viewed more generously as an emancipation of the employee to choose when and where to work, gain new experience and obtain flexibility in work schedules to permit a full out-of-work life. The definitions of employee, employer, workplace and workday are being reformulated in these conditions.

Even the workplace is morphing into a blend of traditional brick-and-mortar elements and cyberspace. Many workplaces are no longer a physical place but a bundle of services and settings that support workers no matter where or when they work. People, organisations, ideas and assets are interconnected with information and communication technologies that span geographical boundaries, creating a virtual workplace.

Virtual offices are emerging as companies are leveraging cyberspace and electronic technology to cut costs like rentals and to boost productivity. In virtual offices workers can stay out of the office but retain contact through high technology gadgets with handheld devices (palm and mobile phone developments) that can receive and send email and faxes. Telecommuting is one form of the virtual office in which workers work from home or just about anywhere outside the office. The virtual office will be mainstream rather than a small-scale operation or experiment within several years' time. The pace of work is going to be much more rapid and the virtual office door will never close.

As physical location is no longer critical, going to work becomes meaningless as work becomes what a person does rather than where a person goes. The 'same time same place' workplace is being replaced by the any time, anywhere work space. Houses are being wired for commerce as well as recreation. Managers/supervisors will have to manage without depending on 'face time' as an indicator of contribution. Performance goals will become more explicit and measurement more objective — results will count.

The development of virtual organisations has HRD implications. Virtual corporations need workers who are highly skilled, reliable, educated, able to understand the new forms of information, adaptable and able to work efficiently with others. Employees don't just need technical skills but also the skill of learning how to cope with the continuous and radical change of virtual businesses. New forms of training that are flexible, on-demand and interactive will have to be devised for the employees of virtual enterprises.

As a result of these technological and economic changes to the structure and processes of work some workers' jobs are disappearing, while, for others who are luckier, new job opportunities arise, although possibly accompanied by the trauma of retraining and/or relocation. Many managers and employees at all levels are finding that their tightly planned career paths are evaporating, job satisfaction is not necessarily guaranteed and that new roles in team leadership and participation in decision making are the preferred skills for the future rather than overt managerial ones. This sort of scenario can be threatening and bleak to many employees, whether at managerial or lower levels. All these changes necessitate new approaches to organising the workplace, with consequent implications for reskilling, educating and motivating all staff in the new procedures, processes and organisational structures. These changes also have impacts on social aspects of living and married life as full-time male employment decreases. As the *Business Review Weekly* bluntly reported (James, 1997, p. 68): 'Unskilled workers once added value to processed goods. Now technology has made the gap so wide that the unskilled are unwanted.'

In summary, changes in the nature and patterns of work are not easily captured in a few words but some striking trends are apparent in Australia as Waterhouse (1998) and Van den Heuvel and Wooden (1999) report, trends also noted in the USA report *Workforce 2000* and in the UK *Social Trends Report* (1992). The Australian trends are the following:

- Twenty-five per cent of all wage and salary earners are casual, this proportion having risen 11 per cent between 1984 and 1998. Outsourcing involves 10 per cent of workers and Australia has the second highest proportion in the OECD of workers in temporary employment.
- Permanent workers are twice as likely than casuals to have participated in in-house training and employer-supported external training.
- Casual workers are 50 per cent more likely to have undertaken self-funded training.

The 'standard employment' pattern of the past is no longer the norm and our education and training system needs to adjust to this and the different learning needs it engenders. According to Waterhouse (1998):

- The workforce has been feminised by a shifting differential pattern of employment for men and women. The universality of the full-time permanent job held by the male breadwinner is increasingly a thing of the past. The 40 hours a week for 40 years for males has joined the quill pen and pay slip in the waste bin of history.
- Unemployment has emerged as a significant factor, particularly with a critical mass of long-term unemployed and retrenched professionals.
- There are increasing numbers of workers employed under part-time, casual, periodic-contract, agency-leasing and self-employment/entrepreneurial arrangements. The full-time permanent job held by the male breadwinner is no longer the norm. Instead a fragmented labour market is evolving that is characterised by an uneven distribution of paid work in which the jobs of many people are part-time and precarious, while those in full-time jobs find themselves working longer hours.
- Employment has shifted across industries, with declining job numbers in manufacturing and increases in service industries. The traditional employment model of unionised male full-time employment in manufacturing enterprises is no longer true.
- Self-employment is growing and, increasingly, individuals are managing a 'portfolio' of jobs.

- The workforce is much less unionised.
- Knowledge has become a significant form of capital, leading to competitive advantage highlighting the significance of lifelong learning. There is an upskilling of many jobs so that employees with strong technical skills are the backbone of most organisations. Even jobs that traditionally were not computerised, such as couriers, dry-cleaning and car maintenance, now contain such components.
- There is rapid growth of temporary cross-functional, multidisciplinary teams, sometimes with globally and ethnically diverse membership. Such teams often have no traditional boss, with members taking on responsibility for planning, organising, etc. Members will be expected to function effectively in a new team from the start. Team building will be no more as time will not allow for it. You have to come off the bench and help the team gain yardage straight away.
- The end of the company man/woman person is in sight with the rise of the portfolio person. These are highly mobile persons who apply their skill and intellectual capital to different projects. They look for a customer, not a job. They have *Heinz 97* careers covering a wide diversity of work assignments to suit their individual talents and interests, in contrast with the traditional career path. Traditional methods of management and motivation will not work. The promise of future promotion or employee-of-the-month awards are nonsense to highly skilled contingent workers whose loyalty is to their discipline not their employer of the moment. Threat of losing a job is also meaningless since they expect no job security. Instead these workers need respect, interesting and challenging work, the chance to further develop their skills and the resources and freedom to use their talents, plus an equitable share in the profits that issue from their contribution.
- A social-benefits loss is developing as business resists the responsibility of delivering social services like pensions, health care insurance and sick leave to many non-core contingent employees. They will argue that these matters are for the individual or government to address. This will lead to an uncoupling of social support mechanisms from employment.
- Placement agencies, career counsellors and employment agencies will redefine their missions and marketing strategies to stress their roles as agents as more people become responsible for managing their own careers with the help of such 'agents'.

These changes have been a mixed blessing for employees. Calls for 'working smarter' might deviously mask a code for doing more with less and home can become a place of work rather than relaxation. Because of the new diversity in workplace operation and employment arrangements, VET needs to make a paradigm shift from delivery of predetermined content to effective dialogue with stakeholders and clients on design and delivery of effective learning in a variety of contexts for a variety of needs.

# ■■■ THE DEMOGRAPHIC TREND

A major factor in determining a nation's development is its demographic structure. Australia, like many European countries, is experiencing an ageing of its population. The birth rate is declining and selective immigration has been one way to offset this diminishing proportion of younger workers. Other policy directions must draw benefit from increasing longevity and direct a learning thrust across the adult age group. Some 46 per cent of the Australian population in 1970 were under the age of 25 years. Now that proportion has dropped to around 35 per cent. There has been a corresponding increase in the percentage of people over 45 years old from 28 per cent in 1970 to around 36 per cent now. This trend will continue when demographic projections are made to 2010 (ABS, 1999). For example, in 2010 the under-25s will constitute 32 per cent, while the over 45s will have risen to 40 per cent. The ABS *Labour Force Projections 1999–2016* supports the development of an ageing profile. More than 80 per cent of the projected growth in the labour force up to 2016 will be in the 45 years and over age group. The average annual growth rate of the female labour force will increase by a factor double that of the male workforce over the same 18 years, with the former contributing 45 per cent of the workforce by 2016. Participation in the labour force by females between 25 and 54 years of age will increase by 7 per cent and of those between 55 and 59 years by 12 per cent over the same period. Male participation will actually decrease from 73 per cent to 67 per cent.

A report by the Federal Government, *Australia's Workforce 2005: Jobs for the Future*, identified trends and developments that will shape Australia's work force and skill needs. It shows that the proportion of people who will complete secondary school or obtain a tertiary qualification is projected to rise from 57 per cent in 1994 to 68 per cent in 2005. As a result the proportion of people with higher-education qualifications in the work force is projected to rise from 22 per cent in 1995 to 26 per cent in 2005. The labour force growth rate is projected to slow to an average of 1.6 per cent per year to 2005. This drop is due to a reduction in the rate of natural increase and decreases in immigration leading to a decrease in the number of people of working age. Consequently, the long-term trend is to a middle ageing of the work force and increased participation of middle-aged women, as indicated in other ABS data above.

After such a shift in the structure of the population, specifically an ageing of the workforce, most employees would have obtained their qualifications some years ago. This brings into sharp relief the need to maintain the relevance of knowledge and skills and for a commitment to the process of lifelong learning, putting the spotlight on the learning and education needs of adults far more than was ever the case. This is the another imperative alongside the economic one for the thorough development of lifelong education. No longer can entry-level education and training be sufficient to provide a skilled workforce. There must be an increasing focus on the reskilling and the learning needs of adult Australians if the country is to negotiate a complex future economically, socially and politically (Robinson, 2000).

# ■■■ EMPLOYMENT PROSPECTS AND CAREER REDEFINITION

When an electronic circuit learns your job, what can you do with yesterday's skills? The concept of career is changing for many employees. Career development is becoming a matter of lifelong learning, comprising the learning of both new work skills and personal skills. Young people leaving the education system in the next decades are unlikely to find access to the traditional jobs or career paths that have been there for previous generations.

Workers entering the labour market today might have up to seven or eight major career changes in their working life. Educational qualifications are no longer a guarantee of a job. Employees and others seeking work will need to become life-long learners, moving in and out of education environments, both formal and informal, in work time and out of work time, acquiring new skills and knowledge for their careers. Unfortunately, neither educational institutions nor workplaces are structured or designed to facilitate adult education and learning. Moreover, knowledge of, and skills in, the methodologies and psychology of adult education are limited among educators, trainers and human resource personnel.

Career development is beginning to occur laterally instead of the traditional ladder-climbing approach. This enables people nevertheless to obtain job satisfaction as they realise and accept that 'up' is not the only way. Lateral career growth is also intended to meet the organisational need of a flexible workforce that can adapt to changing business circumstances. Lateral development or 'new starts' will have to be seen to be as acceptable and attractive as gaining promotion used to be. Recurrent education and training, shorter working weeks, job sharing, term contracts, periods of casual employment, employment and unemployment, cooperative self-help ventures, flexi-time, sabbaticals and early retirement are already forming the building blocks of individually designed and constructed careers.

Work life and home life will become difficult to separate as paid employment 52 weeks of the year eight hours per day ceases to be the norm. There will not be enough jobs for all those who want a full-time job. Women will find the new forms of work more to their liking than will men as white collar and white coat activities replace blue collar jobs and part-time and contract work replace full-time jobs for life. House husbands might become as common as housewives, with new technology enabling even the most incompetent to cope with maintaining a household. More unconventional work and periodic unemployment will make it more difficult to separate work from the rest of life and will make nonsense of categories like 'redundant' and 'unemployed' that are used to define people without jobs in today's society.

In 1970, 60 per cent of the Australian labour force was unskilled. That percentage has halved and will continue to drop. The strongest areas of new jobs growth will be human services, health, education, welfare, property and business services (Workforce 2010). For those without professional qualifications the strongest growth will be in retail and hospitality. Forty per cent of new jobs will go to those with degrees

(Workforce 2010). Over the next 10 years 30 per cent of new jobs will require people to work 49 hours per week or more while 40 per cent will require fewer than 30 hours. Industries most at risk are mining, transport, banking, insurance, storage, gas and water, electricity and communications, due mainly to a slimming of the workforce as new technologies are introduced. According to the Australian Bureau of Statistics, 40 per cent of Australian workers will have changed their job in the past three years. The occupational half-life now in many technical jobs is five years, and 30 per cent of workers are in jobs that did not exist 20 years ago. Twenty years ago 50 per cent of what a person learnt through training was likely to be useful for up to 14 years. Today even core knowledge has to be upgraded every five years. Middle managers in the manufacturing and financial areas are seriously affected by restructuring and techno-logical developments. Their traditional lines of command have been shortened and redefined so that one manager's duty encompasses a wider span of control and more areas. Thus multiskilling at an executive level is also taking place. The training reforms that are occurring are looking to provide a more skilled and flexible workforce, which will improve Australia's international competitiveness.

Dual career couples also face stress as they try to balance the work–home imper-atives. Employers need to face the reality of the conflicting loyalties of such couples and address the organisational implications of these trends. Tensions in one are transferred into the other, there is role conflict and work overload, particularly as work time can spill over into family time. Around 60 per cent of couples are dual income earners. Women constitute approximately 50 per cent of the workforce (ABS, 2000b). Trends in the USA and the UK are the same. Both men and women are pursuing occupations not simply as a means of earning money but as a source of satisfaction, meaningfulness and self-fulfilment. Flexibility on the part of employees achieves more effective utilisation of human resources. Thus we have a proliferation of work patterns that meets employers' desire for instant gratification. Flexibility means you bend one way — the employer's.

Another area of major change is workplace organisation. This is marked by a shift away from closely supervised labour in a rigid hierarchy to jobs that allow more room for taking responsibility for such things as problem identification and problem solving in a network in a flatter organisational structure. New forms of participation are emerging not through traditional arrangements for workers' rep-resentation or by collective bargaining. The concept of management is evolving in many firms that have outstanding records of performance to include continuous learning by everyone in the firm about its markets, products, organisation, etc. This is crucial not only to individual work satisfaction but to making better use of human abilities and potential in the production process.

The employment destinations of employees holding qualifications will broaden as new industries and jobs emerge. The education and training content of these courses will need to address this broadening of employment destinations in terms of content and skills taught so as to ensure competency and relevancy.

## thrivability and planetism

Ellyard (2000), Australia's foremost futurist, believes that 70 per cent of job categories, products and services in the year 2020 have yet to be invented. Rather than survival or coping, he has coined the term 'thrivability' or the ability to thrive not simply survive. 'Training' he indicated is an outmoded concept associated with behaviourism and 'learning' should be employed in its place. From a global perspective, Ellyard emphasises 'planetism' in which Western is not necessarily best or superior. Planetism will mix ideas, knowledge and behaviours and integrate them. Elements of this are perceptible already as we realise that medical healing can come from a range of sources, or that community living and working might make for more healthy relationships, social living and employment prospects than the footloose, nuclearisation of family life.

Success will go to those organisations that are mission-directed rather than problem-centred, that is focusing on getting to the future rather than doing things more efficiently. As Ellyard says, we have to cease concentrating on keeping our current industries strong, for example how far we should invest in the coal industry when the future lies in renewable power. The future does not lie just in working harder and more efficiently and training harder. It lies in developing new industries and the new skills that go with them. Ellyard draws a subtle yet significant distinction between data, information, knowledge and wisdom. Data plus purpose equals information; information plus culture equals knowledge; knowledge plus experience equals wisdom. Information technology is only one leg of the journey; we must move on into the realms of knowledge technology and wisdom technology — these are the growth areas involving information and these will help to get us into the future. For example, the earth repair industry will be a booming one as all over the world countries, organisations and individuals seek to mitigate the damage done to the environment and restore it to sustainable levels.

## ▪▪▪ HUMAN NEEDS AND THE PURPOSE OF WORK

So far we have assumed that the driving force behind industry, work and employment and the motivation to improve one's skills is money. However, it is too simplistic to regard work solely as a way to earn money for either employees or business leaders. Work has a far higher value in human motivation than that. Table 1.2 summarises the present and future role of work. Work satisfies many human needs. Work provides a sense of achievement, developing a sense of responsibility, it gives a time structure to the day, week and even year, opportunities for social interaction, opportunities for the development of self-esteem and identity, occasions for shared experiences and links to goals and purposes that transcend those of the individual, such as participation in a collective/team effort.

Work and education have many features in common. Work is nearly always, formally or informally, a goal of educational activities. Educational activities/ achievements are the most widely employed structure for placing people in work functions and roles. Education and work are both instruments of selection for status, occupational level and quality of life. For many people work is the only form of education that has borne any relevance to what they do, developing and finding aptitudes and interests that other types of education have failed to discover or promote. It is primarily work that supplies people with everyday learning and new knowledge. Work is therefore on a par with other educational institutions, since experience in certain types of work can be accepted as relevant for admittance for further training. This commonality between work and education implies that if managers and organisations can, within a context, use the intrinsic motivation, needs for achievement, success, and self-esteem that drive human development, the development of a learning community and culture can be facilitated.

Persons who lose their jobs are well acquainted with the importance of work in their lives beyond mere financial implications as they adjust to changes in daily routine, diminished social interaction, and a change in identity. The range of its role is a measure of the impact of work as an essential element in human development, life satisfaction and survival. Work is a human bond almost as important as the family. Drucker recognises this when he says,

> *'Management always lives, works and practices in and for an institution,*
> *which is a human community, held together by a bond that next to the tie*
> *of the family is the most powerful human bond: the work bond'*
> *Drucker, New Management, 1988*

However, for many workers work does not provide many of these satisfactions, particularly those in mundane, routine, repetitive activities that reflect the scientific Fordist approach. In the future these human needs are going to be met far more widely at all levels as organisational structures change. This will benefit production as satisfaction and motivation will increase.

TABLE 1.2 THE CHANGING CONCEPTION OF THE ROLE OF WORK

| TRADITIONAL | FUTURE |
| --- | --- |
| Work as a source of income | Work as a source of personal satisfaction |
| Work as meaningless | Work as meaningful |
| Work as reactive; making others rich | Work as a contribution to society; making everyone rich |
| Work as boring drudgery | Work as an opportunity to participate and achieve |
| Work as isolated from rest of life | Work as integrated with rest of life |
| Work as gaining status | Work as gaining sense of community |

# ■■■ IMPLICATIONS FOR EDUCATION IN THE WORLD OF WORK

Technological innovation has moulded the world into new forms. Electronics is shaping our lives in every sphere of activity, as we bank, shop, exercise, travel, work and play and keep our personal records. Paine (2000) uses a very illuminative simile with reference to the knowledge-based world when he compares fireworks that have trajectories with those that have starbursts. The old economy was a trajectory, you could ride it and control it. The new era is a starburst, uncontrollable and going into multidimensional space.

We are moving into a world that is complex, unpredictable, network-based, horizontally integrated, information rich and largely beyond our control. Yet we try to prepare people for this world by sticking them in institutions that are hierarchical, standardised, centrally controlled, based on knowledge transmission and vertically integrated. A large part of the working world uses computers as a basic tool of the trade. But the people who are training and educating employees still tend not to. Obviously, we do not want students and employees going into institutions that are unpredictable and out of control, but there must be some movement towards preparing people to live in the new world with a frame of reference that will allow them to move forward. While it is unlikely that a surgeon from a hundred years ago could walk into an operating theatre in today's world and set to work, there is no doubt that a teacher from a hundred years ago could walk into a modern classroom and pick up the chalk and carry on.

Knowledge is one of the few meaningful resources today. The traditional factors of production — land, labour and capital — are still necessary but can be fully utilised only if there is knowledge. The old economy of high-volume, standardised production run by a small management group at the top, backed by professionals such as accountants and engineers has gone. With it have disappeared the education and training systems that demanded following of instructions and specialised job training.

The new economic paradigm requires flexibility, quality, innovation and knowledge at all levels. Successful competition now depends on how quickly and well employees can transform ideas into better products and services. In the new economy, employees capable of rapid learning and willing to undertake retraining in more complex tasks/skills are critical. But it is not enough to produce people with specific skills, as in the past. People skills, communication skills and skill at problem analysis in a sort of collective entrepreneurship are also essential. Hobart (1999) concluded that the new competitive framework requires a broader set of skills; the 'hard' (technical) and the 'soft' (interpersonal) skills. We must not train the spinners and weavers of the twenty-first century — highly trained employees who cannot apply their skills to innovative methods, concepts or thinking.

The only skills we can be at all confident will be relevant in the future are generic skills such as collecting, analysing and organising information, the ability to reason, the ability to communicate and work in a group context, the ability to know how to learn, resourcefulness and problem solving skills — in other words generalist skills. People with a range of specific and general skills will be the gold collar workers of the next century, as opposed to the blue and white collar workers of the twentieth century with their narrow skill base. Unskilled workers will still be needed, often in low-level service jobs.

Science and technology are developing at an unprecedented pace, particularly in electronic communications and genetic engineering, while economic and social relationships between groups and countries are undergoing dramatic changes. Yet the school of today is still catering to yesterday's society. This is quite understandable. It is essential that all students receive and understand the common, given elements of their own culture and world knowledge, such as the number system and chemical formulae. It is incredibly difficult to predict what might be needed in addition to cope with the future. Moreover, the future isn't what it used to be; it is changing at an exponential pace. This demands that career education prepare individuals, as Toffler (1980, p. 24) puts it, 'to ride the tiger of change' and give them some control over their lives rather than leaving them to be helpless flotsam and jetsam in the tempests of life. Vocational education in the narrow sense of preparation for particular employment is an outdated concept. Yet schooling must have as one of its major aims the preparation of the next generation for employability in a general sense — a vocationally relevant education. The most needed qualities of tomorrow's school leavers will be adaptability, resourcefulness and flexibility, together with basic portable skills that will enable them to undertake new and successful learning throughout their lives.

The main implication of the new conditions is that two elements of workplace-relevant education can be identified. One is the technical or cognitive knowledge needed by the individual to perform effectively in a particular role in a firm or job. This includes multiskilling and the ability to transfer skills to several different tasks. The second is the personal competences and qualities that enable employees at all levels, including management, to meet the new demands required by changed organisational structures and processes and cope with continuing organisational and personal life changes for the rest of their lives. The implications of changes in the workplace are noted in Table 1.3.

The competency-based training currently being established (discussed in Chapter 2) will be a major feature of workplace training in the immediate future. Proactive rather than conventional dependent employees are required. Employees must be capable of self-initiated action and need to know how to learn rather than be taught and to be enterprising in outlook. Organisations that do not possess employees with these characteristics will lag behind changes and eventually suffer marginalisation by virtue of uncompetitiveness.

TABLE 1.3 WORKPLACE CHANGES AND IMPLICATIONS

| YESTERDAY | NOW AND IMMEDIATE FUTURE | IMPLICATIONS |
|---|---|---|
| Mechanical systems | Micro-electronic systems | Conceptual learning |
| Labour intensive | Knowledge-capital intensive | More value added by people |
| Apprenticeship training on time basis | Competency standards to specified objectives | Modular training |
| Training in more physical skills | Learning of systems, social skills | Less manual learning; self-directed and self-initiated learning; involvement in decision-making process |
| Established equipment | Prototypes and development | Experts are trainers |
| Individual tasks fragmented | Team work; holistic view of production; barriers between workforce levels break down | More social skills training in communication and relationships |
| Reactive and passive; routine | Proactive and flexible; initiating and anticipative; monitoring and diagnosing | Learning how to be responsible, make decisions and be involved |

Early vocational specialisation is therefore not the way to go. This is the danger of the training reform agenda and the competencies movement. In the contemporary setting organisations need employees whose abilities extend beyond the performance of specific skills and functional literacy. The competencies movement must ensure a place for learning that enables all employees to participate actively in family and community life, leisure and recreation, further study and productive work, in other words be supportive of lifelong education. A vibrant and productive society requires informed, active participation in each of these domains, not just in the workplace. However, the general skills taught in the workplace in a learning organisation will provide a sound basis for all the others.

No systematic study has been undertaken of the skills needed by the developing countries of Asia and the Pacific in the twenty-first century. However, a number of industrialised countries (e.g. the United States, the United Kingdom, Australia and New Zealand) have worked out the generic skills workers will need to perform well in the workplaces of the future. In the United States there is the Secretary of Labor's Commission on Achieving Necessary Skills (SCANS) with its report *What Work Requires of Schools: A SCANS Report for America 2000* and the American Society for Training and Development's (ASTD) report *Workplace Basics: The Essential Skills Employers Want*. In the case of the United Kingdom, the work on core skills was undertaken under the auspices of the National Council for Vocational Qualifications (NCVQ), while in New Zealand it formed part of the development of the National Curriculum. In Australia the key competencies were developed under the aegis of the

Australian Education Council and Ministers for Vocational Education, Employment and Training. All these reports produced in the late 1980s or the early 1990s, while still relevant, need further development and elaboration and restatement of the requirements in terms of lifelong education rather than in the narrower competency-based ethos for which they were designed.

> Marginson (2000), in his examination of the changing nature of organisation of work and its implications for education and training, identifies the need for more emphasis on skills for continuous learning and innovation:
> * First-rate interpersonal and human relations skills to work well in team contexts and get the best out of their colleagues.
> * Critical analytic and interpretive skills to handle and make sense of the enormous amount of information now available.
> * Entrepreneurial and enterprising skills, whether to run a business or work for others so that new business opportunities and approaches are always being sought.

In addition to competency in specific job skills, the major generic skills most wanted are the following:

1. *Knowing how to learn*
   This is the most basic of all skills. With this skill employees can more easily acquire other skills. The skill involves the capacity to collect, analyse, organise and apply information. It covers techniques, attitudes and knowledge that facilitate processing of information. It includes the ability to use appropriate technology, as well as the capability to apply it in new contexts at work. This skill therefore enables workers to adapt quickly to new demands at work. Employers see the skill of knowing how to learn as the key to retraining efforts and continuing education. Most important, this skill enables people to apply new knowledge more efficiently to their work, thus greatly assisting the enterprise to meet its strategic goals and competitive challenges.

2. *Reading, writing and computation*
   For traditional jobs working often involves going through a regularised process or repetitive interaction with machines. Illiteracy and innumeracy could be hidden or ignored. But today's workplace involves increasing interaction with sophisticated computerised equipment that requires good reading and computation skills. Workers spend an average of one and a half to two hours reading forms, charts, graphs, manuals and computer terminals on any workday. Writing remains the primary form of communicating policies, procedures and concepts and is frequently the first step in communicating with customers, documenting competitive transactions or successfully moving new ideas into the workplace. Computation is used daily to conduct inventories, report on production levels, measure machine

parts or specifications, etc. Higher mathematical skills are required when it comes to the introduction of approaches like statistical process controls.

Deficiencies in these skills will result in a productivity decline, increased accident rates and costly production errors. It will also be difficult to effect necessary job retraining and an employer's ability to meet strategic goals and be competitive will be impaired.

3. *Communication skills: speaking and listening effectively*
Communication is central to the smooth operation of an enterprise. These skills are at the heart of winning and keeping customers. Pitching innovation, contributing to quality circles, resolving conflicts and providing meaningful feedback all hinge on effective communication skills. Success on the job is linked to good communication skills as workers spend most of their day in some form of communication.

4. *Adaptability skills: solving problems and thinking creatively*
Enterprises are increasingly placing a premium on workers who are both problem solvers and creative thinkers. As decision making is decentralised to the point of actual production or service delivery, a company's competitive position might hinge on its workers' ability to solve problems quickly. Competitive advantage is frequently tied to a company's capacity to innovate quickly. This capacity rests in large part on employees' skill at freeing themselves from linear thinking in order to make the creative leap. An enterprise's ability to achieve its strategic objectives often depends on the problem-solving and creative thinking skills of its workforce.

Successful problem solving involves first skill at individual problem solving. Second, skill in group problem solving and, third, practical ability to combine individual and group skills. Cognitive skills, group interaction skills and problem-processing skills are also crucial to successful problem solving.

Creative thinking is the ability to use different modes of thought, to come up with something new, to visualise, foresee or form new combinations of ideas to meet a need. In the workplace creative thinking is generally manifested as creative problem solving or creative innovation. Often a group activity, creative problem solving is characterised by effective team work. On the other hand, creative innovation is either an individual or group activity. It is the development of new activities that expand markets and improve such elements as productivity.

5. *Developmental skills: managing personal and professional growth*
Personal management skills are the building blocks for good morale, a focused work and home life and, even, organisational productivity. A strong foundation of skills such as self-esteem, motivation, goal setting and employability/career development influences the behaviour, attitudes and desires of workers and ultimately contributes to an enterprise's ability to carry out its mission and strategies. Today's workers are increasingly called upon to make decisions at the point of production or at the point of sale and to display good interpersonal

skills when they work in teams or with customers. A positive sense of self-worth is important to success in these areas.

6. *Group effectiveness: interpersonal skills, teamwork and negotiation skills*
At work employees constantly interact with others. To perform work roles effectively requires good interpersonal, team work and negotiation skills. Interpersonal skills include the ability to judge and balance appropriate behaviour, cope with undesirable behaviour in others, absorb stress, deal with ambiguity, listen, inspire confidence in others, structure social interaction, share responsibility and interact easily with others. These skills are essential to the successful negotiation of conflicts, which are a fact of work life. Negotiating skills include the ability to separate people from problems, the ability to focus on interests not positions, the ability to work out compromises for mutual gain, the ability to apply objective criteria and an understanding of the approach demanded by the prevailing circumstances.

Interpersonal and negotiation skills are the cornerstone of successful teamwork. Teams facilitate the pooling of talents and skills relevant to the successful accomplishment of vital tasks and goals. Quality team work results when team members know how to recognise and cope with the various and unique personalities and when each member has a sense of the cultures and approaches that other team members represent. Team members also need an understanding of group dynamics, which evolve and change as the team approaches its goals. Finally, team members must be aware of the technical skills of fellow members and how these skills can be applied. Negotiating, coaching and delegating are new skills that even managers now have to learn. Democratisation of the workplace demands enhanced communication skills from managers, supervisors and employees in order to exert influence and effect empowerment, and for maintaining relationships.

7. *Influencing skills: organised effectiveness and leadership*
Enterprises are a maze of explicit and implicit structures that make up their 'culture'. Good performance can occur only when employees know the culture of their workplace. Both organisational effectiveness and leadership skills are required. Organisational-effectiveness skills include the behaviours, attitudes and knowledge an employee needs to achieve success on the job, both as an individual and as a member of the enterprise. Each employee uses these skills to adapt to organisational expectations, rules and regulations, including expected job performance levels. They provide guidelines for establishing appropriate and effective interrelationships. Leadership skills are necessary at every level of the enterprise from chief executive to the line worker, as all workers might at times need to influence their work group and to present a vision of what the organisation as a whole or a specific task requires.

Education and training institutions will need to incorporate the teaching of these basic workplace skills in their curricula to ensure that future labour market entrants are properly equipped for the world of work. Likewise, enterprises need to teach their existing employees these skills. Enterprises should expand the scope and mission of training from merely upgrading the technical skills of their professional managers to ensuring that all their employees, as well as their key customers and suppliers, understand the company's quality vision and develop the skills and competencies needed for success.

The conclusion is that in order to succeed in the new workplace, employees will have to have the skills and ability to add value quickly. The workplace will reward generalised specialists who have both solid basic education plus portable professional, technical and personal skills in demand across a range of organisations. Given this scenario, it is no wonder that most workers need additional training and education to rise with the tide of the new technological and global age. These trends are placing a competitive premium on education and training, creating more opportunities for those who continue to upgrade their skills and knowledge. Employees with advanced or upgraded skills are a key investment for competitive business performance. Skill is the new source of security in the twenty-first century for employers and employees. Lasch has commented on the major ethical problem arising from all this in his book *The Revolt of the Elites and the Betrayal of Democracy*.

> *'An aristocracy of talent is superficially an attractive ideal which appears to distinguish democracies from societies based on heredity and privilege. Meritocracy however turns out to be a contradiction in terms. The talented retain many of the vices of the aristocracy without any of its virtues...'*

The worry is that current indications prognosticate a society composed of overworked or underworked persons with too little time or too little money to enjoy life watched with envy by those peering in from the outside. This is a description of a society on the way to disintegration. This is why education and training policies, human resource policies and the content of education and training programs need to prepare all levels of employees for what lies ahead. Whatever context education and training occurs in, it should no longer be seen as education to earn a living but as education for living. Additional skills are also needed, such as self-esteem development, survival skills such as stress management and an awareness of alternative employment and leisure skills involving knowing how to use time to develop new employability skills and how to study.

Personal development is a process that enables individuals to devise strategies for the future, develop new strengths and overcome past weaknesses. Organisations will only survive if they meet the needs of the individuals who serve them — not simply in terms of salary but in terms of their inner needs. People want jobs that provide continual interest and enable them to grow personally. Being competent means having the ability to manage the tasks and challenges that life brings. Chapter 2 will take up this theme as an argument for the development of lifelong education that provides for overall development not just that pertaining to the workplace, enabling an individual to be effective in the major roles of our lives (worker, spouse, parent, friend, citizen and consumer), as all these interact. The work role is no longer separate from other roles.

## ■■■ THE CHALLENGES AHEAD

We can no longer train people in a single skill but should rather teach them the foundations on which they can come back to training and education again and again in the course of a lifetime.

### lucky country to clever country

The 'lucky country' has to become the 'clever country'. However, cleverness will not of itself help individuals or the nation. What is needed is certainly some intellectual skill, knowledge and creativity but these by themselves might lead to intellectual virtuosity bereft of emotional and social balance and maturity. What we should seek rather than an 'intelligent country' is an enterprising and hard-working country in which future and established workers and management are provided with satisfying work and work conditions *plus* personal growth skills.

The consequences of failing to adapt to change and inculcate relevant coping skills is illustrated in a famous satire written over 60 years ago, entitled the 'Sabre Tooth Curriculum'. It recounts how a Palaeolithic school curriculum became obsolete when the Ice Age came. The new conditions demanded a different curriculum to be taught to the community so it might survive and prosper. However, all attempts to introduce relevant skills into the curriculum met with stern opposition. 'But that wouldn't be education', the elders of the tribe argued when new subjects were suggested that would enable the tribe to cope with living in the snowy wastes. The inevitable result was that the tribe didn't survive!

The moral of this satire is still pointedly true today. If we do not learn to adjust to advanced technology, new economic conditions and the restructuring of our manufacturing and service sectors by accepting the need to learn new work, technical and management skills and develop appropriate practices with regard to our human resources, Australian workers, their families, communities and the whole fabric of industry and society might deteriorate psychologically, socially, emotionally and physically over the next decade. If we are not prepared to do this then economic and social opportunities will be engulfed in the morass of a society split between rich and poor, employed and unemployed, skilled and unskilled, rural and urban. An embittered and divided society would be a bitter harvest to reap from technological advances and economic change. Our society already has some very unpleasant aspects to it, particularly for those who are unskilled, young, minority group members or those made redundant in their late forties.

The technological revolution has enabled even formerly underdeveloped countries to become internationally competitive. The globalisation and freeing up of trade fosters competition. This means that the only way to remain competitive is to continually develop and refine products that are highly customised and of a higher quality than before. Simply maintaining standards will no longer suffice. The demand in world markets is for high quality, flexible and reliable service. Behind these features must lie a highly skilled workforce, the creation of which requires both a national, systematic approach to developing human resources outside the standard formal education system and awareness by management of new workplace organisational structures and processes. Products have a shorter life cycle now, so innovation and refinement of product or service is vital, as is a workforce that can adapt to changes that preserve the viability of the firm. Training and personal development will be a major strategy for any business that wants to remain in business. But these educational activities must be pursued in ways that are appropriate for adult learners.

The knowledge, skills and values that we have learnt from life experiences are templates that no longer fit a rapidly changing world congruently. They act as constraints on adaptability. New ways of living and working make many people feel that they no longer fit, that they need to change their sense of identity as they move into a different sort of world. Rapid change brings more ambiguity, more options, more decisions, more pressures, more stress and fewer certainties. In order to cope at work and, generally, in life, individuals will need to be resilient, resourceful, confident, positive, skilled, adaptable and able to make decisions and relate with others who are full of personal energy and initiative.

## improving language and literacy skills

An important area to be addressed in any skill enhancement program is remedying the inadequate English language and literacy skills that hamper other skill improvement programs and prevent many workers deriving benefit from them (Mawer, 1999). In Australia one million people are estimated to have literacy difficulties and of these 600 000 work below their skill level because of communication inadequacies. Many of those with language difficulties are migrants from non-English speaking backgrounds (NESB). These migrants are a useful source of cultural knowledge for organisations exporting abroad. Their skills can be used to gain access to local markets in culturally sensitive ways.

Companies might waste up to two-thirds of their training budget on account of workers not being able to benefit from them owing to language and literacy problems. Levels of production and competitiveness are affected and these deficiencies must be remedied. If we are to make full use of available technologies we need more than basic literacy. We also need contextual knowledge, an understanding of technical terminology, troubleshooting, teamwork and data interpretation skills. The textile, clothing and footwear industries have promoted language and literacy as a training priority as most employees are immigrants with non-English speaking backgrounds. Multiskilling and new work practices are putting real pressure on a culturally diverse workforce that finds it difficult to learn new skills because of language barriers. The Australian *Workplace Relations Act* 1996 puts a premium on employees' ability to communicate effectively in negotiating working conditions, and many companies include in their job application and suitability tests material that is highly verbal, requiring strong literacy skills, such as supplying synonyms and antonyms for given words.

The cost of limited language and literacy skills to the Australian economy in lost production and efficiency has been estimated at several billion dollars, around 5 billion in the UK and 40 billion in the USA. There is also a consistent positive correlation between proficiency in English and labour market success (ANTA, 1996).

## bureaucracy or vision?

The problem with monolithic structures and regulatory bodies like the Australian National Training Authority (ANTA), which are overseeing these issues, is how do they represent, support or even enable thinking about potential emergent industries and services since the current post-compulsory training and education system is locked into existing industrial structures? If we continue to focus on this then the future will bypass us. We will miss out on preparing people for the new products and services and jobs that go with the future. So while we repair, re-jig and upgrade the old we also need to be mission directed. Korea is a good example of this. They wished to transform their peasant society and create a modern economy after the Second World War. They envisioned what people would want 25 years ahead and went for it. Their vision was the miniaturisation of electronics. They had no experts and the silicon chip had not yet been invented, but 25 years on they were making 35 per cent of the world's chips. They had a dream and they got to the future. They had another dream — to become a member of OECD by 1995. They got there by asking themselves what they needed to do and going out and doing it as a mission-directed culture. Australia must do the same, as must each and every enterprise.

Australian enterprises are competing in a global market, characterised by intense international competition and sophisticated consumer expectations. To prosper, Australian products and services must be outstanding by world standards. Therefore, Australia's international competitiveness depends on a well-educated workforce. Only lifelong learning can guarantee our standard of living. Thus in relation to continuous reskilling, three key areas need attention (Waterhouse *et al.*, 1999). These are:

- the need to develop learning communities, not just train individuals

- the need to develop collective learning rather than experts
- the need to develop more strategic and effective approaches to workplace learning.

## SUMMARY

This chapter has provided an overview of the technological, economic and social changes that are impacting on the world of work, particularly in Australia. Although it is difficult to understand fully the breadth of the changes that take place during one's lifetime, most of us have some appreciation of the vast changes that have occurred over the past decade and are continuing today. There is incessant technological advance that commenced in the past decade, with newer and more sophisticated systems of work, new ways to deliver products, innovative systems of management and automated technology controlling production and checking quality. Materials delivery and distribution use computerised information systems. This is continually extending in scope and complexity, resulting in alterations to work practices and to the structure of industry even before consolidation of and acclimatisation to previous changes have been effected. There are national and international economic impacts of tariff and trade agreements, the effects of expanding economies in developing countries, economic malaise and recovery cycles in major developed countries, the effects of globalisation, recognition of the change in the nature of our export trade and increasing employment prospects into service industries and away from manufacturing.

Team-based workplaces and decentralised organisations with cross-functional groups replace old rigid stovepipe chain-of-command organisations where there was little or no worker discretion on narrow, repetitive jobs. The basic and technical skill requirements of jobs are changing, whether on factory floors, in small corner shops or in client service operations. Skill requirements at managerial and non-managerial levels are rising. For adults this often means rapid changes in available occupations, employment patterns, career and job opportunities and required skills and in the structure of communities and family roles and relationships, as part-time employment increases, more women enter the workforce, age profiles of employees are transformed and the very concept of work alters to include more flexible non-standard work arrangements such as casualisation, outsourcing, contingent workers and leased-agency workers.

These transforming concepts of career and employment, new work practices and new values and philosophies about work have considerable implications for managers in their management of employees and themselves in this time of change. Flatter business structures, with the emphasis on teamwork and multiskilling, require the development of new skills and different knowledge. The whole economy is more knowledge-based. Future work will require continual updating of professional and technical skills, better literacy skills, better communication skills and new ways of working together at all levels of work. It is evident that these trends are not ephemeral but will be with us for many years to come. Organisations need to be well aware of these trends and make, for their managers and other staff, a commitment to lifelong education and training, including both personal and portable skills, enabling employees at all levels, organisations and society to survive, adapt and prosper.

# chapter 2

# lifelong education: australian policy

**Reflections of the early 1990s:**

**The government believes that an integrated approach to employment, training and education is the key to focussing on and fostering the development of a skilled and flexible workforce.**
John Dawkins, *Industry Training — The Need for Change*

**Reflections of the later 1990s:**
**Today's and tomorrow's workers must never stop learning: learning is not just for children and young adults, it is for everyone and life long.**
ANTA, *National Marketing Strategy for Skills Acquisition and Lifelong Learning 1999*

There is a marked difference in the philosophy expressed by the above quotations. They are stations on the journey from post-compulsory years of learning as training for economic ends to the concept of lifelong learning for all facets of living, which this chapter will attempt to explain.

The twentieth century has seen policies designed to make universal basic education (that is compulsory schooling) a key thrust in education world wide. The final decades of the twentieth century saw universal education and training extended across the teenage years and into early adulthood in many countries. The focus has been on preparing young people for entry to the workforce, and on retaining young people in the formal education and training system for longer periods of time.

However, a continuing focus on the preparation of young people for entry to the workforce as the keystone of post-compulsory education and training will no longer be sufficient, and for the following reasons:

- First, on the demand side, technological innovation and globalisation of economies around the world are having a profound impact on the nature of work, the way it is organised and the skills it requires, as described Chapter 1. These changes are now so rapid that people must expect to be working in several different occupations during their lifetimes. Many specific skills and jobs now have a very short 'half-life'.

• Second, on the supply side, the workforces of most developed countries, including that of Australia, are ageing. In Australia, there has been a two per cent drop in the size of the school age cohort between 1998 and 2000 and the birth rate continues to be low. Fewer young people will be entering the workforce than in the past. Education and training policies will therefore need to be more heavily focused on the adult workforce than previously and include the reskilling of older workers.

As a response, Government, educational and business organisations in developed and many developing countries are making far-reaching changes to the way their workforces and citizens are educated and trained, and to the organisational structures and processes within organisations.

If Australia is to maximise its economic potential, policies to further promote lifelong learning should be recognised as the key direction for the future. The onset of the information age and the knowledge-based economy requires countries to become learning societies. The skills base of a nation, and the speed with which skilling can adjust to meet new requirements, will be as important in the twenty-first century in determining economic success as a nation's natural resources and financial capital base, if not more so. These changes will not be achieved without significant reform to education and training systems. Australia's population is poorly qualified compared with other developed countries. We are seven per cent below the OECD average in terms of the proportion of people between 25 and 64 who completed secondary school. There are certainly high levels of attainment in university education, but low levels for vocational training. In 1999, only 23 per cent of 15- to 24-year-olds, 14 per cent of 24- to 29-year-olds, 12 per cent of 30- to 39-year-olds, 11 per cent of 40- to 49-year-olds and 6 per cent of 50- to 59-year-olds were engaged in publicly provided vocational education and training.

Of course, Australia has been making substantial progress of late. Some 1.7 million people (or about 18% of the 15- to 64-year-old population) were enrolled in publicly funded vocational education and training programs in 2000 (ABS, 2000) and although this was the same as the previous year it marks an increase since 1990 of 70 per cent. Around a third of these are taking courses for their own development by choice, that is not job-related; 40 per cent were at AQF I–III level of study and 19 per cent were on non-award courses (Vetstats, 1999). Most were studying in the business, engineering and services fields. Fifty-two per cent reported that the course was highly relevant to their current job but 15 per cent reported no relevance at all. A further 670 000 people were enrolled in higher education (i.e. 5.4% of the population aged 15–64 years). Some 80 per cent of wage/salary earners reported having undertaken some kind of employer-provided training. Around 77 per cent of the 'economically active' population aged 15 to 64 years undertook some kind of external or workplace education or training during 1997 in Australia, with 61 per cent of employers providing training of some kind. Technical and Further Education institutions accommodated 75 per cent of participants in 1999, community providers served 11 per cent and private providers 14 per cent (Vetstats, 1999). A survey of leading managers (Tegart *et al.*, 1998) reveals that 43 per cent prefer to acquire new skills by recruiting new employees or contracting out rather than training existing staff. Among remaining employers, most favoured on-the-job training, followed by inhouse formal training. Around 70 per cent of employers claim that VET provides its graduates with skills appropriate to employers' needs and that training pays for itself through increased productivity.

Already, Australia is meeting the diverse training needs of nearly 20 per cent of its adult population 68 per cent of whom are already in the workforce, which suggests a sizeable body of people wanting to improve themselves and keep up with a changing world. Australian governments and industry are spending billions of dollars each year on vocational education and training. The New Apprenticeships scheme has doubled those in training since 1995, with more women involved, greater access for older, less skilled workers and a wider range of industries. This scheme provides jobs with a contract of training in industry-relevant skills and employment experience. The User Choice system has been developed for employers of New Apprenticeships subjects, under which employers decide which provider will be used and where the delivery will take place. For more formal tertiary education, Open Learning Australia (OLA) is acting as a broker for around 30 TAFEs and universities. OLA students undertake study for a variety of reasons — to gain skills, to work towards a qualification, for professional development and even for recreational purposes. There are no prerequisites and anyone can enrol, regardless of their secondary education standard, age, disability status or location. TAFE registration occurs at any time during the year, while universities register four times each year. OLA students are distance students, receiving specially developed materials, support from trained advisers and increasing on-line facilities. The qualifications are the same as on-campus equivalents. The OLA web site www.ola.edu.au provides continually updated information on OLA and its courses. OLA was established to improve access and equity in the delivery of tertiary education when and where it is required. It was the first Australian institution to offer four study periods each year and open entrance. By upholding the principles of flexibility it has been quite successful in acting as a change agent in Australian higher education and vocational training. Almost 400 000 people work to provide education and training for over two million Australians 95 per cent of whom are doing education and training for vocational reasons. In recent years, this effort has:

- dramatically expanded the amount of training available to Australians
- been based largely on what industry requires of workers
- made education and training much more accessible to women, Aboriginal

and Torres Strait Islander peoples, people with disabilities, people from non-English speaking backgrounds, remote and isolated people and other traditionally disadvantaged groups

- made trainers much more responsive to industry and people wanting to do training.

The number of people participating in the formal education and training sector will continue to grow but at a slower rate than during the previous decade. This is due mainly to the slowdown in population growth. Current education and training policies therefore represent a consolidation of the large increases in access of the late 1990s.

Impressive as this seems, much more needs to be done to make adult education and workplace training a genuine part of a lifelong education culture. The record of Australians undertaking school or training after their 16th birthday is not good. For example, as we get older, we do less education and training that leads to a qualification. Fifty-two per cent of the Australian workforce does not have a post-school qualification, whereas in Sweden more than 50 per cent of the adult population is involved every year in some form of adult education, 44 per cent in the UK and 37 per cent in the Netherlands. In fact, in some post-industrial countries today, the number of adults involved in training and education exceeds the number of children in primary and secondary schooling. The education scene is coming to emphasise the active participation of the adult population, according to Paul Belanger, Director of UNESCO Institute for Education (1998). Australia, however, ranks only eighteenth among the 22 OECD countries in terms of post-compulsory qualifications  (www.unesco.org/education/educprog/tve/nseou;l/docse/rpllsie.html). People without post-school qualifications are more likely to be unemployed, less able to change jobs, more likely to be retrenched, be worse paid and less willing and likely to do any training. This group could easily develop into an underclass from which it is difficult to escape.

A recent survey of 500 senior executives nation wide (Drake Consulting *Skills/Values Survey*, April 1999) sought to determine, among other things, the skill levels of corporate Australia and how well resourced companies are. In other words, did they have the appropriate mix of permanent and casual staff? The survey revealed that only 24 per cent of the workforce are appropriately skilled to perform their tasks effectively, that 70 per cent have moderate skill levels (but require further upskilling) and that six per cent of employees are sufficiently skilled.

Rapid and widespread social and economic change means that more people across the whole community must engage in more lifelong learning, at more stages of their lives. The National Marketing Strategy for Skills and Lifelong Learning will be Vocational Education and Training's blueprint for turning the Australian community and enterprises on to lifelong learning (see pp. 48–52). There are also issues (taken up in Chapters 7–9) about the appropriateness of existing educational content, assessment approaches and teaching methods for adult learners. If adult learners are to have the opportunity to realise their full suite of potentialities, their needs as well as those of industry and commerce must be met.

## ■■■ THE CHANGING PARADIGM — INTERNATIONAL APPROACHES

The conceptual origins of adult and lifelong education can be found in the development in the late 1960s of the concept of *recurrent education*, then occasionally termed *education permanente*. With its emphasis at that time on equality of opportunity, particularly with the workplace in mind, UNESCO promoted recurrent education. Recurrent education was seen as a framework for enhancing post-school education, especially to meet the needs of those in the workforce who needed new skills and knowledge, and a satisfactory interplay between the world of work and the educational system. Recurrent education was regarded as a possible cure for the persistence of distinctions between traditional liberal education and vocational education, a distinction that tended to militate against self-awareness and autonomous decision making in learners of all ages and preserve the dichotomy of employee/worker–boss/professional that has plagued Australian industrial environments for decades.

### *learning to be*

It was the publication of *Learning To Be: The World of Educational Today and Tomorrow* by Edgar Faure and his colleagues on the UNESCO International Commission on the Development of Education that broadcast a new paradigm of lifelong education to the rest of the world in 1972. *Learning To Be* heralded a sea change from traditional ideas about the purposes and role of education. It placed lifelong education within a humanist framework, emphasising personal fulfilment as a radical, democratising instrument for social and political liberation and consciousness-raising, based on the pioneering work of John Dewey, Montessori, A.S. Neill and contemporary Third-World reformers such as Paulo Freire. The general theme was education as a means of creating the self-awareness that changes the learner from object to subject. Within this philosophy, lifelong education is focused on the creation of equality — democratisation through education. Even in societies with improved educational opportunity, a need was recognised for parity between those currently in formal education and their elders, who needed educational compensation for their previous more limited access to educational opportunities. The emphatic thesis of *Learning to Be* was that true equality in and through education could be achieved only by a continuing process of education over the life span. A secondary message of importance for most countries, including Australia, was that rigid distinctions between different types of teaching — general, scientific, technical and professional — must be eliminated, and all levels of education should integrate the theoretical, technological, practical and manual. The presumed primacy of formal academic and professional education was challenged and such education seen as less relevant for the future for the national, economic and social development of all.

## ■■■ THE CHANGING PARADIGM: AUSTRALIA'S RESPONSE

The flow of this new UNESCO conceptualisation entered Australian awareness immediately after the publication of Faure's work in the early 1970s.

### the introduction of lifelong education to australia

In Australia, the first formal statement on lifelong education as a driving force for a future education system came from South Australian Director of Further Education, Max Bone, in 1972.

Myer Kangan, the Commonwealth official whose 1974 *Report on Technical and Further Education in Australia* effectively created a new national sector of education from the various State technical education agencies, was strongly influenced by *Learning To Be* and lifelong education became a central feature in the emerging Technical and Further Education (TAFE) sector. However, in its transfer from Europe it failed to carry with it the generous 'liberational' and enlightening elements of the model and retained a restricted 'recurrent education' flavour. Lifelong education thus initially masqueraded in Australia as a limited vision specific to TAFE, rather than one that permeated all levels, forms and settings of education.

Business and industry readily accepted the abridged concept of recurrent education since it had the potential to remove barriers to workforce training and retraining, such as age restrictions on apprentices, which had long frustrated employers. Second, if recurrent education was a community value, the expense of adult retraining would be shared by the community as well as by industry and individuals.

### australia abandons recurrent education

Hence, although recurrent education remained influential in Australian education until the mid-1980s it permeated only the TAFE sector philosophy. But as TAFE failed to deal adequately with the problems of unemployment and the disjointed pathways between school and adult working lives, the simplistic philosophy that the solution to unemployment was to be found in better and more education was called into question by government. This view was held by the Hawke Labor Government, which in 1984 established the Karmel inquiry into what benefits could be identified from the massive increase in public investment in education. When Karmel's report indicated very little evidence of increased performance in outcomes for students since the early 1970s, the government sought to sweep away the existing education policy framework and effectively abandoned recurrent education, and with it any immediate embrace of lifelong education.

In 1987 a Ministry of Employment, Education and Training was set up with a new mandate to focus on vocational and instrumental goals with social and individual development objectives, virtually ignoring characteristics of lifelong education. It was a commitment to another simplistic view that economic development is incongruent with the aims of liberal education. It was determined that education must have economic and instrumental objectives. This led to the emergence of the training reform agenda and award restructuring system, based mainly on successive reports from committees set up by the Federal government.

## the training reform agenda of the late 1980s and early 1990s

A sequence of three reports laid the foundation for the national unified system of competency-based training. These were the *Finn Report* (1991), the *Mayer Report* (1992) and the *Carmichael Report* (1992).

> The dominant themes of these reports can be summarised as follows:
> - All young people should complete years 11 and 12, the curricula of which should provide for contextual learning and work experience and be relevant to the world of work.
> - The immediate post-compulsory years should include a broad-based education, employment-related competencies and vocational education and training.
> - The process should lead Australian training away from the time-linked apprenticeship model of narrow specific skills.
> - Credit transfer and pathways between sectors should be maximised.
> - Assessment of competencies should be outcome-based (criterion-referenced).
> - The difference between vocational and general education should be minimised.

Thus in the early 1990s the concept of lifelong education promoted by international bodies did not transfer too well to Australia, where more narrow instrumental goals were sought. However, the new VET policy achieved no better results in ameliorating unemployment and youth transition and skill development than had previous policies, with the chief executive of the Australian National Training Authority (ANTA) claiming in July 1994 that Australia would be 30 years behind leading OECD countries in vocational skill levels if it continued on its current course. The Labor government continued revising and refining policy in the early 1990s, focusing more intently on the development of a behaviourist-toned vocational education system, with its competency-based training fully identified with economic objectives and ignoring social and community objectives.

Australia lagged behind other major countries in its attention to lifelong learning owing not only to the focus on narrow economic aims but also to complications of a federal system where states and territories shared control of education, as well as a feeling that some major policy makers until the second half of the 1990s regarded the general tenets of lifelong learning as something of a luxury or indulgence and marginal to the major economic concerns of the country. In addition, the fragmentation of responsibility among many stakeholders in the private and voluntary sectors impeded progress. The confrontational style of politics and industrial relations on top of it all meant that the difficulties of developing national policy for lifelong education appeared insurmountable by the mid-1990s.

## the Delors report

However, significant progress towards a holistic concept of lifelong education continued to be made in the international arena. In 1993, UNESCO invited Jacques Delors, former President of the European Commission and former Finance Minister of France, to study the diversity of educational contexts and structures around the world, and the large volume of educational research available, in order to construct a conceptual map for the future of education in the twenty-first century. The *Delors Report* was issued in 1996, formally entitled *Learning: The Treasure Within*. It established a new intellectual environment for discussion and debate on education in its expression of a commitment to the importance of education for personal and social development, enabling nations to provide for their citizens an avenue to redress the hardships imposed by inequity and oppression, empowering people individually and collectively to fulfill their potential and contribute to society. The key driver in the report was the concept of globalisation.

## ■■■ LIFELONG LEARNING — WHAT IS IT?

The *Delors Report* provides a useful way of thinking about lifelong learning. It calls for a broad concept of education that is pursued throughout life: flexible, diverse and available at different times and in different places. The report identified four 'pillars' of education for mutually supportive learnings for the future, viz.:

*Learning to know.* The mastery of learning tools rather than the acquisition of structured knowledge. Includes developing concentration, memory skills and the ability to think.

*Learning to do.* Education to equip people to do the types of work needed in the future, be innovative and able to adapt learning to future work environments.

*Learning to live together, and with others.* Education to avoid conflict or peacefully resolve it, through education to discover other people and their cultures, and involvement in common projects.

*Learning to be.* Education that contributes to a person's complete development: mind and body, intelligence, sensitivity, aesthetic appreciation and spirituality.

In its deliberation on lifelong education the OECD also focused on the three inter-locking objectives of economic growth, social cohesion and personal development that contribute to the four mutually supportive learnings of the *Delors Report*. In 1996 the OECD Education Ministers recognised developing globalisation, the massive changes in IT and innovative technological production methods as the impetus for further consideration and overhauling of what was being offered in the form of post-school technical and work-based education. Globalisation involves not only the movement of goods and services around the world but also the trans-fer of investment, peoples and intellectual property, coupled with market deregulation, micro-electronic communication innovations and worldwide finan-cial markets. This 1996 OECD meeting was chaired by the then Australian Federal Minister of Education, Simon Crean, and it promoted the concept of lifelong learning as a means of educating people to meet the massive and continual changes in the workplace and in living itself. To achieve this the OECD empha-sised a good foundation from schooling, the development of smooth pathways and progressions between work and further learning at all ages, and a radical change in the roles and responsibilities of all partners in the financing of lifelong learning for all. This reinvigoration of lifelong learning by the *Delors Report* and OECD has been taken up throughout most of the developed world as it is perceived as the major avenue for facilitating individual and national development. Such interna-tional impetus has impelled Australia to start moving towards recognising lifelong education, accessible to all Australians, as the basis for post-compulsory education it has proved to be in other countries.

## developments in the UK

The UK has set targets for a raft of proposed initiatives in a Green Paper, *The Learning Age: A Renaissance for a New Britain* (1998), including a University for Industry, incen-tives for further study, franchised learning centres, individual learning accounts, a simplified qualifications framework and a Training Standards Council. This followed significant reports on the need for lifelong learning (Dearing, 1997; Freyer, 1997). A further British report *Learning to Succeed* (1999) identified the need to support young people, adult learners and the creation of Learning and Skills Councils.

Other developments include new vocationally oriented foundation degree pro-grams to have started in 2001 in Britain, with universities, colleges, employers, industry and training organisations joining forces to provide 2000 places initially with five million pounds sterling development funding from the Higher Education Funding Council of England. These are designed to attract students from a wide range of backgrounds and equip them with technical and transferable skills, as well as academic knowledge. Twenty-one consortia have been established, consisting of 35 universities, 70 further education colleges and a range of employers, training organisations and industry organisations. The courses are two years in duration (or equivalent part-time) and provide a route to an honours degree after an additional year, which can be completed after a period of employment. The new degrees allow people to develop key skills that are relevant and in demand for a twenty-first-century workforce and will attract those not previously interested in higher education or whose needs were not met by traditional degree courses. The partnership with industry ensures that each program is designed to teach identifiable skills in a particular sector or occupation, and include work-based elements (www.hefce.ac.uk). A University of Industry commenced in late 2000 within a big-top circus touring around the Midlands of England. Other parts of the University of Industry will be formed from consortia of educational establishments and businesses and have a fixed location.

The trade unions are also seeing a role for themselves as providers. A major public sector union UNISON now has 40 education officers offering union members the chance to return to education and study to postgraduate level. For those workers who dropped out of education and who are wary of formal institutions, union-based education provision (validated by standards institutions) provides a source of confidence and support to those returning to the learning environment (Evans, 2000).

## developments in europe

Within the EU, the White Paper *Towards a Europe of Knowledge* plotted future infrastructure in the areas of school-industry links, developing new areas of knowledge, combating exclusion and education investment. This was followed by a conference by the same name held in Manchester, UK, in 1998. The Cologne G8 Summit *Charter of Aims and Ambitions for Lifelong Learning* (1999) adopted by European leaders states, 'Access to knowledge will be one of the most significant determinants of the income and quality of life of people in our communities in the future' and emphasises that 'education and skills are indispensible to achieving economic success, civic responsibility and social cohesion' (www.g8cologne.de/01/00141/index.html). The Charter emphasises getting information to people who need it, who can benefit from it, and who can add value to it. It doesn't matter whether it is in manufacturing, agriculture, services or business, the ability to think and plan ahead is going to depend increasingly on how quickly individuals can tap into the information and ideas needed, take charge of the future and manage change.

## developments elsewhere

In the USA, a summit on 21st Century Skills for 21st Century Jobs was held in 1999, at which Vice President Gore stated 'realising our potential will require investing in education and learning for all of our people throughout their lifetime' (opening address). Such views are also advocated in *Workforce 2000*, a report of the US Department of Labor. In Singapore, the Manpower 21 Plan has been launched to create opportunities for Singaporeans to realise their full potential so everyone can make a meaningful contribution. The vision is for Singapore to become a Talent Capital, a centre of ideas, innovation and knowledge, a hub of continuous learning for lifelong employability, with a comprehensive system, the School of Lifelong Learning, addressing the needs of all workforce levels. The concept of lifelong education was also the theme of a UNESCO meeting in Seoul in 1999.

These pronouncements and conference foci illustrate the fact that there was a growing mandate from the late 1990s for lifelong education to integrate a constellation of individual, social and economic goals. This broader perspective on lifelong learning, involving social, cultural and personal development as well as economic concerns, was exemplified by UNESCO's Conference on Adult Education in Hamburg in 1997.

## ■■■ LIFELONG LEARNING VERSUS RECURRENT EDUCATION

It is now feasible to discern the five major differences that distinguish lifelong education from its predecessor, recurrent education.

1. Recurrent education implied discontinuous learning phases set between periods of work, whereas lifelong learning is considered to be continuous and embedded formally and informally in work and other activities.
2. Lifelong education substitutes individual demand for economic demand.
3. With higher school retention and tertiary education rates, lifelong education must focus more on workers who were disadvantaged by the lack of such education.
4. The government's retreat from full support and the emergence of alternative models of provision and funding for lifelong education.
5. Lifelong education provides a growing focus on social cohesion and civil society.

Lifelong learning emerged in the late 1990s as a very different animal from recurrent education and goes beyond offering adults a second chance. It implies a continuing relationship with education and can occur in formal and informal ways in the home, workplace and community, as well as educational institutions, embracing individual and social development of all kinds in all settings. Recurrent education gave the impression of a stop-start process, a reaction to some immediate need in the training arena. Lifelong education also implies the provision of a sound groundwork in basic education on which all else is built, as well as smooth transitions, pathways and well-oiled linkages between different sectors of education and between sectors and the workplace to facilitate a plethora of often personally tailored lifelong learning routes. A few years ago, all that was needed to travel round the world was a passport and a ticket. In the future, the passport to mobility will be a sound basic education and enthusiastic involvement in lifelong learning. The characteristics that set lifelong learners apart are:

- the necessary skills and attitudes for learning, especially literacy and numeracy skills
- the confidence to learn, including a sense of engagement with the education and training system
- the willingness and motivation to learn.

If education and training programs are explicitly designed with the development or preservation of these characteristics in mind, the number of people who slip through the system or become alienated from it will be reduced. Lifelong learning also implies new roles and relationships for those concerned with education and training, revisiting curricula, goals and teaching and learning methods.

Thus there is growing international consensus that lifelong learning is the key to prosperity in the new millennium. The OECD, UNESCO, Council of Europe and the European Union all give priority to lifelong learning. Lifelong education is a powerful tool for promoting social cohesion in the complex multi-ethnic societies of the modern age in a climate of social and economic change. It also has the potential to foster opportunities for all Australians, including the most disadvantaged, to participate fully in the economic, social and cultural life of the community. The 1996 *Delors Report* noted growing inequality owing to rising poverty and exclusion, not just between nations or regions in the world, but between social groups within both developed and developing countries. Internationally, Donald Johnston, Secretary General of OECD, reported in November 1998 (www.oecd.org/publications/pbserver/214/editorial_eng.html) that, from a survey of 12 OECD countries, at least a quarter of the adult population fails to reach the minimum literacy standards needed to cope adequately with the demands of everyday life and work.

Thus the idea of continuing knowledge acquisition and development of skills for the broad mass of people in society has gained new impetus. Traditional training has limitations that can only be compensated for by learning over the life span of an individual. Though there are distinct economic benefits to society from a population that is adequately prepared to meet a changing economic environment, learning throughout life has an important social aspect, given the increased longevity of the population of advanced industrial countries. It is no longer viewed as an individual right but as a prerequisite for participation in all aspects of society.

All this effort by supra-national bodies and in major competitor countries provided and continues to provide Australia with a challenge to go beyond narrow economic bases for training reform, and pious motherhood statements, and proceed along similar lines or else miss out. By 1996, Australia had linked into the mainstream thinking about lifelong education, with the National Board of Employment, Education and Training (NBEET), claiming, 'Lifelong learning should be concerned not only with a skilled and flexible workforce but also with enabling people to realise more of their individual potential and with "public learning" — enhancing societal awareness and understanding of various critical issues in public policy' (NBEET, 1966). This was prompted no doubt by a desire to spare Minister Crean, who had just chaired an OECD meeting promoting lifelong education, embarrassment at the failure of his own ministry to embrace such a vision.

The challenge in Australia had and still has many foci: first there is the need to integrate three overlapping forms of lifelong learning — workplace education, formal and informal education, and community-based education. Additional to this is the development of financial mechanisms for Federal government, State government, employers, providers and consumers that will support such an approach, plus the provision of alternate and flexible pathways through the system and policies on national recognition, quality assurance and credentialing. A variety of government policies, initiatives, seminars, workshops and conferences have provided the impetus for developing practical ways to resolve all these issues. The most influential of these have been the Adult Learning Australia (ALA) position paper of 1998, the UNESCO–Flinders University Institute of International Education seminar in November 1998, the 1999 National Seminar on Lifelong Learning Policy and the Australian National Training Authority (ANTA) Conference 2000. To stimulate a broader conception of lifelong learning and facilitate its development in practice from the key reports of the early 1990s, which had focused more on economic benefits, the National Board of Employment, Education and Training (NBEET) produced a series of reports on the need to stimulate and develop lifelong education such as *Lifelong Learning – Key Issues* (1996) and *Learning to Learn in the Vocational and Training Sector* (1996). In the former report, the Board argued in almost Freirean terms the need for people to continue their learning for the twin objectives of achieving broad economic goals and creating a society in which people enjoy learning. This was to produce not only a skilled workforce but also to enable people to realise more of their individual potential, enhancing societal awareness and understanding of various critical issues in public policy. ANTA responded to this call and, in developing the current national strategy (1998) *A Bridge to the Future 1998–2003*, established vocational education and training's mission to ensure that:

> *'The skills of the Australian labour force are sufficient to support*
> *internationally competitive commerce and industry and to provide individuals*
> *with opportunities to optimise their potentials.'*

The Federal government agreed to maintain funding levels in real terms for the duration of this national strategy. The annual training plan for year 2000 envisaged around 65 training packages to be endorsed by the end of that year with around 1000 registered training organisations operating within the Australian Recognition Framework. The emphasis in 2000 was on improving provider readiness and responsiveness, including professional development for teachers, trainers and registered training organisations. Another major focus for 2000 was on on-line delivery. Since 1997, 160 000 students are provided for each year in excess of the 1997 level. Enterprise- and industry-relevant training packages have been developed for 60 per cent of the workforce.

However, these developments indicate that the thrust in Australia in practice has been less towards the all-embracing multiple dimensions of the social, personal and economic objectives of lifelong education than to the contribution that it can make to enhancing work skills and employability. There is no real policy on lifelong education and no shared national vision to facilitate concerted action as Kearns (1999) pointed out. Kearns (op. cit.) noted that VET national policy has a mainly workforce focus with mention of lifelong education objectives simply incidental. Only national policy for adult and community education (ACE) contributes deliberately to lifelong learning and to Australia as a learning society. McKenzie (1998) noted this too but argued that it is this narrower focus that is critical and supports the concept as it is seen as the driver of employment-related skill and subsequent employability and economic competitiveness. So while the thrust in other countries, particularly developing countries, is also at citizenship, social development and life skills, these are seen as less crucial since they are already well developed in Australia's democratic lifestyle. There is still the ghost of the training reform agenda in contemporary policies when the Minister of Education, Training and Youth Affairs, Dr Kemp, shows his hand as follows:

> 'There is little doubt that the nations of the world which will succeed in the twenty-first century will be the knowledge societies, societies rich in human capital, effective in their capacity to utilise and deploy their human resources productively and successfully in the creation and communication of new knowledge. In such a world there will need to be greater opportunities than ever before for lifelong learning — for preparation not just for the first job but for succeeding jobs.' (1999)

A more detailed account of the debate relating lifelong education to post-compulsory education and training can be found in McKenzie (op. cit.), Kearns (1999), Kearns and Papadopolous (2000), Ryan (1999) and Watson (1999).

The Australian focus on an intellectual capital approach as a means of at least running with the pack if not leading it continues with a two billion dollar innovation plan unveiled in January 2001. Included is a scheme to extend interest-free loans to postgraduate students doing non-research courses to update their skills in an attempt to prevent the cost of courses being a barrier to anyone wanting to upgrade their skills. The intention is to assist 240 000 students this way over the next five years. But this focus, again, is on the benefits to the economy and the uplifting of those who already have advantages. The challenge now at the start of the new millenium is to continue creating the policy framework that will permit rapid development of lifelong education and adult education within a philosophy that not only brings economic benefits to the entire nation and to individual businesses but equally benefits all citizens by removing barriers to greater opportunity and life fulfilment. The main issues to be tackled include access, equity, quality assurance in training, cross-state recognition, recognition of prior experience and smooth pathways between various sectors. Some headway has been made with regard to access, quality assurance and cross-state recognition.

**1.** *Access*

David Kemp, former Federal Minister for Education, Training and Youth Affairs announced at the ANTA National Conference July 2000 strategies and policies aimed specifically at overcoming the disparities between states, particularly as regards recognition and regulations, and access for disadvantaged groups. In an echo of Freire, the Minister indicated that 'education and training is the foundation of a prosperous and democratic society. It is more than the acquisition of knowledge. Education helps develop analytic and problem solving skills. It helps develop an inquiring mind and promotes innovation. As well as being important skills for the workplace, these are also important life skills.' This shift in priorities in one year from earlier narrow economic objectives.

**2.** *Quality assurance and cross-state recognition*

The Ministerial Council of Education Ministers (MCEETYA) took in June 2000 other significant steps towards addressing issues surrounding cross-state delivery, recognition, quality and national consistency, which effectively lie in the hands of State and Territory governments, in order to advance a quality, fully national training system necessary to skill up Australia. All States and Territories have now agreed to set in place the necessary corresponding legislative provisions to underpin a truly consistent national framework.

The old fragmented framework of training dominated by individual State provision has been dismantled and replaced in the late 1990s with a more flexible, responsive national system, the National Training System (NTS). Smith (1999) has charted the structural developments of the NTS under the aegis of ANTA.

## ■■■ THE AUSTRALIAN NATIONAL TRAINING SYSTEM (NTS)

The Australian National Training System (NTS) — a framework of regulatory agencies, blueprints and policies created in the final years of the 1990s — has moved training into the twenty-first century and has done so by bringing about a significant shift in the locus of power and control of publicly funded training:

- Control of training policy and funding has moved from States to the Commonwealth
- Training agendas have moved from vocational educational institutions to government and peak industry bodies.

These changes are important to note not only because they impact on vocational education structures and processes, but also because they reflect the interests and objectives of the training reform movement. As noted earlier, the stimulus for the reform of Australia's training systems was not essential educational concerns but government worries over economic issues. From the 1980s, Australian political economists, like their colleagues in Britain and the USA, started to compare their productivity with the superior economic outputs of Japan, West Germany and Scandinavia. The general interpretation was that the investment made by these nations in education and training had a considerable effect on their economic success. In particular, investment by individual enterprises in the training of their own employees was a practice that paid dividends. In Australia, however, the move towards a more competitive economy did not start with the enterprises themselves, it was led by trade unions and the Commonwealth Government. The former wished to protect their members' interests in a changing economy and to secure their own institutional survival. The Commonwealth Government, in a small and previously highly protected and regulated economy, has traditionally been a catalyst for change through legislation and targeted funding. So the reformers adopted the rhetoric of enterprise-based training as the official objective for what was in reality a pursuit of government and trade union agendas.

By the mid-1980s, policy and position papers from governments, employer associations and unions suggested that there was consensus among these stakeholders that a national system of vocational training should replace the state systems under which the content and level of courses varied from state to state. From this it was obvious that if the industrial system was to achieve a system of classifying skills that was standardised across all industries, the methodologies for the design of training programs should be radically overhauled. Standardisation of skill classifications in the labour market would need to go hand in hand with standardisation of training. National standardisation messages from overseas indicated the value of greater flexibility in training arrangements, decreased regulation, the matching of horizontal broadbanding of skill classifications with broad-based training programs and, above all, the capacity to customise training to the needs of individual enterprises.

The relationship between industrial and training reform was formally acknowledged by the Commonwealth Government in the late 1980s. It issued three papers from the office of the then Minister of Education (John Dawkins) that announced its intention to develop a new national training system. This new system was to subsume, through agreements and mirror legislation enacted over the next four years, the individual State and Territory systems and replace certification based on time served with certification based on achievement of competencies to prescribed national standards. In 1989 the Committee of Commonwealth and State Ministers for Vocational Education and Training (MOVEET) moved to adopt a competency-based system of training and set up the National Training Board (NTB) to coordinate the development of competency standards for each industry.

In November 1990, a Special Ministers Meeting agreed to adopt a nationally consistent approach to the recognition of skills. This agreement was the basis for the National Framework for the Recognition of Training (NFROT), which represents the standardisation of procedures for accreditation, credit transfer, assessment, registration of training providers and recognition of skills.

The direction taken by the Commonwealth Government in 1989 consolidated into the National Training Reform Agenda, a related collection of government policies progressively agreed by Ministerial Councils between 1989 and 1994, whose common element was that they were all aimed explicitly at reforming aspects of Australia's approach to skills formation (Fitzgerald, 1994, p. 17). At no stage was there any definitive statement of what exactly was on the National Training Reform Agenda, but the overriding concerns have been competency-based training, competency standards, national recognition of training, reform of curriculum, delivery and assessment, a new system of entry-level training, the development of a training market, access and equity and streamlining of funding for training — rather than client needs or changes to teacher/trainer methodologies.

The extent to which control has shifted from the States to the Commonwealth is significant, as illustrated in the case of curriculum development. From the establishment of the state-based Technical and Further Education (TAFE) systems in 1974 up to 1991, curriculum development was the responsibility of each State's TAFE authority, with input from trade committees, local employers and state-based industry agencies. Since 1992, control of the curriculum has moved progressively from the States to the Commonwealth. By 1997 curriculum development had become an ANTA function, and all stages of the process were codified so that no stage could be modified without protracted consultation with the various ANTA curriculum authorities.

As power shifted away from State training authorities, it accumulated in the hands of government and industry peak bodies. By 1994 ANTA had made considerable headway towards the establishment of an integrated national training structure. In its first three years of operation ANTA exercised its control over the various regulatory agencies through a combination of funding and performance agreements. By 1996 ANTA had formalised its control of all decision making and the national training budget, effectively bringing all agencies previously administered under separate arrangements under the ANTA umbrella.

This structure was equally shortlived. Two reviews of ANTA revealed that 'industry' — the primary client of the NTS — was dissatisfied with the service being provided. In particular, there were complaints about the structural complexity of the NTS and the amount of bureaucracy involved in getting training programs developed and accredited. ANTA's response was to develop a slightly more flexible National Training Framework (NTF), the two major elements of which are the Australian Recognition Framework (ARF) and nationally endorsed Training Packages.

These moves appear to reflect less concern on the part of ANTA with teaching quality than with controlling training structures and content. A new Skills Passport system is being proposed as a portable, formal record of an individual's competencies. The post-compulsory education system is now characterised by registered providers using industry-designed and nationally endorsed education and training products.

Seamless pathways are being developed so that people from a wide range of backgrounds can access different types of education. Many vocational education and training providers and higher education institutions have successfully cultivated relationships that facilitate articulation from one sector to another. This applies to movement in both directions and a recent feature is graduates undertaking vocational and training qualifications — a reverse articulation — in larger numbers than students moving on from vocational training to university. Various arrangements allow students to be granted credit toward study in another sector using qualifications already obtained elsewhere. The various sectors are moving towards recognising each others' 'passports' at their borders, rather than through uniformity across sectors.

These changes heralded the removal of the term 'curriculum' from the key national training design structures. This underscores the central point about the NTF — it is a regulatory rather than educational system. Over the past 10 years there has been a significant realignment of power relations in training management, through the creation of a complex plethora of regulatory agencies and artifacts — CBT, ASF, NFROT, ITABs, AQF — all controlled and operated by another acronym — the superordinate ANTA. What we have is a hydra of agencies, regulatory artifacts or tools to serve the national training reform agenda. What this phenomenon does reflect is the extent to which social and political control is manifested through the process of reform and the creation of new institutional and technical forms and tools.

The reform effort has been political and bureaucratic rather than educational. The outcome is a new national system whose chief role is to manage and regulate training through guidelines, blueprints, templates and agreements. The agenda has not engaged educators in reforming processes of teaching and learning and offers no new educational experiences for students or employees. Nor has any new teaching paradigm for the majority of post-school teachers/trainers emerged. Its primary purposes are to enable training outcomes to be certified against a set of agreed standards and to provide a policy and accountability framework for the disbursement of public funds.

It is up to education and training providers to interpret this regulatory framework in the context of educational values, inputs and outcomes so that the design and delivery of training is informed by a set of principles on teaching, learning and cognition, particularly those concerned with the teaching of and learning by adults. It is this that Parts 2 and 3 of this book address.

The current strategic vision of ANTA for the future of Australian education and training for the period 1998 to 2003 has the following main objectives:

- Education and training as the basis of an Australian democracy in which all have an opportunity to be active members of society with equality of access.
- The creation of a learning society with a culture that deeply values skill, knowledge and lifelong learning, with intellectual and human capital recognised as the mainspring of national and individual prosperity, sustainable growth and international competitiveness.
- Enhancing mobility in the labour market.
- Industry playing a major role in the reform of education and training.
- A seamless post-compulsory system of education and training, enabling individuals to move through formal and informal systems in any order and back again with confidence that their qualifications and skills are portable and recognised.
- Maximising the value of public expenditure.

A national policy framework for lifelong learning is now being built on the wealth of information and experience gained from research promoted by ANTA and the NCVER, as well as from experience in other developed countries. The second national research and evaluation strategy for vocational education and training in Australia, covering the period 2001 to 2003, was developed in 2000 following extensive consultations with a wide range of interest groups. The strategy identifies 10 priorities that provide the focus for the national research effort. These include:

- the economics of vocational education and training
- lifelong learning and the social and community aspect of VET
- innovation and the changing skills of the Australian workforce
- the vocational education and training provider
- equity in vocational education
- the quality of teaching and training in VET.

About $2.2m is available annually to support the research work.

## ■■■ COMPETENCY-BASED TRAINING (CBT)

In most English-speaking countries a competency-based approach to education, training and assessment has emerged as a key educational policy, with governments, business and trade unions joining forces to promote the competency agenda (e.g. National Vocational Qualifications in the UK; New Zealand's National Qualifications Framework; National Skills Standard in the USA). Competencies have been seized on as a means of facilitating uniform credit transfer arrangements between sectors, something that can only happen if discrete competencies are taught, assessed and recorded. It has been perceived by some as *the* answer and by others as the wrong answer to the improvement of education and training (Harris *et al.*, 1995). In each country competency standards are driven by a political rather than an educational impetus to prepare the workforce for the competitive global economy. Simultaneously, a growing chorus of critics argue that the approach is conceptually confused, empirically flawed and inadequate for the needs of a learning society (Chappell, 1996; Hyland, 1994). However, CBT is the central feature of the Australian NTS and the focus is on the introduction of competency-based training systems for all recognised vocational courses with incorporation in industry standards of the key competencies outlined in the *Mayer Report* (1992).

The purpose of CBT is to equip people with successfully attained and demonstrated skills that entitle the learner to the relevant qualification under the Australian Qualifications Framework. It is also a means of involving industry in the design, development and provision of training. CBT is outcomes-oriented rather than a 'time spent training' approach — on the old apprenticeship model. CBT is delivered by recognised training organisations, industry enterprises and educational establishments. Typically, a number of units of competency are grouped together to form a qualification accredited at a particular AQF level. Mutual recognition allows a worker to take a completed or partially completed qualifiaction to a different provider or State, where it will be recognised. According to ANTA estimates, around 75 per cent of the workforce is covered by competency standards (see www.austraining nsw.com.au/cbt.html).

The advantages of CBT include:
- a clear statement of skill requirements rather than implicit assumptions
- a broadening of skill classification to encourage multiskilling
- the development of clear skill-based career paths, rather than time spent or seniority
- the clear identification of the skills a person has and comparing these with workplace requirements to provide a common reference point for the individual for industry and for trainers
- the possibility of incremental recognition of competencies achieved
- a basis for recognition of prior learning supporting portability
- qualifications that are gained are recognised nationally as linked into AQF
- a basis for developing relevant training programs that address identified needs and that have clear outcomes
- an opportunity to redress past and present inequities, for example women
- training is responsive to the needs of the workplace.

While CBT is regarded by some as a visionary system that will lead Australian industry into the twenty-first century ahead of its competitors, others view it disparagingly as behaviourism in disguise; no more than a mechanistic, task-oriented system to serve an economic rationalist paradigm. The major criticisms involve issues such as the following.

## defining competency

There are some unresolved issues relating to the definition of competency, the translation of competency standards into effective training programs, the reliable and valid measurement/assessment of competency and the close association of competency with the ability to perform a narrow set of tasks or operations. The most widely held conception of competency is that it is task-based, conceived in terms of discrete behaviours associated with the successful completion of atomised tasks. Competency is not an overt observable behaviour but inferred from performance. In order to make assessment easier, complex work tasks are broken down into components. Competence is therefore assessed within small elements of a complex task using observable and measurable outcomes. The aim is the transparent specification of a competency so that there can be no disagreement about what constitutes satisfactory performance. The task becomes the competency. It is individualised, emphasises outcomes (what individuals know or can do) and allows flexible pathways for achieving those outcomes.

This approach is not interested in connections between tasks and ignores potential transformations that could occur when tasks are integrated or sequenced. This places competency within the Taylorist traditions of the past. This leads to a restriction of education and training programs to behaviours specified in an occupation's competency standards. The checklist approach to determining whether or not a competency is achieved suggests a 'minimum' level of acceptable performance rather than a standard of excellence. The weaknesses of this simple model are clear. It is reductionist, ignores underlying attributes, ignores group processes, ignores complexity of performance, is slow in reacting to factors in the real world and ignores professional judgment in intelligent performance. Behaviourism is criticised for ignoring connections between tasks, the attributes that underlie performance, the meaning, intention or motivation to act, the effect of context and interpersonal aspects. Behavioural objectives can never be achieved in practice with the precision they offer in theory. Studies of the development of expertise as well as the constructivist view of learning suggest that people make judgments, review, reflect on and change behaviour, reconstructing relevant and useful knowledge as they interact with a situation (Hodkinson & Issitt, 1995). Job performance involves more than the performance of a well defined set of tasks in a routine predictable way.

Hager (1995) defends CBT, arguing that it does include more generic or key competencies rather than a simple behaviourist Lego brick system, and these were in fact promoted in the *Carmichael* and *Mayer Reports*. The *Carmichael Report* refers to 'whole work roles', which implies not only technical skills but also communication, relationship, coordination, decision making, time management and contingency management skills. The *Mayer Report* also listed key competencies that promote emphasis on general personal skills but these have been constrained by the tenor of the narrow perception of the competency drive.

The focus on observable behaviour in a scientific management tradition cements competence to industrial standards and locks employees into a static view of what the world of work is like. Given the vagaries of predicting the future we need to ensure that each person is prepared not only with specific skills but with general portable skills to cope with whatever the future may hold for them.

A richer concept of competency is needed that integrates the attributes of the individual and the tasks that are performed, whether these tasks are specific skills requiring a minimum of thought or high-level general skills such as critical thinking or problem solving. Such a concept would help to remove the dichotomy between training and education. Even at the lowest level, workers need to be encouraged to consider the situational appropriateness of the skill as they apply it so that there is no inappropriate uniformity in doing a task. There is discretion for the employee to use in how to approach a task. The standard is not about procedure but about outcome.

## the philosophy

The key competencies advocated by the various reports are shaped by a set of assumptions about the skills that are lacking in the workforce that individuals need in order to participate in it effectively, about the nature of work in the future, about the way work will be organised and about the sorts of jobs that will be available. These assumptions are supported by other beliefs such as the need to be internationally competitive and flexible, that employees at all levels should be able to contribute to their full potential and that technological change requires the acquisition of new skills and higher level skills and a need to bridge the gulf between general and vocational education. Few would argue with this thesis. However, the philosophy and practice of CBT is causing considerable disquiet.

Many critics believe that competency programs will not improve learning. Critics see competency-based training as a tool of administration rather than of instructional reform. That is it provides a means of setting educational objectives and organising program delivery that promises efficiency, effectiveness and responsiveness to the needs of industry. Goals are seen as the epitome of sound management practices. But whether the learning has made the individual more competent in the workplace is rarely evaluated. There is a tendency to reduce goals to those that are measurable and observable. Goals are set only when they can be pursued without risk of failure. The assumptions are that more education and training results in better economic performance and that serving industry needs serves individual and societal needs (Gonczi, 1997). There is an unspoken and often unrecognised power struggle over who controls post-compulsory education goals, standards and curricula. Does it empower individuals to choose what to learn and how to learn it or is the framework a prescription to which funding is tied, students benchmarked and stamped out with particular attributes and employee advancement and pay determined? (Mulcahy, 1996) Who determines which skills, knowledge and values are included or excluded? Since it is industry-driven the answer is reasonably clear. This also means that the role of CBT in developing lifelong learning is limited.

Many advocates are attempting to disentangle CBT from the philosophy of behaviourism, which has tainted the approach. But it is difficult to avoid behaviourist notions in specifying performance-based objectives clearly in advance. There is no way of avoiding either the rational instrumental link between the needs of the employed or government and the learning activities imposed on the learner. Behavioural objectives also impose a top-down approach to designing a learning system in which the needs of the learners are subordinate to the needs of the economy. Skill development and educational achievement are subordinated to job performance objectives. In this context learning becomes a tool of corporate balance sheets and political decisions. CBT can become a highly regulated form of provision. Humanist values do not enter the equation. The CBT approach is essentially located in an empirical analytic paradigm, which takes the view that reality is objective and that individuals and the world are separate, knowledge involves objectively proven facts and what cannot be legitimately quantified is not worth knowing. It is a dominant Western scientific approach exemplified in education and psychology as behaviourism.

The major alternative paradigm is a situational interpretive one, which recognises that people give personal meaning to experiences; meaning grows from the way individuals interact with the world. Events can be interpreted in different ways by different people because they have different past experiences and expectations. Thus in contrast with the mechanistic efficient curriculum of the CBT movement, the experientialists would focus on learner-centred, democratic, problem-solving orientations. CBT in this paradigm is largely compatible with a cognitive view of learning so that competence is not trained behaviour like a conditioned Pavlovian response but a thoughtful process reflecting interaction between context, culture, social practice, experience and personal attributes used to achieved outcomes in jobs located within organisational-particular relationships.

We will be raising these differences again when we discuss adult education in Chapter 7. The differences arise from the balance of emphasis placed on the major elements of a learning situation, that is the attributes and needs of the learner, the structuring of the subject matter and societal influences. A further paradigm that impacts on adult education and that is totally alien to CBT is the critical reflective paradigm. In this paradigm reflective thinking is used on taken-for-granted assumptions and values to aid understanding of fundamental issues impacting on human action and interests. It is the uncovering of the hidden agenda.

## the economic imperative

Critics argue that CBT represents a systematic attempt to restructure much of post-school education around a set of principles that is fundamentally derived from economic pressures. It is a new way of viewing the nexus between work, training and education. Competencies are presented as the cement that will hold together microeconomic reform and industrial relations policy and cure Australia's economic problems. The objective is to reconstitute education and training to serve economic goals. The skills of the employee are viewed as capital that benefits the economic growth of society. This sort of narrow instrumental perception of education serves the interests of social allocation, not the development of human potential. It leads to a dangerous assumption that current unemployment is due to a lack of relevant skills and once this is remedied the jobs will be there. This is a flagrant deception perpetrated on the unemployed. A training-led recovery is very unlikely. Neither is there any validity in the assumption that more skills will lead to higher productivity. In any case, education reforms should lead not only to an economically richer nation but also to one socially and culturally better off. The equation between economic goals and the goals of education is one that needs far more debate and calls into question the aims of education, which, certainly at all levels, should be concerned with a wider proactive role in society than merely the work role.

CBT is in effect a child of economic rationalism, providing a prescriptive and managerial solution, responding to a technicist instrumental agenda — a neat human capital package that can be delivered by education establishments and workplaces and monitored by a centralised bureaucracy, according to criteria that stress the importance of measurable outcomes, uniformity and an instrumental definition of education. Useful general portable and flexible training has been given to professionals and managers, while shop floor employees are given what is needed for the next job rather than general portable life skills. Competency standards can be as restraining as the hierachical Fordist model of work they are seeking to replace by fossilising current skills rather than continually reworking them to meet developing needs.

## role of pedagogy
Scant attention is paid to knowledge about learning and teaching in the CBT rationale. Curriculum development, curriculum articulation, theories of teaching and psychological issues in teaching are all generally ignored. Research in educational psychology reveals that the learning of skills is a complex task that does not always require the mastering of simple tasks as a precursor to learning more complex ones (Porter *et al.*, 1992).

Specific knowledge is located in bodies of knowledge and students and teachers need to understand where that knowledge came from and how it can be understood in other contexts and experiences. Learning is also a social act and happens best where people cooperate. Each learner also brings to the classroom different life experiences and expectations; they consequently learn different things from the teacher and input a variety of their own learnings to modify what is going on in the classroom. Teaching cannot be equated with the transfer of discrete skills.

Many of these issues are addressed in the work of adult educators and their approach to adult education or, as some term it, andragogy. Chapter 7 focuses on the principles of andragogy, which demand a humanist approach. CBT remains constrained by the notion that it is the teacher who issues information to the student, who in turn digests it and manifests competence by a demonstration of satisfying some technical competency standard. As Porter *et al.* (1992) argue, 'with ends determined and assessment standardised, there is little room for pedagogic manoeuvrability' (p. 56).

## industry control

It has been fundamental to the CBT movement that discrete competencies should be determined by industry. By controlling the programs, industry can ensure that only the specific skills it requires at a given time for a given market are taught. This can lead to a dumbing down of the workforce and control of the workforce as industry demands employment flexibility in how many and who are employed. Support for industry control of training in Australia was given the imprimatur of Prime Minister Paul Keating at *The Australian Financial Review's* Conference on Australian Industry, 5 July 1994, when he said, 'it was now up to industry to take control of the training agenda'. He continued by focusing on skills and industry needs — 'industry needs to recognise its role in improving the skill levels of its employees…industry must set the direction of training and drive the administrative processes so that they are simple and relevant to the needs of firms'. He continued by describing training as a mainstream economic issue. Nowhere was education or the role of educationalists mentioned. This high-level dependence on industry is very questionable.

First, industry might not be able to identify and articulate clearly what competencies are required. Research completed in NSW suggests that small- to medium-sized firms have great difficulty in identifying their own training needs, let alone the key competencies for their industry. Thus the wrong competencies might be chosen and several major firms might control the selection for their purposes, which might not suit smaller firms. Second, Australian industry is made up largely of small firms. Small firms are notorious for having short-term planning horizons. Therefore it is doubtful that considering only immediate skill requirements to solve current shortages will really serve the nation well in the future. A constant interplay is required between industry, education and training to ensure that we don't create a population skilled to meet needs that no longer exist and underskilled for emerging needs.

## assessment issues

Assessment is based on competency standards endorsed by the National Training Board. The standards are grouped into units that describe the major functions of a work role. Each unit is composed of a number of elements of competency, which in turn are made up of a number of performance criteria. Thus the standards describe what a worker is expected to do in order to fulfil a major work role (elements of competency). They indicate the level of performance required for each outcome (performance criteria) and the range of contexts and conditions across which performance is to be demonstrated (range of variables). These three components of the competency standard give the trainer and assessor a template for assessment.

How much evidence is required for competency to be inferred depends on principles of good practice, cost, time and practical considerations such as disruption to work schedules. The three most used methods of assessing competency are observation of work activity, examination of work output and asking questions about work activity. Observation of the work activity might involve a simulation. Essential questions about the potential reliability and validity of assessments are not raised. Nor are the assessment procedures independent of the interests of persons making the judgments or decisions as to what is required. The content has been established by industry and is assessed on standards set by industry. Education specialists have been left on the sidelines as commentators on a process that many of them perceive as based on unsafe and untested assumptions. The emphasis on objective, atomistic assessment leaves no room for the concept of education as conversation — as the ability to make or even suspend judgments, to build relations and make decisions — and eliminates consideration of values such as prejudice against those who are different or individual versus group needs, business ethics, etc.

Ongoing technological and economic revolutions are increasing pressure on teachers of trade and professional subjects to raise the levels of performance of those they teach. Maintaining skill and knowledge currency is a major challenge in a period of profound and escalating change. Economic stringency has affected the availability of teaching resources, aids and access to modern equipment and is proving a major inhibitor in maintaining professional teacher credibility. Additionally, the effective teaching of trade and professional subjects and the training of teachers for the teaching of such subjects are made far more difficult when governments implement new administrative structures affecting skill learning and recognition that have not been carefully and extensively trialled before wide implementation.

## research evaluation of CBT

The concerted effort to ensure that CBT is implemented widely throughout TAFE systems in Australia occurred before it was rigorously and extensively evaluated in pilot programs. Cornford (1997) argued that the political decision to implement CBT before reviewing recent empirical studies raises significant questions about CBT's effectiveness and success. It has come to be widely accepted that the decision to introduce CBT in preference to other possible approaches was political (Stevenson, 1995; Ryan, 1997). Even the Australian Federal Parliament's House of Representatives Standing Committee for the Workforce for the Future seems to have accepted that the decision to adopt and implement CBT involved political leaders, business leaders and the trade union movement, with scant consultation of teachers and vocational education experts (Jones, 1995). However, the omission of teachers, vocational education experts and researchers from the consultation process is a serious miscalculation since it denies input from the professionals who are best able to provide well-founded research evidence and experience-based judgments about the practical issues involved. Many concepts that might appear attractive political propositions are unworkable in practice. McBeath (1995) has pointed out that the history of curriculum innovation and change is replete with the failure of new curricula because there was little or no teacher support.

The Australian Federal Government failed to recognise that the CBT model it was imposing was an entirely theoretical model. No real attempts to quantify the effectiveness of this new paradigm or to examine the practical implementation problems of newer concepts of assessment moving from normative- to criterion-referenced forms were made before official moves to implementation. Despite the importance of the effectiveness of competency-based training, only a handful of studies to date have moved beyond the theoretical or anecdotal level. Disillusion had set in sufficiently for a straw vote on CBT at the final meeting of the Australian National Training Authority (ANTA) Research Council conference in October-November 1996 to reveal that the balance of votes was 'clearly against CBT' (Foyster, 1997, p. 32).

The debate on the effectiveness of competency-based approaches in raising the quality of skilling in Australia has intensified (Foyster, 1997) and the focus has shifted from political and economic debate to studying what is actually occurring in vocational areas where competency-based training has been introduced. The limited research that has been conducted has focused on practical aspects of implementation and, for convenience, can be divided into two distinct categories. The first is the issues facing teachers and teachers' judgments concerning the effectiveness of CBT in developing more effective and advanced skills in specific trades and professions. The second is the extent to which CBT is implemented. These are held to be essential issues in evaluating the effectiveness of CBT (e.g. Ryan, 1997; Van Berkel, 1997). Cornford (1996; 1997) details much research that provides telling criticism in relation to both implementation and effectiveness issues.

## effectiveness and implementation issues

Despite the importance of teachers in implementing curriculum innovation, very few studies have investigated the problems that they have been facing with CBT. The two studies by Cornford (op. cit.) sought the views of teachers, chiefly in NSW TAFE in a wide range of trade and professional subjects, who were teaching or had taught competency-based subjects and who had considerable teaching and industry experience. Overall, many similar findings emerged from both the more and less experienced teaching groups. The most striking findings were the following:

- Some 63.9 per cent of experienced teachers considered that the introduction of CBT had hindered or severely hindered their students' attainment of skill performance levels, with 25 per cent considering that performance levels had not changed.

- Some 38.9 per cent of experienced teachers and 33.3 per cent of less experienced teachers considered the information supplied to them on CBT to be poor or very poor.
- In all 57.1 per cent of more experienced teachers saw support in terms of resources and equipment as poor or very poor, and 33.9 per cent of less experienced teachers made the same judgment.
- The logical sequencing of modules was seen to be very good or good by only 25 per cent of more experienced teachers, who were more inclined to see this aspect as average.
- Some 54.3 per cent of the more experienced teachers considered the time for teaching relevant theory as adequate, with none indicating that it was very adequate.
- Only 33.3 per cent of less experienced teachers considered provisions for practice in competency-based subjects or modules good, with 38.9 per cent of experienced teachers concurring.
- Some 59.4 per cent of less experienced and 55.9 per cent of more experienced teachers encountered problems 'often' or 'very often' in teaching students in more advanced competency-based modules/subjects because of insufficient student understanding of previous modules apparently passed. This is a considerable problem. In CBT the issue of skill levels actually attained has great significance, since the whole concept of a statement of competency implies a cast-iron guarantee that the individual awarded that qualification can perform at that level, and presumably move on to more advanced levels!
- In all 37.5 per cent of less experienced teachers saw the standards set in objectives as low or very low, while approximately the same percentage of more experienced teachers (33.4%) made this judgment. Some 44.4 per cent of less experienced teachers and 58.3 per cent of the more experienced saw them as average. However, in terms of standards actually attained by students, 42.3 per cent of less experienced and 54.3 per cent of more experienced teachers considered these to be low or very low.

Roux-Salembien, McDowell and Cornford (1996) examined the effectiveness of CBT with commercial cookery teachers in NSW TAFE. Results generally indicated strong dissatisfaction with CBT and the way it had been implemented, with 58.3 per cent indicating that they were dissatisfied or very dissatisfied and a further 16.8 per cent undecided. Some 50 per cent of the respondents felt that they had not received sufficient training on CBT prior to its introduction, while 72.1 per cent indicated a desire to undergo further training. There was evidence that these teachers did not have a full understanding of criterion-referenced testing and of whether or not recognition of prior learning was a key feature of CBT.

Student motivation also emerged as a considerable concern of these commercial cookery teachers. In all 48.7 per cent either disagreed or strongly disagreed and 26.2 per cent were undecided as to whether or not CBT was improving student learning outcomes. These findings from commercial cookery teachers are cause for serious concern when it comes to considering the suitability of competency-based approaches for increasing the effectiveness of skill learning. Commercial cookery is a subject that appears to lend itself particularly to CBT since the ability to produce readily observed required outcomes has traditionally been a major focus in teaching and assessment in this occupational area.

An NCVER study (Lowrie, 1999) suggests that there is still a variety of understandings about the nature and practice of CBT among teachers/trainers, which were often related to whether they perceived CBT to be suited to their industry area. Billet (1999) noted that the instructional and curriculum practices existing prior to CBT were judged more conducive to the development of required skills as well as the teachers' knowledge in assisting with the development of transferable knowledge plus a variety of instructional processes such as self-directed learning and off-job experiences. The broader reform movement permitting self-direction and self-pacing (see Chapter 8) coupled with teacher expertise and discretion to tailor arrangements and provide appropriate experiences were seen as the way to create adaptable and flexible students. The great challenge for CBT lies in increasing its capacity to get beyond simply achieving pre-set goals (Mulcahy, 2000).

Fitzgerald (1994) surveyed business and industry as a consultant for ANTA on the issue of implementation of national training reforms. Generally, the need for reform was widely accepted. In relation to competency standards and their implementation, Fitzgerald (op. cit., pp. 20–21) raised four particularly relevant points among a number of others:

1. There is conceptual confusion about exactly what constitutes a competency-based system, leading to a failure to address adequately curriculum, delivery and assessment implications.
2. The process of developing competency standards has become far more complicated and resource-intensive than initially thought.
3. Industry standards are being developed by bodies unrepresentative of either experienced key enterprises or experienced teachers/trainers in those industries.
4. The standards development methodology is too task-oriented, detailed and prescriptive and, consequently, reduces enterprise and training provider flexibility and promotes uniformity rather than permitting necessary variations to suit local conditions and the specific needs of enterprises.

Fitzgerald concluded that there was 'evident widespread industry acceptance of, and support for, training based on competency'. However, from interviews and discussions with firms 'it was apparent that this support for the concept does not necessarily translate into support for the reforms as implemented' (Fitzgerald, 1994, p. 20).

In 1995, the ANTA Research Council provided funding for a project to study the nature of learning, the conditions under which learning occurs in the workplace and the relationship between formal training and workplace learning in three enterprises (Taylor). The messages coming through clearly in this study are the following:

- Training is not a lock-step process of individual competency accumulation.
- Effective learning is a complex cognitive and interpersonal process, and highly contextualised.

The implications of the findings for formal training and competency assessment are profound:

- First, if standard patterns of work and learning cannot be assumed, then the operationalising of national competencies in training processes must be done at the site of learning, not in the national centre.
- Second, this process must be undertaken by skilled professionals.
- Third, the design and delivery of training must be informed by a set of psycho-educational principles about teaching, learning and cognition.

These research findings effectively illustrate the limits of standardisation. This is not to say that standards for competency and certification have no place in a system of training. What it does mean is that quality outcomes do not rest on generic guidelines, procedures and packages. These inputs are simply the point of departure — they signal a broad consensus about roles and responsibilities in the training arena and about the bottom line in terms of reasonable client expectations. The real work of training begins when training providers and their clients get together to work out what needs to be done and how to do it, using the resources supplied by the system and, most important, their own individual and collective knowledge and understandings. This is the challenge that educators should embrace.

## recognition of prior learning (RPL)

The move to recognise prior learning (RPL) is a valuable part of CBT. How someone gained a skill or a formal qualification is less important than their ability to demonstrate the competency. This could empower vast numbers of individuals who currently feel locked out of further study and advanced training/education. In this way barriers of elitism can be broken down. Additionally, vocational courses, workplace courses and TAFE programs are being promoted as career options other than university-based ones. Articulation between TAFE, universities and industry does not mean a drop in standards. The exit standard is more important than the entry requirement. This concept has long been in vogue in distance-learning/open-learning contexts. More and enhanced dialogue has developed within and across sectors.

In summary, it could be argued ungenerously that CBT provides a status quo, merely providing access to skills and no real change, ignoring holistic, complex interpretive, problem-solving learning. It retains current practice and existing industry standards rather than developing new and creative ways of doing things. There is no evidence that CBT works in the way intended or promotes successful transfer of knowledge. It omits the teaching of values and culture. There is little personal development or portable life skill learning along the lines of that suggested in Chapter 1. The intention was sound but the reality is limited by the instrumental needs of the moment. One writer over a decade ago sounded the warning bells by describing CBT as a 'process whereby social behaviour is brought within the sanctionable jurisdiction of bureaucratically mandated rules' (Hilbert, 1982). However, where generic competencies have been used, Moy (1999) found that they were regarded as essential for work and life by employers and employees. The nature of work and life is changing so rapidly that to meet the needs of the new millennium, generic as well as specific competencies are necessary.

CBT as a concept was perhaps seriously and grievously flawed from the outset. Hager (1995) has conceded that competency standards are concerned with summative assessment, that is measuring the effectiveness of overall training. Summative assessment and CBT standards thus represent the end product and do not reflect the complex processes of learning leading to this desirable state of training or issues of formative assessment. Formative assessment involves assessment of all learning that leads ultimately to readiness of the individual for summative assessment. It is also apparent that CBT policy making and implementation lack any substantial basis provided by educational and psychological research and theory on such aspects as skill learning, cognitive psychology, adult learning processes and the development of expertise (Stevenson, 1994, 1995). Therefore, it cannot provide any substantial guidance for those who need to develop curricula or teach over a number of stages of learning development across a varying age range of students to ensure students achieve genuinely superior levels of learning and skill performance. Serious replanning of the CBT system must involve broad consultation with teachers and other experts involved in its practical implementation.

The major problem is that industrialists and economists rather than educators are in charge of the CBT drive. There is no real hard research that points conclusively to CBT generating improved industrial performance. It is a bandwagon of hunches, but without research evidence it is hard to refute. It might be that once initial goals of satisfying the overriding concerns of the economy are achieved more holistic concerns will have a place and experts from other fields may have an input.

## ■■■ EQUITY AND FUNDING ISSUES

Access and equity have been addressed in broad terms in the national VET strategy for 1998 to 2003. However, efforts at translation into procedural documents and policy at a lower level are patchy and lack cohesion. Moreover, documents such as *Equity 2001* from ANTA reflect a shift away from strategies for target groups and attacks on systematic barriers to a focus on individuals and remedies to address their specific problems. This entrenches a deficit view of disadvantage.

There are problems investing in skills in that many employers fear high employee turnover after they have spent money training them. Some try to reduce this by providing skills that are unique to their particular firm and avoid portable skills. Smaller firms also meet high training costs per employee compared with larger organisations. Some workers might not be able to participate owing to finances, time, access, family obligations, transport or even a lack of information. There are also unique barriers for certain age groups, minorities and disabled persons. There are still substantial voids in modern training efforts. Time and costs were the major barriers noted in focus reports in the American 21st Century Skills for 21st Century Jobs Summit (1999). Formal institutions need to note these problems and address employees' needs for less costly and more flexible delivery.

A report by NSW TAFE on the current context of vocational training and education (www.tafensw.edu.au/gendequi/inccontx.htm) suggests that unlike other education sectors, females are underrepresented in work-related education and training. Thus there has been a failure to redress the imbalances in their workforce participation and financial rewards relative to men. Women's participation in the workforce is heavily skewed towards lower level skills and part-time work as well as traditionally female occupations. The larger the proportion of women in an organisation the lower the amount of training expenditure and what training there is for women tends to be of the non-accredited induction type or specific product-knowledge courses. Where women enter entry-level traineeships, most are one year long whereas males tend to be on three- to four-year schemes — effectively a dual system of training. Employer-based VET also favours males. Two thirds of those trained by employers in private schemes are men, except in office and clerical/computing skills. There is a danger Australia will have a well resourced training system that caters only for those in full-time employment if a national system dominates. However, if an employer-based system develops more strongly, it is likely to be dominated by relatively short-term exigencies and low-level skill provision. Many women are often part-time employees in small business, which tend not to provide as much training anyway. Thus the involvement of small business in training arrangements is critical. Women and other disadvantaged groups therefore miss out on two counts — through working in small business and often in part-time jobs at a time when the trend is for increased personal provision of training.

If competition for scarce training resources is fierce those chosen are not likely to include many from equity groups, unless some directives or incentives are provided. Employers perceive their financial support for training and education to be aimed at improving business efficiency; they argue that equity policy should be funded by government (Marshman & Assoc., 1996). The consequence of all this is that women more than men take the initiative to fund their own further training, education and qualifications. If current developments, with their greater emphasis on employer involvement and work-based training, continue, it will be at the expense of individual learner-funded involvement, which seriously disadvantages women and other minority groups, such as NESB migrants and indigenous Australians.

This leads to the issue of the cost of lifelong education — a further obstacle in the way of those who want to become lifelong learners. The current focus on 'strategic partnerships' is often code for government wishing to shift some costs onto others. Unless the learning is of an approved vocational type there is no support. Other countries are steaming ahead in this regard, with the UK, for example, providing Individual Learning Accounts to tempt unqualified and marginalised adults back into education. Another British initiative, the Investors In People scheme, could be Australianised (Robinson, 1999b). The USA has tax credits and various forms of scholarships to make education and training accessible, affordable and convenient for all adults. In Australia the current taxation system in both cases would treat such funds as either subject to fringe benefits tax or as income. Australia needs a taxation system that supports lifelong learning. A variety of practical funding methods are available, but what will be put into operation is at present a guess. Should there be entitlement, loans, tax credits? In the USA there is a system of financial assistance for those pursuing lifelong learning, which provides every citizen with a lifetime learning tax credit of 20 per cent of all educational costs up to $5000 each year. In addition, Americans are able to exclude from income tax assessment as a benefit $5250 in college costs paid by their employer. Even in Malaysia, Prime Minister Mahathir's strategy of creating a Multimedia Superhighway to propel the country into the twenty-first century led him to provide cheap loans, tax exemptions and to allow workers to access a percentage of their superannuation funds to buy computers — with an admonition to learn or be left behind.

Businesses in recent times have struggled with the costs of year 2000 technological debugging and more recently with the impact of GST, and are reluctant to spend even more on formal and informal education and training costs for their employees, who might when better qualified move on to another company for promotion. Dockery *et al.* (1997) argue that the lower the skill content and the shorter the learning time the quicker employers can profit from training. This implies that employers have little incentive to invest in training for sophisticated and complex technologies. Therefore, the greater the technical transformation the greater the need for government financing and even training provision. Thus government financing can be crucial in determining whether innovations occur and get diffused. Australian companies are generally small and therefore need to be targeted by public policies. If small firms are to be serious players government intervention is necessary. However, governments should not stand in for the firm in the training role, merely strengthen it. Unless government does share the training costs in areas subject to rapid technological change, training will fall short of what is required, which will have national economic consequences.

Enterprises tend to take a short-term view and to regard staff development as a cost rather than an investment. The long-term view would locate the long-term viability of the business in terms of the quality of their employees and the degree to which they are committed lifelong learners, continually expanding their knowledge, skills and personal qualities to cope with unknown future developments.

Genuine social concern to broaden the social base of participation can backfire by turning opportunities to learn into impositions to be accepted on pain of lifelong inadequacy in a meritocracy that ranks learners (workers and would-be workers) according to their employability at the time. It would seem from this sort of analysis that the hope of Freire and Delors that emancipation be enacted through lifelong learning is a contradiction in terms. In sum, there is a systematic tendency to reproduce social ranking in education and this is exacerbated during periods of increased economic and social inequality associated with the growing role of privitisation and market forces. The State has a role as a social corrector. No other institution can assume this role. The optimum role for government involves a framework of universal entitlement to training coupled with targeted support in particular circumstances. The government needs to draw contingent workers into the policy mainstream. The growing reliance on such workers, particularly in some of the fastest growing technologies, could undermine overall development and the capacity of the whole system. Lifelong learning in reality is in tension between the economic imperative and democracy. Fresh consensus is needed to resolve this situation and it is this very tension the world is witnessing in the contretemps between various groups representing the disadvantaged and the environment and the governmental and business groups ranged on the side of globalism (e.g. demonstrations in Seattle, Melbourne, Davos).

## ■■■ A MARKETING STRATEGY FOR LIFELONG LEARNING IN AUSTRALIA

*A Bridge to the Future,* Australia's national strategy for vocational education and training 1998 to 2003, emphasises the need to develop a training culture through effective marketing. The present question is how can Australia be transformed into a country that not only values education and training but also embraces lifelong learning as a natural and normal activity. The critical need to create a lifelong learning ethic within the Australian community and enterprises led to the development of ANTA's *National Marketing Strategy for Skills and Lifelong Learning.* Marketing strategy has become a major element of ANTA's approach to making skill and lifelong learning a national priority. Marketing is being used as a means of investigating the attitudes, values and behaviour of the general community and employers to skills and lifelong learning so that effective strategies can be set in place to increase demand, provision and interest in lifelong learning.

Three marketing research reports (*National Marketing Strategy for Skills and Lifelong Learning — General Community 2000; National Marketing Strategy for Skills and Lifelong Learning — Employer 2000; National Marketing Strategy for Skills and Lifelong Learning — Training Provider 2000*) have provided quantitative and qualitative data on the attitudes of employers, individuals and providers to skill and lifelong learning. This will guide strategic development to encourage people to learn and maintain an involvement in learning throughout their lives. Detailed information on these projects can be found at www.anta.gov.au

The three marketing studies give an idea of:

- where key sectors fall on a spectrum of attitudes and values towards learning
- how well existing products and services meet market needs and what can be done to improve the fit between supply and demand
- information that can be utilised by government, employers, providers and community bodies in a range of strategies and initiatives to overcome barriers to lifelong learning and increase motivation to engage in learning throughout the community.

Dickie (1999) has reported some early findings from these ANTA surveys. She emphasises that Australians are a mass of contradictions about what they say about what they want and what people will actually respond to in the field of skills acquisition and lifelong learning. Dickie reports that for the majority of people interviewed, learning/training/education does not figure in their personal individual plans for at least the next 10 to 15 years. And then only by necessity, not by desire or design. Australians appear hedonistic — enjoyment and happiness are the primary life goals — not learning. Learning/training/education are seen as important for someone else — my children or grandchildren, colleagues, boss, community — but not for me! This is congruent with findings of a Commonwealth Bank Survey, in which 88 per cent of people thought that access to a good education was the most critical issue facing Australians, but an ABS survey found that 54 per cent of people who hadn't done any education or training in the preceding 12 months said that nothing would get them into education/training now. Most people do not want to be bogged down in institutionalised education. Changing attitudes, values and perceptions to make the whole range of learning opportunities more personally relevant and help people to develop a personal lifelong learning menu from which they select different courses at different times is the critical and difficult task we face.

## two broad goals

In the short term, Australian education and training providers and the government need to understand what different groups of customers want in terms of products and services and what needs to be done to improve the fit between supply and demand. In short, it is about tailoring the capacity of existing learning, training and education systems and networks to supply the market with what it needs and expects, when, how and where it can best be supplied and at an appropriate price.

In the long term, Australia needs a community that is committed and passionate about the idea of learning throughout life, that realises that lifelong learning is not only for work, but for self-esteem, community development, personal fulfilment, parenting, creative development, fun and because it might be useful one day. A 'cultural revolution' is required to turn the vision of a learning society into reality. That means making it easier to access and making it more important, more relevant and more routine for everyone to take up some form of learning at any stage of life.

Now that various consumer and employer segments have been identified from the ANTA surveys, the intention is to use a social marketing approach and behaviour change models similar to those used in health promotion to move segments from indifference to awareness and then on to being ready for change and taking action, feeling positive in their action to continuing to do so. During 2001, ministerial decisions directed that priority will be focused on the employer segments (to lift their investment in training) and on 16- to 24-year-old pessimistic, switched-off young people who regard education as a waste of time and need real pathways, government and employer support and practical career advice. Better recognition of prior learning is another part of the strategy, fuelling the confidence of existing workers by opening doors to higher levels of training. The ACE sector is picking up those who want to learn but have fear barriers. Indigenous and disability blueprints announced by former Education Minister Kemp in July 2000 are focusing on those sections of the community. Thus a range of initiatives and policies are starting to drive Australia slowly towards lifelong education.

## ■■■ LIFELONG EDUCATION — A SELF-EVIDENT GOOD OR DISGUISED CONTROL?

Not only has CBT attracted criticism, even the concept of lifelong education has been placed in the firing line. The prevailing orthodoxy in the developed world about lifelong education seems to involve the following argument (Coffield, 1999):

1. A nation's competitiveness depends on the skills of its people.
2. Therefore, governments have no choice but to introduce workforce upskilling policies.
3. This means education must be 'modernised' and become more responsive to the needs of employers.
4. Education is therefore an instrument of the economy.
5. But the responsibility (and cost) is increasingly borne by individuals if they are to renew their skills regularly and become 'employable' (self-development).

This is no more than an updated version of human capital theory, which unfortunately leads politicians, planners and business managers to focus solely on updating employee skills as a means of maintaining sustainable economic advantage.

Even a Labour UK government had for a period a Minister for Lifelong Education, who claimed, 'if we do not create a learning society, if we do not find the means of generating the appropriate skills and craft and expertise then we will fail to develop our most important resource — our people — and we will fail as an economy in an increasingly globalised market' (Howells, 1997).

Such an approach blames the poverty of undeveloped nations and peoples on a failure to develop human capital and avoids consideration of structural inequalities and injustices. It also ignores the many other factors that interact to determine economic growth and development, such as investment, cooperative industrial relations, new managerial approaches, new methods of production and distribution, cost cutting and new technologies. By reinforcing employers' beliefs that the main obstacle to success is the poor education of the workforce, comprehensive strategies incorporating all these other factors are ignored or delayed.

Lifelong learning also appears in educational and political discourse in a bewildering number of guises. Which is it?

- Is it an instrument for change in individuals, organisations and society? (Darmon *et al.*, 1999)
- Is it a means of increasing national competitiveness?
- Is it a social policy to combat social exclusion and ease the re-entry of the unemployed into the labour market?
- Is it a way of 'updating' skill levels, of promoting the professional and social development of employees and of acquiring new knowledge through the labour processes?
- Is it a means of promoting personal development?
- Is it a strategy to develop the participation of citizens in social, cultural and political affairs, and so on?

There is also a sceptical outlook on lifelong learning that has received little attention up to now in Australia, namely that it is a form of social control and has the potential to become more powerfully so (Tight, 1998). Such criticism makes us aware that we are not discussing an unambiguous or neutral concept, but one that is currently being used by numerous interest groups for different purposes.

The expressions of hope that promoters of lifelong learning and adult education offer for increasing conscientisation, and equality of educational, social, economic and political opportunity (as exemplified in the work of Freire, Knowles, Rogers [see Chapter 7]) have been dampened by critical educators. Coffield (1999), for example, argues that there is a conflict between the rhetoric of lifelong learning and the benefits of flexibility and multiskilling as experienced by employees and required by employers. The employer/government vision of lifelong learning and the learning society continues the depressing picture of social control in disguise and demonstrates the power of the global market as it is operationalised among political and business elites. Coffield supports his argument with reference to the Rover car debacle in the UK. In 1996 the CEO of the Rover Group stated that 'We at the Rover Group Ltd are proud to be among the world's foremost Learning Oganisations...The strength of a company lies in the strength of its people...' The CEO went on to claim in an 'evangelical' message that employees at Rover were more fulfilled, mature, committed and prepared to take responsibility than they had been five years earlier. Three years later it became a horror story, with a massive financial crisis, voluntary redundancy for 2500, the scrapping of overtime and extra work hours without pay for small periods of heavy demand. The moral appears to be that:

- individuals might become lifelong learners, yet remain powerless to affect major decisions that impact on their lives
- the vision of managers and workers being part of the same team might be a fiction peddled by managers and politicians
- lifelong learning can be used to create new forms of control, limiting employability to those who are chosen/willing to enhance their skills to make themselves flexible and employable
- educators need to be aware of the political and economic uses of lifelong education.

Multiskilling, flexibility and increasing self-employability are creating split societies and greater inequality — as updating and learning new skills lead to social control — between those who have and those who haven't, between those who can and those who can't, between those who overcome hurdles and those who meet insurmountable barriers — an educational apartheid between valuable and non-valuable people. Lifelong learning as a philosophy of empowerment seems to have been taken for a ride into a very narrow economic version of 'learning for earning', according to Coffield (op. cit.). As regions and nations outbid each other to attract business investment, employees have little power to deal with peripetetic and shell companies whose main aim is profit maximisation (Barnett & Cavanah, 1994; Greider, 1997).

Heinz (1999) adds the insight that lifelong learning is also becoming a moral obligation on the individual, as well as a social constraint. In Europe, America and Australia both the State and employers are using the rhetoric of lifelong learning first and foremost to make workers more flexible and more employable — 'portfolio workers'. In the words of the Tavistock research team within the UK Learning Society Programme: 'This new discourse on flexibility and employability legitimates the already well-advanced shift of the burden of responsibility for education, training and employment on to the individual, and implicitly denies any notion of objective structural problems such as lack of jobs, and the increasing proportion of poorly paid, untrained, routine and insecure jobs.' (Darmon et al., 1999, p. 38). It also implies that those with learning difficulties might well be excluded from post-school learning as a poor investment at the same time as inclusion is a major policy at school level. Education is moving away from the Delors' concept of individual and social emancipation to an 'investment' that has 'inputs' and 'outputs', with 'stocks' that appreciate.

In the UK and North America, Heinz (op. cit.) argues that lifelong learning is being used as a substitute for a decent system of initial vocational education and training. However, some European countries are trying to create more equity. The French social compromise, for instance, seeks to limit flexibility by, among other things, issuing regulations to make firms more socially responsible (e.g. the same working conditions and entitlements to training for part-time, fixed contract as for full-time staff). Meanwhile, in Spain the social partners agreed to a new training tax on employers and employees, which devotes 50 per cent of all funds to the training of the unemployed in accordance with the principle of solidarity. What does seem to be common in all countries is that trade unionists are reluctantly accepting increased flexibility in return for training to improve employability. But such deals are not 'so much a trade-off as a trap' (Darmon op. cit.), particularly in view of the estimated more than 25 per cent redundancies over the next 10 years. The term 'employability' also disguises the tension between training workers to meet the short-term needs of employers and the preparation for frequent changes of job for which high-level general education might be more useful.

In short, critics of current lifelong education policies argue that lifelong learning is not a self-evident good, but is becoming contested territory between employers, employees, unions and the State. Lifelong learning is being used to socialise workers to the escalating demands of employers, who use:
- 'empowerment' to disguise an increase of workloads via delegation
- 'employability' to make the historic retreat from the policy of full employment and periodic unemployment between jobs more acceptable
- 'flexibility' to cover a variety of strategies to reduce costs, which increase job insecurity.

Lifelong learning, if we are not careful, could simply become debased to 'learning for earning'.

This dismal cynicism can be countered by positive achievements, with lifelong learning heading in the right direction and trying to avoid an all-consuming devotion to satisfying the temporary instrumental needs of industry, ensuring that lifelong learning is as much the property of the individual as the deliverer or system. For example, the London Open College Network has since 1992 attracted back into formal learning via credits large numbers of students from groups under-represented in the past, especially women (63%), the unemployed (43%), the unwaged (23%) and ethnic minorities (39%). Credit-based learning appears to be working because it meets at a number of different levels a huge variety of student needs (Davies, 1999).

# ■■■ THE WAY AHEAD

The country needs to develop a new learning culture — one of lifelong learning for all. The rationale for lifelong learning is multisourced. Primarily owing to the growth of the knowledge-based global economy, the threshold of skills being demanded by employers is rising. Migration from farm to factory was easy compared with that to the knowledge economy. Persons with low skill levels will be penalised. Second, technological development demands continuous renewal and updating of skills as career jobs with one employer become fewer and as job descriptions evolve and diversify under shifting market conditions. Thirdly, irresistible social arguments can be invoked that demand that the current uneven distribution of learning opportunities be remedied, particularly between the unemployed and employed, between genders and between levels of employment. A polarisation between knowledge 'haves' and 'have nots' will pose pressing future political challenges that will weaken the very fabric of democracy if lifelong learning strategies are not introduced. Other issues of mal-distribution of learning opportunities stem from employment in small companies where cost and ability to provide become problems. Lifelong learning could play a major role in breaking the cycle of marginalisation, disadvantage and in delivering increased economic security and an ability to respond to change for individuals and enterprises provided governments oversee and set in place procedures that deter a social control approach by business organisations. One factor that might prevent serious social control lies in the fact that new technologies are shaking up old power relationships with new competencies, not possessed by senior staff, but often by junior staff, being strongly in demand. As a result, there is genuine uncertainty in management and grey areas are opening up, providing space for alternative visions of the workplace, of workplace and lifelong learning and of more radical options to be explored.

Australia's vision for lifelong learning involves a drive for seamless pathways between sectors to create an environment where all Australians are able to access education and continuously upgrade skills and knowledge. This vision is seen as essential in a pursuit for better lives for all and a transition to a knowledge-based economy. It is also about opening doors to those who for a variety of reasons have been disadvantaged. The developing system represents a collaborative effort by governments, industry, unions, private enterprises and communities to address the learning needs of individual Australians in a context of globalisation, technological advance and knowledge explosion in the spirit of the *Delors Report*. Unfortunately, Australia was late in recognising that many clients in post-compulsory education and training are not at entry level and requiring intensive initial-skill training, but are mature adults owing to the changing age structure of workers. Very creative options are needed to cope with and encourage involvement of post-entry-level mature adults, particularly in terms of methods of study to meet the psycho-educational-social needs of this increasing older and often experienced market, as Parts 2 and 3 of this text indicate. There might well be an underlying economic imperative but meeting it will require sensitive approaches to these more human aspects of personal development.

As in most countries there is competition for the scarce resources of government funding and policy making. In Australia, current issues concerning the environment, reconciliation with Aboriginal inhabitants and micro-economic reform are dominant. Thus while motherhood statements are made about the worthwhileness of lifelong learning and the provision of overarching federal policies to lay the foundation for the future education direction, there has been a tendency to place such issues lower down on the priority list. Those issues perceived as important always tend to be sacrificed to those designated 'urgent' as politicians seek expedient, immediate and publicly acknowledged results to boost their careers and government popularity. Putting out brush fires is a political metaphor for standing in most countries. However, educators would argue that it is precisely lifelong education that would facilitate the resolution of many of the other burning issues that will continue to haunt Australia in the future. Adults able to regenerate their knowledge, develop new skills, show critical awareness of issues and generally move towards greater conscientisation could move ecological problems, ethnic tensions and other issues to some degree of resolution more productively and effectively within a national regional and local setting.

The evangelical rhetoric claims that lifelong learning will secure our economic future, civilise our society, develop us spiritually, promote social cohesion and active citizenship and build individual self-confidence and independence. This might be too much to demand at once as massive tidal waves sweep over our shores, erode the past and leave large deposits of everchanging new economic, cultural, and social material for us to use to create the next vision of what Australia should be and do. There are obvious economic benefits to society from a population that is adequately prepared for the future environment but lifelong learning has an important social aspect given the increased longevity of the population. Lifelong learning should be concerned not only with a skilled and flexible workforce but also with enabling people to realise more of their individual potential and with public learning enhancing awareness and understanding of various critical issues in public policy.

While some impressive training initiatives have been made, such as the Hunternet Training Group, which matches training with the developing needs of the Hunter Valley, creating multiskilled tradespeople, a more comprehensive system of lifelong learning in Australia is required, moving beyond policy statements and giving real grunt to a concept which in reality is largely still unstructured, informal, spasmodic and minor. Many educators and institutions might say they are already engaged in lifelong learning, and for some of their students this might well be true, but the challenge is to reach those who are outside the silos of learning — the one in four who never return to education. The bottom line for lifelong learning is policies and programs that reach out to all adults and make education an engaging part of their lives.

Kearns (1999) identified some future directions for promoting and putting into operation lifelong education for all, viz.:

1. *Foundations for all*
   - Provision to ensure that everyone achieves the foundations of lifelong learning from the compulsory years of schooling, for example basic literacy, numeracy and computeracy.
   - Learning to learn skills.
   - Motivation and desire for learning.
   - Personal mastery to drive lifelong personal development.
2. *Strengthening and developing pathways, bridges and transitions*
   - Strengthen and extend reciprocal pathways between education/training, workplace and home. This will require substantial reform of the post-compulsory education and training system to ensure a wider range of appropriate learning options.
   - Support the key transitions individuals face.
   - Ensure support and safety net provision for disadvantaged groups and individuals.
   - Recognise prior learning (learning passport system?).
   - Place the focus on the needs of the learner, not the needs of the system.
3. *Foster learning organisations and institutions*
   - Encourage enterprises, institutions and government agencies to develop as learning organisations.
   - Integrate work and learning in enterprises.
   - Build strategic partnerships, for example VET and community organisations like ACE.
   - Orient VET to lifelong learning objectives.
   - Recognise informal learning in the workplace and community.
4. *Extend the role of information and learning technologies*
   - Ensure everyone achieves basic information literacy.
   - Continue process of making modern learning technologies widely available through the community.
   - Support and encourage individuals lacking confidence in the use of these technologies.
   - Extend use of modern technologies to widen equitable access to education and training opportunities.
5. *Develop learning communities*
   - Encourage and support communities at all levels to develop as learning communities: towns, cities, local communities and common interest networks.
   - Foster partnership and network development as a key component of learning communities, linking organisations, workplaces, institutions and communities.
   - Provision for a variety of consumer segments based on marketing data.
   - Generally, foster a learning culture to underpin economic activity and quality of life for all in a learning society.

**6.** *An increased national investment in skills and knowledge*
- Even though successive governments in Australia have ensured that we have a comparatively sound level of national investment in education and training, it is difficult to see how we can become a world-leading skills nation, as we must, without raising national investment further, not just from public but from private sources too.
- Lifelong education cannot be thought of in isolation, and for the policy to work at all stakeholders must work together in coherent partnership to mobilise the necessary resources.

The challenge is to develop a more inclusive vision (or preferably competing visions) of lifelong learning, more comprehensive social theories of learning and more democratic and socially just policies for lifelong learning than currently exist. Parts 2 and 3 of this text review the educational and psychological bases for developing lifelong education, with special reference to adults.


## SUMMARY

The growing consensus on the need for lifelong learning grew out of recurrent education, prompted strongly by OECD and UNESCO, and involved social, cultural and individual objectives as well as educational and economic ones. Australia has tended to emphasise the economic benefits of training reform and has only since the mid-1990s moved towards the more enlightened vision of the *Delors Report*. Now lifelong learning is promoted by ANTA and MYCEETA as vital to Australia's international business competitiveness, the employability of individuals, the inclusion of all Australians in society and the life satisfaction of all. Lifelong learning does not mean recurrent training but a constant relationship with education. A large bureaucratic structure has been erected to ensure the aims of the NTS are met, a structure that is more to do with control than with educational processes.

The competency-based approach is the government's response to the changed economic and technological environment and it is aimed at facilitating a nationally cohesive training system that is responsive to industries' needs and allows flexible training arrangements. While it is important that education, training and the workplace are linked more effectively than in the past, it seems unlikely that CBT can create a sufficiently flexible education structure and process, based as it is on standardised, national competencies within an instrumental behaviourist framework, to facilitate lifelong eduation with a more humanist mission.

Evidence from a range of studies indicates that CBT has not been successfully or extensively implemented in either the public or the private sector. There are wide differences in degrees of implementation in TAFE in different States, while in business and industry there appears to be a very limited adoption of CBT. Many

TAFE teachers surveyed in NSW do not believe that it has improved levels of performance. Major practical problems in implementation stem from the complexity of the issues, confused conceptualisation and failure to engage in extensive pilot studies to identify weaknesses and to prepare teachers for the implementation of a new system involving distinctly different philosophies.

Lifelong education has not been greeted by radical educators as the blessing it has been heralded as by others, such as Freire. Its application to control entry into the labour market and stratify people according to skills has been seen as a way employers and governments can manipulate employability. The Federal government is meeting this challenge by taking steps to increase equity and access for all groups to post-compulsory years of training and education as a countermeasure. Three other challenges also exist: the challenge of creating social cohesion, the challenge of creating proactive partnerships between stakeholders and that of developing smooth pathways between workplaces, home, education sectors and training throughout life.

Marketing surveys have been conducted to determine attitudes to lifelong education among consumers, employers and training providers, and these facilitate the segmentation of these constituencies, enabling the drawing up of specific marketing plans to meet particular needs.

# chapter 3

# learning organisations and learning communities

**The illiterate of the year 2000 will not be the individual who cannot read or write but the one who cannot learn, unlearn and relearn.**
Alvin Toffler

**A learning enterprise...requires a shift away from the bums on seats training mentality to innovations interlacing work and learning; to the sharing of development, transfer and use of knowledge and skills; and to continual improvements in what is provided, how it is provided and when it is provided.**
Ford, 1991, p. 60

The first two chapters presented argument that the pressure of global forces is already imposing considerable change on learning and working. It was emphasised that the response of the Australian government, like others in the developed world to the changing business and economic environment, has been to invest effort and money in training the workforce, with particular emphasis on CBT and the start of a policy drive towards lifelong learning. However, the response of organisations, whether in business or other fields, has to be wider in scope than CBT to encourage the involvement of all employees in lifelong learning. The challenge for all organisations is to create adaptive, cohesive, equitable, integrated, participative, productive environments; encouraging learning communities and a learning culture in collaboration with other partners to develop scarce resources of people, materials, land and energy. The narrow, quantity-driven production modes of the past have left legacies of wasted human, social and environmental resources.

Lifelong education, involving both work-related and personal skills and knowledge, is an inevitable response, enabling not only individuals, enterprises and the nation to benefit economically but also the possibility of enhancing social cohesion through access and equity policies at a time when social divisions could increase. Thus we are looking at the creation of a learning society, based on a learning culture. This requires efforts not only from government, education providers and organisations but also from communities. All organisations, informal and formal, community, social, academic and the like, not just those in the business field, need to become learning organisations if a learning culture and society is to flourish. This chapter considers briefly issues and considerations surrounding the development of learning organisations and learning communities as the main elements in the process of creating a knowledge-based society.

## ■■■ THE LEARNING ORGANISATION

The *learning organisation* is a concept that is becoming an increasingly widespread philosophy in modern business organisations from multinationals to small ventures, but it needs to encompass all organisations to create a learning society. The learning organisation has its origins in companies like Shell, where Arie de Geus described learning as the only sustainable competitive advantage. The key characteristic for the success of any organisation is its ability to learn. The fundamental source of competitive advantage is shifting from resources to knowledge. The fundamental challenge is for each organisation to develop the capacity to create and diffuse knowledge throughout itself. There must be a focus on how to create conditions for learning instead of investing in precisely defined organisational structures quickly made obsolete by changing conditions. Focusing on the original business concept, the learning organisation is seen as enabling an organisation to become more responsive to an increasingly unpredictable and dynamic environment. It seeks to promote collective and organisation-wide learning, skills and knowledge that transcend boundaries of departments, areas and hierarchies. Here are some definitions by key writers:

> *The essence of organisational learning is the organization's ability to use the*
> *amazing mental capacity of all its members to create the kind of processes*
> *that will improve its own* (Dixon, 1994)

> *A Learning Company is an organisation that facilitates the learning*
> *of all its members and continually transforms itself*
> (Pedler, Burgoyne and Boydell, 1991, p.1)

*Learning Organisations — organisations where people continually expand their capacity to create the results they truly desire, where new and expansive patterns of thinking are nurtured, where collective aspiration is set free, and where people are continually learning to learn together (Senge, 1990, p. 3).*

Drawing on these, a generic definition of a learning organisation that could apply to all forms of organisations, not just business ones, would be:

*A learning organisation is one that has in place systems, mechanisms and processes enabling people at all levels individually and collectively continually to enhance their capacities to produce results they really care about — for themselves and the communities in which they participate as part of an ever changing environment.*

The important points to note are that learning organisations:
- adapt to their external environment
- continually enhance their capability to change/adapt/transform themselves
- promote and develop continual individual and collective learning
- employ the results of learning to become even better at what they do
- view problems as a challenge to be met.

Contrast the above definitions eulogising the need for educated, involved and innovative employees with the following quotation from Frederick Taylor, the original guru of management from the early twentieth century, who once wrote:

*One of the first requirements of a man who is fit to handle pig iron as a regular occupation is that he shall be so stupid and phlegmatic that he more closely resembles in his mental make up the ox than any other type.*

# ■■■ THE NEW PARADIGM

A new paradigm is developing from a variety of innovations in organisational practice. Industrial democracy, worker participation, participatory management and quality management have all come together from a variety of sources to power a drive to assert the processes as well as the outcomes of work as an integral part of human life, and to structure the organisation of work accordingly. This paradigm requires a change in thinking by managers about work, education, training and learning. Table 3.1 lists the most striking shifts that need to be made in moving from an outcome-driven organisation to a process-oriented organisation.

TABLE 3.1 THE SHIFT TO A LEARNING ORGANISATION

| TRADITIONAL ORGANISATION | THE NEW PARADIGM |
| --- | --- |
| Training | Learning |
| Hierachical, top down control | Collegial and networking |
| Work isolated from life | Work integrated with life |
| Structured | Interactive |
| Organisations as mechanical structures | Organisations as dynamic organic systems |
| Control | Commitment and co-operation |
| Rules and values | Shared goals and procedures |
| Adversarial | Mutuality; win-win |

The term *learning organisation* is used to describe attempts to apply the notion of self-development more holistically to organisations, rather than focusing on specific aspects. Barham *et al.* (1988) saw learning organisations as those where training and development had become intrinsic to the organisation; where learning was not restricted to discrete skills taught in chunks of training activity. In the learning organisation learning about job and self becomes a continuous process — a way of life, an environment where individuals learn about the process of learning itself. It cannot be strongly hierarchical, as hierarchical organisational structures do not lend themselves to people taking responsibility for their own learning, to self-development, to team-based structures. This has implications for the way managers perceive their roles and for the process having to be driven as much by joint ownership by employees as by economic considerations, or else the system will not work.

In a learning organisation, strategy and policy will ensure that education and training are well integrated in the planning process to make plans a reality. The organisational structure features the devolution of responsibility to groups and teams requiring project management skills and management expertise as general learning needs for most employees or members. Individuals are given responsibility with support, and mistakes are tolerated. Problems become the basis for self-development and collaboration with others. There must be a double loop of learning that allows reciprocal feedback, information flows and monitoring of changes in the external and internal environment.

The development of a learning organisation requires more than a few training programs for employees at all levels, more than multiskilling and CBT credentialing — although these may be elements of it. It requires a strategic rethink of the whole arena of management and a shift in how we view work. The rate at which an organisation and individuals learn will be a fundamental advantage in a future that is information-based.

The current response to workplace-based training needs in Australia is focused too strongly on the top-down competency-based, structured approach to training. There is a need to move rapidly from structured agendas to facilitated group learning processes with joint ownership and willing involvement. Organisations can only learn as fast as the slowest 'link'. Change may be inhibited unless all players learn together and share the beliefs and values associated with the change. Organisational learning must be seen as a continuous process of events or projects where the results are reviewed and embedded in further changed work processes. A fundamental feature of a learning organisation is that it not only adds value to services and products but to the lives of the people involved.

Senge (1990) argues that we have to cease perceiving the world as a collection of separate unrelated forces and perceive its wholeness as a system; changes in one part influence changes in many others. Only then can we build learning organisations where people can expand their capacities, where collective aspiration is set free and where people are continually developing as a group engaged in a joint enterprise. The only competitive advantage for organisations in the future may be to learn faster than the rest. Organisations that will go from strength to strength will be those that invest in people's commitment and capacities to excel through providing structural, educational and personal development that facilitate involvement and learning. The organisation must become a team of people all pulling together — the power of one — complementing each others' strengths and directing effort to a common goal. It must also be an organisation that satisfies higher aspirations for working or membership such as belonging, self-fulfilment, self-esteem — not just financial ones. As long as employees feel about work as Terkel (1975) expressed it — 'as a Monday to Friday sort of dying' — then organisations will simply stumble on, drained of motivation and quality of life, and will slowly crumble. Thus a newly developing role for managers is to create an ethos and structure in which willing participation is engendered for the benefit of all. Imposing new forms of operating can be easily undermined as employees subtly ignore, avoid and even work against the imposition. High-level personal skills will be needed by managers to generate the willingness and interest to work together and develop appropriately tuned participative systems.

## key features of the learning organisation

Four major factors distinguish a learning organisation from a non-learning organisation. These are:

1. *A learning culture* — an organisational climate that nurtures learning. Its characteristics mirror those associated with innovation.
   - Work and learning are integrated so that an educative workplace is created that is supportive of on-going learning.
   - The organisation is adaptive and able to respond to changing conditions.
   - Learning is valued and actively fostered.
   - The organisation is well connected to its environment and applies systems thinking.

- Staff are empowered and there are active strategies to foster personal mastery.
- Learning is linked to knowledge generation and management.
- There is a common vision and sense of ownership that bonds staff.
- The organisation must accept a need for change at all levels, not just management.
- Future, external orientation characterises these organisations; they develop understanding of their environment; senior teams take time out to think about the future; widespread use of external sources and advisors, for example customers on planning teams.
- Free exchange and flow of information — systems are in place to ensure that expertise is available where it is needed; individuals network extensively, crossing organisational boundaries to develop their knowledge and expertise.
- People learn how to learn — particularly how to learn together.
- Commitment to learning, personal development — support from top management; people at all levels encouraged to learn regularly; learning is rewarded. Time to think and learn (understanding, exploring, reflecting, developing).
- Employee empowerment is valued.
- Commitment in terms of allocation of resources (money, personnel, time) on a long-term basis as this determines quality and quantity of learning.
- Valuing people — ideas, creativity and 'imaginative capabilities' are stimulated, made use of and developed. Diversity is recognised as a strength. Views can be challenged.
- A new philosophy encouraging openness, reflection, acceptance of error and uncertainty must prevail. Centralised structures stifle learning and individuals never gain a comprehensive picture of the whole organisation and its goals.
- Climate of openness and trust — individuals are encouraged to develop ideas, to speak out, to challenge actions, without fear of reprimand. Such questioning often highlights problems at an early stage and reduces time-consuming errors.
- Learning from experience — learning from mistakes is often more powerful than learning from success. Failure is tolerated, provided lessons are learnt.
- Learning is essentially problem-centred. Identified problems determine exactly what must be learnt and who ought to become involved. The process is cyclical, involving acting, reflecting, thinking, deciding and acting.
- There is a mutually shared vision that provides a firm identity, which is maintained as development occurs.
- Communication transcends vertical and horizontal boundaries, counteracting fragmentation.

2. *Key management processes* — processes that encourage interaction across boundaries. These are infrastructure, development and management processes, as opposed to business operational processes.

- Strategic and scenario planning — approaches to planning that go beyond the numbers, encourage challenging assumptions, thinking 'outside of the box'. They also allocate a proportion of resources for experimentation.
- Competitor analysis — as part of a process of continuous monitoring and analysis of all key factors in the external environment, including technology and political factors. A coherent competitor analysis process that gathers information from multiple sources and sifts, analyses, refines, adds value and redistributes that information is evidence that the appropriate mechanisms are in place.
- Information and knowledge management — using techniques to identify, audit, value (cost/benefit), develop and exploit information as a resource (IRM); use of collaboration processes and networking, both human and electronic, to categorise and share expertise.
- Capability planning — profiling both qualitatively and quantitatively the competencies of the organisation. Profiling these on a matrix can be helpful to planning adjustment.
- Team and organisation development — the use of facilitators to help groups with work, job and organisation design and team development — reinforcing values, developing vision, ownership, cohesiveness and a climate of stretching goals and sharing and support.
- Performance measurement — finding appropriate measures and indicators of performance; ones that provide a 'balanced scorecard' and encourage investment in learning.
- Reward and recognition systems — processes and systems that recognise acquisition of new skills, team work as well as individual effort, celebrate successes and accomplishments and encourage continuous personal development.
- Empowerment of employees who become responsible for their own actions. Managers do not forfeit involvement as they need to enthuse, sustain, encourage and coordinate. People learn from each other.

3. *Tools and techniques* — methods that aid individual and group learning, such as creativity and problem-solving techniques.

These are too numerous to cover in detail, but include a wide range of learning and creativity skills in the following groups:
- Inquiry — interviewing, seeking information
- Creativity — brainstorming, associating ideas
- Making sense of situations — organising information and thoughts
- Making choices — deciding courses of action
- Observing outcomes — recording, observation
- Reframing knowledge — embedding new knowledge in mental models, memorising.

Collective (i.e. team and organisational) learning requires skills for sharing information and knowledge, particularly implicit knowledge and assumptions and beliefs that are traditionally 'beneath the surface'. Key skills to note here are:

- communication, especially across organisational boundaries
- listening and observing
- mentoring and supporting colleagues
- taking a holistic perspective — seeing the team and organisation as a whole
- coping with challenge and uncertainty.

Many (but not all) of these will be found described in Senge (op. cit.) within his five disciplines of Personal Mastery, Systems Thinking, Team Learning, Shared Vision and Mental Models.

4. *Skills and motivation* — to learn and adapt. This involves a willingness to want to improve personally and organisationally. As employees feel they are appreciated for their skills, values and work, feel respected and become aware of their importance to the organisation, they are more motivated to 'add their bit'. This brings increased job satisfaction.

It must be emphasised that the learning organisation is not one that runs a lot of courses — it is one that is capable of self-transformation or double-loop learning (see below), which changes current operating assumptions, norms and values. It accepts and creates responsibility for an ever-widening constituency: quality service for customers; quality working life for members; performance for owners; and quality social responsibility for the community. The learning community is a group of people who meet as peers to satisfy personal learning needs primarily through the sharing of resources and skills offered by those present.

Members of organisations can no longer define their roles narrowly but must take a broad interest in the activities of all those who contribute to the organisation's overall operations. Employees and members must learn and act together as they face the same problem of enhancing the performance of the organisation. When staff are cross-trained for a range of skills, they come to understand the roles and skills of the other workers.

Within learning organisations people develop because:

- there is greater motivation
- there is emphasis on learning and taking on board new ideas and methods
- the workforce is more flexible
- training is done within the company by those who actually do the work and is an integral part of team work
- people are more creative
- there is improved social interaction.

Teams and groups work better because:
- there is knowledge-sharing.
- members value each others' opinions more
- interdependency improves relations and trust between people at a personal level
- knowing about others' roles and tasks means members can plan their work better
- traditional communication barriers break down
- information resources grow
- innovation and creativity can come from any member or part of the organisation.

## double-loop learning

The learning organisation employs double-loop learning rather than single-loop learning. Single-loop learning rests on an ability to detect and correct error in relation to a set of operating norms. This involves scanning the environment, comparing this information with the operating norms and then initiating the appropriate action. Here is an example of single-loop learning:

**Step1**  Strategic planning for long-term unemployment programs reveals an increasing demand for certain services and staff.

**Step 2**  Workforce planning, using standard operating norms, indicates the specific increases of trained staff that are needed.

**Step 3**  Resources are committed to recruit and train the required extra professional staff.

Double-loop learning occurs when the problem is set in a wider context. For example, in Step 2 above, we might ask whether the operating norms are appropriate. It is a more creative process. Here is the double-loop version:

**Step 1**  Strategic planning for long-term unemployment programs reveals an increasing demand for certain services and staff.

**Step 2**  Workforce planning, using standard operating norms, indicates the specific increases of trained staff that are needed.

**Step 2A** Existing staffing norms, professional boundaries and numbers are questioned and the skills mix is weighed against service needs.

This feeds back into Step 2.

**Step 3**  Resources are committed to recruiting or training staff in different skill and number combinations.

## why the interest in 'learning organisations'?

The underlying cause for the recent emphasis by business on the learning organisation is the increased pace of change. The workplace has been a rather conservative place and learning has been something divorced from work and innovation something of a disruption. The current and future context requires an organisation to learn quickly and innovate in order to perform better in a kaleidoscopic environment. So now organisations are searching for the (unattainable) Holy Grail to improve existing products or services (continuous improvement) and innovate (breakthrough strategies). An array of new management processes have been deployed in the search for continuous improvement such as TQM (Total Quality Management) and BPR (Business Process Re-engineering). But companies are finding that the success or failure of such programs depends on human factors, such as skills, attitudes and organisational culture. It also appears that many implementations are geared to highly specific processes, defined for anticipated situations. The current interest in the learning organisation stems from the recognition that these initiatives, by themselves, are not the answer and a more comprehensive approach applicable across a wide range of environments is needed that can:

- cope with rapid and unexpected changes where existing 'programmed' responses are inadequate
- permit flexibility to cope with dynamically changing situations
- allow front-line employees to respond with initiative based on client needs instead of being constrained by processes/structures established for different circumstances.

With the pace of change increasing all the time organisations must develop the capacity for rapid innovation that can be facilitated only by being organised around people who believe they can meet challenges through knowledge, a sense of control and belief in what they are doing.

Consider organisations you know, work in, or of which you are a member. Answer 'yes' or 'no' to each of the following questions and you will easily recognise an organisation that needs to become a learning organisation.

1. Are employees/members unmotivated or uninterested in their work?
2. Do the employees/members lack skills and knowledge to adjust to new jobs/roles?
3. Are you the only one coming up with new ideas?
4. Do others simply follow orders?
5. Do teams argue and lack real productivity?
6. When the leader is away do things get put on hold?
7. Do the same problems occur over and over again?
8. Are you always the last to hear about the problems?
9. Is there a lack of communication between people and between teams?
10. Are you the first to hear about clients/members complaints?

Workplace reform is no longer merely a matter of cutting costs or reskilling through CBT. The business organisation of the future requires a highly skilled flexible workforce, modern technology, plus a structure and culture that nourishes learning, thinking and community. Continuous learning must be built into the job, with the worker and work group given sufficient responsibility and authority to perform the job effectively. Regular feedback permits continual revision of objectives, roles and priorities that can be incorporated into the managerial process.

## the development of learning organisations

Derived from case studies in Europe and Japan, Bolwijn and Kumpe (1990) have proposed a four-phase model in the developmental life of an organisation, detailing the cultural and structural requirements of each phase. The four phases and their characteristics are listed in Table 3.2. These changes represent the move towards flatter management structures, greater autonomy and responsibility at lower levels and skill upgrading. The phases overlap as changes occur and the time scale is variable. This overlapping and variable development is illustrated in Table 3.1.

TABLE 3.2 THE FOUR PHASES OF ORGANISATIONAL DEVELOPMENT

| PHASE | PERFORMANCE CHARACTERISTICS | OGANISATIONAL REQUIREMENTS |
|---|---|---|
| THE EFFICIENT ORGANISATION | Efficiency | Specialisation and hierachical organisation |
| THE QUALITY ORGANISATION | Efficiency plus quality | Communication and co-operation |
| THE FLEXIBLE ORGANISATION | Efficiency plus quality plus flexibility | Integration and decentralisation |
| THE INNOVATIVE ORGANISATION | Efficiency plus quality plus flexibility | Participation and democratisation plus innovative drive |

In the *efficient organisation,* cost reduction is the aim. This sort of organisation is usually involved in the mass production of a narrow range of standard goods that are competitively priced. The organisational structure is based on the need to undertake many simple repetitive tasks with cheap labour. Staff are separated into work units with specific responsibilities and specialised staff who can learn tasks very quickly. Planning and control are the functions of management, who must ensure that the organisation functions as a sleek, smooth-running machine.

The *quality organisation* recognises quality as a strategic issue for which top management's involvement and commitment are necessary. The whole organisation is involved in improvement — doing the right thing the first time in the best and cheapest way. Customer orientation is a strong focus and it is assisted by improved feedback and data collection. Close coordination between technical, production and sales staff is essential for product and service quality. There must be a cultural and structural change to permit increasing communication and cooperation in both horizontal and vertical dimensions. The hierarchical control is looser to permit this, and discrete work groups start to come together.

The *flexible organisation* adds individualisation to provide a wide and assorted product range. It keeps abreast of external events and developments, producing small batches and introducing new variations and generations over a short period. The organisational design is based on fast feedback loops to facilitate quick reactions but also to maintain reliability of product and delivery. Autonomous product-business team units contain all supporting functions, flattening the hierarchical structure and limiting the involvement of central staff. Extensive use is made of task forces to deal with unforeseen events and problems. This leads to an ethos in which changes are regarded as a challenge.

The *innovative organisation is* characterised by its capability to coordinate technological developments used in separate business units. Outsmarting competitors by changing the game or the strategic management of technology is an important part of the company's success. Ad hoc multidisciplinary teams are used and managers are employed as coordinators. Team ethos removes line management distinctions. Supplementing the horizontal and vertical communication of the flexible firm is an 'open door' policy, the employment of mavericks and diagonal communication bypassing hierarchical levels. This is a learning organisation.

> Creativity is not restricted to new services, products or technology but envelops new markets, new missions, new ways of working together and new ways of thinking. The know-how of individuals determines their contribution, rather than their position. The tension between hierarchy and expertise no longer exists, as participation and human resource management are maximised in an informal open atmosphere that encourages contribution. The knowledge and expertise of all employees are used.

Table 3.3 indicates some of the fundamental cultural differences between traditional hierarchical organisations and the emerging learning organisation.

## creating the right environment

The goals in a learning organisation are to:
- pursue the promotion of the image and vision of the organisation
- demonstrate actively the value placed on all employees who provide higher quality services
- ensure that staff at all levels are free to display initiative in the organisation of their daily tasks
- recognise and build on the organisation's good practices
- encourage better two-way communication both within and outside the organisation

**TABLE 3.3** COMPARISON OF FUTURE AND TRADITIONAL ORGANISATIONAL CULTURES

| FACTOR OF ORGANISATION | TRADITIONAL CULTURE | NEW CULTURE |
|---|---|---|
| STRUCTURE | Hierachical and rigid; chain of command | Flexible; multiple lineages; functional collaboration; team base of command |
| AUTHORITY | Based on position, hierachical | Based on knowledge, cross-functional networks |
| ATMOSPHERE | Impersonal, cold and task-centred | People-centred, informal, caring, warm and trusting |
| MANAGEMENT PHILOSPHY | Control through coercive power; cautious; error to be avoided | Function to release energy of personnel high risk-taking; errors are to be learnt from; emphasis on personal development; sharing of resources |
| DECISION-MAKING | Top levels; decisions are final | Close to required action; collaboration; decision-making by problem-solving |
| EMPLOYEE | Limited skill and knowledge | Enhanced knowledge and multiskilled |
| SUPERVISION | Watchdog | Resource |
| STATUS | Differences in facitlities, dress, eating, perks | Differences muted and even eliminated |
| REWARDS | Individual performance rewarded | Teamwork and collaboration rewarded |
| INFORMATION | Closely controlled restricted flow one way downwards; facts are used to control | Shared widely; multidirectional; facts are used for learning |
| RESPONSIBILTY | Perform or else | Based on trust |
| HUMAN DEVELOPMENT | Indoctrination | Enabling and empowering |

- recognise more clearly areas of creative tension or potential conflict within the organisation and establish clear mechanisms to resolve conflict
- establish and maintain mutual trust throughout the organisation.

The elements of a learning environment that will facilitate the achievement of goals include the following:
- The senior management team allocates time for its own development, which is pursued both collectively and individually.
- Team decision making always recognises the learning that will have to occur if the change resulting from the decision is to be effective.
- Staff at all levels are aware of their responsibilities for prompting continuous and relevant learning, both for themselves and for their team members.

- Innovation is encouraged at all levels.
- There is a clearly expressed and widely supported aim of improving organisational effectiveness through personal development.
- Learning-supportive systems are in operation (e.g. performance review, counselling).
- There is recognition at all levels of management of the freedom that individuals require to manage their own self-development.
- There are training and development staff available to offer advice and support who can use a wide range of learning strategies and who can respond to learning initiatives from others.
- Individuals take responsibility for identifying their own learning needs and for pursuing ways of satisfying these.
- Informal learning networks exist, and do so with the approval of management.
- Evaluation and feedback is regular and frequent at individual and group level.
- The organisation's rate of learning is equal to or greater than the rate of change, increasing the organisation's chances of survival.

Within this model of a learning organisation individuals will be exercising choice and experiencing feelings of ownership. They do not have privileges; they do have the freedom to operate within an agreed framework, which they and management have created in accordance with agreed values and beliefs. Individuals may therefore:
- make proposals
- challenge colleagues and managers
- be heard
- be allowed to learn and have responsibility for their own learning
- identify their own learning needs
- hold views at variance with others and debate these views freely
- receive feedback and have open discussions with supervisors about their own performance
- give direct feedback about ways in which the supervisor's or manager's performance assists or constrains their own performance
- feel supported by management.

Workplace education has considerable advantages. The acquisition of knowledge can take place continuously where the integration of theory and practice is possible. Given realistic educational opportunities, participants come to realise they possess valuable knowledge, and learning becomes a natural part of the daily activity. Learning becomes a group process as all realise how dependent they are on one anothers' skills and knowledge. Using these skills and knowledge as a basis for future development and solving workplace problems can only improve morale and productivity. The individual employee should be regarded as a producer of knowledge derived from work experiences and these items of knowledge should be fed back into the work situation to improve production and work conditions. The worker is best qualified to identify problems in structures and processes but, in order for the organisation and the individual to benefit, there must be open channels of communication and a commitment to permitting workers to use their knowledge on the problems and work towards solutions individually or in teams.

## ■■■ MANAGEMENT AND LEADERSHIP

*The most appropriate leader today is one who can lead others to lead themselves. The more traditional image of a leader as a shining figure on a rearing white horse crying 'Follow me!' represents an incomplete view of leadership.* Manz and Sims, 1991

In times of change and insecurity, the common belief is that we need dominant and strong leaders to control events. However, bureaucratic control and managerial constraints are unlikely to generate the inspiring capacity for creativity and flexibility that is essential to transform Australia into a value-adding post-industrial economy. There has been too much emphasis on tasks and structure, and too little consideration of the abilities of people. The workplace has been designed to provide a necessary minimum level of intrinsic reward and career security to ensure compliant and committed employees. This approach assumes goals are known and accepted, and that leadership involves simply galvanising employees into action within a stable environment. The current and future complexity, ambiguity and change in the environment will not bear out such pre-programmed views of management and organisation.

Australian management ranks low in leadership and quality and is probably not good enough to meet immediate and critical challenges, according to David Karpin, the chair of the Industry Task Force on Leadership and Management Skills. He quotes the 1993 *World Competitiveness Report*, in which Australian management ranks seventeenth among 22 countries on whether organisations are managed in an innovative, profitable and responsible manner. Australia may be ahead of Turkey, Greece and Portugal but it lags behind New Zealand and the UK. Karpin also indicated that in terms of quality of relations between managers and employees, Australia ranked nineteenth among 22 countries.

One of the Karpin research studies found that the ideal manager assessed from the industry perspective was strong in people skills, a strategic thinker, a visionary, flexible and a team player. These are exactly the characteristics that have been identified as being essential in the successful organisation of both the present and the future — the learning organisation. When asked in the Karpin study what sort of management courses should be offered by universities, the industry response focused on programs that would challenge underlying beliefs and assumptions held by managers, enabling them to understand themselves and others, facilitating managing in an international context, including practical training in interpersonal skills, communicating, negotiating, resolving conflict and, finally, strategic thinking. It is apparent that industry knows which way it should travel, but, as we have seen, CBT is not for managers and those who progress through the ranks to management will not be provided with the necessary skills under CBT.

The conventional wisdom that perceives business as war and holds that organisations or subunits within organisations must be mutually hostile is also wrong. Operating towards others as if boundaries were minimal creates conditions for interchange and productivity that are hard to beat. The central issue is not how you can keep the product or service to yourself, but how quickly you can generate something new or refine existing products. This requires openness, stimulation and interchange, where boundaries within an organisation are non-existent or extremely flexible. In these changing times, an organisation must evolve or die. This is why all organisations, whether or not they are businesses require:

- flexible employees/members at all levels, who are able and willing to learn new jobs
- creative employees/members at all levels, who are able and encouraged to think beyond apparent boundaries
- healthy employees/members at all levels, who have a balanced rather than stressed approach to responsibility
- to be a learning system
- a sense of common purpose.

Bass (1990) has claimed that the future form of leadership must be transformational: this involves charisma and inspiration, intellect and individualised consideration of employee needs and aspirations. A leader with these qualities is proactive, innovative and less inhibited in their search for solutions. Personal presence, visionary zeal and inspiration were the motivational forces behind this new kind of leader's impact. However, even this transformational leader has their difficulties as they are still a model of the Leader as Actor with followers as unthinking responders. Manz and Sims (1991) claim that such leadership qualities are inimical to organisational effectiveness in the future, for the following reasons:

- Highly complex technology is concentrating specialist expertise that managers cannot hope to comprehend fully in the hands of employees.
- Extended international operations make close supervision impossible.
- Microelectronic information and communications systems provide almost complete knowledge at a local and base level in the organisation.
- A highly educated workforce has a developed sense of its own ability and worth.
- A volatile environment requires spontaneous initiative and creativity at a local level.

In such a context the leader's role is that of developing employees, facilitating operational integration and articulating shared visions. These visions act as a coordinating focus for day-to-day decision making, and at the same time provide an overriding purpose for the activity. The shared vision of learning is one of the criteria that marks the learning organisation (Senge, op. cit.). The vision may be initiated by one individual, but only when it is assimilated by other/all employees can it energise and direct them. As Senge (op. cit.) points out, as a vision is shared it gets weakened through distortions and variations some of which may conflict. This diversity must be able to be expressed so that while the vision may be modified, it is still shared coherently.

The new model of the learning organisation envisions that no single person is in control — all employees are. As a result, issues need to be managed in a four-step process:

- Leadership — a combination of passion and responsibility.
- The creation of a vision.
- The establishment of a sense of community.
- Management (which may become a non-issue when the previous steps are working); if you want to get something done, forget about organisational charts.

From what has been presented already in the opening chapters, it is certain that employees, including managers, need to have both skill-based and personal and attitudinal skills, such as critical thinking, problem solving, teamwork, communication and decision–making skills, developed in a pragmatic, work-related manner, rather than in theory. Employees are expected not only to respond to events but also to anticipate them. Commitment to work is needed for this — and commitment to an organisation stems only from the satisfaction of feeling involved and needed. Many managers have been specialists or technicians in a particular part of the organisation. Few are provided with the education or skills that facilitate the personal transformation that being a manager requires.

## organisations satisfy human needs

The typical scientific behaviourist management approach, emphasising the division of labour and a hierarchy of authority and responsibility, has gone. Organisations are starting to take the human element into account and to envision any organisation as a human community, where people experience learning, dignity, meaning and security as they coordinate their activities for the achievement of some common, explicit purpose or goal. This view removes the misconceived notion that an organisation exists purely to get things done. This is only one of an organisation's purposes. An organisation is also a social system that enables members to meet human needs and achieve human goals. People involve themselves in work and community organisations not merely to subsist, but also to satisfy human needs of affiliation, self-esteem, achievement and acceptance. Organisations have vital human purposes beyond that of the economy. People in organisations should be at the centre of the creation of knowledge and meaningful activity. Organisations must do justice to the human ability to use language, to be aware of themselves and their capacity to attribute meaning to events and to make sense of things. Ideally, education and training for adults in the workplace and other organisations further both work and human purposes in that employees develop competencies required to accomplish the goals of the organisation and also develop competencies that will enable them to satisfy their human needs both in work and in the outside community.

How can an organisation enable individuals to get their needs met? This can be achieved only in collaboration with others. The individual is always enmeshed in a social world. The dilemma is that in entering social relations each of us surrenders some individuality. This can raise anxiety in individuals, who must ask 'Who am I? What can I become? What am I becoming?' How then is it possible for an organisation to achieve effectiveness by utilising the potential aggregate effectiveness of its members? It can do so by developing a climate in which the needs of its members carry at least the same weight as the market position. It must have sophisticated ways of seeking out, listening to, interpreting and taking account of the needs and aspirations of members. It must enable, empower and empathise with each of them. The organisation that can achieve this becomes a learning organisation.

## ■■■ TRAINING, LEARNING AND EDUCATION

Education is as wide as life experience itself and involves all formal and informal influences and processes that facilitate the development of the individual. Learning is a general term covering all the experiences, processes and activities by which a person may gain new behaviours. Training is a subset of learning, limited to the acquisition of specific skills through deliberate classes and structured instruction. CBT falls under this subset. A learning organisation is not about 'more training'. While training does help develop certain types of skill, a learning organisation involves the development of higher levels of knowledge and skill. Learning organisations also embark on meta-learning or how to learn. The old adage that knowledge is power now needs to be rewritten as shared knowledge is power.

Study, training and education are almost pejorative terms for most people. Associated with formal schooling, they have become synonymous with taking in information, a diet of predigested material that is later elicited as a response to the appropriate stimulus. Learning appears more acceptable if the ANTA surveys (Dickie, 1999) are to be believed. Yet even here, there can be a debasing of the concept with the 'I learnt it at a course yesterday' approach probably meaning that its successful application in the real world is a forlorn hope. Real learning involves understanding and the personal assimilation of information, processes and ideas within ourselves to create a difference in our thinking and behaviour in our relationships with the physical and social environment. It is learning that Senge (op. cit.) calls generative learning — that which enhances our capacity to be creative.

The distinction between vocational and general education is no longer valid since conventional workplace training programs cannot provide the adaptability and flexibility across skill areas nor general portable skills like decision-making or communication skills. A vocational education system that points its students towards a specific range of employment is not only misjudging the fluidity of the contemporary labour market but is denying them the opportunity to develop the adaptive behaviour that will help them survive in those markets. Human skill must be added to occupational skill. 'Quality of work' must be subsumed within 'quality of life'.

The cultural norms that have developed within an organisation may need to be explored and changed for education and training to provide an acceptable return on investment. In many organisations it is not the done thing for staff to admit incompetence; it is kept a secret, no training occurs and the company suffers. In other organisations, staff are sent on courses without formally assessing or establishing their training needs. Then the trained staff are expected to be instant experts on return. They feel cynical and angry when sent on irrelevant courses. Anger also results when management fails to support them in the implementation of their new skills. So the new skills fall into disuse and the whole exercise proves to be a waste of time.

Training must be perceived as an investment rather than a cost, organised on a cumulative and organisation-wide basis and not as an uncoordinated occasional activity. Training must no longer be equated with courses, so that many types of training currently unrecognised or those that find little application in the workplace are recognised as valuable both for work and living. The long-term objectives of any adult workplace learning must be to improve organisational effectiveness and efficiency as well as enhance staff morale and motivation through development of action plans geared to personal growth and provision of opportunities for staff to display individual potential for growth. Planned organisational development and employee development are inextricably linked. A 'sheep dip' mentality about training, in other words that one exposure to education and training is sufficient for healthy job maintenance for life, can no longer be excused.

## ■■■ MANAGING RESISTANCE TO CHANGE

Change happens when something starts or stops or occurs in a different way. It can usually be managed by a rational approach. Transition is a psychological process that extends over time and cannot be managed by rational formulas. This means that people have to change in attitudes and values as well as behaviour, and these demands may engender resistance.

These are some of the most common obstacles to becoming a learning organisation:

- Operational/fire fighting preoccupation — constantly responding to brush fires and not creating time to sit back and think strategically.
- Too focused on systems and processes (e.g. ISO9000) to the exclusion of other factors.
- Reluctance to train (or invest in training), other than for obvious immediate needs.
- Too many hidden personal agendas among both management and employees, for example status-seeking behaviours and individualism; an 'us' versus 'them' mentality.
- Too top-down driven, bureaucratic and overly tight supervision, all of which adds up to a lack of real empowerment.

But the most obvious sign of resistance is slowness to meet agreements or even total refusal to cooperate. This resistance can be intentional or unintentional, overt or covert. Managers who are flexible and adaptable have the best chance of dealing effectively with resistance. It is easy to provoke increased resistance if the manager tries to insist, criticises or makes other negative moves.

Resistance can even be valuable if it leads those involved to consider options, which aspects of change are essential and how change should be managed. An unemotional response to resistance should be adopted. Some objections can be based on realistic thinking and a sound appreciation of the issues. There may also be a communication problem. Clear communication and involvement are generally sound procedures to ensure support. Feedback and the contribution of ideas must be encouraged. The task is to listen and guide colleagues and workers to a reframing of their own perceptions. The resister may have a different definition of what is required; of what the problem is. Only through discussion can mutual understanding be achieved. Acknowledging contradiction and conflict is not giving way to it. A light touch that enables coordination of these difficulties and differences into an integrated whole allows all those involved to contribute both negative and positive views without damaging the process.

To analyse resistance it is necessary to discover the categories of behaviour. Is it overt (open) or covert (concealed)? The former allows for debate and permits individuals to work together to solve disagreements. The latter often involves secret activity with a private agenda for personal ends. This resistance is often not discovered until too late. Unconscious motivation occurs when the person is unaware of their behaviour. Employees may be acting through habit, or lack of awareness of the situation and its requirements. Some unconscious resisters may believe they are not resisting.

Conscious or deliberate thwarting of a project is most difficult to counter. Entering into debate can sometimes help. Combining these four types of behavioural response to organisational change results in a cross-classification of the kind shown in Table 3.4 (O'Connor, 1993).

By considering colleagues in relation to these categories, decisions on how to react and deal with them are facilitated. Those who are unaware need to be asked questions to bring them to a state of awareness and an understanding of the nature of what is going on around them and what they are doing. No accusation is implied. One simply asks them to reflect on what they are doing:

*What do you think is the goal of this change? How do your actions contribute to this goal? Is there incongruity between what you believe to be the goal and the real goal? How can we bridge that gap?*

TABLE 3.4 FORMS OF RESISTANCE TO CHANGE

| OVERT AND CONCIOUS | OVERT AND UNCONCIOUS |
|---|---|
| THE PROTESTER<br>This is a resister who protests, pointing out the failings of the plan; who believes it is wrong. It is possible to discuss and debate with this person. | THE ZOMBIE<br>This person is locked into ingrained habits and has neither the will nor the ability to cope with change, they simply avoid change, although verbally will acknowledge their need to change. |
| COVERT AND CONCIOUS | COVERT AND UNCONCIOUS |
| THE SABOTEUR<br>This person sets out to undermine change. They might just wish not to have to put up with change. Others might have agendas they wish to impose. | THE SURVIVOR<br>This person carries on regardless, blissfully unaware that what they are doing is wrong. They may believe they are doing a good job. |

When resistance is overt and conscious, open debate is recommended to achieve agreement on the end goal. Those who are resistant to change in a covert manner could be asked to explain their reasons without accusation or judgment — simply so that both sides understand the position of the other.

Experience shows that middle management and technical staff are most threatened by attempts to change the work organisation to one that fosters a more participative and educative environment. A climate of sharing is not one they are used to or comfortable with. They have acted as experts and knowledge custodians. Hoarding for career-building purposes restricts the flow of information to others. But in a learning organisation all knowledge should be made available, short of compromising the enterprise's competitiveness and confidential financial conditions. The profusion of monitors and computers enables rapid and broad access to information needed in the work process, creating a climate in which the understanding and efficiency of the workforce is raised in relation to the work process as a whole.

## ■■■ GETTING STARTED

Growing a learning organisation is not an easy process. It requires determination and commitment. It is also a never-completed process as learning organisations are constantly growing and becoming refreshed. As with many 'interventions', there are many good places to start, depending on the specific context. Some often recommended are:

- Start at the top — it is usually essential to have impetus from senior management who are fully behind the process.
- Start with a chronic problem — always a good place to get the thinking caps on; involve participation.
- Initiate a task force — a common response, but they will need drive and vision.
- Start with an organisational diagnosis — the HR consultants favour this one!
- Link to an existing process or initiative — go where there is existing energy.
- Review existing systems and processes — an audit to identify a 'capability' gap.
- New product development.

The last-mentioned is a great starting point as it is tangible, provides an opportunity to be innovative and needs a lot of 'boundary crossing' to succeed. It draws on many of the processes, tools and techniques to become effective at learning. However a start is made, five processes that form the core of learning organisations must be present:

- Engaging in team learning — to achieve greater ability and potential
- Building a shared vision — to increase motivation, commitment and direction
- Adopting systems thinking — better control of actions and decisions
- Achieving personal mastery — to attain results
- Changing mental models of the world — to encourage new behaviours.

## ■■■ LEARNING SOCIETY/CULTURE/COMMUNITY

Rather than limiting the concept of *learning organisation* to the business world, many consider that all organisations outside the sphere of business, such as community, social, educational and political, can and must be learning organisations too. The aggregation of these then constitutes a learning society, permeated by a learning culture that captures the necessity for continuous and progressive adjustment to change of all parts of society and emphasises the need for an educational system based on a powerful and practical understanding of learning for people at all ages and stages of their development. The urgent need for productive and progressive adjustment to change places increasing burdens of relevance, efficiency and effectiveness on educational systems and invests learning as the core concept of our time. The emergence of the concept of a learning organisation within one sphere of human endeavour has focused attention on the way in which other organisations need to change in order to promote lifelong learning. Learning organisations are one of the key building blocks of a learning society, and their relative absence impedes the achievement of such a society.

A learning culture can be defined as a focus on ongoing, lifelong learning at the individual, team, organisational and societal levels. A recent survey conducted by ANTA revealed that Australians prefer learning to training and so we can see emerging a change of language, with learning communities, learning organisations and learning networks replacing the *training* culture. But even at the ANTA 2000 conference there was a training culture workshop and one of the main speakers stated that 'A training culture is a set of instinctive behaviours, beliefs and values...'. 'Instinctive' is certainly an erroneous adjective, suggesting such behaviour is innate. Old concepts and thinking are hard to eradicate, leaving Australia still plagued by ghosts of top-down training agendas when the vision should be of lifelong learning that is owned jointly by the deliverer and the receiver.

In order to transform the concept of the learning organisation into a learning society that professes a learning culture, there has to be added to its characteristics two major processes. First, the focus of change becomes the culture, not just the organisation, so that the culture, its underlying cognitive and affective determinants that influence individual thinking, behaviour and the subjectively perceived social worlds are changed. Second, traditional norms need to be challenged, diversity valued and open feedback facilitated. In effect, added to the concept of the learning organisation is a cultural lens that transforms it into a learning culture or learning society.

A learning culture is a culture that treasures, nourishes and advances not just narrow economically focused objectives but those that emancipate people and allow them to be involved in determining their own and their societies' futures, lifestyles, values and feelings through collaborative, problem-solving, visionary community action. Such adult learning approaches that are integral to learning-organisation and learning-community development are derived from a foundation of humanism. Humanism is a philosophy associated with beliefs about freedom and autonomy, the belief that humans are capable of making their own choices, that individuals have a drive towards self-actualisation (or becoming what they are capable of becoming) and that individuals have a duty of responsibility to themselves and others (e.g. Rogers, 1969). Thus the humanist perspective supports the essence of the learning organisation and the learning community. Adult learning theories also fall into this ambit and provide a foundation for many human development strategies that support the development of learning organisations, cultures and communities. The work of Mezirow (1990) on transformational learning and Knowles (1984) on andragogy (adult learning), both of which will be considered in detail in Chapter 7, are underpinning strategies for all this. Just as a learning organisation permits internal renewal and transforms itself as it empowers people, encourages team learning, promotes open dialogue and acknowledges the interdependence of individuals so too does the learning community and learning society at a macro level outside the purely more economic purpose. The learning organisation, learning community and learning society are all reflections of an underlying learning culture in which there is a commitment to learning as a continuous process built into all aspects of life.

A learning community is not simply a physical region well endowed with well patronised educational institutions. In a learning community the learning that takes place in an educational institution is only part of the broader learning that takes place in homes, workplaces, public libraries, community organisations, social clubs and the like. A learning community plans, develops, articulates, manages and delivers its programs and methods of learning based on its currently assessed learning needs. A learning community has the following characteristics:

1. People have access to learning opportunities when they need them and in an appropriate setting. This requires flexibility on the part of formal and informal providers.
2. People are motivated to seek these opportunities.
3. Education and training are seamless, that is providers abandon their boundaries.
4. The learning community manages its own learning.
5. The learning community uses new technology to provide access to the benefits of learning at a distance and removes the digital divide. Flexible learning networks use technology to deliver learning in workplaces, homes and community settings. They are targeted to increase access for disadvantaged groups such as isolated persons, NESB persons and those who are disabled. This sort of infrastructure places formal and informal providers in a position to deliver flexible programs to the community.

A learning community is one with strong networks between community organisations, public organisations and enterprises. The Victorian Government has instituted a Learning Towns program, which creates collaborative learning partnerships by linking adult community education, TAFE, industry, other education providers and community activity. On a regional level, it has been found that where this occurs, there is a growth of the regional economy (Hugonnier, 1999). In Australia, communities and regions could be vital in environmental management policies, economic development and reconciliation as individuals and groups achieve new perspectives, transform their understandings and gain emancipation from old beliefs just as happens in organisations. The community and region can build intellectual and social capital through the learning interactions of members as they go about everyday life, attend meetings of all sorts of formal and informal bodies, and undertake joint activities for mutual benefit. Social capital is the networks, norms and trust present in a community that facilitate cooperation. Most people can bring two types of resources with them when they interact — knowledge resources and identity resources.

Knowledge resources are the knowledge of who, when and where to go to for advice on other resources or knowledge on how to get things done. Identity resources are the ability, motivation and commitment to act for the benefit of the community and its members. These two kinds of resources allow community members to combine their skills and knowledge with those of others to produce action or cooperation for the benefit of the community. However, some people may need building up of their self-esteem and confidence before they can contribute as these are prerequisites for the use of other interpersonal skills (Kilpatrick, 2000). Partnerships and collaboration in communities mean that a wider range of skills are available to solve local problems and enhance the community capacity to manage change. Obviously, accessing, sharing and creating knowledge skills and values among communities has a significant role to play in regenerating regional Australia and well as communities within urban areas as adults come to realise their potential to work together, learn and change conditions (just as Paulo Freire found he could do within impoverished communities in South America). Such learning communities are also able to construct intercommunity networks and create ties with other public and private groups, increasing access to wider ranges of skills, knowledge and resources. There is a reciprocal relationship between a learning community and the construction of social capital in that the former facilitates the latter but a community with social capital will continue to develop as a learning community. Adult community learning is the way to a more sustainable future for all communities, especially regional ones.

Public libraries can act as a major feature in community learning not only through the obvious provision of books, but by providing a centre for the use of computer technology and access to a virtual library, rooms for meetings and community activities. However, libraries will have to modify their culture and services to meet the learning community's needs. Libraries need more flexible opening times. They need to establish a service profile not tucked away in an intimidating building but using, for instance, library kiosks in shopping centres, community centres and clubs. They need to offer a range of learning resources and have the capacity to act as learning brokers, customising delivery to suit the information needs of particular groups and linking groups into other groups. For example, in NSW, licensed clubs cashed up with poker machine profits are moving into the provision of community education using this funding. As a first step they are setting up Internet cafes to help working class members gain a facility in using the new IT tools. Libraries can link into this as new learners find they need to seek other information. This is an effective way of breaking down negative attitudes to education among adults. The NRMA motoring association is planning to introduce mechanics courses in some disadvantaged areas. This is an opportunity to excite people who do not normally participate in education. Initiatives of this kind have a snowball effect and can open the door to other opportunities and interests. Again, the library service can be proactive and link into these programs by offering relevant materials, information, videos and Internet material on motor vehicles etc. Libraries are an obvious focal point for the delivery of numerous State services and ACE activities. But no longer can libraries wait for clients to come to them — they need to be involved in outreach programs.

Learning communities are thriving in formal education organisations and settings as well as community ones. In the USA profound changes are moving schools and colleges from teaching factories into learning communities, where staff, students, administrators, parents and interested parties in the community work collaboratively to share significant academic goals in environments in which competition is de-emphasised, often connecting learnings from across discipline and course boundaries (www.ntlf.com/html/pi/9612/sev_lev.htm). In London, a credit system of learning has attracted non-traditional adults into learning (Davies & Bynner, 1997).

Learning communities are important for three major reasons:

1. First, they are important to economic competitiveness. This is not to be seen as a narrowly focused short-term priority but as a way of ensuring in the local setting that successful businesses remain, providing a basis for the prosperity of the area and supporting other productive activities and services that maintain community life.

2. Second, they have a unique capacity to offer tailored local solutions to emerging issues such as a local industry trend or one of international or national importance, for example an environmental issue such as land salination. Many of these problems are only visible at local levels. Local communities are able to respond quickly when centrally prescribed solutions will be too late and not wholly appropriate.

3. Thirdly, they provide a key to individual social and economic opportunities and inclusiveness.

A learning community can exist in physical or virtual space. Community meetings, pubs, sporting clubs and educational institutions are being replaced by chat rooms, online forums, bulletin boards and news groups. A learning community can be geographical, such as a town, small settlement or a business enterprise or organisational such as UK Learning Cities network, Victorian Learning Towns Network and the Glasgow Learning Alliance. What is common to all these learning communities is that they mobilise economic, social, educational, intellectual and physical resources to advance personal fulfilment and social development and create economic prosperity and resilience through lifelong learning.

They are places where individuals are supported and encouraged to achieve personal growth, develop self-esteem, build a portfolio of knowledge, skills and values and assist them to fulfil life's purpose. In learning communities, educational institutions, businesses and other organisations commit themselves to creating and maintaining a culture of experimentation, risk taking, curiosity and continuous improvement. Learning is seen as an investment in competitive success and productivity through the processes of teamwork, devolved decision making and systems thinking.

Successful learning communities require the following:

- *Dispersed leadership.* Communities and organisations need to encourage local leadership models that are polycentric, with a range of people sharing the work towards a common vision of their community.
- *Innovative culture.* Organisations and communities need to utilise the creative potential of all members to solve problems; developing, diffusing and applying new knowledge through their activities. This is the culture of innovation that permits survival.
- *Decision-making mechanisms.* Organisations and communities need to utilise a range of methods to facilitate discussion and decision making on issues that concern them, such as learning circles, discussion groups, town meetings, etc.
- *Social capital stockpiling.* Social capital is the structure of human relationships and is essential to community activity. Social capital arises from interconnected webs held together by sharing, commitment and values. New technologies will aid this.
- *Future orientation.* Organisations and communities must focus on the future. Issues such as environmental protection, health and welfare and economic security are all-important.

## practical strategies for building a learning community

Kilpatrick (op. cit.) suggests the following strategies:

- Create opportunities for interaction.
- Schedule events and meetings (can include Internet and phone).
- Determine communication sites, including electronic and physical sites.
- Develop leadership skills and confidence.
- Foster externality by building ties with other groups.

Building sustainable learning communities requires, above all, a deep understanding of human nature and motivation, the challenges of individual growth, the processes of lifelong learning, effective teaching skills for group, meaningful learning and transformational/moral leadership.

## adult community education (ACE)

The strongest base for the development of a healthy learning community and society that is focused on lifelong learning through adulthood is the Adult and Community Education (ACE) sector, the most decentralised of the education sectors. It refers to the provision of those general adult education programs and activities that fall outside yet complement the formal programs and qualification pathways provided by other sectors. The focus is on learning opportunities at community level rather than work-related training. Fully 82 per cent of recreation, leisure and personal enrichment enrolments in 1999 were with ACE, but a considerable and increasing number of clients are taking vocational, remedial and basic education courses, with business, health, community services and hospitality as growing fields (ABS, 2000). Community education providers have strong local bases and can provide the flexibility needed to complement central agencies. The major future source of adult and lifelong education will be Adult and Community Education (ACE) as this is itself a response to the lifelong learning needs of the community. Its key features are that:

- it is learner-centred, actively involving adults in decisions about their learning and providing learning in ways, at times and in places to suit learners
- it is for everyone, with about one million Australians involved every year — ACE accepts a special responsibility for those who have had difficulty in the past participating in education
- it covers a wide variety of learning, involving not only leisure, self-improvement and general education but also employment skills, preparation for vocational training and other learning needs
- it responds to the community, working with people to support personal and community development.

ACE recognises that adults have a diverse range of learning needs and does not confine itself to standard learning and teaching methods.

Recently, some ACE organisations have become part of the delivery of vocational education and training to people who need a more supportive context in which to learn new skills. This is made possible by making the community-based organisation a Registered Training Organisation or by entering into partnership with an existing RTO to deliver the training. ACE merges recreational and vocational education as part of lifelong education. The ACE sector, with its flexibility, is ideally suited to changing its courses and programs as new trends emerge.

The Government has recognised its importance by establishing a Task Force on Adult and Community Education (under MCEETYA), which was due to report in early 2001 and provide advice on current and emerging educational matters, as well as advise ANTA on its responsibilities in funding certain adult and community education.

## adult learning australia (ALA)

General adult community education activities have been in operation for over 100 years. A national association was first formed in 1960, and soon became a quasi-professional association in which university staff from Departments of Adult Education and Extra-Mural Studies were prominent. During the 1970s and 1980s it was enlarged and enriched by the growth of a distinctively Australian community-based adult education — strongest in Victoria and NSW. This included the Neighbourhood House and Learning Centre movement, which now has some 900 centres across Australia. During this period the Association absorbed the Australian

Association of Community Education and evolved into the national peak body for adult and community education — Adult Learning Australia (ALA).

In the 1990s, the ALA progressively assumed a third role — that of a national advocacy body for adult learners and lifelong learning. This role has been most clearly expressed in its initiation and leadership of annual Adult Learners' Week. They have also become active advocates of 'Third Age Learning'.

## adult learning australia (ALA) position paper (1998)

The ALA position paper suggests that while there is still a need for additional funding for Adult Community Education (ACE) providers, it is now appropriate to place more emphasis on the demand side. This means identifying and attending to the conditions that alert, encourage and support adults to take up learning, and those that enable them to make sound choices about what they learn and how. They emphasise this to address the challenge of the 25 per cent of adults who do not participate in any further structured education and training after leaving school. Generally, the typical ACE customer is generally better off, well educated, predominantly female, more likely to be employed, but not in the lower skilled occupations. Many of them are already 'lifelong learners'. Underrepresented groups the ALA wants to draw from include:

- low-skilled manual workers
- people without qualifications
- unemployed people
- some groups of women (e.g. lone parents)
- some ethnic groups
- older adults (>50)
- people with learning difficulties/disabilities
- people with literacy/numeracy difficulties
- ex-offenders.

The ALA suggests a national policy framework for lifelong learning that recognises and attends to the issue of non-participation by specific groups by providing incentives and support for more members of the 'non-participant' ranks to take the first steps back into education and training, thereby becoming active learners. The ALA has developed a bundle of proposals for its *Lifelong Learning Initiative* for the stimulation and support of increased participation in adult learning.

One of these in particular, a learning cities network, would assist and speed the take up of other lifelong learning initiatives, such as employee development schemes, and the implementation of effective advisory services for adult learners. For example, Canberra is already exploring its role as a learning city. Regional communities have started developing learning circles on such topics as salinity, reconciliation and crime prevention. New technologies are opening up opportunities for those in remote areas and for seniors who have transport or mobility problems to join in these ACE programs. These initiatives could usefully be considered as part of a wider government policy framework for lifelong learning.

A study by Volkoff (1999) of the involvement of ACE in VET showed that learners were motivated mainly because the course interested them, gave them knowledge or skill at levels appropriate to their needs and the class time suited them. The latter seemed to be quite important in providing for ACE students. The overall picture was one of ACE learners making conscious, informed, positive choices of courses, environments and teaching styles that suited them. It was a provider of last resort for socially and economically disadvantaged persons who were seeking to improve job prospects and valued hands-on supportive environments in which they could gain confidence and competence. ACE gives participants confidence to move into formal education, opening up job opportunities. It also picks up young persons who slip through the net of more formal provision and gets them back to more effective learning. For mature people to embrace lifelong learning it is crucial that early experiences of study be personally rewarding, self-affirming, empowering as well as useful. The ACE has the capacity to provide this, encourage lifelong learning and play an important role in vocational preparation and orientation.

Kearns and Papadopoulus (2000) investigated policies, strategies and practices in five OECD countries (Britain, the United States of America, Sweden, Germany and the Netherlands) with which learning cultures were built to determine the implications for Australia. Strategies to build partnerships between stakeholders for ongoing learning were central to the innovative responses across all countries, leading to new forms of public–private partnerships. This study also noted that economic objectives were not the sole focus of policies for building a learning culture in these OECD countries, but that key social, civic, cultural and educational objectives with more integrated, whole-of-government strategies were the foundation of policy. These broader policies were directed at combating social division and polarisation, at community regeneration, at combating exclusion and at mobilising civil society for these purposes. Terms such as the *digital divide* and *information divide* have been used, but fundamentally it is a learning divide with the risk of excluding those who lack the capacity and motivation to be involved in lifelong learning. The goal of lifelong learning as it is developing in the socio-economic context of the new economy in major Western countries is central to all of these objectives. Partnerships between stakeholders at the local level were being built in order to address these objectives using infrastructure, financial incentives, information and marketing and technology policies. In all countries there was a paradigm shift from training to learning. This provides a basis for policy strategy in Australia, which according to Kearns and Papadopoulus (op. cit.) has five interlocking directions:

- The skills imperative — winning the skills race
- The social imperative — creating a just and cohesive society
- The learning imperative — building a learning society
- The technology imperative — addressing the challenge of technology

- The partnership imperative — linking policy and concerted actions by stakeholders.

The report identifies the absence of local infrastructure to foster collaboration and partnership among stakeholders as the major problem. A shared national vision of Australia as a learning society is required to engender concerted partnership action involving all stakeholders, including unions, business associations and training companies. Other issues raised included the remediation of literacy and basic skills deficiencies of many adults in the workforce and an insufficient range of incentives to induce stakeholders (employers, individuals, communities) to invest in learning on a whole-of-life basis. These gaps in policy and vision impede adult education from playing a more strategic role in opening pathways for lifelong learning and supporting the building of a learning culture.

## ■■■ PROBLEMS WITH A LEARNING SOCIETY

Three problems present themselves — all of them raising ethical and value-laden issues and concerns about what learning is of most value and who the clients should be.

1. What is learnt could be regarded as important and relevant or wrong and wasteful of resources, depending on your perspective. For instance, on the Net powerful learning sites include those that teach visitors how to make bombs, abuse children, commit suicide and defraud others. If there is to be a public policy about resourcing a learning society for lifelong learning it needs to have some ethical basis for discriminating between things that are 'valuable' to the community and nation and those that are 'dangerous' or 'immoral'. The values implicit in this are obvious, yet we cannot avoid the issue. No attempt will be made to adjudicate on this here, but the issue should be raised for discussion elsewhere.

2. The second question is to whom should the resources for learning be directed? Who should benefit — those who have missed out, those who have shown that they do well in an education context and from whom the nation may get most benefit for each dollar spent, or those whom business and industry need to retrain, etc.? Moves towards a participatory learning community can perpetuate exclusion, reinforce existing socioeconomic divisions — a powerful legitimising mechanism — and produce a growing gulf between knowledge-rich and knowledge-poor members of society. What is the criteria for some basic entitlement? A learning society is not as inherently benign as it sounds.

3. What is the purpose? Is it for the benefit of business and industry? Is it for the benefit of society as a whole? It is to help individuals? There is an obvious tension between the objectives as seen from the perspectives of a

variety of stakeholders, which stem from the multifaceted role of education, which seeks to produce participating citizens, responsible parents, discriminating consumers, sceptical thinkers as well as reliable, skilled workers. To what extent should the moral purposes of education be subjugated to the demands of business? These questions need raising and serious debate.

However, depending on policy, education could be a powerful weapon in the battle for inclusion and bring about the delayed opening of a door to greater life chances for many adults. The answers to these dilemmas may lie in government working closely with many other stakeholders, such as business, the unions, community groups, educational institutions at all levels, private providers and voluntary movements to achieve balance in provision and allow the real action to come from professionals and committed citizens who have a generous and inclusive vision of how our learning society may look in the future.

## ■■■ THE CHALLENGE

The challenge facing organisations, members, managers and employees today is to make the effort needed to learn some of the new skills and techniques, and to implement processes that engage them in programs of continuous capability development.

Learning should be integrated in doing, as part and parcel of everyday work. It should also be energising, stimulating and fun — getting the best out of everybody to meet the challenges ahead. The concepts of the learning organisation and knowledge management are increasingly seen as two sides of the same coin — as you learn you gain knowledge, which you apply and in the process learn more.

The perfect learning organisation is not an attainable goal, but a desirable concept. Nor is there any correct implementation of the learning organisation. Every organisation can continuously adapt and adjust to its own particular context and circumstances.

In the business sector, there is an incredible tension apparent between the need to develop learning organisations in order to compete in the global market and the managed flexibility that demands a lean and mean approach to achieving profitability and competitive advantage.

There is a clash between initiative, assumption questioning and critical reflection in employees and managerial authority in a world populated by agile competitors, short technology and information life spans and demands for higher quality at lower cost. Yet, in this threatening environment, the only way to keep ahead seems to be transformation of the organisation into a continually relearning and evolving system.

# SUMMARY

The concept of the learning organisation is becoming popular as organisations realise that to maintain competitiveness and even continue to exist they must harness the most valuable resource they have, the human resource. Moreover, it is not simply a matter of providing employees with specific job skills or multiskills, but one of providing personal skills involving employees' attitudes to work and to themselves in terms of positive thinking, self-esteem and competence in communication and relationship skills. These will all be required to enable employees to cope with the workplace of the future.

A learning organisation is a system that will bring people together at all levels to develop skills, plan future strategies and maintain an educative environment. It is characterised by a commitment to lifelong learning and the continual growth of people in terms of both specific and general skills, the latter including personal psychological growth. The sharing of new ideas, brainstorming and opening up ideas to the criticism of others are supported so that planning becomes learning and corporate planning becomes organisational learning. There is a shared vision involving an agreed destiny and identity. With genuine ownership, most employees or members make a commitment and seek to excel and improve themselves. A flat management structure with work organised through self-managing teams and team learning are corollaries of the previous characteristics. The capacity of the team for coordinated action far exceeds that of the individual. Teams are the fundamental unit of the learning organisation, enhancing capabilities to innovate and be creative.

By becoming a learning organisation there is a greater chance of recognising new opportunities, understanding threats and achieving competitive advantage. The learning organisation not only meets the organisation's need for a rapid response and collective learning, it also creates a context for humans to act as human beings.

All organisations need to become learning organisations to develop the nation into a learning society, imbued with a learning culture. This will enable lifelong education to triumph, leading to greater inclusion, the solution of local problems and the development of communities in which people are constantly seeking to improve quality of living. The adult community education sector can provide the impetus for this extension of the learning organisation.

# part two

## the adult learner: psychological background

**Any attempt to provide** effective lifelong education for adults must take into account what we know of adult psychological and social development. There is a tendency to assume that adulthood is a lengthy period between adolescence and old age in which there is a slow but inexorable decline in most capacities. This negative attitude needs to be banished by an understanding that adulthood is as full of change and development, of uncertainty and triumph, of successes and problems and of risk and challenge as any other period of life. This section therefore considers the psychological characteristics of adulthood that affect the capacity to undertake education and training activities with success.

# chapter 4

# the psychology of learning

**If you think education is expensive try ignorance.**
D. Bok

**Learning is not just knowing the answers. That is master mind at its best, rote learning at its most boring and a conditioned response at its most basic. It does not help you change and grow; it does not move the wheel.**
Handy *The Age of Unreason* 1989

## ■■■ WHAT IS LEARNING?

Many authors and texts have set out to define this term, mostly with a conspicuous lack of success. This is because it is difficult to formulate an all-inclusive definition of learning that covers all the activities and processes that are involved. The best definition is to conceive of learning as a *relatively permanent change in behaviour,* with behaviour including both observable activity and internal processes such as thinking, attitudes and emotions. By contrast, training is a far more restricted concept involving a set of arrangements external to the learner in which the environment is deliberately shaped by an instructor with respect to some predetermined learning outcomes, usually of the skills variety.

There are many situations in which what is learnt may not manifest itself in observable behaviour until later. For example, it is possible to learn how to do something by watching someone else do it. The learner's behaviour does not change at the time but this does not mean no learning has occurred. This is apparent in learning to undertake some simple word processing command. Watching how someone deletes a file or clicks on a mouse after placing the cursor on a button may only have effect in later behaviour. In fact, observational learning, whereby behaviour is produced later based on behaviour displayed by a model earlier, is a major way in which much socialised behaviour is learnt.

Learning theory provides some of the most exciting, important and practical knowledge in psychology. To possess knowledge about how people learn is to possess power, for through that knowledge one can modify behaviour. Most people think of learning in a very narrow sense of acquiring a correct set of facts. But learning is concerned with more than knowledge.

For example, there is the equally important acquisition of social skills, such as how to get on with others, and the learning of attitudes and values, such as what value do I place on beating a business competitor by unscrupulous means or what attitudes do I hold towards trade unions, how do I best encourage others to do well and how do I show assertive behaviour?

Emotional learning is vital too in our everyday activities so that we can express appropriate emotions in the correct context and in response to the relevant stimuli. While guilt, happiness, fear and anxiety all have their appropriate places in our lives, it would be embarrassing to show happiness at a funeral or anger towards a newborn child. Motor or physical skills such as walking, keyboard typing and using complex machinery are also learnt. So the range of learning is extremely wide and it is involved in virtually every piece of behaviour humans can exhibit, since very little behaviour is innate and present at birth.

It is also apparent that learning may not necessarily be correct or even appropriate. We can learn incorrect facts, for example in the amount of stock we believe is held in the warehouse; we can pick up bad habits such as taking long tea breaks; we can respond maladaptively to situations such as showing frustration when equipment breaks down. Young children often learn the wrong behaviour such as hitting another child to get a turn with a toy. Adults can learn to show fear inappropriately, for example showing anxiety when walking past a barking dog or being fearful of using a lift. Learning can thus be emotional and social, as well as concerned with factual knowledge or physical action.

Nor do we set out deliberately to learn most of our behaviour. Much of our learning has been attained surreptitiously through the process of socialisation in our particular culture. From childhood we soak up the norms of our family, neighbourhood and society simply by being involved in them. There may be no explicit teaching but we may learn or pick up the norms that 'black people can't trust the police', or that 'I am seen as clumsy (or unintelligent or noisy, etc.) by parents/peer group/employers', etc. We copy others, and we interpret things about ourselves (sometimes inaccurately of course) from the way we believe other people are responding to us. In these ways so much of our learning is non-deliberate and just occurs through personal interpretation of what is going on around us in the home, workplace and classroom.

Learners learn far more than the teacher/trainer ever sets out to teach. There may be specific content being taught but learning context is replete with uncontrolled learning — learning about the teacher's attitudes to the subject from their verbal and non-verbal cues; learning about oneself, such as how intelligent one is, etc. Through verbal and non-verbal cues each member of the class learns about the teacher's attitude to each of them — whether the teacher believes them to be competent, unable to learn the required skills or a nuisance because of the awkward questions they put to the teacher. They learn how to work together, to share and to accept each other; they learn about how other class members react to them and what expectations each starts to develop about themselves. While there is intentional learning in a formal educational setting there is also a plethora of chance learning of a personal nature, which strongly influences self-esteem and personal views of self.

So the concept of learning involves both the planned learning we intend to occur through structured and more informal education and unplanned fortuitous learning as part of our daily experience of living. Many educationists regard this unplanned and often internal learning as the more important since it affects our approach and attitudes to the planned aspects of learning.

While many theories have been produced by psychologists to explain how people learn, they can all be split somewhat crudely into three discrete camps:

1. The behaviourist (stimulus-response) approach, with varieties developed by Pavlov and Skinner.
2. The cognitive–Gestalt approach, based on work by, among others, Kohler, Piaget, Bruner and Hebb.
3. The humanist or phenomenological approach, exemplified particularly by Rogers.

Each applies to different sorts and areas of learning and all overlap at the edges. It is not a case of one being correct and the others wrong. They each have their particular range of applications. It is not the intention of this text to offer an exhaustive treatment of learning theories.

What follows is a summary of major approaches and their relevance to adult and workplace education. Described are some of the central themes that learning theorists have explored, particularly the different philosophical, theoretical and practical themes and how these impact on the conceptualisation of what constitutes appropriate teaching of mature persons for lifelong learning. In grouping theories of learning into three categories we are guilty of oversimplification and artificiality, but this structure does provide a means of imposing order on a diverse array of theories.

What primarily distinguishes the three groups is their philosophic view of man in his environment. Is the human being a passive learner, ready to be moulded, functioning largely in reaction to stimulation from the environment, does the human being operate on the environment in an intentional thinking way or is the human being endowed with a positive self-directing drive to grow psychologically and 'become' whatever they are capable of becoming?

# ■■■ THE BEHAVIOURIST APPROACH

The behaviourist approach attempts to study learning and behaviour within a scientific tradition. Only those elements of human behaviour that can be observed, experimentally controlled, measured reliably and that are capable of replication are worthy of psychological study. The study of 'mind', a vague, mystical, quasi-religious concept, was studiously avoided since no such phenomenon could be observed. The brain is a 'black box' in the sense that response to stimulus can be observed quantitatively, totally ignoring the possibility of thought processes that might influence interpretation of stimulus or decision making on how to respond. What was studied was the overt response, or human behaviour. In this way, argue behaviourists, can the study of behaviour achieve scientific respectability, enabling psychology to be located within the realm of the natural sciences. Major behaviourists include Pavlov, Watson, Thorndike and Skinner.

Behaviourists assume we see and experience the world exactly as it is in the physical sense — a real world that is the same for everyone. This view also assumes that the world and the things in it function according to natural laws and changes can be explained in terms of cause and effect. Human behaviour can therefore be understood in terms of cause and effect. Thus behaviourism focuses on how environmental stimuli (S) elicit responses (R) (the behaviour). Another name for behaviourism is *stimulus-response or S-R theory*.

To the behaviourist, learning is the modification of behaviour through the application of specific stimuli, which shape the response in the desired direction as a result of the reinforcement of the behaviour elicited. Learning is demonstrated through the response or behaviour. Behaviourism is based on a mechanistic view of the world in which man is a reactive, passive robot that responds predictably and unthinkingly to stimulation. This view is consistent with an emphasis on training as a means of education and lies behind much of the thinking and rationale of CBT. Internal functions such as thinking, wishing and perceiving are either ignored as subjective, and therefore not amenable to quantification, or else are reduced to more simple phenomena. Skinner, a major proponent of behaviourism, once stated, 'man is a machine in the sense that he is a complex system behaving in lawful ways' (1971, p. 197). Although Skinner claimed in his utopian novel *Walden Two* that behaviourism is applicable to all types of education, this philosophy has had its greatest success in vocational and technical education, particularly the development of skills. Concepts and methods closely associated with this philosophy in adult education include reinforcement, shaping, programmed instruction, behavioural objectives, computer-assisted learning and competency-based education. These give a good clue as to what behaviourists believe to be the purpose of adult education.

Two major learning theories lie within the ambit of behaviourism: *classical conditioning* and *operant conditioning*.

## classical conditioning

Pavlov's experiments were the first to show how stimuli come to elicit responses (or behaviour) that originally may not have evoked them, that is learning (or conditioning) or a change in behaviour has occurred. Figure 4.1 illustrates this phenomenon using Pavlov's original experiment.

FIGURE 4.1 PAVLOV'S BASIC EXPERIMENT OF CLASSICAL CONDITIONING OR ASSOCIATION LEARNING

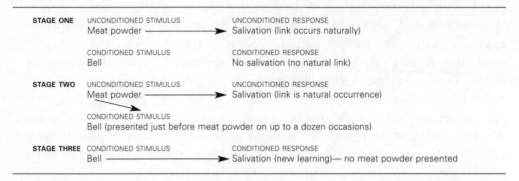

This shows that the learner is conditioned (learns) to emit a response, originally attached quite naturally to another stimulus, to a new stimulus after the presentation of that new stimulus when the latter has been presented on a number of previous occasions fractionally before the original stimulus-response linkage.

Figure 4.2 depicts another example. The anxiety response originally evoked in the dentist's chair can be elicited by a pneumatic drill. In this case we have learnt an inappropriate response to the road drill. We have become conditioned. This demonstrates that responses generalise to similar stimuli or other stimuli present at the same time as the original stimulus.

FIGURE 4.2 CONDITIONING GENERALISING TO OTHER ELEMENTS IN A SITUATION

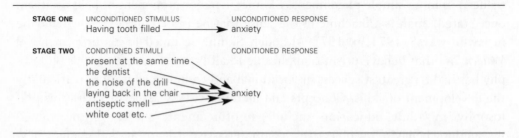

While Pavlov tended to concentrate on reflex responses, classical conditioning is most potent in humans in emotional learning where we attach the response to other stimuli that are around at the time. Examples would be the antiseptic smell of the surgery or the presence of a person in a white medical tunic evoking the same feelings of anxiety as above. In another example, anxiety originally attached to a barking dog running and jumping up can transfer to a generalised fear of all dogs. This is common in young children and is a classical conditioning–learning situation (Figure 4.3).

FIGURE 4.3  AN EXAMPLE OF GENERALISATION

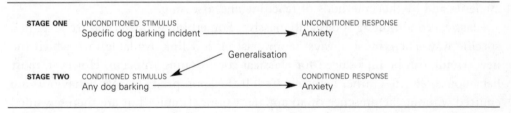

This means that an anxiety response can generalise very easily to a wide variety of stimuli. If you experienced anxiety, loss of self-esteem or failure because you did poorly in a test at school or just didn't cope with academics then these feelings can return and impede opportunities for further study that present themselves later in life. Many employees who had deleterious experiences at school try to avoid learning situations, taking tests and other events that might cause a recurrence of unwanted emotional trauma. The very mention of having to learn a new skill, enter a classroom-type situation with rows of desks or having to go on a course immediately causes unease and discomfort. In many cases early schooling experiences have built up a self-concept or self-image that says, 'I am not able to succeed in these sorts of activities'. The self-concept is a very important element of everyone's personality and will be dealt with later in Chapter 6 . Figure 4.4 opposite shows how this can come about.

FIGURE 4.4  GENERALISATION IN A LEARNING CONTEXT

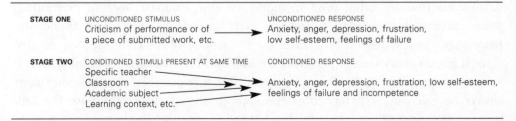

Thus a response can generalise not only to similar stimuli that evoke that response but also to any other stimuli that happen to be around at the time. Here is another example taken from an organisational setting. At a certain factory, every time management was due to make a visit all the windows would be washed and a general clean up effected. This went on for years so that long-serving staff would turn on their best behaviour and look prim and proper whenever the windows were cleaned or there was a general clean up, even when the top brass were not scheduled to visit.

Classical conditioning can be used in this way to explain why Christmas carols evoke pleasant memories of childhood, the songs originally being linked to happiness at opening presents, or why re-entering education can provoke anxiety and other negative emotions in adults. Many people have read a book or seen a play because they liked the last one they read or saw. Teachers condition their students to enjoy, endure and even hate education whether or not they intend to by the emotional climate they create in the learning environment, by the way they treat students and by their methods of teaching and assessing.

Classical conditioning is basically passive. Something happens and we react in a specific way. There must always be an existing S-R link available into which the new stimuli can be introduced for classical conditioning to occur. However, most behaviour is emitted rather being elicited. If the appropriate learner behaviours are emitted without the presence of an apparent prior stimulus but are then rewarded (reinforced) for being produced, the response will become habitual too. This latter situation falls under another type of conditioning, termed operant conditioning.

## operant conditioning

Skinner was the major proponent of operant conditioning, which argues that behaviour is a function of its consequences. People learn to behave in particular ways to obtain what they want or to avoid something they don't want. Operant conditioning differs from classic conditioning in the fact that the stimulus–response link is not present initially and the experimenter has to find some way of generating the behaviour to bring it under stimulus control. The stimulus that is used to bring responses under control is reinforcement, which is sometimes regarded erroneously as synonymous with rewards.

RESPONSE (BY CHANCE) ⟶ REINFORCEMENT ⟶ INCREASES PROBABILITY OF THAT RESPONSE

Reinforcers that are often used include food (for animals), money, promotion, praise, attention from others, success, certificates, head nods and friendship. Reinforcement is that which increases the probability of the response. Say we give a dog a biscuit every time it performs a trick. This increases the probability that it will repeat the trick again when prompted. But it is essential that reinforcement always be given immediately after the appropriate response otherwise the link between the two will not be made. Teaching to Skinner is 'simply the arrangement of the contingencies of reinforcement' (1968, p. 20).

Examples of operant behaviour are all around us. For example, a trainer indicates that if you want a high grade on a course you must attend all classes and submit all course work. A salesman finds that to earn a sizeable income he must generate large sales in his territory. Your boss indicates that if you are willing to work overtime as required you will receive a more positive performance appraisal. However, if the reinforcement fails to be delivered, on the next occasion you are asked to work overtime you will not comply. Similarly, the salesman will reduce his workload if the promised commission payments are not forthcoming.

In other words, behaviour that is not reinforced will die out or, to use the technical term, 'extinction' will occur. Furthermore, one can extend this and show that to prevent a response being learnt in the first place, it is essential that it is never reinforced. Since there is no reinforcement for producing the response, it will tend not to be used again. An instructor can stop students asking questions in class by ignoring those who raise their hands. Hand raising will extinguish as a response because it is not producing the effect desired by the students.

Reward, however, is not quite synonymous with reinforcement. A reward may not have any effect on behaviour because the reward offered was either not desired or noticed by the person. A reward only becomes a reinforcer if, after giving it, there is an increase in the emitting of the response that has been rewarded. Promotion to supervisor that takes an employee away from his mates may not be seen as a reward and the employee may try deliberately to get demoted to rejoin the peer group. The reward of promotion was in these circumstances a punishment for the recipient.

## negative reinforcement

Negative reinforcement involves knowing what to do to avoid something unpleasant or escaping from personally evaluated dangerous consequences. Some trainees will work hard to avoid failure or job loss. They are not working hard because they want to but merely to avoid unpleasant consequences. Many people offered a chance to avoid redundancy by retraining reject the offer and accept unemployment as the lesser evil rather than destroying their self-esteem by showing incompetence on the training course. Acceptable social behaviour is maintained by the threat of legal punishment. Turning up to work on time means one avoids losing pay for lateness. The reinforcement in all these cases is not a positive reward but avoidance of unwanted experiences or consequences.

## punishment

Punishment is the imposition of unpleasant conditions in an attempt to eliminate an undesirable behaviour. Punishment can be of two types. In type I an aversive or undesirable consequence is given (e.g. jail sentence). At work, coming late may be punished by making the person stay after the normal finishing time to complete their required time on the job. Type II involves taking away a privilege or benefit (e.g. loss of driving licence). At work a bonus can be forfeited or the grade level of the appointment reduced (e.g. supervisor down to ordinary worker level). Suspending an employee without pay for two days for failing to turn up on a required course is a type-II punishment too. Avoiding the punishment in future and receiving full pay is the reinforcement for the employee turning up the next time. Punishment type II is regarded as more effective than punishment type I as the subject can regain the privilege by manifesting the required behaviour again over an agreed period. Once punishment type I is given it is given.

Punishment is distinguished from negative reinforcement because it marks a moment for the learner when things get worse, either because positive reinforcers are lost or because an unpleasant state of affairs such as pain or social rejection is to follow.

## shaping of responses

Some responses we want learners to make are unlikely to be made frequently by chance so they are difficult to reinforce. Remember we can only reinforce the behaviour after it has been exhibited, so how do we make this happen the first time? Shaping is the technique used to get round this problem. Reinforcement is given to all responses that approximate more and more closely the desired behaviour. For example, a new employee needs to be shaped into competent use of the word processor by reinforcing each small step that leads to complete proficiency. In starting to learn word processing, logging on is reinforced, then using the arrows to move the cursor around and so on. By having their instruction arranged in small steps learners can acquire the correct response quickly, obtain reinforcement and move on to the next step. This sequence builds up to the desired state of competence, and provides a basis for future learning.

When an adult learns a skill, the aim is for the extrinsic reinforcement from the teacher shaping the skill to be supplemented and eventually replaced by the reinforcement gained from feedback that comes from an increasing level of performance in the skill itself. Reinforcement from feedback makes it possible for the learner to train themselves once they can evaluate the feedback and to learn the skill without the help of another person. Training does not always require the presence of a teacher.

## schedules of reinforcement

In the initial stage of learning something, a continuous schedule of reinforcement is necessary. That is every time the correct response is made it must be reinforced. But once established, many behaviours need reinforcing only from time to time. Most human behaviour is reinforced on this sort of unpredictable basis. The radar operator never knows when an image may appear on the screen. The lotto player never knows when their numbers might come up.

Moreover, it is not humanly possible to provide reinforcement every time the required behaviour is exhibited. A teacher cannot reinforce every person who puts up their hand to answer the question. But randomly, most people will get asked during a lesson. This seems enough to keep the behaviour level of hand raising high. If you phone friends they will not always be in, but you don't stop phoning them. Reinforcement in real life occurs only on some occasions. However, it is this random reinforcement that is found to be most effective in maintaining behaviour. This is because the human being never knows when they are going to be reinforced again and therefore continue to respond, hoping it will be the next time. It is this variable characteristic of reinforcement that makes gambling hard to eradicate — you might be lucky next time (i.e. get reinforced).

## feedback

Feedback is also a central concept in behaviourist learning. The role of feedback is one of providing reinforcement. Feedback is any information that tells the student how well they are doing. There are many examples in the workplace, such as the quality of a finished product, the level of functioning of a piece of equipment that the learner has repaired. A teacher must draw the learner's attention to the relevant cues so that the learner obtains the feedback. Learners must be clear about what they are trying to achieve so that they can monitor their own practice by understanding what the feedback is telling them. Feedback must be given as soon as possible after the performance to be effective. As with all reinforcement the timing is crucial. Too long a time delay between response and reinforcement prevents the link between two being made. In fact, the person may link the reinforcement erroneously with some other response if there is a delay. Structured and positive feedback is vital at the start of learning a new task to maintain motivation and to ensure that wrong techniques or methods are not learnt at the outset.

## criticism of the behaviourist approach

The problem with these behaviourist approaches to learning is that they are somewhat mechanical and rigid. It is the control of learning by the management of reinforcement. The role of the trainer/teacher is to manipulate and control the situation so that the learner learns the correct S-R links that have been designated. There is no concern with the internal state of the person, such as feelings and attitudes.

Reinforcement tends to be extrinsic to the learner, that is offered or provided from outside. For animals, food is the major reinforcer. For humans, extra pay, praise and promotion are extrinsic motivators in the workplace. However, intrinsic reinforcement, that is reinforcement from within the person, such a sense of achievement, self-esteem, a sense of recognition and enjoying meeting a challenge, is more likely to lead to lasting motivation and high performance. Behaviourists are limited in their consideration of intrinsic motivation as internal feelings, beliefs, perception and thoughts are not amenable to scientific scrutiny and are therefore not measurable and objective. Thus behaviourism provides only a partial answer to the role of reinforcement in learning. Extrinsic and intrinsic motivation will be considered in more detail in Chapter 6.

Behaviourists also lay scant emphasis on the human ability to interpret and evaluate incoming stimuli and to decide which response to give or whether to respond at all. Behaviourism tends to regard each stimulus and response as individual building bricks rather than looking at the different sorts of buildings that can be created using the same elements in different ways. We don't receive sensory input in discrete stimulus packages, with each inexorably tied to a discrete response. Life is a continuity of experience, a flow of subtle combinations of stimuli that can evoke a variety of responses depending on the individual interpretation of the incoming information.

In terms of learning of skills and knowledge, through repeated encounters with the same stimuli in the same context, people become conditioned. That is they develop patterns or habits of response that in time become automatic. Instruction, which provides repetitive practice at skills, falls under this banner as does a wide range of learning activities from learning multiplication tables and foreign language vocabulary to learning workshop safety practices or operating a sophisticated computerised machine. It is apparent that much of the skill learning envisaged under CBT will be of this nature, leading to the criticism that CBT is really limited to no more than the inculcation of specific skills currently deemed necessary by industry. Higher order learning is not involved.

The following principles are emphasised in behaviourist theory:
- The learner responds actively — learning by doing.
- Frequency of repetition of responses is important in acquiring skill — that is much practice is needed to achieve high skill performance levels.
- Positive reinforcement is vital to obtain repetition of required or correct behaviour.
- Generalisation suggests the importance of practice in varied situations to facilitate transfer.
- Immediate feedback of results is strongly motivating.
- Shaping behaviour by the reinforcement of approximate responses is essential in learning new skills.
- Moving to a random or variable reinforcement schedule is necessary to maintain behaviour.
- Learning is facilitated when objectives are clear — expectations must be expressed in behaviours that can be measured.

## ■■■ COGNITIVE–GESTALT APPROACHES TO LEARNING

The emphasis in this approach is on the significance of the role of experience, the development of meaning and the use of problem solving and insight as the sources of learning rather than the effect of training in set routines. The individual perceives organised wholes, not disconnected parts or individual stimuli. We evaluate a context as a whole, not the individual myriad of visual, acoustic and tactile elements that impinge on our sense organs. We see a house not the individual bricks; we can enjoy a painting, in other words we see the pattern and harmony not the brush strokes. The response is not a knee-jerk one as in the behaviourist model but a thoughtful response to the individual's subjectively structured wholeness of the experience. Each person learns and behaves in terms of what is real to them.

A behaviourist interpretation of behaviour as a chain of stimulus response links is at a disadvantage in accounting for integration of the parts of behaviour when integration occurs simultaneously at several levels. This cognitive–Gestalt approach accounts for the different ways in which individuals make sense of their environment because it takes into account each person's differing past experiences, needs, expectations and aspirations. Because needs differ from time to time, different issues become more salient and different concerns may vary in importance from one context to another, one can never assume that any two situations will be psychologically similar and therefore one can never predict behaviour accurately. The interpretation of the stimulus aggregate is the determiner of the response, not the individual stimuli, nor their conjoint objective characteristics. Learning in this approach is therefore based on the reorganisation of experiences into systematic and meaningful patterns that lead to problem solving and insight.

Cognitive–Gestalt psychologists believe there is a uniqueness that characterises each person, which comes from the special way they engage in purposeful interaction with their environment. The term *life space* is used to convey this special way of interpreting one's environment. Persons showing insightful learning are able to modify their behaviour as and when necessary in the light of the situation as it obtains at any given moment or context. This suggests that behaviour is strongly under the control of how the individual perceives, structures and interprets their environment in terms of that environment and of past experience. This subjective interpretation provides goal-directed tendencies for behaviour.

## meaningfulness

Meaningfulness is an important concept in Gestalt psychology. Gestalt is a German word for pattern. Our brains tend to look for pattern and completion. For example, most people when they hear 'one, two, three' will have to fight the impulse to add 'four'. This is an example of the built-in tendency of the brain to obtain completion that is satisfied by the structure of the mind map. The mind map helps the brain get a firm grip on a new subject or idea. It can unlock the memory, stimulate ideas and creativity and assist in problem solving. Our brain has the capacity to associate anything with anything else and it will find associations if we allow it to. These will aid problem solving and promote creativity.

The Gestalt psychologists believe that human beings will attempt to create meaning out of the myriad of stimuli that impinge on their sense organs continuously. The Gestalt psychologists formulated some 'laws' termed the 'laws of pragnanz' or meaningfulness. These laws suggest that a person will structure the perceptual field in as simple and clear a way as possible in order to impose meaning on it. Some simple examples of this can be found in Figure 4.5. In (a) we can structure the lines either into groups of two or as a series of individual lines. In (b) we see either rows of similar shapes or columns consisting of alternating shapes. In (c) we try to create a meaningful whole by interpreting the drawing, even though this is not an accurate reflection of the stimulus in behaviourist terms.

FIGURE 4.5 THE LAWS OF PRAGNANZ

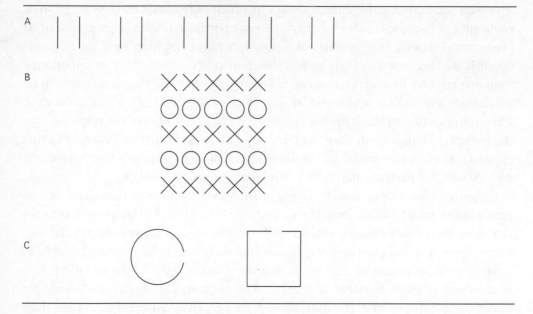

Each person will create their own particular meaning based on the current context and their past experience. To be told that one must learn a new skill by the boss may be interpreted by one individual as 'If I don't I'll be sacked', by another as 'What a great opportunity' and by a third as 'Another situation in which I'm going to make a fool of myself and fail'.

Every situation is capable of individual interpretation in unique yet really meaningful ways as people put patterns around or structure the incoming information. This restructuring into different combinations and arrangements is an important concept as it leads to new ways of organising a complex problem and to insight into possible solutions.

## insight

The cognitive–Gestalt approach also stresses insight — that sudden realisation of how to solve the problem by a cognitive restructuring of the environment. By imposing a different structure and organisation on the issues and context, a fresh new solution is brought forth. The main characteristics of insightful learning are:

- surveying, examination and inspection of the problem
- some tentative trial solutions
- a suddenness of solution — the Eureka moment
- the ability to repeat the solution without error on successive presentations of the original problem
- the ability to transpose the solution onto situations exhibiting similar features and into new contexts.

We often fail to solve problems because we look at them in conventional ways using old modes of thinking. Until we start thinking round the problem in different ways (restructuring and reorganising) we will not achieve any insight into how to solve it. The person's ability to solve a problem is determined very much by their perception of the environment.

Wertheimer demonstrated this effect of restructuring and insight with children in a problem-solving situation. He describes how he visited a classroom in which the teacher was teaching the class to find the area of a parallelogram after revising the area of rectangles. With the aid of Figure 4.6A the teacher used the conventional method of dropping two perpendiculars and the explanation was given that the area of a parallelogram is the base multiplied by the vertical height. Examples were set and successfully completed by the class.

FIGURE 4.6 WERTHEIMER'S PROBLEM

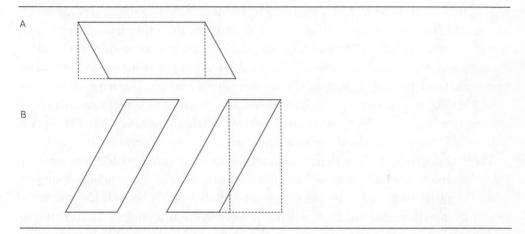

Wertheimer then set a problem. He drew a parallelogram as in Figure 4.6B. The pupils attempted with the old method and became puzzled when it did not work. After looking at the diagram for a few minutes one child realised that the drawing was the same as Figure 4.6A but it had been rotated 45 degrees. He turned his page 45 degrees and obtained the original diagram and successfully solved the problem. This anecdote stresses that insight and restructuring will occur only if we make an active attempt to look at a problem in a variety of ways.

## meaningful and rote learning

Cognitive psychologists emphasise meaningful learning. Ausubel (1963) differentiates between meaningful and rote learning. New material is only meaningful when it can be incorporated in existing knowledge and existing concepts understood by the learner. Ausubel recognises that meaningful learning involves relating new ideas to existing knowledge. Rote memorisation occurs when no relationship to existing concepts can be made or is attempted such as when Ohm's Law is learnt by rote but the learner has no idea what is implied, how it could be demonstrated or how the frormula has been derived. Rote learning is not integrated into existing knowledge and therefore is more easily forgotten. It tends to be learnt superficially and is less efficient than meaningful learning.

The most important contribution a teacher can make to the adult's learning of cognitive information is to select, organise, translate and present the new material in such a way as to enable the learner to appreciate its relationship with ideas, concepts and principles they already have in their memory.

## advance organisers

Ausubel (op. cit) advocates the use of advance organisers to aid meaningfulness prior to the introduction of new material. The function of the advance organiser is to provide a scaffold of ideas or cognitive structure that will bridge the gap between what the student already knows and what they need to know before the new material can be learnt in a meaningful fashion. Advance organisers are material at a higher level of generalisation and abstraction than the new material to be learnt. This scaffolding of higher level ideas allows the incorporation of the more detailed and differentiated material in a stable structure. Advance organisers draw upon whatever relevant concepts the learner already has, make it possible to fit new learning into a conceptual framework and provide key ideas on which to anchor new learning. They are most effective when the learner has little prior knowledge that can subsume the new knowledge or help to organise it.

The teacher/trainer must therefore determine which concepts learners need to know for the new material to be meaningful to them. The sequencing of subject matter must be such that new concepts can be related to old ones. If there is nothing to tie new learning to, then much will be forgotten as it will be difficult to understand. Advance organisers exploit the hierarchical nature of human conceptual structures to promote optimal learning and retention. This leads to the concept of progressive differentiation, whereby the most general and inclusive ideas of a subject are presented first. These are progressively differentiated until finally the most specific details are presented. This has implications for the sequencing of subject matter by a teacher. The second principle is that of integrative reconciliation in which the teacher draws the learner's attention to cross references between related ideas, with significant differences and similarities drawn out. This will prevent artificial barriers being erected between topics and increase the possibility of generalisation and insight.

While we have only touched on some aspects of cognitive–Gestalt theories, there are important implications for learning and teaching. Learning in this approach is concerned with helping learners develop insights or patterns of relationships among elements of a situation, which permits them to see how to solve a problem or extend their learning and understanding. These insights change through experience and have a personal dimension, making such meanings individual. Discovery of meaning is the essence of learning, with motivation, knowledge and creativity combining in its promotion. Insight and meaningfulness aid transfer and learning how to learn.

While cognitive–Gestalt approaches to learning promote the power and flexibility of human perceptual, interpretive and thinking processes, they present a subjective account since there is no scientific basis for qualitative data, such as experiences, feeling and perceptions that are unique to the individual. The environment is the personal construct of the perceiving individual built out of past experience, needs, expectations and current interpretations. Behaviour is a function of this totality. There is a purposive and directional character to behaviour. We may not be fully aware of the purpose and direction of our own behaviour and certainly not of that of others, but we must attempt to understand as much as possible so that we can use the motivation that is there and an understanding of how others see the world to develop strategies for creating a learning environment in the workplace. Each worker perceives the workplace, their role in it and the role of training and education career opportunities in different ways. The modern workplace requires persons who can solve problems, seek insightful solutions, restructure the environment and innovate.

In cognitive–Gestalt learning, the challenge for the teacher is to accommodate the uniquely personal nature of each student's life space, based on the assumption that each student will perceive the learning situation differently and interpret the material in subtly varying ways. It may be asked that if each person has their own view of reality how can we avoid 'anarchy' and remain able to communicate with each other. The answer is that there is a physical reality that is subject to physical laws that we all know in much the same way because those physical laws are perceivable by humans in pretty much the same way. Differences in interpretation occur mainly in social settings, that is what is going on, what agendas are involved what was meant by utterances, etc.

The cognitive approach is a half-way house between those of the behaviourist and humanist/phenomonological views (to be discussed next), emphasising that man is a thinking organism and not just at the whim of stimuli. However, critics claim that it ignores non-cognitive factors such as personality, motivation and feelings and focuses too much on the role of language and information processing.

The following principles are emphasised in cognitive–Gestalt theory:
- Knowledge is constructed from experience.
- Learning is a personal interpretation of the world.
- Learning is an active process in which meaning is developed on the basis of past and present experience.
- The perceptual features of the problem as interpreted by the individual affect what is learnt.
- A learning problem should be structured by the teacher so that the essential features are open to the learner's inspection — well

organised material is easier to learn.

- The organisation of knowledge should move from simple to complex to create a meaningful whole — logical relationships should exist between key ideas and concepts.
- Prior knowledge is important — new material must 'fit into' existing knowledge structures (schemas, advance organisers).
- Feedback as hypothesis testing is a basis for correcting faulty learning, that is providing information rather than 'reward'.
- Learning with understanding is the aim, not learning by rote.

## ■■■ LINKING BEHAVIOURIST AND COGNITIVE– GESTALT APPROACHES

Several processes and theorists link the cognitive approach with the behaviourist approach. This shows the continuity in the range of learning theories, which do not lend themselves to neat compartmentalisation. Transfer of learning, learning how to learn and social learning theory are three particular issues that reveal this link. Links between these two approaches to the development of learning from basic elements to more complex levels illustrate the continuity of learning processes and the need to go beyond S–R learning in the education of adults, who have a greater fund of experience they can bring to bear on educational activities and problems to create insights and new meanings than do young people.

### transfer of training

Transfer of training (or learning) is a process by which the effects of training or learning in one activity are transferred to another form of activity. For example, does learning mathematics improve the learner's ability to solve problems requiring logic, whether or not these are of a mathematical nature? Practically all educational programs are built on the premise that transfer does occur. If it did not then every element of skill, knowledge and capacity would have to be taught separately, like teaching animals to perform tricks. If transfer is possible there is a considerable saving of time and effort. For example, once a person has learnt to write with a pencil they can transfer this skill to using a biro or a felt-tipped pen without further learning.

When training in one task aids performance of another task the transfer is positive; if the training in the first task hinders the performance in the second then the transfer is negative as when a person has learnt to use a PC and is then given a Mac. Sometimes, of course, there is no effect either way.

Most educational activities are based on the premise that what is learnt today will have some relationship to a fact or skill learnt tomorrow and the learning today will facilitate the understanding tomorrow. The major problem is to find ways of facilitating positive transfer and reducing negative transfer.

The behaviourist approach to transfer suggests that what transfers is the common or identical stimuli and responses so that the amount of transfer is related to the number and importance of the elements common to both tasks. However, people do not learn isolated S-R links; they learn general principles — so that the child who has learnt that 12-5 = 7 using beads understands that principle equally when counting people, chairs or apples. Language learning is the closest that one can get to an S–R approach to transfer. Here, there is positive transfer as the response is the same to two different foreign words, but negative transfer if two different responses have to be given to the same stimulus as this causes confusion.

| S | R | S | R | This usually promotes transfer |
|---|---|---|---|---|
| Chien | Dog | Hund | Dog | |
| S | R | S | R | This usually impedes transfer |
| Dog | Chien | Dog | Hund | |

Since to transfer in most situations the learner needs to derive principles, a cognitive–Gestalt approach is better suited as an explanation of how transfer occurs. Some classic experiments by Judd (1908) and Woodrow (1927) revealed that transfer occurs when:
- the learner's attention is drawn to components capable of general application
- practice is supplemented by enlightened training
- the learner understands the general application and seeks opportunities or is provided with opportunities to practise.

These three points illustrate the difference between pure mechanical routine and clear intellectual awareness. Method is as important as content. The Gestalt psychologists, of course, argue that insight, generalisation and meaningfulness must be present for transfer to occur. Obviously, the learner's desire to apply relevant principles is important since potential applications can be missed if the learner is lazy or indifferent. Nor will transfer take place unless the initial learning is thorough and has become meaningful. Notions that are hazy, obscure and inaccurate have no transfer power. Transfer is a function largely of the person and not the situation. What seems clear is that transfer is most effective and consistent when learning emphasises the understanding of relationships and concepts rather than the acquisition of discrete responses or items of factual knowledge that are left hanging in the air.

There is an affective element in transfer that brings the humanist philosophy of education into play. Transfer involves risk taking or going out on a limb, since by definition one is exploring and creating new possibilities. So if we wish to encourage transfer, the teaching context must avoid sarcasm, rigidity and threat and encourage risk-taking and the right to make mistakes. Considerable emphasis is placed on transfer in vocational education and training, yet such training is usually undertaken with a structured behaviourist approach and very little opportunity is provided to practise transfer in the workplace or in a range of situations.

Although organisations spend considerable sums of money on training their employees there is often little transfer to the work situation. Having learnt a new behaviour, employees must be given an opportunity to apply the skills frequently in the workplace, they must be provided with a mentor/coach to help them adjust/amend the skill where necessary, they should be provided with a role model who uses the skill appropriately and be given appropriate rewards for applying the skill in their work. While training schemes get trainees up to scratch and induce them to perform at the desired level fairly effectively, the lack of follow up, guidance and encouragement to utilise the skills is a major problem. The more closely a training program matches the demands of the job, the more effective training will be as transfer to the workplace will be rapid given the high degree of concurrence with the training context. This is particularly true of simulation devices.

## learning how to learn

It appeared that the Gestalt school had discovered a different kind of learning. However, work by Harlow and others has shown that insightful learning is in fact dependent on past experience. The apparently sudden solution to a problem is only likely to occur when the learner has had the opportunity to become familiar with the main features of the problem situation on earlier occasions. It is dependent mainly on earlier trial-and-error learning. There is a natural progression from random trial-and-error to apparently insightful learning. The learner develops a strategy for solving types of problems. Harlow calls this a learning set. Thus many sudden flashes of inspiration that enable us to get the car started on a cold morning or to use a familiar industrial technique in a new application are the result of previous experience and learning. Human learning appears to be hierarchical, with the mastery of simple kinds of learning being a requisite for more complex learning.

Learning how to learn is a prime example of transfer. The work of Harlow demonstrates that stimulus–response learning and insightful learning are related, with the former dominant in the early stages of learning and problem solving and insight following restructuring of the elements as trial and error fail. Harlow showed with students that once the principle of some problem had been grasped, insight occurred but this happened only after initial trial and error using an S–R approach had been employed.

They are two different phases of one continuous process. Some people pass from one stage to the other more quickly than others, depending on past experience and intelligence and willingness to think laterally.

Harlow's demonstration of S–R learning acting as a basis for later insightful learning is paralleled by Hebb's theory about simple and complex brain cell linkages developing in childhood (see Chapter 5). S–R learning is dominant in early childhood while insightful learning becomes more possible with increasing age as there is continued development of brain linkage complexity derived from stored experience.

## learning by discovery

Bruner adds learning by discovery as another way to make material meaningful and therefore learnt and understood so that people can act more competently in relation to their goals. Discovery is a rearranging or transforming of evidence in such a way as to enable one to go beyond the evidence and so reassemble it to create new insights. Discovery becomes a reward in itself and thus motivates further learning. This is intrinsic motivation, which will be discussed in Chapter 6. Discovery and meaningful learning improve the retention of the material since it is related to existing information in the form of rules, concepts and understandings. The primary objective with all these cognitive theorists is to emphasise the need for the learner to gain insight and understand and relate new knowledge to past knowledge for it to make sense to them. This is a repetitive cycle for once organised this new knowledge then acts as a basis for the organisation of further new knowledge.

Bruner sees cognitive development as an attempt to construct a model of the world from which an individual can make sense of their own personal world. In the light of the escalating pace of change, he argues that education needs to place more emphasis on teaching learners to develop more generic strategies for solving problems — learning how to learn — rather than expanding the curriculum. In this way learners are fully involved in an active role in the learning process and the problem-solving strategies they develop are more transferable as they have personal meaning and value in terms of the learner's own purposes and intentions.

## social learning theory

This theory integrates behaviourist ideas about reinforcement with cognitive processes of understanding the behaviour of others and identifying with it. Bandura (1977) promotes this form of learning. His two key elements are experience and expectations. Experience enables us to learn the consequences of our responses and expectations derive from the anticipated consequences of our responses. Bandura sees a major role for reflection, that is reflecting on our own and others' experience

As we indicated earlier, much learning is non-deliberate and obtained simply through the process of living in a social setting. Social and interpersonal behaviour particularly is learnt in this manner, often fortuitously through imitating models for a variety of reasons and then being reinforced for that behaviour. The role of a model is vital and can be a peer group member, family member, pop star, work colleague or, in fact, anyone whose behaviour is attractive to emulate, including those on television or in motion pictures. A model must be a significant other to the person doing the modelling. Quite a bit of workplace learning is based on copying the techniques of others as demonstrated by a skilled exponent or trainer. The phrase, 'sitting by Nellie' was commonly used in the past before training programs were in vogue to explain how newcomers learnt their tasks.

Modelling is an extension of operant conditioning into a cognitive framework, for while behaviour is seen as a function of consequence it is not the consequence itself but how a person perceives and defines that consequence subjectively that matters.

Four processes have been found to determine the influence the model will have on the individual:

1. *Attention*. Attention must be focused on the critical features of the model and the model's behaviour. Influential models are those who are perceived as attractive, influential, repeatedly available and successful in achieving presumed ends in the eyes of the observer.
2. *Retention*. A model's influence depends on how well the behaviour is remembered; how striking it is once the model is no longer present.
3. *Reproduction*. The watched behaviour must be turned into action, so that practice can be effected and the behaviour effectively emulated.
4. *Reinforcement*. Individuals will be motivated to exhibit the modelled behaviour, perform it more often and practise it if reinforcement is provided for reproducing the behaviour.

The model is imitated because the imitator obtains reinforcement from imitating. The reinforcement may be extrinsic, that is praise, peer-group membership, acceptance, etc. Or it may be intrinsic such as feelings of success, raised self-esteem or the belief that one is approved of by others. But, of course, what is felt to be rewarding is an individual matter. We are all well aware of the modelling effects of violent films, pop star behaviour and football hooliganism on some but not all observers. The model must be a significant other to the observer.

Research suggests too that while there is a high level of modelling where aggressive activities are concerned there is also a high level of modelling when warmth and support are in evidence. Caring, support and affiliation are likely to be imitated in group situations and this can build up team cohesion.

As part of teaching, the teacher behaves in ways that they want the learner to model or imitate. In order for adults to learn how to develop self-directed and problem-solving behaviour in the educational context, the teacher must model those behaviours. The teacher shows others how to listen empathically by listening empathically to them. The teacher teaches the art of receiving and giving feedback by inviting learners to criticise their own performance. The organisation itself serves as a role model. If methods of organising and working in teams are being taught then the organisation should be also using that method. If a young executive is being taught how to involve subordinates in decision making then their superiors should be using the same practice.

So far we have been discussing the copying of a model. Identification is a further stage than this and occurs when the behaviour becomes a natural part of one's own behaviour. Our roles as son, daughter, father, mother, colleague, friend, employee, etc., are learnt through observing and playing those roles so that over time identification occurs as a consequence of constant exposure, frequent opportunities to play the role and effective reinforcement. Each role contains a different set of expectations about behaviour. Learning these distinctions facilitates us operating within society. We know what behaviour is expected from us as we play different roles in each day's activities. Some roles that are learnt restrict rather than expand our repertoire of behaviour. This is particularly true of the stereotypes of the female and male roles, which in part suggest that certain occupations and jobs in the workplace are gender-appropriate and that, for example, the genders have different learning capacities in the science and language areas.

## skilled and unskilled performance

Much of the education of adults in the workplace consists of skill learning. In performing a skill the person has to process information and then make appropriate responses. Car driving is a skill. The driver notices the road conditions and traffic signs, anticipates the actions of others on the road and responds to these conditions. The skilled driver makes so much more of the information that reaches them than does the novice. Performance is smooth and without hesitation, movements are precise and economical and lead to a predetermined outcome. They have learnt to overcome the processing limits imposed by the nervous system. If we asked the skilled driver what was going through their mind as they were driving they would probably describe thoughts mostly unconnected with the immediate task in hand. The novice driver, on the other hand, would be closely focused on the rear-view mirror, remembering which lever is the direction indicator and which the windscreen wiper, and steering a proper line. The demands of the instant are so great that there is no possibility of planning ahead. They are monitoring their own actions as they occur, almost talking themselves through car driving skills step by step.

The novice driver makes considerable use of visual information while the skilled driver uses more kinaesthetic information about whether their hands and arms are in the right position. The novice must watch the consequences of their actions on the steering wheel to know what effect they will have on the car's path of travel. The experienced driver can tell from the engine noise and the feel of the car whether or not they are in the right gear. In isolation the novice can perform all the subroutines, such as starting, changing gear, turning, parking and emergency braking. But what they lack is the ability to organise and coordinate these separate skills together into a smooth efficient sequence.

This illustrates the development of most skills as they are organised in a hierarchical way, with many sequences carried out by the skilled performer being subroutines that are repeated time and time again. These subroutines are called forth by higher level programs, which control the overall plan of action. Each subroutine has to be learnt and may consist of other, even lower level subroutines. Responses become more and more automatic, needing less conscious attention with continued practice.

Although different skills are acquired at different rates and follow different patterns, a typical learning curve shows that learning may at first be rapid, then level off or plateau. This alternation will be repeated several times as the skill level increases and is followed by a consolidation phase.

To carry out any skilled task an individual needs three different kinds of information. First, they must know what they are expected to achieve. This information may be provided by instructions, plans, objectives or defined standards. In a teaching context the teacher must give a clear indication of the performance level expected. Second, the person requires sensory input from the task itself. This is feedback from the equipment and the environment. Discrimination is required so that the person learns what they must take note of and what information is irrelevant. Third, the learner requires feedback from the consequences of their actions. The skilled performer makes use of two types of feedback. Internal feedback is generated via the kinaesthetic sense receptors in the muscles, joints and tendons whenever a physical response is made. External feedback derives from the effect of the action on the environment and is detected by the eyes, ears and sense of touch.

## knowledge of results or feedback

Knowledge of results is essential for skill learning. The teacher will provide much feedback in the early stages, providing as much praise as is reasonable and shaping the skill through this reinforcement. Knowledge of results is necessary in order to modify behaviour. Action feedback provides us with current knowledge of our progress as we observe ourselves shaping a piece of wood or parking a car in a confined area. Feedback may also help us with our next attempt. This is learning feedback. Having made an error in shaping the wood or parking the car, we will understand where the problem lay and rectify it for the next occasion. This pattern of learning resembles trial-and-error learning as successful actions are reinforced while unsuccessful actions are eliminated. This does not mean that the learner has to be left to their own devices to learn a skill through trial and error. Indeed, if this were to occur, most skills would be learnt only up to a passable level, not an efficient or competent or economic level. Left to practise on a keyboard we may become passable two-finger typists but we will never master the skills or the speed of a trained word-processor operator. Another function of the teacher is to ensure that bad habits are eliminated early.

Feedback should focus on positives rather than negatives, even though the positive aspects may be minimal. Recognising small/partial accomplishments provides reinforcement to improve rather than causing the recipient to withdraw from the context owing to negative (punitive) comments. This also raises self-esteem and the expectations that one can succeed. Even if the positive aspects are minimal the benefits of positive reinforcement will likely increase the amount of success from that minimal level. Feedback should state what has been observed and be specific, such as, 'I particularly like the way you started the machine correctly and put in accurate settings', rather than 'That was good'.

# ■■■ THE HUMANIST/PHENOMENOLOGICAL APPROACH

Humanism generally emphasises that psychology should study the whole person, not a fragmented reductionist analysis, and also describes learning and behaviour from the viewpoint of the person, not that of the observer. It is also associated with beliefs about freedom and autonomy and that humans are capable of making significant personal choices within the constraints imposed on them by heredity and environment. Humanists do not view with any favour society planning what individuals should do, think or achieve. Gestalt psychology was the start of this approach but it has developed much further into a focus on experiential learning and phenomenology in which the individual is seeking ever-greater personal adequacy, self-esteem and self-actualisation — that is becoming whatever they are capable of becoming. Self-actualising or becoming is a state that never ends as one is always in the process of becoming.

This is the polar opposite to behaviourism and represents the universe as a total interactive system. Man is active and spontaneous. Learning is synonymous with human growth and the development of potential is mediated through symbolic interaction with the human and physical environment, as subjectively and idiosyncratically interpreted by each individual.

This approach rejects the dehumanising stance of behaviourists who equate people with automatons who can be shaped into functional members of a better society by scientifically controlling the environment. In contrast, humanists place a high value on each individual's innate need to achieve personal worth, dignity and creativity and believe a better society will evolve by nurturing these human qualities.

Psychologists who adopt this philosophy are rather a mixed bag. They have in common a concern for the person as an end in themselves. Terms such as 'person-centred', 'self-direction' and 'caring' are commonly used as concentration is focused on the development of the individual as a free and autonomous entity. Humanism is the concern for the growth and full development of the whole person. The most concise statements on humanist approaches to learning and education come from the originator of humanist psychology, Maslow, who differentiates between intrinsic education and extrinsic education by defining the former as that which changes the person and enables him to move towards his unique potential; extrinsic education is education that is only an end in itself. Maslow's theory of motivation will be detailed in Chapter 6. Maslow describes the self-actualising person as realistic; they accept themselves and other people; they are problem-centred, autonomous and independent; they are creative and resist conformity. The goal of education to Maslow is 'self-actualisation' or helping the person to become the best that they are able to become by developing 'full use and exploitation of talents, capacities, potentialities, etc.' (1970, p. 150). He identified a number of characteristics of self-actualising people, which include tolerance of ambiguity, acceptance of self and peak experiences that lead to personal transformation through new insights. Concepts of adult education that reflect this philosophy include self-directed learning, student-centred learning, development of human potential and lifelong learning. Other goals of education are the development of identity and vocation.

Humanist educators would create a positive classroom climate in which students can grow psychologically to meet the aim of humanist education: that of the creation of self-actualising persons, in other words becoming fully developed and complete persons. A self-actualising person is free from anxiety, not dogmatic, less conformist, more inwardly directed, able to accept others despite their differences, more creative and spontaneous, open to new experiences, has healthy interpersonal relationships and a greater sense of purpose. Self-actualisation is concerned not just with intellectual learning but with emotional and social learning too.

Real learning enables the learner to discover their own unique qualities and to find in themselves those features of caring, doing and thinking that makes them one with all mankind. Learning in this sense is becoming and learning how to be fully human is the only true learning. Humanist psychologists claim that educators have the weighty responsibility of helping students to become more fully developed persons.

In this context, the roles of both students and teachers are markedly different from those in traditional classrooms. The student is seen as having a very active role throughout the education process, including making decisions about what is to be learnt as well as how and when it is to be studied. Such self-direction according to Rogers is not a selfish 'doing your own thing' but being 'able to choose and then learn from the consequences' (1951, p. 171). That is, the person is not a parasite but a contributor to society. The teacher is characterised as a helper who provides a climate in which the student can feel free to develop emotionally as well as intellectually. Of low importance are the usual notions of the teacher as an authority and source of information.

What is learnt reflects not the goal of the teacher but the values and ends of the learner. This is precisely what most adults feel does not happen to them when they are required to or voluntarily engage in education and training particulary under CBT industry requirements.

> The central assumptions then in humanist psychology are the following:
> * Humans live in their own personal subjective world — reality is defined by each person.
> * Individuals are basically positive and inherently good.
> * Humans are free and autonomous and capable of making personal choices — there is no determinism.
> * Individuals will seek ways to enhance themselves and society through self-actualisation.

- Each person's self-concept plays a significant part in their personal growth, fulfilment and development.
- All humans need personal fulfilment.
- All humans need close personal relations with others.
- Individuals have a responsibility both to themselves and to others.

Like the cognitive psychologists, humanist psychologists believe human beings respond to the environment as each experiences it. Part of the environment is the person themselves so that the self becomes a very important element in determining behaviour to maintain and enhance that self. All behaviour then is an attempt of the organism to enhance itself. This is the process of self-actualisation or the process of continually developing oneself or, as Rogers calls it, the process of becoming.

Feelings and emotions play an important part in the learning process. This is why behaviourist processes are a limited approach to learning. Humanist approaches seek to understand and use the affective dimension of learners as well as the intellectual. Adults not only are but feel unique, able and independent. A teacher who does not realise and recognise these feelings will miss many opportunities to facilitate learning. An adult who returns to education with painful memories of earlier schooling will feel insecure, fearful and inadequately equipped. Such feelings may interfere with learning, unless the teachers provide a climate of encouragement and understanding.

If learners are to function in a healthy creative manner their personal worth must be valued in the learning situation. Humanist teachers keep their exercise of power and control to a minimum, adopting the role of a learning facilitator who is characterised by three essential attributes.

First, facilitators must be *sensitive and empathic* or able to see reality from the perspective of the learner. Second, facilitators are *accepting,* which means conveying confidence in the personal worth of the individual. This allows learners to express their perceptions and understandings without inhibition and to go about learning in their own way, with guidance and direction available rather than imposed. Third, facilitators are *genuine*. This implies presenting oneself as authentically as possible without a barrier or mask associated with the role or an image that obscures the real person and limits the building of trust with the learner.

Educators need to view the student as a whole person. Very frequently, an educator/trainer only sees part of the student, often as an academic problem. The school/work counsellor sees the individual as an emotional problem; the principal/boss sees them as a troublemaker. As Maslow said, 'if the only tool you have is a hammer you treat everything as though it is a nail'. Research has shown that self-actualising persons are better at learning, are more creative, more open-minded and more academically successful than non-self-actualising students. Similarly, self-actualising teachers are significantly more open-minded, less dogmatic, warmer and more encouraging of self-directed student learning than non-self-actualising teachers.

Humanists like Rogers place the concept of the self centrally in their theory. They believe there is a real self and an ideal self — that which the person would like to be. The discrepancy between the two can provide a stimulus for learning. Rogers attempts to answer the question, 'If education were as complete as we would wish it to be in promoting personal growth and development what sort of person would emerge?' He answers, 'a fully functioning person' and to get to this state education must be self-initiated with personal involvement and with the experience incorporated in the person's total experience. This emphasis on self-initiated learning is operationalised through student participation in planning, delivering and evaluating learning. It presupposes self-responsibility and independence and removes adult fears of re-entry into an authoritarian, regimented and bureaucratic milieu that is associated with schooling.

The main thrust of modern lifelong adult education is based on a humanist approach, directed towards involving adults into the self-diagnosis of their own needs, of formulating their own objectives for learning, in sharing responsibility for the learning activities and evaluating progress towards their goals (see Chapter 7). It is a lifelong process the purpose of which is to develop individuals who are able to live humane and meaningful lives.

From humanist approaches numerous principles of learning are apparent:

- Learning is a natural process as people are by nature curious.
- Persons learn by relating the world to their previous experience, that is learning by doing.
- People learn in a free environment that permits and encourages development of potential self-expression and self-determination — self-actualisation.
- Social situations affect learning as learning is rarely an isolated event — people learn cooperatively, which includes constructive feedback in a non-competitive environment.
- The learning that has most meaning for people is that which is constructed by the individual out of personal experiences — meaning is a personal thing.
- Learners have needs, goals and purposes for learning so that choice, relevancy and responsibility are important.
- Self-regulation — monitoring one's own learning — is an important skill.
- Learning is not just a cognitive process — it affects one's emotions and feelings, which creates very pervasive and long-lasting learning.

## criticisms of the humanist approach

Humanism is not without its critics. The primary complaint, raised by religious fundamentalists, is that it denies a god, original sin and offers a highly self-centred, selfish approach to life. However, it is quite easy to celebrate the good of humanity and engage in practices that facilitate self-direction without abandoning traditional theologies. In fact, the aim of self-actualisation is to find the highest good in working for the good of all. For example, Mother Theresa is regarded as having expounded the qualities of self-actualisation.

Phenomenological or humanist psychologists have raised questions about methods of instruction, about who should set goals for the individual and who should determine educational objectives. There are several untested assumptions though. First, is it true that only feeling free when learning will free a student to be creative? Second, is the approach unlimited in its application to all students and subject matter? Also, while one can accept the idea that a person may be expert about their own needs, feelings and beliefs one may rightly question whether or not the student is expert about what they should learn.

Humanist psychology provides some insight into how the adult learner should profitably be engaged in educational pursuits. Independent and self-directed, an adult can guide and promote much of their own educational development with the support of an empathic and accepting teacher. Whether one is striving towards self-actualisation, maturity or being fully functional, the emphasis is on continued self-improvement through learning.

However, it is not always sensible to develop awareness and understanding and facilitate growth regardless of the circumstances, institution or relationship. Often institutional or program goals are not congruent with those of individual learners or with adult education approaches. There are other drawbacks to approaching an adult as an independent learner. Some adults do not handle the role maturely; they may not know what they need to know. It may not be feasible to try to translate each individual adult need as perceived into a learning program. Satisfying an identified need may not lead to the adult's long-range goal. For example, training to be a teacher or a lawyer may not lead to a job in today's market. So while it is desirable that adults direct their own learning it is the responsibility of those who educate adults to guide learners within a framework of possibilities.

The adult does have a huge fund of experiences on which to draw. However, if this causes them to be closed and rigid in their thinking then they are an impediment rather than an aid to their future learning as they close off new experiences, values and attitudes.

Some educators argue that humanist approaches to learning overemphasise personal experience, emotions and feelings at the expense of intellect. Self-actualisation is an indulgence that must be tempered by the need to live in a social setting. Effective education for adults must assist them with managing the social and work roles in which they are engaged and with coping with new roles. The teachable moment for an adult depends not on physiological maturation, as with a child, but in large measure upon the immediate problems or tasks associated with social and work roles. Humanist learning approaches tend to avoid consideration of developmental factors. Positioning the adult learner within a developmental framework enables us to view adult education as more than a drive towards self-actualisation or a simple mechanistic response to a stimulus. Adult learning becomes a complex phenomenon involving biological, social and psychological factors.

## SUMMARY

Teaching can be conceived of as:
- telling or transmitting information that needs to be remembered — *a behaviourist approach*
- organising a learning environment to facilitate student activities that lead to discovery, understanding and problem solving — *a cognitive approach*
- developing individual potential by making personal learning possible through self-direction and valuing personal experience in a supportive teacher interaction – *a humanist–phenomenological approach.*

We have introduced three major families of learning theory and drawn out some of the implications for teachers. It is apparent that the organisational imperatives of instructional efficiency and resource conservation will tend to favour the behaviourist approach, which focuses on the conditioning of learning through S–R links, whereas consideration of learner characteristics brings teachers to employ more cognitive and humanist approaches.

The behaviourist approach sees learning as organised by the teacher, who controls the environment, particularly the application of reinforcement, so that learners are simply reactive organisms having their behaviour shaped.

The other two approaches to learning presume three major characteristics common to all persons. First, that all humans are active participants in their own learning, possessing potential resources to cope with situations they encounter, and can develop a critical way of interpreting reality and the ability to change it. Second, humans are dynamic and are continually developing in an ongoing interplay with their environment. People look for opportunities to develop their potential and find outlets for their abilities. Third, people want to be involved in personally meaningful and satisfying activities and be able to have some control and influence over their lives.

The behaviour of an individual in this context is dependent on the meaning a situation has for the individual. In Gestalt theory, learning is based on the development of insight and of more effective ways to use the elements of a given situation to achieve a goal or solve a problem.

Cognitive theorists emphasise the need for meaningful learning, insight and the perception of principles capable of generalisation. These are central to understanding and the ability to transfer learning across situations. Items of skill or knowledge must be located within a rich network of related items and must make sense in various contexts. Principles underlying a skill or technique must be explained to aid positive transfer. This eliminates rote learning and the explanation and understanding of principles ensures the active searching for and application of learnt skills in the workplace.

In humanist theory the individual aims to enhance their self-concept and interpret the environment in terms of its effect on the self. Thus feeling, emotion and attitude are important determinants of learning to a humanist.

# chapter 5

# intelligence and memory

**We remember**
**10 per cent of what we read**
**20 per cent of what we hear**
**30 per cent of what we see**
**50 per cent of what we see and hear**
**80 per cent of what we say**
**90 per cent of what we say and do.**

## ■■■ INTELLIGENCE

The term 'intelligence' has been used generally by laypeople, educators and psychologists to explain why some people appear quicker at learning than others and why some people are able to succeed in academic and employment activities while others fail. Of course, picking things up quickly and coping with learning tasks does not depend simply on intelligence. Motivation, interest, the learner's subjective assessment of their own competence, the stimulation or lack of it in the family and social environment and a host of personality factors interact to determine successful learning, achievement and high-level performance.

Intelligence is often taken to mean current ability or how a person performs now. Intelligence can also be thought of as being predictive of potential for the future. It is the capacity to learn, solve problems and apply knowledge and experience. Because intelligence cannot be observed apart from the way it influences behaviour, it is regarded as a hypothetical construct like justice or love. It is better to use 'intelligent' as an adjective to describe behaviour rather than use the noun 'intelligence' to refer to an abstract quality a person possesses. Thus some ways of performing are judged in our culture to be more intelligent than others. We say a person's behaviour is intelligent when they are more purposive than haphazard, more intentional than accidental and more foresightful than impulsive and stereo-typed. We measure intelligence by measuring performance on items that are 'judged' to measure intelligent behaviour. The difficulty is that these judgments are culture-bound. A university professor might well appear highly unintelligent trying to cope with living with Aborigines on 'walk about'. The professor would not know the berries and leaves that are nutritious from those that are poisonous, nor would they be able to find water in an apparently waterless desert. The Aborigines are far more intelligent in their own culture than the professor, just as we appear to be in ours when we compare our test scores with those produced by peoples from undeveloped non-Western cultures that do not value logical abstract problem solving of a mainly verbal kind.

So while intelligence is a frequently-used concept, it is also a misunderstood one. Most psychologists would be hard-pressed to come up with a definition of the term that would be generally acceptable to a majority of them. The problem is that intelligence is an abstract concept and simply a way of trying to label a particular type of culturally defined behaviour, that is what our Western-type culture regards as intelligent. Definitions of intelligence have ranged from, 'an innate general factor' through, 'ability to learn' to, 'ability to adjust to the environment'. Some definitions consider intelligence as 'the ability to carry out abstract thinking' (Terman, 1959). Other psychologists accept a definition of intelligence as 'the ability to discern relationships' (Spearman, 1927). This last definition has been used as the principle behind most intelligence test items, which is usually one of seeking relationships. What follow are some examples of such test items. Figure 5.1 is an example of a verbal item.

**FIGURE 5.1** VERBAL INTELLIGENCE TEST ITEMS

---

1. INSERT THE MISSING WORD:

    GRINS   (LOIN)   ALONE

    SWILL   (. . . .)   ATONE

2. INSERT THE MISSING NUMBER:

71, 68, 77, 74, 83, . . . .

---

Figure 5.2 below is an example of a non-verbal item. Both examples (Figure 5.1 and 5.2) illustrate the relationship-seeking basis of intelligence text items and ultimately the scores derived.

Notice the requirement to realise what the relationship is in order to produce the single correct response. Intelligence tests are often termed convergent thinking tests as there is only one correct answer to each question. Thus such tests can be marked objectively as there is no judgment to be made as to the degree of correctness.

Criticism has been levelled at the speeded and child-oriented nature of most intelligence tests, which make them unsuitable for adults. The major adult intelligence test is the Wechsler Adult Intelligence Scale. It includes verbal and non-verbal/performance items.

FIGURE 5.2 NON-VERBAL INTELLIGENCE TEST ITEMS

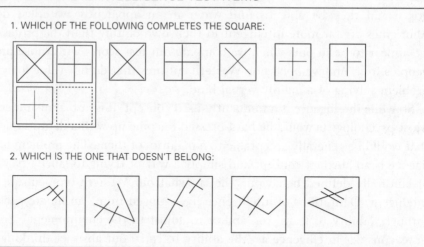

1. WHICH OF THE FOLLOWING COMPLETES THE SQUARE:

2. WHICH IS THE ONE THAT DOESN'T BELONG:

## one general intelligence or many intellectual abilities?

A central question in the debate is whether mental competence is a single ability, applicable in many settings, or whether competence is produced by specialised abilities, which a person might or might not possess independently of other abilities. Almost equally important is the question of how cognitive skill, as evaluated by intelligence tests, translates into everyday performance. There are no simple answers. Although we know a good deal about individual differences in human cognition, there is no monolithic, agreed-upon, all-purpose theory to organise these facts, nor is there likely ever to be one. There are a number of different theories that are neither right nor wrong, but are useful for different purposes.

## psychometric approaches to intelligence

In popular discussions of intelligence, the term generally refers to scoring well on tests that have been developed to measure mental ability as psychologists have come to see it. This emphasis on test scores is the psychometric view of intelligence. Its core belief is that individual differences in human cognition can be adequately measured by performance on intelligence tests, and that intelligence itself can therefore be defined by variations in test scores, across people. This notion was expressed most pungently when the psychologist Edwin Boring (1923), in a public debate with the columnist Walter Lippman, said that 'intelligence is what the intelligence test measures'. It turns out that that statement is not quite so arrogant or self-serving as it sounds. To see why, we have to look at what intelligence tests are and how intelligence measures are inferred from test scores.

## role of heredity and environment

Some psychologists (e.g. Herrnstein & Murray, 1994) view intelligence as mainly innate, that is you are born with a particular level of intelligence that cannot be altered, while others (e.g. Howe, 1997) take the opposite view that intelligence is developed as a function of the level of stimulation in the home and neighbourhood environment. Studies comparing the intelligence scores of identical twins raised in the same home with those of identical twins raised apart in different homes suggested that heredity is the dominant factor in determining intelligence since the intelligence scores of each pair reared apart produced high positive correlations (i.e. scores within pairs were very similar), almost as high as those for each pair reared together (scores within pairs were even more similar). This indicated that the different environments of the twins reared apart had little impact.

These studies now appear to offer unreliable evidence for a variety of reasons. First, it is becoming apparent that both heredity and environment are intricately enmeshed in determining the level of intelligence that develops in any individual. For some people heredity might be the stronger factor, while for others a high degree of environmental stimulation received, particularly in the early years, is the vital factor. Second, while we know what heredity is, it is incredibly difficult to define environment. It is not just the physical environment but includes subjectively interpreted subtleties such as the emotional and social tone. It is the psychological environment as interpreted by the experiencing person. Whether the environment is stimulating or not, whether the person feels socially accepted and whether the person feels comfortable there depends on the idiosyncratic way in which that individual construes their environment. Even people within the same family home will interpret the psychological environment of that same home in different ways.

There is surprisingly little evidence for influences of cultural experiences on intelligence — once again as measured by intelligence test scores — in spite of many efforts to find such effects. Two well-documented findings capture the gist of the results. Studies of adopted children have repeatedly shown that the IQ of the biological parent is a better predictor of the child's IQ than is the IQ of the adopting parent, even when adoption is virtually at birth. Consistent with this observation, the quality of home or school environments appears to have relatively little relation to permanent changes in test scores, once one has taken account of the correlation between genetic and social variables. Put a slightly different way, genetic predictions based on parental or sibling IQ can account for IQ variability in children, after social factors have been taken account of, but social factors are not related to children's IQ after genetic variability has been accounted for.

Herrnstein and Murray's *The Bell Curve: Intelligence and Class Structure in American Life* made its authors household names, sometimes accompanied by four-letter words. (The bell curve is the normal distribution curve to which scores from intelligence tests are standardised). Herrnstein and Murray maintained that America was splitting into the intelligent, who will move and shake society, and the less intelligent, who will be moved and shaken. They thought the split inevitable, because technological society requires intelligence to run it. Finally, taking a bravely academic rather than politically correct stance they affirmed that intelligence is largely hereditary, and affirmative government programs are undesirable because they amount to discrimination against the capable.

The first reactions to *The Bell Curve* were expressions of public outrage. In the second round of reaction, some commentators suggested that Herrnstein and Murray were merely bringing up facts that were well known to the scientific community, but perhaps best not discussed in public. A Papua New Guinea language has a term for this: 'mokita'. It means 'truth that we all know but agree not to talk about'.

The uproar over *The Bell Curve* replayed a debate from the early 1970s, prompted when Arthur Jensen (1969) wrote that educational enrichment programs were inherently limited by the immutability of intelligence. Counterattacks followed, and by the early 1980s widely read books and articles maintained that there is no such thing as general intelligence (Gardner, 1983), or that if there is it is largely a statistical artifact of the way that tests are constructed (Gould, 1983), and that even if IQ exists it has little to do with life outside of a few narrow academic settings (Ceci and Liker, 1986). Some of these authors have recanted (Ceci & Bruck, 1994, p. 79).

## Hebb's model of intelligence

Hebb (1949) provides a sensible model of intelligence that helps in clarifying the confusing ways in which the term is used and that indicates the roles of heredity and environment. He argues that from birth stimulation from the environment, for example sensation, experience and perception, builds up patterns of electrical discharge or *cell assemblies* in the cerebral cortex — a sort of programming.

The cell assembly is a collection of nerve cells that function as a circuit to record and store each experience. Activation of a cell assembly would constitute memory or recall. Through early childhood these cell assemblies builds up rapidly as the child is flooded with new experiences.

Cell assemblies start to link together to form more complex circuits termed *phase sequences* so that experiences 'a', 'b' and 'c' (or cell assemblies 'a', 'b' and 'c') can be evoked by the activation of only one of the elements. This is the start of thinking and the ability to relate thoughts together in a sequence. Thus early learning in infancy is the building up of cell assemblies, which permits the stimulus-response type of learning of discrete items. Later learning combining cell assemblies is the characteristic of insightful learning and problem solving as propounded by cognitive–Gestalt psychologists. Insight is therefore the sudden activation of an effective link between experiences/knowledge stored in the brain. Intelligence, as it is generally measured, looks at this ability to perceive relationships. Hence, degree of insightful ability is a quality of a person related to degree of intelligence.

The absolute necessity of a rich, stimulating environment during infancy and preschool years is indicated in order to build up a plethora of basic cell assemblies. Poverty of early experience might therefore underlie differences in measured intelligence. Intelligence might not be able to be taught, but intellectual stimulation will provide the best climate for its growth.

Hebb goes on to suggest that there are two types of intelligence:

1. *Intelligence A* is the innate potential, the possession of a good, healthily functioning brain. It is the wiring diagram genetically specified and laid down at birth. It is only in this sense that functions of the brain might be said to be hereditary. Individuals will differ with respect to this. There are noticeable differences between children within one family. It can never be measured.

2. The second type is *Intelligence B,* which is actual, developed mental skills and determines level of performance. Intelligence B develops out of the interaction of innate potential (Intelligence A) and environmental stimulation. It is therefore possible for a person with high innate potential to function at a lower level than they should because of the debilitating effects of early environment. Equally a person with average innate potential could function at their optimum if their early environment was highly conducive.

Vernon carried this model one stage further. He proposed *Intelligence C,* which is the actual score obtained on a particular intelligence test on a particular day. It is an amalgam of Intelligence B, with the effects of anxiety, motivation and other social and situational variables impacting at the time of testing. Of course, intelligence tests have to use elements of the environment such as words, shapes and numbers in order to pose test questions. Therefore, it is obvious we must also be measuring prior learning in measuring intelligence. Also any intelligence test is only measuring a small sample, often a biased sample, of skills we describe in our culture as 'intelligent'.

Intelligence test scores will give a fair idea of the extent to which development has occurred but say nothing about how much undeveloped potential there is left. Hypothetically, intelligence will rise to the limits set by heredity or that set by environment, whichever is the lower. Only in a perfect environment will innate potential be the limiting factor. It is Intelligence A we would like to measure but the closest we can get is Intelligence C.

## factor-analytic approaches — models of intelligence

Currently, psychologists do not regard intelligence as a single trait. There appears to be a variety of elements that compose overall intelligence. Initially, however, psychological thinking and research did propose a unitary conception of intelligence as something that underlies all manifestations of behaviour and skill. This was labelled intelligence or simply 'g', meaning general intelligence. The conceptualisation of 'g', which has always been inferred from the strong intercorrelations between batteries of tests, has changed over the years from reasoning ability in the early days to information processing in the present. Spearman, in giving a large number of tests to children, was the first to note that if the children did well on one test they would do well on them all or if they did badly on one they would fare badly on them all. He therefore concluded that all the tests had something in common. He devised the label 'g', or general intelligence. But because all the tests did not produce identical results, each had a small specific component, or specific ability 's', required to perform in them. Thus Spearman proposed a two-factor theory of intelligence involving a predominant general factor 'g' and a smaller 's' factor specific to each test. Arguably, 'g' flows into every activity but specific abilities like verbal and numerical ability are only demonstrated in activities in those areas. This approach exemplifies the factor-analytic approach to intelligence.

Factor analysis is a technique that attempts to explain, in this case, the degree of correlation between performances on tests or on test items. In other words are they highly correlated, less so, not at all or do they bear a negative relationship. If intelligence items or tests are highly correlated then we assume they are underlain by the same ability or factor. If correlations are minimal then we assume that each test is underlain by a different ability or factor. This argument, as you see above in Spearman's case, was the basis for postulating a general ability (or general factor of intelligence) and a specific ability for each test.

The contrary tendency towards a pluralistic notion of intelligence has resulted in this two-factor theory being replaced by theories that suggest intelligence is composed of a large number of specific abilities. Using other factor-analytic techniques, American psychologists have split 'g' into a number of mental abilities. Thurstone argued for nine primary mental abilities, such as word fluency, numerical facility, perceptual speed and spatial ability. He claimed that he could find no evidence for 'g'.

Guilford stipulates 120 specific mental abilities. Guilford's model of the intellect has been useful for suggesting types of intelligence that can be translated in different types of test and test items. He distinguishes five types of mental operation: cognition, memory, divergent production, convergent production and evaluation. His second dimension is the four content areas: figural, symbolic, semantic and behavioural. Finally, he identifies six types of products: units, classes, relations, systems, transformations and implications. The various combinations of operations, contents and products make up the 120 intellectual abilities (6 x 5 x 4). Tests have been devised for 82 of the 120. In fact, ignoring the practical considerations of devising the tests and carrying them out, it is conceivable that there are even more abilities, for example to sing a note in tune, to track a moving object on a computer screen using a joystick and ignoring information from one sensory modality when using another.

## fluid and crystallised intelligence

Cattell (1976) has proposed a different structure of intelligence, consisting of the following:

- *Fluid intelligence (Gf)*, which is the biological inheritance.
- *Crystallised intelligence (Gc)*, which is capable of growth through the influence of environment, mainly individual experiences and social processes.

Cattell's (op. cit.) proposal of fluid and crystallised intelligence has much in common with Hebb's A and B. Fluid intelligence (Gf) is rather formless, similar to Intelligence A, relatively independent of education and experience. It can flow into a wide range of intellectual activities. Innate in nature, it is our ability to perceive complex relationships, to form concepts and to engage in abstract reasoning and solve problems. The basis of this fluid intelligence is neurophysiological structure, which in turn depends on heredity, but it can be adversely affected by injury and disease.

Crystallised intelligence (Gc), similar to Intelligence B, is the result of fluid intelligence being mixed with cultural knowledge. It is termed crystallised because it is a precipitate of experience and therefore based on acculturisation. It enlarges with education and life experience. The sorts of abilities that demonstrate crystallised intelligence include general knowledge, verbal comprehension, numerical skills and coping with social situations. Interacting together, these two types of intelligence are involved in much of our daily activity. One person might solve a problem by applying fluid intelligence to discover an original solution; another person might solve the same problem by applying accumulated experience or crystallised intelligence.

They both develop during childhood and adolescence but on reaching neurological maturity there is a decrease in fluid intelligence as diseases and neurological loss occurs. Crystallised intelligence will continue to increase through increased experience. The older person replaces brilliance with wisdom. Crystallised intelligence is largely influenced by the extent to which an individual continues to seek information and engage in stimulating and educational activity. The most important factors in the environment necessary for intellectual development are those concerned with language and parent-child relationships. Much of the difference in measured intelligence later in life can be traced to lack of appropriate verbal stimulation and poverty of perceptual experience. Thus involvement in learning activities in later life is valuable as a means of maintaining intellectual level or even improving it. We will see that the better educated tend to show a stability of intelligence as they age. Most adults in their forties onwards have the ability to learn new tasks if they can control the pace or the rate of learning. Taken together, both types of intelligence cover the learning tasks that confront adults. As people grow older, they compensate increasingly for loss of fluid intelligence by relying more on crystallised intelligence: that is they substitute wisdom for brilliance with an end effect of apparent intellectual stability or even improvement in those still engaged in stimulating activity. For a person who maintains their health and avoids debilitating disease or injury, and engages their mind with the problems and activities of life around them, the chances are good that they will experience little if any decline in intellectual performance.

In childhood new connections between nerve cells might be made by the actual growth and development of new cell processes and synapses. As the brain reaches full development it loses its capacity for further growth, yet one still goes on learning and showing adaptive behaviour in new situations until senility because by opening new synaptic links new pathways are possible and new circuits available. In this way we can continue to store information. Almost certainly no-one has ever remotely approached the theoretical limit set by their brain. With 10 000 million cells, each with its 10 000 separate synapses, there is ample potential for coding all the information the brain is likely to need to store over 70 plus years. What sets the limit is not the wiring diagram but the peripheral blocks that prevent information ever arriving, the irreversible deficits introduced by a socially, emotionally and physically deprived childhood and deficits arising from declining visual and auditory acuity in the older person.

## resolving the issues

There is no necessary conflict between the views of Spearman and Cattell and multiple-factor views if they are all considered as part of a hierarchical system. The question of how many abilities there are might depend solely on the level of analysis one wishes to consider. For example, numeracy might be a specific factor, which is possible to split into mechanical mathematics and problem solving. If the purpose of testing is to assess some specific ability then tests measuring lower down in the hierarchy are the obvious choice, such as perceptual speed for clerical tasks, whereas if a more general appraisal is needed one can simply measure general ability. The level one chooses is a matter of convenience.

FIGURE 5.3 SIMPLIFIED HIERARCHICAL DIAGRAM OF THE STRUCTURE OF INTELLIGENCE SHOWING RELATIONSHIPS BETWEEN LEVELS

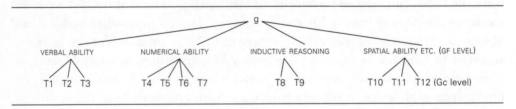

One of the most interesting contributions to the specific-general debate has been that of Fodor (1983), who argues that the mind process information in both generic and specific ways. For example, visual, auditory and linguistic data are analysed by specifically dedicated neurological systems — autonomous and hard wired. By contrast, central processes in 'non-specific' areas of the cerebral cortex serve general problem solving purposes and can relate to any information on hand.

In a highly technical report, Carroll (1993) used somewhat different methods to re-analyse a great many important data sets that have been collected over the past 60 years. The results of these independent analyses were quite consistent. Skipping over some details, human intellectual competence appears to divide along three dimensions: fluid intelligence (Gf), crystallised intelligence (Gc) and visual-spatial reasoning (Gv).

- Fluid intelligence is the ability to develop techniques for solving problems that are new and unusual from the perspective of the problem solver.
- Crystallised intelligence is the ability to bring previously acquired, often culturally defined, problem-solving methods to bear on the current problem.
- Visual-spatial reasoning is a somewhat specialised ability to use visual images and visual relationships in problem solving.

Crystallised- and fluid-intelligence measures are substantially correlated. For instance, Horn reported a study in which the correlation between Gf and Gc measures was 0.61. Such findings have led believers in just one intelligence to argue that Gf and Gc are simply different flavours of a general intelligence (IQ) factor. This argument cannot be answered one way or the other solely by looking at correlations between tests. However, it can be attacked by stepping outside of factor analysis and looking at how Gf and Gc measures respond to manipulations that might change mental competence. It turns out that they respond differently. The most striking example is ageing. Measures of Gf generally decrease from early adulthood onward, whereas Gc measures remain constant or even increase throughout most of the working years (Horn & Noll, 1994). This is not surprising. Experience counts; most of the key leadership positions in our society are held by people over 40. On the other hand, middle-aged and older people do take longer than younger people to understand new problem-solving methods and to deal with unfamiliar tasks. Age is not the only variable that can be shown to have different influences on fluid and crystallised intelligence. Alcoholism shows similar effects.

## speed of processing hypothesis

One possible explanation for the high correlation between different types of ability tests is that some individuals are able to process information quicker than others. So 'g' is simply the basic property of the nervous system that affects all cognitive operations. Several studies have measured neural conduction velocity and have found a significant correlation with 'g' in the order of $r = 0.42$ and 0.48. Other measures of neural speed such as choice reaction time and inspection time also show significant correlations that suggest about a quarter of 'g' is explained by neural speed (Deary, 1997).

## other theories of intelligence

Other significant theories on the nature and measuring of intelligence were posited by Sternerg, Gardner and others.

## Sternberg's triarchic theory

Sternberg (1985) uses a very broad definition of ability and is not interested just in intellectual tasks that are abstract and decontextualised (as in IQ tests) but reaches out to include practical, social and tacit (knowledge learnt through experience and not deliberately taught) forms of intelligence as well as experiential theory to explain how we come to use previous experiences to perform complex behaviour smoothly and automatically. His social intelligence includes the skills and abilities we use in everyday life to deal with people. His theory is so named because it explains how three different types of intelligence operate.

1. The componential subtheory tries to model how people conceptualise and solve problems and perform basic mental operations to reach a solution. This is similar to standard approaches to intelligence

2. The contextual subtheory examines how people adapt to their environments and adapt their environments in an intelligent manner. He claims that it is impossible to identify intelligent behaviour without taking context into account. Running away as fast as possible might be appropriate when a large bull is chasing you but not too appropriate if the chaser is an armed policeman. Winning at golf in a competition is generally sound but not if you want to clinch a business deal with your competitor. This is where intelligence is enlarged to include social factors, motivation, expectations, personality, etc. Evaluation of a particular response as intelligent therefore depends on a wide range of factors, including the perspectives of the person behaving and the observer, and becomes a complex procedure. In this sense intelligence might have been widened so much as to become meaningless and a layperson's theory. Traditional tests have decontextualised in order to remove the noise of variables such as prior experience, and involve objective scoring, standardised instructions and time limits, etc. Solving anagrams and remembering a sequence of digits is far easier to test than real-life abilities like placating a dissatisfied customer or transferring maths skills to investment decisions.

3. The experiential subtheory implicates the role of experience in problem solving.

Sternberg developed instruments to assess tacit knowledge (everyday life problems) and found that it does not correlate with standard IQ scores, but predicts school and job performance better than the latter measure. In fact, for rural Africans the correlation was negative, indicating that they saw their path to success not through schooling but by acquiring tacit knowledge that enabled them to adapt to rural village life. The difference is due to Sternberg focusing on practical abilities while standard IQ focuses on analytic thinking. Thus successful intelligence is that which enables people to adapt successfully to their environment, capitalising on their strengths and correcting their weaknesses where possible. There is no one path to success, and the job of the teacher/trainer is to help students chart their own path. Most societies tend to focus on analytic ability and memory as the criteria of intelligence but in doing so create a self-fulfilling prophecy that identifies those with these qualities as the able group. Choose another criterion like tacit intelligence and other individuals will come to the fore.

Sternberg's theory is valuable in moving away from the arbitrary tasks usually considered to index intelligent behaviour and tries to explain what is going on when people meet problems in real life. However, it has an unlimited complexity about it that in most instances defies testing in practice. Overall it is a radical redefinition of intelligence, involving social context and high-level planning skills and it reminds us that there is more to being intelligent than abstract reasoning.

> The principles that derive from Sternberg's work include the following:
> - Training in intellectual performance must be socio-culturally relevant.
> - Training must be linked with real-world behaviour.
> - Training should actively encourage individuals to manifest their differences in strategies and styles.

Sternberg stresses that it is not enough just to have these three types of intelligence, rather that people are successfully intelligent when they are able to choose how and when to use these abilities effectively.

## Gardner's theory of multiple intelligences

Arguing that 'reason, intelligence, logic and knowledge are not synonymous', Gardner, like Sternberg, is careful to indicate that what is regarded as intelligent might depend on culture. He views intelligence as that which provides adequacy of performance at whatever is valued in the culture and disputes the idea of one intelligence. Memorising a Holy book, making money, being an expert at making an igloo or hunting with a blow pipe are valued differently by different cultures. Intelligence 'is the capacity to do something useful in the society in which you live', in other words it is what a person can do. The values of a particular society often dictate what is seen as intelligent or not. Not all societies value linear, logical, problem-solving skills. Gardner (1993) proposed a multiplicity of intelligences. His theory, which draws on a number of sources of evidence, including the effects of brain damage, the phenomenon of gifted persons and evidence from other cultures, provides an alternative to factor-analytic findings, encompassing eight different types of intelligence:

1. *Logico-mathematical* — an ability to solve problems in a logical way.
2. *Linguistic* — the mastery of language; capacity to use language well, like a lawyer or orator.
3. *Spatial* — the ability to represent the spatial world in your mind, like a navigator or architect; to create and manipulate mental images.
4. *Musical* — the capacity to hear musical patterns and think in music; to recognise pitch, tone and rhythm.
5. *Body-kinaesthetic* — the capacity to use the body, as in the performing arts and sport, or to make something.

6. *Personal* — understanding self and having empathy with others (this links with Goleman's concept of emotional intelligence — see below).
7. *Naturalistic* — the ability to understand the natural environment (e.g. the talents of Darwin); sensitivity to the environment and living things.
8. *Spiritual/existential* — the strengths of spiritual and religious persons.

He ignores 'g' and claims the multitude of abilities are independent and the supposed relationships between them found by others exist only because all the tests rely on language skills. Interestingly, there is substantial overlap even though his work and the factor-analytic models use different sources of data. So while Gardner's work is interesting, it really only reinforces what other theorists have said. It is a popular theory with educators since it paints a more egalitarian picture than the factor theories in that if there are independent sorts of intelligences a person who has limited ability in one cannot be considered limited in general and might have strengths elsewhere. Jean (1999) found that learners in her Gardner-based choices classroom chose activities that matched their strongest intelligences, which helped to overcome their resistance to learning. Multiple intelligences theory might well provide better insight into the nature and needs of adult students to help them in their learning than an approach that simply looks at one IQ score. Many workers have considerable skills and abilities (e.g. designers, musicians, carpenters and mechanics) but these are rarely recognised by standard intelligence test measures. Recognising multiple intelligences and helping mature adult students to recognise the intelligences in which they individually excel raises their self-esteem and motivates them to continue learning. Teachers are also enabled to use these intelligences as a way of conveying a focus for development and applying more relevant teaching strategies. Teachers should think of all multiple intelligences operating in the classroom and consider them of equal importance, thus recognising and teaching to a broad range of talents. Material and methods of teaching must engage as many of these intelligences as possible. Traditional testing should be modified to permit students to show their knowledge in their own rather than in predetermined ways.

## emotional intelligence — the caring and sharing way to success

Studies of emotional intelligence originated with BarOn's work in producing the first validated EQ scale. BarOn addressed the personal, emotional, social and survival dimensions of intelligence in his definition: 'an array of personal, emotional, and social competencies that influence one's abilities to succeed in coping with environmental demands and pressures' (p. 3 EQ-i manual).

Salovey and Mayer defined emotional intelligence as, 'the ability to perceive accurately, appraise, and express emotion; the ability to generate feelings when they facilitate thought; the ability to understand emotion; and the ability to regulate emotions to produce emotional and intellectual growth' (1997, p. 10). This definition centres on identifying, using, understanding and managing emotions.

It was Goleman's book that popularised the concept. Goleman based his work largely on Salovey and Mayer's ideas. Within his emotional competence framework he addresses personal competence through self-awareness, self-relation and self-motivation, and social competence through social awareness and social skills. The common theme is emotions. In summarising all these ideas a generic definition would be 'emotional intelligence is the array of emotional and social abilities and skills that support our ability to succeed in life'. Given the stressful nature of the workplace environment currently, a high emotional intelligence is needed.

Emotional intelligence consists of five components:

1. *General mood.* The ability to be optimistic, cheerful and create a positive atmosphere.
2. *Adaptability.* The ability to be flexible, realistic; and to identify and solve problems.
3. *Intrapersonal.* The ability to know yourself, know your feelings and feel positive about what you are doing; to have positive self-esteem and to seek to develop potential, free of emotional dependence on others.
4. *Interpersonal.* The ability to interact well and manifest good social skills; demonstrate empathy; and be a constructive member of a group.
5. *Stress management.* The ability to work well under pressure without losing control.

The real value of emotional intelligence is now being recognised in the business world, where increased performance and successful leadership are seen to be based on healthy relationship skills and a healthy emotional intelligence to complement technical and business acumen. Most workers from managerial level downwards to the shop floor agree that most business or work problems are people-related. Improving relationships, building productive teams, increasing team spirit and improving leadership skills would seem to involve emotional intelligence. Goleman (1955) shows that in over 300 studies, 'star' or excelling performers in the business world have more than sheer intellectual ability in their favour. He found that they have considerable emotional competencies, which cover a broad range of skills from empathy through to self-awareness and social skills. He analysed 181 different positions in 121 worldwide organisations and concluded that 67 per cent of their abilities identified as superior were emotional competencies. That is, emotional competence matters twice as much as IQ and expertise. He also determined that the importance of emotional intelligence increased with the seniority of the position. Among machine operators the productivity of the top one per cent was three times greater than that of the bottom one per cent; among sales personnel productivity was 12 times greater. The top one per cent of computer systems professionals were 1272 per cent more productive than the bottom one per cent. The message is obviously: get in touch with your emotions if you wish to do well and also enjoy life.

Fortunately, emotional intelligence can be learnt. Whereas IQ tends to be static, EQ can be increased by suitable training in the skills of self-awareness, emotional control, empathy, self-motivation and positive relationship development. With these skills, managers, supervisors and team leaders start to lead, not just manage and control. They expand their focus, boundaries become more flexible and the good of the business is seen as the overriding vision. EQ is also an integral part of creating a learning organisation (see Chapter 3). It is the catalyst that oils relationships and communication, enabling employee satisfaction, motivation and responsiveness to change.

A high EQ for workers is necessary because of the increasing demands placed on them in the twenty-first century, such as managing their own careers, recognising opportunities, being prepared for change and upgrading themselves in multiskills. Workers will also want organisations that can provide purpose and meaning for what they do and avenues for creative expression and facilitate the development of their potential. BarOn's research showed that EQ accounted for 50 per cent of job success, while Goleman implies even more at 67 to 80 per cent. Leadership Quotient = IQ + EQ + SQ where SQ is the strategic quotient.

Slaski (2001) found that managers with high emotional intelligence were rated as the best performers by co-workers and were also more sensitive to the needs of their staff. The problem is that many employees at all levels are reluctant to talk about their emotions or allow development of emotional skills for their work. They feel they have to be seen as strong and decisive, whereas their performance and that of their colleagues would improve if they were able to express and understand their emotions and recognise the same emotions in those around them. All would then feel greater self-worth and optimism and be socially skilled, treating each other in socially sensitive ways to get the best out of each other. There would be lower levels of stress and fewer negative health effects. As a worker's EQ increases their creativity is expressed and they are more inspired by nourishing surroundings and will work more effectively for the organisation. While IQ is essentially static, EQ can be enhanced and developed to contribute to greater personal and organisational success. In the demanding workplace of the twenty-first century, successful organisations will be those that provide a work environment that nourishes emotional development.

## test your emotional intelligence

Answer each of the statements below and give yourself the points associated with your response, as follows:

Never = 0, rarely = 1, sometimes = 2, routinely = 3 and always = 4

1. Are you aware of your strengths, weaknesses and emotional boundaries in relationships?
2. Do you present yourself with self-possession and warmth?
3. Do you know which emotions you are feeling and label them?

4. Can you celebrate diversity in teams, tolerating and voicing views that are unpopular?
5. Do you make time for self-reflection?
6. Do you recognise the chain from experiencing an emotion to taking action based on it?
7. Are you decisive, making sound judgments using both emotional and analytical information, despite uncertainty and pressure?
8. Are you open to candid feedback, new perspectives and continuous learning?
9. Do you recognise how your feelings affect your performance and your relationships at work?

*Score 27-36*   Excellent. You have a high emotional awareness of yourself.
*Score 18-26*   Well done, but reflect on reasons why you recorded a 'sometimes' response.
*Score 9-17*    Try to develop a plan to develop more self-insight.
*Score 1-8*     Thank you for being honest. Integrity is a great strength too. You are not really aware of how or why you behave as you do. Enrol in a course that will increase your self-awareness.

## the cognitive psychology view of intelligence

Cognitive psychologists see intellectual activity as a process of creating a mental representation of a problem, retrieving information that appears relevant and manipulating that representation in order to obtain an answer. The problem, its solution and some of the methods used to solve it are then stored for later reference. The cognitive-psychology view is that cognition is a process, whereas the psychometric view makes it a collection of abilities. Perhaps because it is more dynamic, the cognitive-psychology view is often seen as more appealing but it has the disadvantage of not lending itself to easy summarisation. When cognitive psychologists try to characterise a person's thinking, they are not likely to use numbers to place the person in a 'mental space' defined by factors derived from IQ testing. Instead they frequently use analogies to computing systems.

To solve a problem a computing system must have sufficient 'number crunching' power to attack the problem, programs that are appropriate for solving the problem and access to the data required to solve the problem. Cognitive psychology draws an analogy between computing power, programs and data access and the cognitive functions of being able to process ideas — any ideas — quickly and accurately, knowing how to solve certain classes of problems and having access to the knowledge needed to solve particular problems. In psychological terms, human number-crunching is a physiological capacity, whereas knowing how to solve problems and knowing key facts are both products of learning. Each of these aspects of thought are legitimate parts of intelligence. The physiological capacities are clearly part of Gf, knowing key facts is part of Gc and having acquired certain problem-solving strategies is a bit of both Gc and Gf. A person's capabilities are determined by the interaction between power, knowledge of how to use that power and access to required data.

The cognitive-psychology account complements the psychometric distinction between fluid and crystallised intelligence and Hebb's distinction between Intelligence A and B. Both accounts stress how a novice's performance depends on their ability to develop new problem representations (Cattell and Horn's fluid intelligence) and how with experience one shifts from problem representation to pattern recognition, by applying past solutions to present problems. Since developing a representation is more demanding of working memory and attention than is pattern recognition, learning to do an intellectual task will generally be harder than doing it. The theory also implies that people who do well on tests of fluid intelligence should have a large working-memory capacity and, indeed, they do (Carpenter, Just & Shell, 1990).

When cognition is viewed this way it is not surprising that IQ tests, and especially fluid-intelligence tests, are associated with academic performance. By definition, students are novices. So are apprentices in workplace settings. Data from the military (Wigdor & Green, 1991) has shown that performance on the Armed Forces Qualification Test (AFQT), which is used to screen military recruits, has a strong relation with performance on the job in the first few months. After two years the relation is reduced, but not eliminated. Similarly, the US Department of Labor's General Aptitude Test Battery (GATB) has been shown to be less valid for older than for younger workers. This is consistent with laboratory studies and theoretical analyses in cognitive psychology, all of which show that experience reduces but does not eliminate the relation between general intelligence and performance (Ackerman, 1996).

Jean Piaget has also advanced a view of intelligence that implicates both biological inheritance and the role of the environment. He was interested in identifying the stages in the development of thinking. He insisted that adult thinking was not a more extended version of childhood thinking, but a completely different type of thinking. Through new experiences and interactions with the environment, children come to modify the way they think. So to Piaget the dynamic interplay between an individual and the environment is the foundation of intelligence and this interplay depends on the child being active, that is acting on its environment, weighing, throwing, twisting, cutting things, etc., and seeing the results. In this way, learning and intelligence go hand in hand through encounters with concrete experience.

Adults, he claims, are able to think hypothetically as well as concretely; the former skill does not become available until late adolescence. This ability to think hypothetically, to reason and manipulate statements or symbols at an abstract or theoretical level is clearly a different form of thinking from that of the child. The adult is able to set up a hypothesis and follow through its implications. Piaget terms this formal thinking. With formal thinking comes the possibility of building new and second order concepts such as acceleration, proportion, density, metaphor and the implicit meaning of proverbs. For example, children will take metaphor and proverbs at an explicit level. The proverb 'you can't make a silk purse out of a sow's ear' means just that to a primary-school-aged child. Judgments take into account all possible situations, not just those that are observed. Reality is a subset of possibility. The understanding of experimentation with its isolation, control or manipulation of variables becomes available to the formal thinker. Theoretical models and symbolic representation can be developed and understood.

Considering what Hebb, Cattell and Piaget have proposed, it is best to consider intelligence as a set of skills fashioned out of environmental interaction, which a person uses to cope with the environment and which are continually refined and developed in this ongoing process of activity and feedback.

A certain amount of intelligence seems to be needed to gain entry to an intellectually demanding field, but beyond that point success is determined by sheer experience, the effort put into the job and social support. In economic terms it appears that the IQ score measures something with decreasing marginal value. It is important to have enough of it, but having lots and lots does not buy you that much more. Regrets to Mensa!

Psychologists now accept that environment plays a much stronger role than once thought in intellectual development and that if environment can be made more stimulating then even in adulthood people can still develop more of their potential and reveal greater intellectual capacity.

## measuring intelligence

When we talk of intelligence we are usually referring to a person's score on an intelligence test. Still more difficult than defining intelligence is the problem of measuring it. The results of a person's performance on an intelligence test are reported as a numerical score relative to the average performance of individuals of the same chronological age.

This is possible because the raw scores on an intelligence test obtained from a representative sample are rescaled or standardised into a normal distribution with a mean of 100 and a standard deviation of 15 to form a standard set of scores. This enables the performance (or raw score) of an individual to be compared with that of the representative group from which the norms were derived. It also means that people who take different tests can be compared because raw scores from any test distribution can be converted to the standard scale. The normal distribution means that scores tail off in a regular and systematic fashion on both sides of the mean (Figure 5.4).

FIGURE 5.4 STANDARDISATION OF INTELLIGENCE TEST SCORES

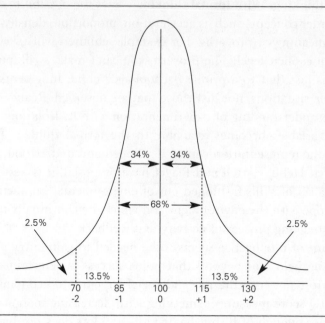

A person with a standardised score of 100, whatever test they took, is average. A person with a score of 130 has a score that is exceeded by only 2.5 per cent of the population. Similarly, a person with a score of 70 has a score that is exceeded by 97.5 per cent of the population. While intelligence test scores are deliberately standardised to a normal distribution curve, there is no good reason for supposing that intelligence is normally distributed in nature.

Because of the need to measure different expressions of intelligence, and because a heterogeneous sample of behaviours produces greater validity, most intelligence tests have traditionally comprised a number of subtests, for example verbal, numerical and spatial, the overall intelligence score being a weighted aggregate of the various subtest scores.

As noted above, supporters of Spearman and Guilford dispute whether the various subtests measure the same type of intelligence or many different types of intelligence. Subtests generally do correlate highly with each other, suggesting the existence of a common factor of intelligence, but the various subtests also show different age-related trends, suggesting that there are different expressions of intelligence.

Verbal intelligence tests are closely correlated with academic performance and are good predictors of academic success. Non-verbal tests using pictures and symbols are useful when the person has a poor grasp of English, such as those from working-class and migrant groups. The poor verbal intelligence scores of these groups are more a reflection of their inability to understand the question and even read it than of intelligence. While intelligence test scores do indicate potential ability, other factors such as motivation, self-concept and personality affect the degree to which a person is willing and able to direct their ability to produce expected performance levels. Without motivation, self-confidence, a reasonable degree of conscientiousness and reliability, even a bright person can have scholastic and career failure and generally not succeed in life, while a person of average ability with a high degree of motivation and belief in themselves and a balanced personality can be a sufficiently high achiever to gain career and life satisfaction. A major problem in using intelligence tests for selection, for training and for undertaking further education is that minority and low socio-economic groups tend to score less well on them owing to the impoverished environments in which they were raised, where reading and number skills were not practised and where dietary and health problems abound, rather than owing to real lower intelligence levels.

Intelligence is not the be all and end all, particularly as it cannot be measured all that reliably and validly, and reflects certainly in adulthood the accumulation of life experience, not just innate factors.

## creativity or divergent thinking

Creativity was a major element of Guilford's 120 mental abilities. The term can refer to both the creative process or to personality. It is just as reasonable to talk about the creative personality as it is to consider creative thinking. Creativity is often judged against four criteria: novelty, appropriateness, transformation and condensation. By novelty we mean unusualness and originality. However, the innovation must also be appropriate. Furthermore, it should involve a transformation or radical shift in thinking or in dealing with an issue/material. Connected to this, there should also be condensation — a summary power of the product such that continued contemplation of it fails to exhaust its meanings and implications.

Creative capacity is not found just in genius, it is widespread and everyone possesses it to some degree, as with intelligence. Creative acts, no matter how insignificant or minimal, can be expected from anyone.

Creativity was neglected by psychologists until the 1970s because the intelligence-testing movement, with its objective measurement, held sway. Intelligence tests with their single correct answer did not provide any scope for detecting creativity either. In intelligence tests sometimes referred to as convergent thinking tests, the information leads to the one right answer. There are no possible alternatives, for example to complete the sequence A:C:E:G:?: the only correct answer is 'I'. However, in creativity tests, which are often equated with divergent thinking tests, there are a variety of possible responses and equally acceptable solutions. However, because there is no one correct answer, creativity is difficult to measure reliably and validly. Creativity is by definition open-ended. Creative tests or tests of divergent thinking invite a variety of responses; some answers are simply more creative than others, but by how much is a subjective judgment.

Guilford identified four major aspects of creativity: fluency, flexibility, originality and elaboration. As an example of fluency you might like to write down as many words as you can that are similar in meaning to the word 'high'. Flexibility involves the degree to which a person can alter their mental approach to a problem and derive solutions using a new perspective. Originality is the unusualness of a response, such as might be given to a question like 'What would have been the consequences for Australia if the Japanese had won the Second World War?' Elaboration refers to developments that could be made, say, to a product to make it more interesting or sellable.

Research (e.g. Haddon & Lytton, 1968) tends to show that for intelligence scores over the average, that is over 100, there is little relationship between intelligence score and creativity score. This means that above average intelligence levels, people might possess any level of creativity from minimal to very high. However, there is a high degree of relationship between intelligence and creativity at less than average levels of intelligence. In other words, as intelligence rises so too does creativity but, on reaching average levels, they diverge. This means that unless a person has some degree of intelligence it is unlikely they will manifest creativity. Some studies of schoolchildren (e.g. Ogilvie, 1974) show that creativity levels are higher in schools that adopt a more informal approach to teaching and in which students work on projects with self-initiated learning and teacher support/guidance, than in traditional schools with their passive children and teacher instruction models. This suggests not only that creativity can be nurtured in the right environment but also that teaching methods that promote creativity parallel the approaches recommended for adult education by Rogers and Knowles (see Chapter 7). It is therefore likely that using these learner-centred approaches in the education of adults will help to promote more divergent and creative thinking among older students too.

In order to encourage creativity, teachers should be respectful of unusual questions and imaginative or unusual ideas, and indicate to learners that their ideas have value. There must be tolerance in the educational environment. But creativity does not simply occur as informality increases or because an unstructured curriculum is in place. A creative person needs a reasonable basis of knowledge. Creativity is not fashioned out of thin air. It needs the right soil and the right seed. Creativity is an outcome of sound knowledge deployed in new ways and its production depends on the establishment of associations between different items of subject matter content. It is the reorganising of the usual.

Scientists tend to be convergent thinkers while arts students tend to be divergent thinkers. Convergers see themselves as dull, conventional, hardworking and reliable. Divergers see themselves as warm, imaginative and exciting.

Sternberg and Lubert (1995) have developed a confluence theory of creativity. They argue that creativity requires the confluence of six distinct factors: intellectual ability, knowledge, personality, style of thinking, motivation and environment. With regard to intellectual ability, seeing problems in new ways, recognising which ideas are worth pursuing and the ability to sell one's ideas to others are the main components. Good knowledge is a basis on which these can operate but the person also needs a personality that will tolerate risk and uncertainty and a willingness to stand up for their views, coupled with intrinsic motivation (a love of what they are doing). Finally, the social and work environment must provide some support.

External factors that inhibit creative thought include high stress levels, the discouragement of risk taking and situations where individuals are pressured to work beyond their capacity and where confidence is undermined by insensitive management. Internal factors that inhibit creativity appear to be those brought on by the individual's own beliefs and expectations. Poor self-esteem, fear of making mistakes and believing that one is not capable of creative activity all conspire to dampen the creative spirit. To generate creativity we must collect as much information as possible, then allow the mind to rest. This incubation period permits a rearrangement of our stored knowledge in a way logical processing cannot. Practical creativity is a process of moving between thinking modes from left brain analytical to right brain intuitive.

The person who is restricted to left-brain thinking is likely to be rigid, intolerant and closed to new ideas. Those restricted to right-brain processing tend to be caught up in flights of imagination that prevent them seeing whether or not their ideas are practical. The most effective individual is one for whom both hemispheres are actively involved and complement each other. This provides power and flexibility as logic, imagination, creativity and practicalness combine as working partners. We noted in the opening chapters that the organisations that will survive and prosper best are those that are prepared to encourage new ideas and foster creativity. It is people who innovate, create direction and solve problems, not organisations. Staff development schemes need to develop creative skills.

A benefit of teaching creativity and creating conditions in which creativity can flourish is that this pushes less creative people into acceptance that they too can be creative and they develop a willingness to plan with new concepts. Brainstorming and synectics are two techniques most people can involve themselves in without too much effort or ability. The aim is to reduce negative thinking that puts sanctions and inhibitors on new ideas, such as 'we don't operate like that here'. Brainstorming is a way to generate creative ideas, an attempt to produce a free flow of ideas. No idea is too ridiculous to put forward. Negative remarks like 'that would cost too much' or 'that wouldn't work' are banned. After the ideas and suggestions have been recorded the group goes back over the material and evaluates it in terms, for example, of cost and feasibility. In this way a new and unusual solution might be found to a problem.

The pay-off of developing and supporting a creative environment is that the workplace is more receptive to new ideas and change, more open in its thinking.

The characteristics needed for nurturing creativity include:
- freedom and a sense of control
- encouragement and support, without destructive criticism
- resources and time
- recognition and reward
- challenge.

Creative people see authority as conventional rather than absolute. They tend to be less dogmatic and more relativistic in their view of life, show more independence in judgment and less social conformity. They are driven by intrinsic motivation, excited by the challenge itself; they have good knowledge of the field, are willing to take risks, and have high energy, curiousity and persistence levels.

For adults, creativity tests would be a better indication than intelligence tests of potential to solve problems, to be innovative and to operate autonomously and proactively. While it is difficult to assess creativity, a few assessment procedures do exist. Here are a few examples.

1. Name as many possible uses for a common object like a brick.
2. Suggest improvements to this toy dog that are novel and unusual.
3. What could we do if Australia were cut off from its overseas supply and sales markets by an anti-Australia worldwide trade war?
4. What would be the consequences if world sea levels rose by three metres?

Taking example 1, the reasoning is that most people will give answers using the brick as a component of construction. Creative persons will suggest such uses as putting them behind the wheels of a car when the brakes fail or standing on them to reach a high shelf. Such suggestions can be weighted in score terms for their likelihood of being made through comparison with frequency of sample responses and by the number of alternatives generated.

We don't know though whether these measures do actually tap creativity. Other tests involve the use of wooden blocks in a variety of shapes, colours and sizes. The task is to discover how many different ways they can be sorted. Bromley (1967) administered these block tests to a range of intellectually superior adults and found that the group in its sixties produced only half of the responses those in their late twenties did. The intelligence mean score for both groups was around 122. Bromley suggested these results were a function of either decreased persistence, flexibility or abstraction or a combination of all three. Similar results were reported by Alpaugh and Birren (1977).

## ■■■ USES OF INTELLIGENCE TESTS

Ability tests are big business as many organisations have found them useful for employee selection and promotion, as well as for identifying those who will benefit from a training course. Depending on the job, either a general 'g' type reasoning test will be used or, for a more specific task, a more specific test will be used. As tests can often be given in booklet form a large number of persons can be tested at the same time if need be. The main advantage of using standardised tests is that there are tables or norms that indicate how often each score is obtained in various groups of people. Such tests usually have a measure of predictive validity so that we know that if a person does not achieve a certain minimum score they are unlikely to do well at the job or on the course. Kanfer (1995) suggests that, overall, companies have saved billions of dollars by using ability tests to assure a merit-based selection process.

IQ does not predict all aspects of job performance, such as motivation, entrepreneurial flair, initiative or interest. Most intelligence tests make valid predictions about ability aspects but have almost no relation to motivational aspects. This is not surprising, but it does make any focus on a unitary index of job competence seem simplistic. In summary, it appears that IQ is an important factor in getting into a job or profession, but is less important (although not negligible) once you have learnt to do the job. Further improvement is then achieved by acquiring experience, rather than improving upon an abstract knowledge of what the job requires.

Even if we do not know how to improve intelligence, as indicated by the test scores, the economic issue is what skills people possess, not what their IQ scores are. We might not be able to destroy the linkage between IQ scores and the relative possession of cognitive skills (and it is not clear why we would want to), but improved education and training can raise the average achievement of all students.

## ■■■ THE MYTH OF AGE-RELATED INTELLECTUAL DECLINE

The direction in which psychological research is now moving seems to be casting an encouraging light on human abilities throughout our life span, which is providing a scientific counterbalance to the dead weight of myth and impressionistic, subjective opinion that inevitable and escalating age-related intellectual decline cannot be avoided. However, the final word on this is still unavailable since there is a lack of consistent research methods and instruments being applied across the age span, making age comparisons difficult. The problem is that myths produce powerful images whether they are grounded in fact or not and it is difficult for educators to abandon the stereotype that young equals sharp and old equals dull.

Given such stereotypes and attitudes, what we need to consider is the social and environmental conditions in which adults operate and which make them appear to decline intellectually, underfunction, reveal low motivation and show low self-esteem. This has implications for how educators and trainers should approach their methodology for developing new skills and attitudes so that both they and adult learners are positive towards learning. Confidence, self-pacing and personally acceptable goals are vital. The old adage that you can't teach old dogs new tricks is misleading as older people can and do learn new things.

There is no denying that ageing is a gradual and immensely variable process of bodily decline and it is easy to assume that as the body grows less spritely so too does the brain. There is a widespread view that brain cells are lost increasingly from adolescence and never replaced. This evidence came from studies of animals, since it is impossible to access living brain tissue from healthy human adults. Many of these studies reveal that there are insignificant losses in animals but those given an enriched environment actually show a thickening of the cerebral cortex (Diamond, 1978). While some physical capabilities decline through adulthood such as strength, reaction time, sight and hearing, and there are changes in muscle tone and skin texture and a gradual decline in overall energy, these are not significant factors in the process of adult learning. Perhaps only loss of visual and auditory acuity and reaction time need to be taken into account by a teacher or trainer.

There are two ways researchers study changes owing to age: *cross-sectional and longitudinal designs.* Much of the folklore of declining mental ability has been derived from studies that cast light on age differences rather than age change.

*Cross-sectional studies* take samples of individuals of different ages and compare these different age cohorts at the same point in time. This is a popular method since it is a relatively rapid method for determining age differences. Such studies generally find decreasing score with increasing average age of the cohort. However, there are many social, cultural and environmental reasons why this can be expected. Because the individuals are of different ages and grew up at different times it is likely they differ in many respects besides age. The education system has improved in quality, range of content, resources and teaching methodologies. Developments in and general availabilty of communications such as video, television, books, computers and foreign travel provide an increasingly enriched environment. Improvement of health standards and care and nutritional factors all conspire to make younger persons appear more intelligent than older persons. It is hardly surprising that younger generations attain higher scores on intelligence and knowledge tests. The present day forty-year-old had a more limited environment. A similar argument holds with height. Younger generations are on average taller than their parents. This does not imply that individuals grow shorter as they age. It is an effect of improved health and dietary conditions.

Another problem with the cross-sectional method is that it is often difficult to obtain representative samples of individuals from each age group. To the extent that different age samples are not equally representative of their age groups, it is impossible to separate age effects from the effects of representativeness. For example, if a group of college rugby players were compared with a group of sedentary 50-year-old office workers on a measure of physical coordination, the differences would not be due wholly to age. The college rugby players are not representatative of young people as a whole, whereas the office workers might be more representative of their age group but, because they were not highly selected, differences in representativeness are confounded with difference in age.

*Longitudinal studies* are better able to reveal change owing to age as they follow the same individuals through a lengthy time span from the commencement of the study to its end. These individuals are repeatedly tested. Longitudinal studies have two major advantages. First, the same individuals are being used throughout the experiment. Second, there is greater statistical power when the same individuals are tested and compared with themselves as there are no extraneous individual differences that could complicate the interpretation of results. Such longitudinal studies show that there are no appreciable changes over the human life span.

In fact, in many cases, as exemplified by Burns (1963), variations in performance in numerical ability and verbal ability seem to depend on whether there is continuing use of these particular skills in daily life, which supports Cattell's notion of fluid and crystallised intelligences. Studies of youth who leave the education system at school-leaving age can reveal decline in test performance within a year of leaving simply because they cease to engage in certain verbal and/or numerical mental gymnastics. As with physical attributes, if you don't use it, you lose it. In one study in Australia, a group of students aged 60 to 90 volunteered to learn German from scratch. In only six months half of them reached a level that is normally achieved by school students after four years of study.

Early influential studies by well-known researchers such as Thorndike in his book *Adult Learning* (1928) and Wechsler (1958) showed that performance peaks around 21–22 years of age and then declines. These were cross-sectional studies. Thorndike's studies and others that revealed decline in intelligence as measured were faulty not only because of the cross-sectional design but also because the test items were not relevant or meaningful to adults and tended to be timed tests. At that time, however, it was still assumed that intelligence was genetically fixed for life and therefore differences in education and environment between young and older persons in cross-sectional cohorts didn't really matter. Another problem that led to the belief that intelligence declines in adulthood was that intelligence tests for adults tended to be little more than upward extensions of children's tests, with more difficult items. These tests tend to assess process, whereas adult intelligence needs more stress on content. Adult intellectual performance is greatly influenced by prior topic and domain knowledge (Ackerman, 1996). The problems that an adult needs to solve almost inevitably draw on accumulated knowledge and skills.

However, other studies from the mid-1950s onwards using a longitudinal method (e.g. Terman & Oden, 1959; Owens, 1953; Eisdorfer, 1963; Burns, 1966) show that the adult subjects continue to improve gradually in performance on the tests. In Owens' study, the same subjects were tested at ages 18, 50 and 61. At 50 they showed a slight gain over their performance at 18. At 61 they maintained that gain in general and revealed only a slight decline in numerical ability. These were all American studies. However, Burns' study in the U.K. produced similar results to Owens'. Burns (1966) found that educated adults actually increased in IQ score from their twenties into their fifties and the effect was particularly noticeable in intelligence items relating to their daily activities. For example, scientists showed increases in ability to manipulate number items while those involved in language activities increased in their ability to respond to verbal items.

It should be noted that all the subjects were of above-average intelligence who had remained in intellectually satisfying occupations using their verbal and numerical skills on a regular basis and, of course, that the general environment is becoming more stimulating and educative with the passage of time. How well these results would be replicated among persons holding manual and unskilled labouring jobs is a moot point. But the study does suggest that intelligence as measured by test score is not doomed to decline with age in those of average and above average intelligence who operate within a stimulating or challenging environment.

Studies using Weschler's intelligence scale for adults reveal that different subtests are differentially susceptible to the effects of ageing. Different types of verbal subtests show remarkable resilience and even produce improvement over the years, while various types of performance on speed tests can reveal decline. We might have in this differential a parallel between Cattell's fluid and crystallised intelligence and Intelligence A and B as postulated by Hebb. Fluid intelligence is genetically based and not affected by environment, peaks in adolescence and declines in adulthood. Crystallised intelligence, however, increases with age, is dependent on experience and interaction with the environment. Changes in verbal learning ability depend more on attention, motivation and perception than on age. Zwahr (1998) showed large declines, increasing with age, on information processing and perceptual speed tests, while verbal ability and comprehension were not affected. In fact, verbal ability increased between the ages of 20 and 70. The general conclusion is that age places a penalty on timed tests and if time constraints are lessened then there is no intellectual decline and adults perform poorly with age simply because of slowness, lack of practice with tests and lower motivation to do tests.

Adult intellect is far better conceptualised by the tasks a person can accomplish and the skills they have developed than by the number of digits that can be stored in the working memory or the number of syllogistic reasoning items that can be correctly evaluated. Even in the artificial intelligence field, researchers are discarding ideas of a General Problem Solver in favour of a knowledge-based expert system. No amount of processing power could overcome deficiencies in domain-relevant knowledge. In an examination of expert-novice systems, Glaser (1991) found the typical expert to differ from a novice in terms of experience and knowledge rather than intellectual processes. This all suggests that current methods of assessing adult intelligence are deficient. In assessing adults for further study we need to take into account not only traditional assessment information but also what they know.

Two issues that prevent results from these longitudinal studies being accepted as totally reliable are, first, that repeated testing leads to test wiseness, that is scores will increase with practice. As the same tests must be given on every occasion the subjects might become sophisticated and knowledgeable about the tests. Alternatively, because of the repetitions low motivation might reduce scores. However, the usual time span between testings is such that subjects would be unlikely to gain advantage from multiple testing.

Second, many intelligence test items are percieved as meaningless exercises for and by adults, such as working out reversed sequences of letters or code substitutions. These items are, of course, well-meaning attempts by psychologists to devise measures to eliminate any influence by the subject's education and cultural background on the outcome.

Other drawbacks include the long time span over which the experiment must be conducted. It is almost impossible for one experimenter to start and finish the study. Long assurance of funding is also necessary for such longitudinal research. Another major problem is obtaining subjects who will make such a long-term commitment. There is always a high drop-out rate so that towards the end of the study the size of the sample is greatly diminished and, with it, its representativeness.

FIGURE 5.5 COMPARISON OF CROSS-SECTIONAL AND LONGITUDINAL STUDIES

| DESIGN | DISADVANTAGES | ADVANTAGES |
|---|---|---|
| LONGITUDINAL | Time consuming | Individual trends can be studied as comparing same individuals |
| | Expensive | Increased statistical power |
| | Participants might not be representative | |
| | Selective attrition might bias results | |
| | Familiarity might improve scores | |
| CROSS-SECTIONAL | Different environmental exposure for different age groups | Quick data collection |
| | Difficulty in obtaining representative samples at each age group | |

Studies of mature students (e.g. Richardson & King 1997) show that they have better time-management skills than normal-aged students and that other learning strengths come from their greater maturity and experience. Hartley (1997), summarising 11 British studies, concluded that mature students perform as well if not better than younger ones and also show better time management and deep learning.

## causes of the differential decline in intellectual functioning

Some physiological changes might start in the early twenties but are hardly noticeable at first and we are able to compensate during the middle years of life by wearing glasses and turning up the volume of the television. Such declines are unlikely to affect learning a great deal. Most decrements in intellectual functioning associated with increased age appear attributable to a reduction in the speed of neural processing and to the decay of the nervous system and decreased cerebral blood flow. Therefore, adults will be slower at discriminating stimuli and responding to stimuli. Adults might also be slower at complex activities. However, neural functioning speed losses and decreased cerebral blood flow will affect memory performance as we shall see below because less time is available for memory organisation and attention-paying activities, particularly when attention has to be diverted between several sources of information. The work of Wesnes and Semple (2001), based on over 2000 healthy people, suggests that reaction time, concentration span and memory decline from the age of 45 onwards. By the time people were in middle age they were 10 to15 per cent slower to react than 20-year-olds. So life doesn't end at forty, it just slows down! However, this cognitive decline is offset by the fact that 'old dogs' have strategies and tricks they can use, derived from their experience. This links in with Deary's recent finding (2001) that adults repeating spelling, grammar and arithmetic tests they took originally in 1932 scored a little better when they were on average 77 years old. Other researchers claim that a narrowing of interests and work-related skills leads to a lack of practice and familiarity with certain types of test items. We know that the reverse is true, for teachers generally increase their verbal subtest scores throughout their life span. Thus it is fluid intelligence that might decrease in adulthood. This is reflected in spatial tests, memory span tests and induction — while crystallised intelligence or stored experience increases.

Testing of memory ability using digit span tests shows that the decline with age is such that a person at 50 is on average performing at about 80 per cent of the level of an individual at 20 years. Spatial abilities as measured by object assembly, block design and picture completion show a decline of about five per cent per decade after the age of 25. Perceptual motor speed as measured by digit symbol substitution declines by 10 per cent per decade. Reasoning ability declines by about seven per cent per year beginning at 25 years. Non-verbal reasoning as measured by Ravens Progressive Matrices declines from 40 years of age onwards at about 10 per cent per year. Since non-verbal tests are less contaminated by environmental and experiential factors they might be the best index of the biological deterioration that underlies all mental performance and fluid intelligence.

Fluid intelligence is most affected by ageing. Performance at tasks that are unfamiliar, that involve strict time limits, require understanding of abstract principles or interpretation of symbolic material is adversely affecting by ageing. Complex abilities such as operating complex equipment, muscular strength, coordination and reaction time suffer with advancing age. This is all caused by the slowing down of the speed of response of the central nervous system, particularly in receiving signals and in selecting actions in response to them. Most people cope with this by using familiar and well-practised routines. However, the learning of new and complex activities will become slower and more difficult with age. Retraining programs need to take account of the age of the learner in terms of demands made and period of learning. With a well-designed program there is no reason why an older worker cannot achieve a standard of performance equal to that of a younger worker, although the older person might be operating closer to their limits. Work by Baltes and Lindenberger. (1997) reveals that older adults perform less well than younger adults and children at coping with two tasks at the same time and switching between tasks.

Crystallised intelligence, as the cumulative end product of information acquired by fluid intelligence, is the sum total of culturally-dependent information stored by a person as a result of their interaction with their environment. It is measured by verbal, comprehension, arithmetic and reasoning tests with understood information, and there is little evidence of decline if the abilities continue to be used.

This maintenance of performance in abilities underlain by crystallised intelligence suggests that disuse causes loss of measured intelligence. This theory recognises that differences in interests, attitudes and experiences cause changes in performance with decrements in those activities that are not being used or that are used irregularly. Practice is necessary to retain performance levels. A function will atrophy like a muscle if not used. So differential frequency of usage is the basis of this theory and test scores in activities that are no longer used will show a decline.

So while verbal abilities appear to remain stable over the adult years, this might reflect the cumulative effect of stored experience as crystallised intelligence more than current status. Thus this might be more indicative of past attainment than present ability. Number ability appears stable till around 50 years, after which a decline appears to set in.

There is no basis as yet for identifying the neural processes that are responsible for fluid and crystallised intelligence, so it remains a theory that helps to explain the facts. The question of whether intelligence declines with age or remains stable depends on the intelligence subtests used. We can predict from the information already provided that verbal subtests show stability, while non-verbal subtests reveal a decline. Thus a global intelligence measure is not a valid way to indicate change in intelligence, since it is a multifaceted concept, composed of an amalgam of these different types of subtests, each contributing its own variation.

We must also remember that intelligence tests are mostly timed tests that militate against adults as their speed of neural processing declines and the content is frequently uninteresting and irrelevant to older persons and more suitable to children for whom they were mainly designed. Age-related slowing is a reflection of central nervous system deterioration but to eliminate this by allowing no time limit would remove all genuine effect of ageing. Moreover, evidence suggests that there is no improvement in scores on average when the time limit is removed. It might simply reward those who have patience and persistence, rather than reflect intellectual competence.

In conclusion, there is mixed evidence on the effects of age on intelligence. Intelligence covers too wide a range of activities and the roles of speeded tests, motivation, practice and interest all combine to confuse the issue. With age, it would appear that:

- there is a decline in fluid intelligence ( reasoning, speed of perception)
- there is no decline in crystallised intelligence (accumulation of knowledge through education and experience), with increases for those still cognitively active
- adults who are less intellectually active suffer greater declines in fluid intelligence earlier (use it or lose it — lifelong education has a part to play here!)
- there is a decline in reaction time, but if adults can control the pace of learning they can compensate

- vision and hearing loss makes learning tasks more difficult and decreases confidence.

The diversity of factors impacting on intelligence test scores suggests that no single factor can ever be shown conclusively to be the determinant of intelligence. Decline in mental ability does not seem tied to increasing age but to the quality of the environment. Generally, we notice that the creative output of scholars, scientists and artists does not occur in their students days but much later in life. The relationship between age and mental ability is small and the claim of massive decline in intellectual performance cannot be substantiated on current evidence. Our concern should be with how we can help older learners to maintain their performance rather than with studying decline.

## ■■■ MEMORY

Memory is another function alleged to decline with age. However, most of our subjective experience with our own or others' memories and with research evidence suggests that memory is highly selective at all ages. It depends on what interests and motivates the individual. A teenager might remember perfectly the top pop songs of numerous singers and musicians but fail dismally to recall historical dates or chemical formulae in a school exam. Similarly, an adult will not remember chart-busting successes if they are not interested in the contemporary pop scene, but might well recollect notable events from their past in great detail. Most of us who were adults at the time of President Kennedy's assassination can remember what we were doing when the news was broadcast.

Stereotypes also contribute to the folklore of memory lapse. A twenty-year-old forgets where they put their car keys and merely elicits some jocular remarks. A forty-year-old doing the same thing can elicit snide comments about being on the slippery slope of decline.

The blanket term memory has often been used to describe the activities of acquiring, retaining and recalling and at one time was thought to be a faculty capable of being trained in order to improve the quality and quantity of its performance. The use of mechanical memorisation at school by learning passages of the Bible, poems or pieces of literature was hailed by some teachers as a means of improving memory. Memory experiments have shown that this improvement does not occur simply by practising memorising.

### the structure of memory

A early conceptualisation of memory was the stage approach, which distinguishes between registration or encoding, retention or storage and recall or retrieval.

## stage approach

Encoding refers to the initial establishment of a neural code for the information. Storage is the preservation of the encoded material over time and recall refers to the ability to produce the information when required. It is the encoding stage that seems to present most problems for the adult and relates to the pace of stimulus presentation. The less time allowed for encoding the greater the age-related difference in subsequent tests of memory. This means that material is not registered in the first place. This then reflects an inability to recall. Additionally, older adults tend not to use mediational processes to aid recall, so imagery, mnemonics, etc., are not used. This also contributes to poorer recall performance. The meaningful structuring of material as it is presented coupled with a slower pace of presentation aids recall and storage but older adults tend not to use beneficial techniques of creating their own meaning out the material.

It is difficult to study storage if adults have greater difficulty encoding because much material might never be stored in the first place. What evidence there is suggests no age deficits for periods of less than 30 minutes but that older adults might be impaired with intervals of over 24 hours. Evidence for age-related changes in recall is not strong and there are contradictory results. Similarly, the difficulty of investigating retrieval is that, again, if the encoding has not occurred then nothing can be retrieved in any case. Encoding, storage and retrieval are not separate processes and questions are being asked about the appropriateness of distinguishing memory in this way.

## depth of processing

A recent interpretation of memory focuses on the depth of processing of the to-be-remembered information. Those stimuli receiving the deepest level of processing — the semantic level or conceptual level rather than the sensory or structural level — will have the most durable and strongest memory representation. This perspective maintains that older adults either do not or cannot engage in the deep levels of processing that are responsible for good memory performance. A popular method for investigating levels of processing is to request recall of various characteristics of presented material. For shallow processing the request might be 'How many letters are there in the word you have seen?'. For deep processing the question might be 'What is an antonym for the word...?'. Results show poorer performance for older adults at the deep-processing level, for example Erber *et al.* 1980. Other evidence is based on the difference between recall and recognition. Some items might not be recalled but recognised. The inference is that the difficulty is in retrieval. However, experiments comparing recall and recognition show no age-related effects. Thus, in sum, evidence is equivocal.

## primary and secondary memory

Another approach in memory studies has been to draw distinctions between two types of memory storage systems, particularly primary memory and secondary memory. Primary memory is thought to be a temporary holding or organising buffer through which all information that will be subsequently remembered must pass. It is roughly the span of consciousness or immediate awareness or current attention. Information is maintained in primary memory only by rehearsal of that information. Without attention or rehearsal the information decays. Secondary memory refers to all the durable knowledge that one possesses that is not in immediate consciousness. It does not require active attention for its maintenance and storage capacity is not limited as it is for primary memory.

It is assumed that any age-related differences will be found in secondary memory performance, since information that is recalled is stored there. However, depth of processing studies do not reveal age-related decrements.

## information processing mode

The most popular model of memory process is the Atkinson–Shiffrin (1968) information processing model. In a simplistic form, the eyes, ears and other receptors receive information that is turned into electro-chemical energy. This, in turn, is transmitted to the brain via the nervous system. In the brain this information is analysed into forms suitable for storage in the memory. We are fairly certain that there is a chemical basis to memory in that the stimulation of nerve cells alters their chemical constitution and it is this change that encodes memory (and by extension learning, intelligence and thinking) but the physiological aspects of memory are not well understood and our memories appear to be distributed across large areas of our brain.

New material might be analysed at different levels. If we are listening to a lecture we might be paying careful attention to every point being made to reach complete understanding. On the other hand, if the radio is on while we are driving to work we might not register anything of a political discussion other than that it was between members of the main political parties.

Researchers tend to distinguish between short-term and long-term memory, in which a sequence of processes operate. These are input (reception), storage and output (recall or retrieval). Age does not appear to affect our ability to store information. Therefore long-term memory is not affected by age. However, short-term memory appears to be affected by age — possibly through sensory impairment of sight and hearing, decreasing speed of neurological functioning, which also manifests itself in older adults taking longer to retrieve stored material. Experimental evidence suggests that there are three stages to the memorisation process. *A sensory memory, a short-term memory and a long-term memory,* with specific processes linked to each. These are represented in Figure 5.6. These three stages of memory must not be thought of as having three discrete, separate locations in the brain, they are too closely interrelated for that. It is also misleading to imagine that there is a straightforward progression, with information moving from sensory through to long-term memory.

FIGURE 5.6 SIMPLIFIED FLOW CHART OF INFORMATION PROCESSING MODEL

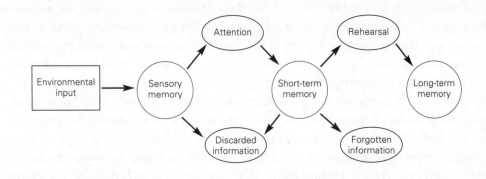

## sensory memory

The sensory memory appears to hold information only long enough for some of it to be transferred to the short-term memory, for around several seconds in all. There is nothing we can do to extend or improve the sensory memory. It involves selective perception of things going on in our environment and we are selective about what we see and what we process before it disappears.

## short-term or working memory

If we are buying an ice-cream we need to remember how much to pay for it; if we are catching a plane we need to remember the departure time; if we are phoning for a taxi we need to remember the number while we phone. Short-term memory would involve holding a telephone number in storage long enough for the number to be dialled but not long enough to use again later. However, if we know we will need the number again we can commit it to long-term memory by rehearsing it. This is the material held in short-term memory. This memory has a limited capacity. It can only hold six to seven items at a time. This can be shown by dictating strings of digits and requesting a subject to recall them immediately. On average only around seven will be remembered. The way to improve the short-term memory is to link individual items together to form a unit or chunk of information. In this way far greater numbers of items can be remembered. We do this with telephone numbers, for example the international dialling code 0011 can be remembered as one item.

Information in short-term memory is very vulnerable to loss through reception of new material from the sensory memory. Because its capacity is limited, something must be displaced if we try to add more information. So information is lost from the short-term memory unless some effort is made to rehearse it. In the case of a telephone number, it will remain if we say it over and over again. Another characteristic of short-term memory is that it is immediately available for use. That is why it is also termed the working memory.

## long-term memory

Long-term memory appears to have unlimited capacity and indefinite duration. Older persons can remember events from their childhood. Sometimes we are surprised by the information we do hold in our long-term memories. Some trivial stimulus jogs the memory and we find we can recall scenes and events apparently long forgotten. Under hypnosis or psychotherapy people recall with considerable accuracy detailed happenings from their past.

Evidence of long-term memory in older adults is difficult to assess for recall of events 40 years ago is impossible to verify and much of the information could be inference rather than reality. The other problem with long-term memory is that many significant events are remembered because we reminisce and so some childhood events have been rehearsed many times on these story-telling occasions. Therefore, they are only as old as the last repetition. Memory of historic events has been used to remove idiosyncratic memories available only to one individual. However, it has been found that some adults who were not born when an event took place apparently remember that event. There are no adequate ways as yet to assess differences in long-term memory and evidence remains at an anecdotal level for the present.

The problem we have with long-term memory is to retrieve the information that is held there. The ease or otherwise with which we can recall information from long-term memory seems to depend on how the information we seek is organised and on the extent to which it is integrated (made meaningful) with other things that we know. The capacity of long-term memory is limitless. But there is a limit to the rate at which new information can be added to long-term memory. It is limited to about one item of new information about every four or five seconds. An unfamiliar seven-digit telephone number will take about 30 seconds to get into long-term memory, that is it needs to be rehearsed in short-term memory for 30 seconds. The limitations of short-term memory and the rate of entry into long-term memory limits learning in adults.

The content of long-term memory does often come from short-term memory but what is already in long-term memory might influence what is extracted from the sensory memory for closer attention in short-term memory and how it is interpreted. The three stages can be better thought of as different operating characteristics of a single memory system.

## why do we forget

A number of major theories have been proposed to explain forgetting in humans.

## trace decay

The trace decay theory suggests that the chemical trace that links neurons together (cf. Hebb's cell assembly) gradually extinguishes over time and gets overlain by other traces.

## motivated forgetting

The theory of motivated forgetting is related to Freudian psychoanalytic theory (see Chapter 6). This theory suggests that some experiences are repressed deep into the unconscious and therefore cannot be recalled. These memories are repressed because the experience they relate to was threatening, embarrassing, shameful or in some way damaging to the integrity of the person. The person, in fact, does not want to remember.

## interference

The third theory is interference theory. It holds that the interplay between and possible confusion in the build up of memories causes forgetting. Interference has been used as the major explanation for memory loss by older adults. What exactly this term means has never been precisely defined but it appears to cover three things: unfamiliarity, concurrent activity and prior or subsequent activity.

Unfamiliarity suggests that new, unfamiliar associations are difficult to establish in a memory system containing well-used, established associations. Studies show that this is so with stimulus familiarity related to age differences. Unfamiliar material is more interfering.

Concurrent activity suggests interference occurs when there is a requirement to perform some activity while simultaneously attempting to remember other information. This is particularly pronounced as an age trend when listening to two conversations at once.

Prior or subsequent activity interferes with the retention of current material. The acquisition and retention of the task is evaluated as a function of the amount and type of prior (proactive interference) or subsequent learning (retroactive interference). The major assumption of this type of explanation is that memory is finite and once the storage limit is reached new information can be retained only by displacing old information.

Experiments show that interference is a function of the similarity of the tasks to be remembered and their closeness in time, as susceptibility does not differ across the age span. The research on interference suggests that there should be breaks between periods of study or lessons during which activities that are totally unrelated to the academic material are undertaken, and that subject matter in successive periods of learning should not be too similar. Learning just before going to bed at night seems to be beneficial for many people since there is little to interfere with it during sleep.

## restructuring

The fourth theory is related to Gestalt learning and meaningfulness. Bartlett suggested (1932) that new learning is interpreted in terms of existing knowledge. His experiments showed that new cognitive material is compared with what is already known. In one experiment he had his British subjects read a passage of prose that recounted a Red Indian ghost story. There are many features of the story that are peculiar to the Red Indian culture but not to the British culture. When the subjects were asked to recall details of the story, many of the details that could not be accommodated into the subjects' existing knowledge were 'lost'. Likewise gaps in the recall were often filled with culturally familiar material that was incongruent with Red Indian culture. Subjects drew on what they expected to happen from their own experience. It is this phenomenon that causes witnesses to invent evidence when recalling events in the witness box. Piaget in his work also emphasised the way in which new material is assimilated into old knowledge so that the store of information is altered with the incorporation of the incoming material and the individual, as a result, more able to deal with a wider range of events. You no doubt remember the laws of pragnanz introduced in Chapter 4. We are not essentially forgetting the stimulus but modifying it as we interpret it to make it congruent with expectations and past experience.

## other reasons

Many of these are obvious and include such things as not paying attention, the effects of grief and depression, fatigue, medications that cause confusion/drowsiness, vision and hearing problems and drug abuse.

## improving memory

Psychological research has provided educators with some significant knowledge and techniques about how to improve learning, retention and recall.

## massed or distributed practice

Massed practice occurs when there is no rest period during a session of learning. When intervals are allowed during the learning session we have what is termed distributed practice. Massed conditions of learning are less productive than distributed practice. A possible reason for this is the effect of both proactive and retroactive interference in massed practice as more and more material is transmitted through the memory system. Teachers need to be on the look out for a drop-off in work or attention on the part of learners. At that point it is useful to have a break. To prevent interference from new material the start of the next session should revise the material covered in the previous session.

## curve of forgetting

Experiments plotting the rate of forgetting show a rapid drop-off of material that has been learnt within the first few hours. After 20 minutes only 58 per cent of material is remembered, after one hour only 44 per cent and after one day 33 per cent. Different types of material are affected at different rates, but the general curve is similar (Figure 5.7).

FIGURE 5.7 THE CURVE OF FORGETTING

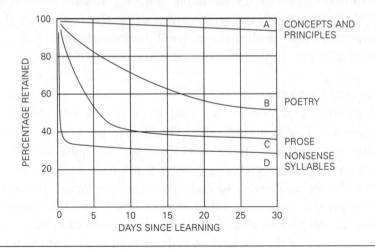

serial learning
The position of material in a learning session affects its retention. Experiments reveal that we remember best things presented first and the material presented most recently. The material in the middle is much less well remembered. This again could be due to interference. In devising learning sessions teachers should consider the order of presentation of their material and ensure the important issues are at the beginning or end of the lesson. An overview at the beginning and a summary at the end aid recall.

meaningfulness of the material
Grasping the meaningfulness of a task is essential for effective learning and retention, as we have already noted in discussing learning theory in Chapter 4. Organising material around existing concepts or categories seems essential (as Piaget, Ausubel, Bruner argue). Some material that has to be committed to memory unfortunately has no obvious meaningfulness unless the learner can deliberately attribute to it some personal, idiosyncratic structure or meaning. Biological systems like the order of the cranial nerves, formulae and laws are often memorised by means of props such as rhymes or mnemonics to make them easier to memorise and recall. For example, *SOH, CAH, TOA* are used for remembering the mathematical rules for finding sines, cosines and tangents of angles. The colours of the rainbow are remembered by the phrase, **R**ichard **O**f **Y**ork **G**ave **B**attle **I**n **V**ain. The more meaningful the material can be made the lower the amount and rate of forgetting. As the curve of forgetting (above) showed, laws and concepts are best remembered. Meaningful associations can also be created by visualisation — a word, picture or colour that can be linked to the event/knowledge item. Some people find making up a story around a sequence of thing they must do quite helpful.

## active versus passive learning

In order to remember material better, it is advisable to work at it actively, for example making notes of the material being read, or practising the task rather than passive learning involving simply reading the material. In tutorials and discussions learners should try to take part rather than just sit and daydream.

## whole versus part learning

Given a task that involves large amounts of material, it is better to divide the material up into segments. This is part learning. Whole learning involves reading through the information to get an overall view of the topic. The pros and cons of the two approaches have been researched for many years without any clear-cut result. The nature of the material seems to be the determining factor. The whole approach is useful when the amount of information to be learnt is sufficiently small to be absorbed at one time. It also results in a better grasp of meaning and continuity between elements of the material once the overall pattern of the information is understood. Part learning is more effective when there is a large body of material to master and when it can be broken up into convenient chunks without damaging its continuity. Part learning also helps to avoid interference as a section of the material can be thoroughly learnt before proceeding to the next section. It is also useful if the parts are small enough to fit into a short learning session to enable distributed practice (see above) to be used.

## analysis, organisation and recall

We do have ways of overcoming some of the limitations of the capacities of the memory system. One way is to code the items into larger chunks. In childhood, learning to spell involves committing one letter to long term memory every five seconds. The adolescent learning a foreign language will hold individual words in short-term memory and try to get a new word into long-term memory every five seconds. An experienced adult reading at a rate in excess of two hundred words per minute will hold the meaning of a passage in their short-term memory rather than individual words and will commit the gist of the passage to long-term memory.

The size of the units or chunks of information that can be dealt with depends on the existing knowledge of the learner. The more the learner's past experience can be drawn upon to enable them to analyse and organise information into familiar patterns the easier it will be for the new material to be committed to memory. If a mass of information can be seen as another illustration of a well-understood principle then it will be accommodated in both short- and long-term memory more readily than if all the detail had to be retained.

New information that has no meaning for the learner in terms of the familiar must be learnt in its entirety. Likewise, it will need to be recalled in its entirety since there will be no cues from the familiar to help in its reconstruction. The greater the adult's formal educational level the better they are likely to cope with most learning tasks in adulthood. This is due to the size of the intellectual framework as there is more existing learning into which it can be integrated.

## ■■■ ASPECTS OF AGEING AND MEMORY

Investigations into memory in conjunction with ageing are beset by difficulties in separating learning ability, intellectual ability, memory, motivation and a host of other situational and physiological variables such as pacing or speed of presentation, the time a person has to respond to an event, sensory deficits, meaningfulness, expectancy to name a few.

It is conventional to draw a distinction between learning and memory although the two are closely linked. Learning is the acquisition of information while memory involves the storage , retention and retrieval of that information. While verbal tests show that there is little decrement in verbal ability with ageing, comprehension, which is not just static information but an understanding and relating of old information to new information, shows a decline. Adults appear to have less ability to relate back material that has just been presented to them. This suggests immediate understanding of verbal material declines. Cohen (1981) shows that this might be due to older adults being unable to access and integrate stored information while simultaneously registering new information. The deficit appears not to be structural in nature since older adults are comparable in performance to younger adults in integrating and accessing information when only one task has to be performed. The time needed to activate information from memory increases by over 60 per cent between the ages of 20 and 50 although extensive practice reduces this difference (Salthouse & Somberg, 1982). Age-related performance for verbal and visuospatial working-memory tasks showed continuous growth up to 45 years of age, then decline. This suggests that older adults have more difficulty preserving new information, which is indicative of age-related performance being related to general processing constraints. Working memory does decline in older people because processing speed is reduced (www.hope.edu/academic/psychology/335/webrep/workmem.html)

Memory is not a unitary process but consists of many diverse processes with a variety of age trends. One particularly dramatic example is the difference in performance on a paired associate task and a digit span task (Dixon *et al.*, 1982). The former requires learning to associate stimulus–response pairs so that the individual will be able to produce the response when presented with the stimulus. The digit span task involves measuring the number of unrelated digits that can be immediately repeated in the original sequence. Paired associate learning declines by as much as 20 to 40 per cent between 20 years and 70 years of age, while the difference on the digit span test is negligible to non-existent. This suggest that some aspects of memory are more likely to decline with increasing age than others, for example Winograd *et al.*, 1982. However, caution is urged as it is difficult to make each task of similar difficulty and theoretically it would be possible to make up a very difficult paired associate test and a very easy digit span test, which could reverse the results generally obtained.

Interference effects are prominent in adults owing to the huge range of information and experiences that have impacted and are continually impacting on adults. Parts of this welter of information interfere with other parts. Teachers of adults therefore need to allow time for the consolidation of new material, rather than keep the information flow going. New material needs to be related to material already stored in order to make sense of it. It needs to be made meaningful. This requires time for transfer from short-term to long-term memory. There is also the problem of unlearning old material that is stored in the memory as new, more current material replaces it. Previous ways of learning might inhibit more self-directed approaches if the latter are imposed suddenly. New knowledge and skills usually require the unlearning of old ones, yet these are deeply ingrained in the memory in terms of facts and procedures. New learning is likely to be remembered in terms of the old or be modified to meet the old conceptions.

## SUMMARY

This chapter has examined the different meanings of the concept of intelligence and looked at various theories about the structure of intelligence. Despite a variety of theories about the structure of intelligence, it is apparent that most psychologists agree that there are multiple intelligences, structured from specific skills and abilities to more general skills/abilities in a hierarchical fashion. More recent ideas of cultural appropriateness and socio-emotional abilities extend the earlier limited, intellectual models.

Despite problems associated with the definition and measurement of intelligence, the conventional view that there is a general decline in intellectual performance with age can be refuted for adults who are of average intelligence and above and who maintain a stimulating work and life style. Research using adult intelligence tests reveals that for bright persons in longitudinal studies there is a high degree of stability in scores up to 50 years and beyond. Less intelligent persons tend to decline slowly with age. Generally, it is fluid intelligence that declines in all persons, but crystallised intelligence more than makes up for the loss in most cases.

However, it is clear that the various components of intelligence tests exhibit quite distinct development trends. Acquired verbal skills appear not to change across the age span, whereas spatial and number abilities start to decline in early adulthood. There are no generally accepted explanations for the differential decline patterns. In general, increased age seems to be associated with a decline in acquiring and using new information. This fits into the dichotomy of fluid and crystallised intelligence suggested by Cattell (1976). On the basis of the evidence there is little doubt that age-related change occurs in reasoning, decision making, memory of material that cannot be organised or elaborated to integrate into existing knowledge, spatial abilities, perceptual, motor and cognitive speed and sensory processes. These declining abilities are based on fluid intelligence and/or neurological functioning. Generally, age-related differences relate to the overall complexity of the task.

Memory involves in general a three-stage sequential process of input, storage and retrieval. Short-term and long-term memory structures appear to offer a plausible explanation for how information is ultimately stored. Mental operations do appear to require a little more time as age increases. This reduced processing rate has an obvious effect on encoding, which then determines how much is stored and eventually what can be recalled. Evidence is limited, but what there is seems to support the hypothesis. Older adults also tend to use less efficient strategies of remembering by not employing mediators. This points to meaningfulness as a prime factor in assisting a person to remember. Other causes of forgetting such as interference, repression and trace decay generally affect all people, not just adults.

Given the context of the widely varying experiences people have during adulthood, the discovery of the systematic effects of ageing among such experiential variability attests to the potency of age-related factors in these areas. On the other hand, if research findings are valid one is struck by the remarkable absence of age effects in most normal activities. Older adults are not defective in coping with daily activities at home or at work. It might be that the research tasks are so remote from everyday living that they measure trivial aspects of behaviour not ordinarily important in normal functioning. It could be argued that these daily tasks are well rehearsed and are therefore less demanding that they might appear. Age-related differences in everyday life might only become apparent when an extra load is placed on the person in terms of increased environmental input and increased processing speed required.

# chapter 6

# motivation and personality

**A person who doubts himself is like a man who would enlist in the ranks of the enemy and bear arms against himself. He makes his failure certain by himself being the first to be convinced of it.**
(Dumas: *The Three Musketeers*)

## ■■■ MOTIVATION

The human being is a marvellous organism, capable of performing a wide range of behaviours such as perceiving, remembering, learning and problem solving. Yet none of this will be done without motivation. Motivation is that which impels an organism to activity. The uses to which a person puts their capabilities depends on their needs, drives, desires, loves, hates, fears, and their feelings about self and others.

Motivation is not a characteristic that some people have and others don't. Motivation depends on the needs of the individual and the situation. A worker who is unmotivated pulling the lever on his drill press might pull the lever on a one-armed bandit in their local club for hours without the slightest hint of boredom.

> Motivation is the willingness to exert high levels of effort towards goals.
> These goals might be organisational or personal. The art of management is to
> ensure that both sets of goals match. The individual's needs must be
> consistent and compatible with the organisation's goals.

Motivation is the key to learning. Differences in performance between individuals of equal ability and aptitude are due mainly to motivation. One person might have a powerful desire to succeed; another is quite content to live a quiet life. Some people enjoy trying to overcome difficulties or solve problems, while others might quit at the first sign of difficulty. The cliché that holds you can lead a horse to water but you cannot make it drink is readily appreciated in education. There is no guaranteed way to motivate a person to study, learn or work; no formulae, no rules. All we have are guiding principles and assumptions about the way a person is likely to respond in particular situations to praise, appeals and even threats.

A working definition of motivation would be that it consists of internal processes that spur us on to satisfy some need. A need is some internal state that makes a particular outcome attractive. An unsatisfied need creates tension that stimulates drives within the individual that produce search behaviour to attain the goal to satisfy the need.

Thus the initiating factor for motivated behaviour might be a felt need like hunger, which will motivate us to find food. Other initiating factors are the desire for acceptance by others and the need for self-esteem, power, promotion, a better salary and lifestyle, etc. The felt need leads to behaviour that will involve pursuing goals that are capable of satisfying or removing the original need. The hungry person seeks food; the person in need of social acceptance will behave in ways they believe from intuition or experience will ensure acceptance by those from whom the person seeks acceptance. Once the goal is achieved, motivation might diminish to a level that will maintain the desired degree of satisfaction. Figure 6.1 illustrates the sequence.

FIGURE 6.1 THE MOTIVATIONAL SEQUENCE

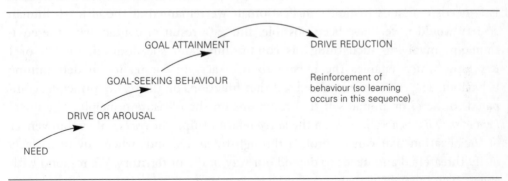

There is obviously a reinforcement value in obtaining satisfaction and achieving a desired end goal. Success will lead to a repetition of that behaviour when such a need recurs. This implies learning has occurred. However, the behaviour that satisfies the need might not be appropriate; it might even be neurotic. A person might well seek attention in unwelcome ways. The behaviour might be very successful as far as they are concerned, but not socially useful for the rest of us.

## theories of motivation

Because human motivation and behaviour is so complex, no single theory of motivation has been found to be entirely satisfactory. Many early theories regarded human motivation as controlled by innate drives or inborn tendencies mainly to satisfy biological needs. We are now aware that very few human behaviours are motivated through biological or innate drives. Most of our behaviour is learnt, with our motivation stemming mainly from desires for power, success, acceptance, social approval and for the reduction of anxiety, rather than from biological imperatives.

## Freud's psychoanalytic theory

Freud's theories range from the sublime to the ridiculous. They constitute theory of human motivation and of human personality. They were based on the verbalisations of patients, mainly middle-class Viennese women under psychoanalysis. These reports are not highly reliable and the interpretations are often more flights of fancy than valid. The patients were not a random sample and because the theory deals mainly with unconscious activity or activity involving interaction between conscious and unconscious activity, it is impossible to set up experiments to test it as the unconscious is by definition unknowable. However, his ideas have made humans look at themselves in a new light and some of the concepts are extremely relevant to explaining aspects of everyday behaviour.

Freud regarded man as an energy system with the energy divided between three components of personality: the *id* (or it), the *ego* (I or me) and the *superego* (the conscience). At birth all the motivational energy is *id*, in other words all the basic instincts preserving life such as eating, elimination of waste matter, sleeping, but including sex and aggression. This seething mass of instinctive drives and animal-istic needs demands instant gratification. If we remained at the *id* level, human society would never have been possible. But as a result of contact with the environment, involving such things as conditioning and socialisation, the *ego* or I develops, which enables the person to take account of reality in determining behaviour. The *ego* is the socialised self that functions on the reality principle, compared to the *id* or animal self that functions on the pleasure principle. The novel *Lord of the Flies* is an allegory on the *id-ego* relationship. The *ego* is only a thin veneer of socialisation that can be broken through by *id* demands when any of us feels really threatened and needs to defend our way of life or territory. We respond with anger, even outright verbal and physical aggression.

The third element of the personality, the *superego*, is the conscience. As a result of conditioning processes, the morals and values of the family and society are internalised during childhood and become a controlling feature of behaviour, even when others are not present. The *superego* can punish the person with pangs of guilt, shame and embarrassment. Extreme *superego* can lead to obsessive compulsive behaviour as the person attempts to ward off or purge guilt and anxiety. At the other extreme, the psychopath experiences no feeling of guilt at any act.

These three elements of personality are hypothetical and simply attempts by Freud to explain the things his patients were reporting to him. What Freud was saying in his model of personality and motivation was that the person is a reflection of the balance of energy between the three elements — the impulsive, the realistic and the moralistic. They are often at odds with each other, causing behaviours ranging from minor ego defence mechanisms to major neurotic behaviour. In particular, the *ego* often feels overwhelmed by the *id* wanting gratification now, the *superego* being censorious and the *ego* feeling the pressure of these conflicting forces. Neurotic symptoms and defence mechanisms are attempts to cope with these conflicts. The personality is in a constant state of civil war.

While these three elements are hypothetical they do bear some relation to reality, as we know. Many of us have on occasion lost control of our temper and later felt somewhat guilty. At a physiological level the *id* might well correspond to the 'old brain' that controls basic life-maintaining functions in the body. The *ego* might well correspond to the cerebral cortex, where individual life experience is stored and reflected in learning, memory and intellectual activity.

The conflict between the *id, ego* and *superego* leads to psychological mechanisms called defensive mechanisms being invoked to protect the *ego* from feeling threatened. The threat might come from knowing what the *id* would really like to do or from feeling the wrath of the *superego*. Quite a number of defence mechanisms can be seen in the behaviour of people around us everyday, and also in ourselves if we are willing to look closely enough. Here are some common defence mechanisms that are used as part of our motivational systems.

## sublimation
Sublimation redirects instinctive drives into socially acceptable ones. The employee who rids himself of pent-up feelings by naming his golf ball after the boss and driving it with venom is displaying sublimation. Success in business can come from sublimation as the hostile energy is channelled into more positive proactive endeavours. Even choice of career might reflect a sublimated drive. For example, aggressive and authoritarian drives can be expressed within the armed services, prison guard service and even teaching. A thwarted maternal instinct can be channelled into nursing, child care, etc. The theatre and ballet allow participants to play roles that might not be socially acceptable in society, for example the cross-dressing found in many Shakespeare plays.

## compensation
This allows a person who is deficient in one talent or skill to substitute another to disguise the deficiency. Thus a student who is poor at sport might study even harder to achieve eminence in their field. A physically handicapped person might try to overcome the handicap by persistence and effort. However, not all compensatory behaviours are constructive. A person who feels inferior might bully or tell tales to down another. An insecure person might eat and drink too much or boast about their behaviour. Some adults return to learning to obtain a sense of achievement and compensate for areas of their lives in which they are unable to perform well or gain self-esteem.

## rationalisation

Rationalisation has two major defensive objectives. It helps us to invent excuses for doing what we know we should not be doing but want to do and aids us in softening the disappointment in not reaching a goal we had set for ourselves. Typically, it involves thinking up logical, socially acceptable reasons for our past, present and future behaviour. With not too much effort we can soon think up a reason for not going to work on a cold wet day (I feel a bit off-colour) or for attending a drinks session with colleagues rather than the evening class (I won't miss anything because I'll borrow someone else's notes). Many people rationalise about why they don't try to improve their skills or knowledge by study — 'I don't need it'; 'Learning's for nerds'; 'Study's a waste of time'; 'I'll miss sport on TV as the evening class time clashes'.

These excuses are ways of justifying our behaviour and protecting our sense of adequacy, self-esteem and conscience (superego). Rationalisation is often presented in alibis or excuses (I didn't get promotion because the other candidate was a relative of the boss). Sour grapes is also a form of rationalisation for it is easy to claim that what you didn't get you didn't want anyway. Some degree of rationalisation is common in most people's behaviour. The danger is that, carried to the nth degree, it leads to the development of false beliefs or delusions that are sustained in the face of contradictory evidence.

## projection

This is an obnoxious defence mechanism that enables us to attribute blame for our failures, shortcomings and mistakes onto others. We also attribute to others our unacceptable impulses, emotions and desires. An employee might justify their failure at work to gain promotion by claiming that everyone was trying to do them down and saying negative things about them to the boss behind their back, or that you have to have a degree to get on. Projection can develop into paranoia, where the person believes everyone is against them, and also into prejudice, where a minority ethnic, religious or social group is the target or scapegoat for unwarranted accusations. Again, projection is another technique for maintaining our self-esteem and adequacy.

## repression

Repression is a technique for putting distasteful, guilt-producing, painful and shameful experiences out of the conscious mind (ego). We eliminate them as though they did not exist but they still do deep down in the recesses of the id. We hate ourselves for criticising another colleague so that we might gain promotion ahead of them. We want to forget the horrible blunder we made trying to demonstrate the equipment we were trying to sell to a customer. Repression is not always complete. We can have vague feelings of unworthiness, unease and guilt. Confronting problems head on is often the more healthy way to go. Repression was mentioned as a form of forgetting in Chapter 5.

## withdrawal

Some situations are so traumatic that the individual has to remove themselves physically from them. A person who cannot cope with new technology or a course they are meant to study might absent themselves with a range of illnesses. If one is unable to remove oneself physically, one can withdraw psychologically, for example by not joining in conversation. Many people who have been deprived of security, love and affection in early childhood find it difficult to form relationships in adulthood and frequently withdraw and become loners.

## displacement

Displacement refers to the shift of emotion away from the person or object that is the real target to a more neutral, safer target. An employee criticised by the boss might suppress the anger felt for fear of losing their job but vent that anger on a subordinate or their spouse later. Displacement occurs when we swear after hitting our thumb with a hammer.

Some forms of displacement involve the conversion of tension into physical symptoms such as tummy upsets and headaches. In the extreme, paralysis, blindness or deafness might occur. This is termed conversion hysteria. An older, skilled tradesman might develop paralysis of the arm to prevent self-knowledge that fine, dexterous movements are not as easy as one grows older. The paralysis enables a physical illness rather than loss of skill to be used as the reason for early retirement. Accident proneness is also seen as a form of displacement behaviour. It might in some cases be deliberate self-punishment.

## reaction formation

Reaction formation is the development and display of behaviour that is opposite to the behaviour one would really like to display. We might be excessively kind to a person we do not like to hide that fact or adopt an air of bravado when our adequacy is threatened. People who have a strong desire to censor sex, alcohol and other presumed vices often have high impulses in the same direction themselves, which they have repressed. Unconventional hairstyles, clothing and music are used by young people as a reaction to the establishment, which they would really like to be part of. Reaction formation can lead to excessive harshness and severity in dealing with others and is recognised by extreme and intolerant attitudes.

## behaviourist theory

Skinner's concept of reinforcement, although located in learning theory, is in fact a motivational concept. It is a mechanism that increases or decreases motivation to repeat responses. However, it is limited to external incentives and several crucial criticisms seem to counter its general applicability too. For example, Bexton, Heron and Scott (1954) paid students quite well to do nothing in an environment of controlled minimum sensory stimulation. They wore blindfolds and ear muffs and lay on a bed. Despite the reinforcement of money very few of the students could last the experiment and opted out after a short period of time. Reinforcement as a motivational techniques has been savagely criticised by a number of psychologists (e.g. Kohn, 1993).

Kohn provides a thought-provoking criticism of extrinsic rewards and their effects on performance, particularly the 'do this and you'll get that' strategy, which leads to a 'what will I get if ...' student or employee bribe mentality. Promising goodies produces little more than temporary performance/obedience — token reinforcement evokes token learning. Gaining a reward becomes the goal rather than challenge or achievement, intrinsic interest, curiosity or a sense of self-esteem. Eventually, if extrinsic reward is removed or not on offer, performance decreases to the minimum necessary to avoid the prospect of 'punishment' such as loss of pay, demotion or verbal criticism. Thus intrinsic rather than extrinsic motivation is seen as the best promoter of adult motivation, particularly in the area of lifelong learning. We want learners to want to learn, not do it simply because they are told to or will receive some 'present' for complying.

## intrinsic motivation theory

In contrast with the principle that behaviour requires extrinsic reinforcement, it has been found, frequently in conditions of no obvious external reinforcement, that children and adults will continue to work at some problem despite growing hunger and tiredness. Children might want to solve a jigsaw; adults a crossword puzzle. This persistence occurs because the task itself is motivating, that is there is intrinsic interest present. The deprivation experiments also indicate that reinforcement by external goodies is not the only way to motivate behaviour. In fact, the whole edifice of lifelong learning cannot be built solely on assumptions that increased knowledge and skill bring money and promotion, it must also rest on human needs for feelings of self-esteem, a sense of achievement, involvement and interest in the topic itself. Thus intrinsic motivation theories appear to explain motivation more generally than extrinsic reinforcement theories and also take into account the personal construing of the environment. To understand why people behave as they do you have to get into their skin and view things from their perspective. Like the cognitive–Gestalt learning approach, motivation seems to depend on personal experience and interpretation of the context. We noted the problem of reinforcement in learning theory: that the reinforcement must be something that is reinforcing to the individual to whom it is being applied. If the reinforcement is not desirable to the individual or not recognised as reinforcement then it will have no effect. It is equally apparent that much motivation is not based on extrinsic reinforcement anyway but on aspects of the environment intrinsic to the individual, like the need to succeed, to develop self-esteem and to avoid boredom.

Hebb (1949) claims there is only one basic motivating principle, that of a state of arousal which corresponds to an optimal level of stimulation. If there is too little stimulation the person will seek more; if there is too much the person will attempt to reduce it. This motivation is manifested in the behaviour of organisms to seek weaker or stronger stimulation.

Hunt (1961) builds on Hebb's motivating principle of arousal by claiming that it is the stimulus properties of the situation that provide the arousal and are intrinsically motivating. He adds that the kind of stimulation sought is that which is incongruous with previous experience. It is the attempt to understand and solve the incongruity by modifying existing behaviour stored as past experience in the brain (Hunt calls this stored past experience *plans*; Hebb terms them *cell assemblies* and *phase sequences*; Piaget used the word *schema* — see Chapter 5) that motivates the individual. (This also has resonance with the problem-solving and insightful learning of the cognitive–Gestalt approach.) It follows from this that organisms are continually motivated to more complex environments; those that are too familiar have lost their complexity and become boring.

What becomes increasingly motivating is incongruity within a context of the familiar, a slight change to the usual conditions. Hunt identified three main standards by which incoming information is tested for incongruity. The first is that of *comfort/freedom from pain*. Hunt accepts that this is a homeostatic need that is concerned with obtaining extrinsic reinforcement to satisfy the incongruity, which could be a need for food. The other two standards are intrinsically motivating.

The second standard is the *information standard,* which consists of information stored in the brain from past experience. It enables us to recognise previously encountered events and the level of incongruity between past experience and new stimuli. The third standard is an *action standard* consisting of a repertoire of responses we have made in the past. We try these out on new events that we recognise in terms of past experience in order to test which response is appropriate. In all these standards there is a process of assessing incoming information against what we have stored in our brain. If we can deal with the situation using familiar and well tried methods, then we go ahead. However, after some time the familiar can become boring and insipid. What becomes increasingly motivating is finding some changes in our environment so that we have to become more active physically and/or mentally in order to solve the problem. Incongruity becomes the mainspring for action.

The difficulty in motivating learners is judging what degree of incongruity a person can cope with and still solve the problem. Too great an incongruity and the person will probably give up as they meet failure. Too little incongruity provides no challenge. The mismatch should be such that the skill, knowledge and capabilities a person has are potentially capable, with restructuring of the environment, of mastering the new situation. Teachers are always trying to achieve this mismatch in order to move students through the work step by step, always ensuring that the student has the necessary skills and background, which, if deployed in a critical manner on the task, will ensure success and increased motivation to continue.

Intrinsic motivation demonstrates the need for the environment to be stimulating through novelty, complexity (but not so complex as to cause defeat) and change in order to encourage its denizens to respond to it and succeed in it. There is a need to be able to control the environment to demonstrate competence. For a beginner in any sphere, mastery over even a limited and simple environment is motivating. The first paragraph typed on the word processor and printed, the first sales made or the first weld made all create a sense of competency and are intrinsically motivating. They have demonstrated a shift in the level of incongruity that can be imposed and permit a gradual introduction of more complex behaviours step by step (incongruity by incongruity). Such success also produces positive attitudes to work and to self.

Individuals will engage in work simply for the pleasure of manipulating objects or ideas or solving problems. The need to explore will manifest itself in the desire to read, to study and to learn about scientific advances. Individuals seek out intellectual activity such as solving crossword problems or playing bridge.

A variant of this approach can also be seen in the need for achievement theory proposed by McClelland. The need to achieve is composed of three elements:

1. a drive to know and understand
2. self-enhancement, which represents a desire for increased prestige and status gained by doing well
3. affiliation, which is the desire for approval from and association with others.

Obviously, the intrinsic motivation of staff is the aim of any organisation. With it staff are more willing and able to solve problems, involve themselves in affiliative team activities and demonstrate positive attitudes towards the organisation as it provides for their intrinsic needs of self-esteem, of doing a good job, of being appreciated and of being challenged. These are major characteristics of a learning organisation, so intrinsic motivation is an essential ingredient in setting these up and motivating staff. Underlying this ideal is the realisation that to achieve skills in problem solving, to set tasks that are potentially solvable by particular persons, to provide immediate feedback on performance and to ensure harmonious relationships within a team requires trainers and managers who are aware of how to establish this context.

Perhaps the most difficult part is to initiate intrinsic motivation in staff who have low self-esteem, who need new skills and who have negative attitudes to training and learning as a result of previous failure at school. While extrinsic motivation has its limitations, initial motivation often needs to be provided through extrinsic rewards. Once the behaviour has been started then it can become self-energising, with previous success, developing self-esteem and interest promoting further development while the extrinsic motivation declines in potency. The same happens when teaching a child to read. Parents offer extrinsic rewards — lollies etc. — at the start but as skills develop and interest increases, the intrinsic motivation of feelings of competency and achievement, enjoyment of reading and curiosity to master an interesting story maintain skill development. Obviously, adult learning might need extrinsic lures at the beginning to encourage involvement. These exist quite potently as increasing salary, promotion, job retention, etc. However, if lifelong learning is to take root in individuals and communities, it can only be maintained by the intrinsic motivation to want to know, to understand and to satisfy curiosity and by internal feelings of success and competence and these personal feelings are driven best in a context of some degree of ownership, choice and participation.

Bruner (1966) enlarged on the theories of Hebb and Hunt and indicated that the three principal parts of intrinsic motivation were curiosity, competence and reciprocity. Curiosity is the need for novelty; competence is the need to control the environment and reciprocity is the need to cooperate in group activity towards a common goal.

In recent years, adult educators have begun to place more emphasis on the learner than the teacher in terms of using the learner's experience and the process of reflection. The adult might experience a discrepancy with their environment, feel out of phase and harmony with it, that their expectations are not being met. Motivation to learn is located within this awareness of a learning need and arises as a result of reflecting on the situation. This is congruent with Hunt's approach above. Reflection on experience is a crucial factor in motivating the adult and in the learning process itself in the andragogical paradigm, as detailed in Chapter 7. Within that philosophy Freire, too, emphasised the importance of reflection in the learning process in order that individuals should become aware of their social situation and the imbalances and incongruities there. Experiences and reflection are essential parts of the learning cycle in adulthood and are elements of motivation theory as expressed by those who promote intrinsic motivation as a mainspring of human behaviour.

## theory X and theory Y

McGregor's theory (1964) Y commences with the conception of a self-motivated adult who seeks to fulfil their own potential, whereas theory X assumes that the adult dislikes work and needs to be controlled and directed. A teacher who adopts the former perspective is more able to develop the potentials of an adult in the learning context, even though they might vary their approach and method to suit the material and the context. McGregor believed managers hold these two assumptions about employees too. Under theory X managers believe:
- employees dislike work and will attempt to avoid it
- employees must therefore be coerced and controlled to achieve goals
- employees avoid responsibility and always seek direction
- employees display little ambition.

In contrast, under theory Y managers believe:
- employees enjoy work and gain satisfaction from it
- employees will exercise self-direction and self-control if they are committed to goals and objectives

- employees can learn to accept and even seek responsibility
- employees can make innovative decisions if allowed to.

These theory-Y characteristics are consistent with humanist adult education approaches and with the thrust towards the learning organisation. McGregor advocated moves towards encouraging managers to accept theory-Y assumptions, which would lead to more motivated employees, provide employees with training in decision making and group responsibility and reorganise jobs so that they would provide greater responsibility and challenge.

## Maslow's hierarchy of needs

Maslow (1943) explores the hierarchy of needs of individuals by linking biological and homeostatic needs with social and esteem needs, rising ultimately to the pinnacle of human expression — self-actualisation — in a hierarchical model (Figure 6.2). There is a predetermined order of motives that distinguishes needs in order of their importance, so that, in general, physiological needs must be satisfied before attending to other more social needs. The significance of the pyramidal shape is not only to demonstrate the hierarchy but also to show the broad base of lower needs. Progress through the hierarchy occurs only as needs lower in the hierarchy are satisfied. People living in Somalia, Sierra Leone or Kosovo (at the time of writing) are obviously more motivated by physiological (e.g. food) needs and safety needs (sheer survival) than by self-actualisation. It is only when a person is living in conditions in which they are presumably not in obvious danger that higher levels of motivation are triggered. To move up the hierarchy a lower need does not have be totally satisfied, only satisfied enough for attention and energy to be diverted to other needs.

FIGURE 6.2 MASLOW'S HIERARCHY ADAPTED

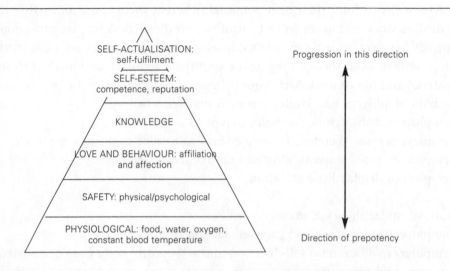

*In some situations the need that prompts the learning might be easy to recognise. This is true for biological needs like hunger and thirst. In other instances, the need might be much more complex and have its origin in social processes and the personal view of the individual of themselves as a person. It would be impossible to describe in simple terms what might motivate a 30-year-old to change the whole course of their life by leaving a well established career and starting a full-time degree course. It might be that their career was something they had drifted into; their career had never extended them; they never felt a sense of personal achievement; they might feel the need to prove to themselves that they can succeed academically; or they need to improve their self-esteem.*

The hierarchy adapted from Maslow runs as follows. It is slightly different from that Maslow originally proposed in that knowledge and understanding have been added before self-esteem needs.

## physiological needs

These are the starting point for all motivation. These needs are fundamental biological needs such as that for food, air, water and shelter required to maintain human life. Consequently, they assume prime importance and only when they are satisfied can thinking and behaviour turn to other less basic needs. If physiological needs are unsatisfied they will dominate consciousness and cause the individual to organise their resources to meet them. It would be rare for an organisation to find its employees at this level (e.g. at times of war, natural disaster, pandemic). However, many larger organisations do ensure that such needs are met by allowing rest breaks and providing physical fitness/exercise programs. This is recognition that employees who stay healthy are more motivated towards higher goals of achievement, intellectual knowledge and self-actualisation.

## safety needs

These involve protection from potentially threatening objects and events. Normal members of our society prefer to have a safe, orderly, predictable and organised world that they can be confident will not become dangerous, unmanageable or unpredictable. Although most of us live in well ordered societies, Maslow suggests that our preference for the familiar, and our tendency to promote science, religion and philosophy in order to increase meaningfulness, are in part motivated by our safety needs. Organisations often include savings, health and insurance plans in their contracts and psychological security is enhanced by the provision, voluntarily or by law depending on the country, of job security agreements and laid-down processes for terminating employment, etc.

## social needs

These needs involve the desire to belong, gain acceptance and to give and receive friendship and affection. Insecurity occurs if these needs are not satisfied. The individual wants friends, marriage and children. After all, no man is an island (John Donne).

The work context can provide friendship and, if organised in terms of teams, the potential for acceptance and personal contact is enhanced. Not only can colleagues meet some social needs, so can supervisors who can feed back messages of acceptance. The work context can in out-of-hours time provide through sporting and social events other means of meeting social needs. Many organisations spend considerable sums on out-of-work activities for staff. Even studying part time or attending hobby classes can be used for social motivation such as meeting others with similar interests or, for a lonely single, getting out in the evening. Education can serve many needs.

Maslow's first three needs are known as deficiency needs. If they are not met, the individual will fail to develop into a physically and psychologically healthy person. The remaining needs are growth needs, which help a person to develop to their full potential.

## knowledge and understanding

This is a bias need to learn and acquire knowledge and understanding. Our search for meaning is lifelong and leads into our need for self-esteem and personal identity. There are no totally mature people, only maturing ones. The rapid changes in the structure and processes in the workplace and the responses of government and industry all noted in earlier chapters of this book create a need for employees to extend their knowledge, skills and understanding. The organisation also gains, and starts to be propelled towards the learning organisation concept.

## esteem needs

These needs include those of self-confidence, competence, respect, recognition and status. Their satisfaction leads to feelings of worth, capability and of feeling useful. Thwarting of these needs results in feelings of inferiority and helplessness. Everyone has a need to be able to hold themselves in high self-esteem and feel that they are esteemed by others. When the individual is able to satisfy their self-esteem needs they derive feelings of confidence, worth and capability and a sense of being a useful and necessary person. When these needs are thwarted the individual will feel weak, helpless and inferior. Although our needs start at a physiological level, what is clear is that the higher-order needs are closely related to the individual's self-concept.

Industrial organisations adopting a Fordist and/or bureaucratic structure are not conducive to satisfying esteem needs. The learning organisation ethos, again, would be far more productive in providing conditions of work that enable employees to satisfy their self-esteem needs.

Most organisations offer awards and identify employees of the month but if the general ethos of the organisation is not person-centred, these acts are viewed cynically and regarded as no more important than the company Christmas card everyone receives annually. Inflation of job titles, perks and other awards are often on offer too. Most organisations rarely get beyond this token effort to reward and recognise employees. More subtle yet of greater importance are the feelings of worth and recognition that come from the manager actually knowing your name and showing interest in what you are doing. The presentation of the company tie never comes close to doing this.

## self-actualisation needs

At the peak of the pyramid are the individual's needs for realising their own potential for self-fulfilment and for continued self development. This involves trying to attain whatever the person is capable of attaining. This, of course, is never actually achieved since attaining one level provides the basis for further development. This is Rogers' concept of self-actualisation.

Self-actualisation is a need to fulfil one's potentialities — an artist must paint, a computer programmer wants to write programs, a mechanic wants to improve the working of a machine. A man must be what he must be, maintains Maslow. Effective self-actualisation depends on being able to recognise one's own capabilities and on being able to appreciate what one is able to become. Put alongside a typical bureaucratic organisation as a place where millions of workers spend a large proportion of their lives, it is impossible to see how paid employment can meet these basic needs for more than a relatively small group. For blue collar workers, in particular, the opportunity to learn and grow in the work situation is very important given their frequently experienced lack of success in previous schooling situations. By operating at their maximum creative potential, employees who are self-actualised are very valuable assets to their organisations. The definition of self-actualisation is not clear and cannot really be operationalised for ease of measurement. Few jobs provide unlimited scope for employees to achieve full self-fulfilment.

Organisations' ability to contribute to the satisfaction of self-actualisation needs among its employees will depend on whether organisations have been able to meet in fair degree lower level needs. Organisations with different structures and management philosophies would be found at different levels of the hierarchy. Presumably, Fordist/bureaucratic organisations would be located no higher than the border between safety needs and social needs. The future organisation with devolution of responsibility, team activity and encouragement of all levels of staff to involve themselves in education, training and personal development will lift the organisation into much higher realms of need satisfaction to the benefit of the individuals and the future viability of the organisation.

Maslow had an optimistic view of human behaviour compared with Taylor's scientific-management approach, which promotes a very negative view of human motivation and therefore places a different slant on how people should be conceived of and treated in the workplace. He claims that the proper management of the work lives of humans can improve them and improve the world. Maslow's theory reinforces McGregor's (1964) more corporate view that organisations are either theory X or theory Y in their underlying management style and assumptions about human motivation. Theory X organisations believe that workers need to be managed with a capital M. Theory Y organisations have a culture of trust and a belief that individuals will develop if given some sense of ownership in decision making. In this context managers are facilitators and not control freaks. Theory-Y organisations are attempting to meet Maslow's higher order needs rather than manipulate the lower order needs to motivate their employees.

The fact that the theory is all embracing has ensured its acceptance across a wide spectrum. There is, however, little evidence that the needs are activated in the order suggested or that lower level needs, for example for food, cannot be sublimated if a person wishes to pursue higher needs. It is not certain how or when gratification of one need activates movement to the next higher need. It is a theory that, though difficult to test, does provide food for thought and recognises that different people are activated by different needs and that a work situation might or might not satisfy these needs to various degrees to the benefit or detriment of the organisation.

## Herzberg's two factor theory

This was proposed by Herzberg (1959) in the belief that an individual's relation to their work is a basic one and that attitude to work determines a person's success or failure there. From surveys, Herzberg concluded that some work characteristics are related to satisfaction at work while other factors are related to dissatisfaction at work. Intrinsic factors such as achievement, recognition, responsibility, advancement and growth were related to satisfaction. Herzberg terms these motivator factors and they are basically Maslow's higher order needs.

Extrinsic context factors such as working conditions, company policy, administration, salary, supervision and interpersonal relations were related to dissatisfaction. Herzberg argued that factors leading to job satisfaction are therefore different from those leading to job dissatisfaction. Therefore, organisations that remove dissatisfiers will *not* increase motivation. They will only be placating their workforce. These factors were termed *hygiene factors* by Herzberg and are similar to Maslow's lower order needs. When hygiene factors are positive, barriers to job satisfaction are removed. Herzberg compared hygiene factors to water pollution control, where although such control does not cure disease it does prevent outbreaks.

Motivation is dependent on the content and organisation of work itself. If we want to motivate people and improve job satisfaction while increasing work rate and commitment then we must focus on intrinsic factors — essentially those factors that humanists and those promoting the learning organisation have emphasised. These satisfiers, labelled by Herzberg as motivators, focus on personal growth, recognition and responsibility. Monotonous, heavily fragmented work needs to be broadened to include other operations and more qualified tasks (job widening and job broadening).

Herzberg's theory has been criticised because all it says is that when things are going well people take credit themselves but when they go badly they blame the external environment. He failed to show the relationship between satisfaction and productivity but simply assumed it existed. However, his work has had an on-going influence on the structural and managerial process changes that are leading towards the learning organisation model. The introduction of job enrichment, involvement in decision-making processes, responsibility, autonomy and opportunities for further training and education as required by changes in the economic and technological environment are consonant with Herzberg's theory.

## McClelland's needs theory

McClelland focuses on three needs, viz. *achievement, power and affiliation*. The achievement drive is the desire for personal achievement, not the rewards of success. People with high achievement needs seek situations where they can assume personal responsibility for finding solutions to problems and receive rapid feedback on what they are doing. They are not gamblers and avoid easy and very difficult tasks. They prefer moderately challenging goals and are strongly motivated.

Some people seek out opportunities for new learning, while others avoid such opportunities, even though they are to their advantage and nothing stands in their way. The sources of this variation in motivation are complex. It might be due to previous negative experiences in education or the early influence of attitudes to education and achievement in the home or to personality factors. Origins of high levels of achievement motivation do seem to be found in childhood. People high in achievement motivation often come from families in which the parents encouraged the child to be independent. Those low in achievement motivation tended to have parents who believed in routine compliance with instructions, allowing little leeway in behaviour. Thus parents define how their children should play their roles and how ultimately they come to value achievement.

The need for power is the desire to have impact, be influential and control others. Individuals with power needs enjoy being in charge and are more concerned with prestige and gaining influence than with effective performance. Affiliation is the need to be accepted by others; individuals with this need therefore strive for friendship and cooperative situations and seek mutual understanding.

Individuals with high achievement needs are attracted to jobs with personal responsibility, such as more entrepreneurial activities. They are not necessarily good managers as they are more interested in how they do personally than in team effort or assisting others. Affiliation and power are more closely related to managerial success. Employees with these needs should be selected and trained for appropriate activities.

## ■■■ PERSONALITY

While a complex interplay of biological, social and emotional factors determines the characteristic level and direction of individual motivation, personality also strongly influences the manner in which a person interacts with their environment.

Personality is the way in which the individual habitually responds and interacts with their environment. This is usually described in terms of descriptive traits such as happy, inflexible, anxious or friendly, to name but a few of the myriad ways we can describe people. Personality, like intelligence, is an amalgam of heredity and environment, moderated by current situational conditions.

In terms of heredity, such elements as hormonal balance and physique are involved. Environmental factors include the culture we were raised in, the behaviours, values, norms and attitudes to which we were conditioned from living among our family, peer group, etc., and general life experience, particularly the ways in which others react to one as a physical and social being — often in stereotypic ways. Thus physique, a result of heredity, can imply particular stereotypes, with the fat person supposed to be a happy, easy going, generous person. Some theories of personality have been based on body build. But it is not so much the particular body build that determines personality as how others react to it. This then leads to a self-fulfilling prophecy that the bearer will live up to.

An individual's personality, while generally stable and consistent, does vary within limits, depending on the situation. Through acculturisation we know that we can be boisterous, noisy and sing bawdy songs at a sports club bar after winning a competition. However, the next day at a reception for the new general manager, we are able to conduct a quiet, refined conversation while sipping sherry.

Personality characteristics create the parameters for behaviour and are therefore the framework for predicting behaviour. Individuals who are shy, introverted and uncomfortable in social situations would probably be ill suited to sales jobs. Psychologists have tried to isolate the personality characteristics that are related to job success in particular occupations. This makes selection more effective and aids decisions as to whom should be trained in which new skills and new roles in the workforce. Retraining a person with an extroverted, independent, non-conformist and creative personality for a highly structured but skilled job on a computer-controlled assembly line would not be appropriate. Therefore, training plans for individuals should be based largely not only on the skills required by the job and the skills of the person but also on the match between the job requirements/environment and the personality of the worker.

Personality characteristics often influence the degree to which we use our intelligence. Many personality theorists claim that the individual can be placed somewhere on a continuum that extends between two extremes (personality dimensions), for example happy–sad, cowardly–brave. However, the number of dimensions of this nature that each theorist believes to be the minimum required to provide a complete description of a person's personality varies.

## personality traits

There are around 18 000 terms to describe personality traits, many of them synonymous. The statistical technique of factor analysis has been used to reduce this number to the minimum possible needed to describe all possibilities of personality. For example, the technique enables synonymous or near synonymous personality descriptions such as sad, unhappy, glum, etc., to be replaced by one term. Using factor analysis, Cattell reduced the plethora of terms to 16, which he termed the source or primary traits of personality (Figure 6.3). Every person possesses each factor to some degree. Variations in personality between individuals reflect variations in the amount of each of these primary traits. His 16PF test provides a profile of an individual's standing on each of the 16 personality traits or factors.

These 16 have been shown to be fairly consistent across individuals and cultures and allow prediction of behaviour in specific situations by weighting the characteristics for their situational relevance. For example, Cattell has provided various equations to compute the efficacy of people at various jobs based on their personality scores from the 16PF. The pattern for the successful wholesale salesperson is:

$$0.21A + 0.10B + 0.10C + 010E + 0.21F + 0.10G - 0.10L - 31M + 0.21N - 0.31Q2 + 0.21Q3 - 0.21Q4 + 3.80.$$

The pattern for teaching effectiveness is:

$$0.34A + 0.34B + 0.34C + 0.68M + 0.43N + 0.17Q3 - 17Q4 - 5.72.$$

Even some of these source traits can be grouped together into four personality types, which isolate introversion–extroversion and high anxiety–low anxiety as the major characteristics. An individual with high anxiety and extroversion would be tense, excitable, unstable, social and dependent. However, predictions are better for individuals who hold a trait at its extreme. Unfortunately, most people are in the mid-ranges.

## introversion and extroversion

In contrast with Cattell's 16 basic traits, Eysenck (1967) has claimed that only two major personality dimensions are needed to explain difference in personality between individuals. One continuum stretches between the extremes of extroversion and introversion, while the other ranges between the extremes of neuroticism and stability. The typical introvert is quiet, shy and private, preferring books to people and planning ahead for eventualities that might never occur. They keep their emotions under tight control. Life is a serious affair and a pessimistic view is taken. They are reliable and set high ethical standards. The extrovert is very sociable and outgoing. Impulsive and preferring action to words, they give free reign to their emotions and are not very reliable. The extreme neurotic is an anxious and insecure person, while the stable person is quite calm and relaxed. According to Eysenck, a person's position on one dimension does not affect their position on the other; they are independent dimensions. These two factors relate strongly to social behaviour, including health behaviour such as smoking, criminality and learning.

Eysenck claims that physiological differences underlie these extremes. The extrovert has a lower level of arousal in the cortex, which means more input is needed from the environment to make an impact on their nervous system. Thus to achieve this higher level of arousal, the extrovert seeks extra stimulation, resulting in highly social, noisy, brash behaviour. As a result the introvert and extrovert respond differently to the world. Introverts are more easily conditioned than extroverts as they pay more attention to their environment than extroverts do. As a result of greater conditioning, introverts have more of a conscience and will stick more closely to requirements and instructions.

These personality differences affect the way these two types should be taught. Introverts prefer highly structured material that has a logical structure. Extroverts prefer material that provides for greater tolerance of uncertainty. Extroverts put their own structure to the material. Neurotics are poor students. They are worried by tests, they are sure they will fail and tend to avoid any challenge. In terms of assessment, introverts work slowly but steadily through a test with error spread evenly through the test, while extroverts work quickly and will guess more, with the rate of errors increasing as they proceed through the test.

Many studies (e.g. Bendig, 1963) reveal that introverts prefer scientific and theoretical jobs, whereas extroverts expressed more interest in occupations involving social contact. Extroversion and neuroticism are related to lower ability to handle routine work activities, with poorer attendance records and more absconding compared with introverts and more stable persons.

The reasons are believed to lie in the greater susceptibility of introverts to conditioning. Since extroverts are slower to condition, they are less able to tolerate routine tasks and cannot sustain task performance. Extroverts are seekers of arousal and therefore do not function as well as introverts in conditions of minimal or moderate sensory variation input. Introverts might become overaroused if their jobs involve considerable organisational contacts, noise and/or a relative absence of routine. In fact, introverts function less efficiently than extroverts in the presence of distractions owing to their preference for a quiet, solitary environment. Extroverts show improvement in performance when distractions are present. Kim (1980) showed that introverts are less dissatisfied on a non-stimulating task than extroverts, who showed greater satisfaction on a stimulating task than introverts. Introverts work better to avoid a threatened punishment, while extroverts are more motivated by a promised reward. Thus bureaucracies motivate introverted staff with sanctions and manufacturers motivate their sales staff with performance rewards. Organisational incentives in training and education should be tailored to suit the personality traits of the employee. Management and training systems must be sensitive to these differences.

Paying heed to these preferences in a learning situation will ensure optimal performance from both groups, as will ensuring that these differences are taken into account when retraining or upgrading employees for a variety of types of tasks and work environments. It is a matter of ensuring square pegs are placed in square holes. In general, research shows that extroverts prefer jobs with higher levels of task demands, greater pace of task demands and more extrinsic rewards. In conditions of organisational change, neurotic extroverts and stable introverts had the most posi-

# FIGURE 6.3  CATTELL'S 16 PERSONALITY FACTORS

| LOW SCORE DESCRIPTION | HIGH SCORE DESCRIPTION |
| --- | --- |
| **Reserved** . . . . . . . .<br>critical, aloof, detached (Sizothymia) | **Outgoing** . . . . . . . .<br>warmhearted (Affectothymia) |
| **Less intelligent** . . . . . .<br>concrete thinking (Lower scholastic mental capacity) | **More intelligent** . . . . . .<br>abstract-thinking, bright (Higher scholastic mental capacity) |
| **Affected by feeling** . . . . . . . .<br>easily upset (Lower ego strength) | **Emotionally stable** . . . . . . . .<br>faces reality, calm, mature (Higher ego strength) |
| **Humble** . . . . . . . .<br>mild, conforming, accommodating (Submissiveness) | **Assertive** . . . . . . . .<br>aggressive, stubborn, competitive (Dominance) |
| **Sober** . . . . . . . .<br>prudent, serious, taciturn (Desurgency) | **Happy-go-lucky** . . . . . . . .<br>impulsively lively, gay, enthusiastic (Surgency) |
| **Expedient** . . . . . . . .<br>disregards rules, feels few obligations (Weaker superego strength) | **Conscientious** . . . . . . . .<br>perservering, staid, moralistic, (Stronger superego strength) |
| **Shy** . . . . . . . .<br>restrained, timid, threat-sensitive (Threctia) | **Venturesome** . . . . . . . .<br>socially bold, uninhibited, spontaneous (Parmia) |
| **Tough-minded** . . . . . . .<br>self-reliant, realistic (Harria) | **Tender-minded** . . . . . . .<br>overprotected, clinging, sensitive (Premsia) |
| **Trusting** . . . . . . . .<br>adaptable, free of jealousy, easy to get along with (Alaxia) | **Suspicious** . . . . . . . .<br>self-opinionated, hard to fool (Protension) |
| **Practical** . . . . . . . .<br>careful, conventional, regulated by external realities, proper (Praxernia) | **Imaginative** . . . . . . . .<br>careless of practical matters, bohemian, wrapped up in inner urgencies (Autia) |
| **Forthright** . . . . . . . .<br>natural, artless, unpretentious (Artlessness) | **Shrewd** . . . . . . . .<br>calculating, wordly, penetrating (Shrewdness) |
| **Self-assured** . . . . . . . .<br>confident, serene (Untroubled adequacy) | **Apprehensive** . . . . . . . .<br>self-reproaching, troubled, worrying (Guilt-proneness) |
| **Conservative** . . . . . . . .<br>respecting established ideas, tolerant of traditional difficulties (Conservatism) | **Experimenting** . . . . . . . .<br>liberal thinking, analytical, free-thinking (Radicalism) |
| **Group-dependent** . . . . . . . .<br>a joiner and sound follower (Group adherence) | **Self-sufficient** . . . . . . . .<br>resourceful, prefers own decisions (Self-sufficiency) |
| **Undisciplined self-conduct** . . . . . . . .<br>follows own urges, careless of protocol (Low integration) | **Controlled.** . . . . . . .<br>socially precise, following self-image (High self-concept control) |
| **Relaxed** . . . . . . . .<br>tranquil, unfrustrated (Low ergic tension) | **Tense** . . . . . . . .<br>frustrated, overwrought, driven (High ergic tension) |

tive attitudes to change and the lowest levels of discontent. Neurotic introverts, as might be expected, were most discontented at change and negative attitudes.

Extroverts are superior to introverts at primary school age and up to around 14 or 15 years of age. At that point a transition occurs and beyond that age introverts' education performance is superior to extroverts'. This might be because the early stage of education, with its social group work and variety of activity, suits the extrovert. Whereas at later adolescence and post-school study, learning is more an individual task, requiring quiet, little distraction, conformity and intense concentration. This type of activity would suit the introvert more. These differences occur when intelligence is held constant.

The vocational choices of introverts are clearer than those of extroverts. Introverts are oriented towards careers and jobs that involve structured and detailed work and aspire to traditional high-status professions, whereas extroverts prefer more practical person-oriented activities. Extroverts are also more liberal and less socially conforming, with aspirations governed by immediate status and monetary considerations.

## the Myers-Briggs Type Indicator

The major test used in industry to assess personality is the Myers-Briggs Type Indicator (MBTI). It consists of 100 personality items, which ask people how they usually feel or act in particular situations. The test labels people as either extroverted or introverted (E or I), sensing or intuitive (S or N), thinking or feeling (T or F), and perceiving or judging (P or J).

These are then combined into 16 personality types. For example, INTJs are visionaries with original ideas and great drive, critical, determined and stubborn. ESTJs are organisers, realistic, practical with a hard business head and like to run organisations. ENTPs are conceptualisers with quick and ingenious minds, resourceful in solving challenging problems and possibly neglectful of routine assignments. The test can be used to improve employee and manager self-awareness and to identify which types of activities are suitable for career development.

## ▪▪▪ SELF-CONCEPT

A theme that has consistently emerged in much of our discussion has been that self-esteem or feelings about the self affect a person's approach to and level of performance in education activities. This self-esteem image is often termed the self-concept.

### what is the self-concept?

The self-concept has three main dimensions:
- the present self-image, or how we see ourselves now
- the ideal self, or how we would like to be

- the self we believe others see us as (the other self).

The self-concept is therefore the image each of us holds about ourselves, the characteristics and attributes we believe we possess. The self-concept is not a singular; we really should refer to self-concepts as we all hold a huge collection of attitudes to ourselves, each relating to a particular role, activity or event in our lives. For example, you could have different self-concepts of yourself as a spouse, a parent, an employee, a driver, a DIY person, a computer user, a learner, etc. Self-image and self-esteem are often used as synonyms for the self-concept, although self-image is really the picture while self-esteem is the evaluation (or positive/negative judgments) of the picture. The self-concept involves both knowledge and feelings (emotion) because beliefs about ourselves are highly personal and central to our individual behaviour and way of life. In fact, many psychologists see self-concept as the major factor behind individual behaviour. That is we behave in a way that is congruent with the way we perceive ourselves, our characteristics and attributes. The self-concept is also learnt, therefore it can change with experience.

People with positive self-concepts tend to do well at most things because they are more positively motivated. They believe they can achieve. Of course, achieving success reinforces their existing view of themselves; behaviour becomes self-validating. They usually have an internal rather then an external locus of control. That is they see themselves as responsible for their own success or failure rather than seeing their behaviour as controlled by such external events as luck or the whims of others. They have more friends and form relationships more quickly and firmly. Persons with positive self-concepts tend to be happy, congenial, self-reliant persons with lots of self-confidence. They accept themselves, including their strengths and weaknesses. They feel secure in themselves and can therefore tolerate criticism, express feelings appropriately and have the confidence to cope with most situations.

People with poor self-concepts tend to be unhappy, anxious, self-critical people who have difficulty building up positive relationships with others. They depend on others for approval and conform to those in authority. Poor self-concept people avoid others but might try to boost their self-esteem by boasting and showing off. They are often depressed, with little confidence in themselves. Such behaviours usually have the opposite effect, driving others away so the person feels even more unworthy and incompetent, avoids trying anything for fear of expected failure in all aspects of life and sets easy goals for themselves. If a learner says 'I'll never pass that test, I just know it' they are expressing something not only about their potential behaviour but also about how they feel about themselves. All things being equal, the chances are good that this student will not pass the test in question because they are self-defeating. Much research in the area of the self-concept tells us that how a person feels about themselves affects their performance. Indeed life success might depend less on the qualities a person has by virtue of genes and circumstance than on how they feel about those qualities.

## development of the self-concept

The self-concept develops from infancy throughout the school days, but by adulthood it is relatively permanent and difficult to change. Every child has experiences that bend them towards future ways of acting, thinking and feeling. Feelings of trust or mistrust, pride or shame, confidence or doubt result from experiences and become part of the individual. This development is determined largely by the nature of the person's relationships with others. What you come to think of yourself is based largely on what you believe significant others think of you. Other people such as parents, teachers, colleagues, managers and friends act like a mirror reflecting back at you how they see you. The way they respond and react to you is a major part of this reflection. Their words and their non-verbal signals (smiles, head nods, frowns, etc.) are interpreted by you as an indication of how they feel about you. In other words self-concept is an interpretation of the common features of all our personal experiences.

Of course, your interpretation might be correct or incorrect because you are making a subjective assessment. But either way this is the picture you have of yourself and you behave in accordance with that picture. You might have decided not to stay on at school because some teacher gave you the impression that you were not very bright. This ruined your career prospects and could have been based on an incorrect perception. An accurate picture of how you come over to others is vital if you are to develop competent social relationships. So as we interact with our environment we receive powerful messages about how successful we are and how well we measure up to society and group standards and we gain a sense of our own energy, skill and industry.

The evaluative significance of self-concepts is obtained from interpretations of how we think others think of us, from objective evaluations like examinations and sporting triumphs and from the surrounding culture. Many of these evaluations become normative. Dull, unemployed, overweight, immature all have negative connotations, while intelligent, motivated, muscular, dependable and healthy are all positive. By self-observation of where one stands in relation to society's standards and by interpretation of feedback from others such evaluations come to be applied by the individual to themselves. Much of this learning of what oneself is like and how one is evaluated occurs in childhood and adolescence. But the process of developing one's self-concept never ends; it is actively proceeding right through life as the individual discovers new potentials and enters new phases of their life. As Rogers says, the individual is always in a state of becoming.

Our roles as adults are very important elements of our self-image. Roles as parent, spouse, worker, citizen, friend, manager or supervisor all add substance to our self-concept as we gain self-esteem and perceive ourselves in the eyes of others. This is why redundancy, retirement and unemployment can have such devastating effects on a person's self-concept. The lowering of self-esteem following such damaging events reduces the individual's readiness to put their self-esteem further at risk on training courses.

The initial response to unemployment is often one of denial and a feeling that nothing much has happened. The individual tends to see themselves as having the same occupational identity as they had when they were employed and continue describe themselves in these terms. Once it becomes clear that a replacement job will not be quickly found the individual alters their self-concept to accept that they are unemployed. After about nine months the individual adjusts to a domestic and economic routine consistent with accepting long-term unemployment. The loss of confidence that goes with the loss of an occupational identity results in a tendency to withdraw from social contacts. The economic consequences also alter the self-concept as club memberships and other activities are abandoned. The role of the male unemployed becomes more domestic with an increasingly historically feminine element, which can bring sexual identity under attack. After a period of unemployment such a person might lose confidence in their ability to cope with retraining and some might turn down the opportunity to return to learning rather than risk further battering of the self-concept.

While we have seen that most people are motivated intrinsically to seek out intellectual challenge, a person with low self-esteem will, in Maslow's proposal, need to achieve more self-confidence before aiming for personal development and the full realisation of their potential. Such a person will need careful help and support with a program designed to provide measurable success at each stage. The person must come to realise that they are capable and able to succeed. This is where initial behaviourist approaches using extrinsic motivation and reinforcement lead into intrinsic motivation and humanist approaches, when the person is seeking to enhance the self.

## the self-fulfilling prophecy

Positive self-concepts and negative self-concepts are maintained through a feedback system that validates the level of self-esteem almost like a self-fulfilling prophecy. Figure 6.4 illustrates this. The circular system is used because self-concept, self-expectations, expectations from others, actual performance and feedback all interact. If at the outset you have a self-concept that includes seeing yourself as a failure, then your expectations are that you will fail. Your actions and attitudes will tend to make that prediction come true and further validate the original belief. If you say to yourself this is beyond me, I'll never manage it, then the odds are loaded in favour of your failure. You might never even try to succeed. It is important to realise that these beliefs and expectations are subjective and might not be true. But they come to pass simply because they are believed. Much research on self-concept tells us that how a person feels about themselves in fact affects their performance more than their actual ability. This is why teachers must be warm, accepting, genuine and show empathy in order to get the best out of their students, especially adult ones who might have had deleterious experiences in their school days. These teacher characteristics encourage students to see themselves as capable, worthy and accepted.

FIGURE 6.4 HOW THE SELF-CONCEPT PERPETUATES ITSELF

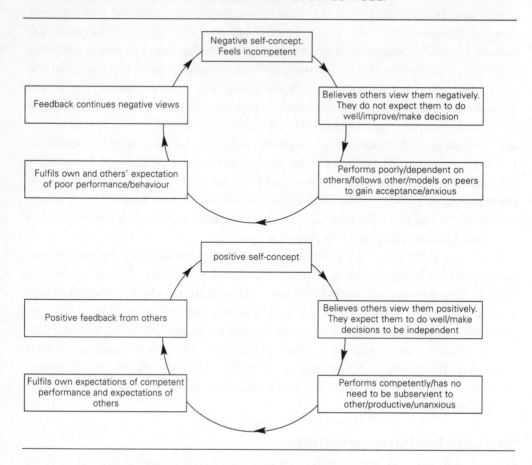

Imagine how a person feels if they are the target of putdowns like, 'Any fool could do that' or 'You are a waste of time'. Their self-concept is lowered tremendously as they believe there must be some truth in the comments. Success brings further success while failure brings further failure. Of course, success can mean a variety of things and can be obtained in many ways. You can feel successful if you gain 50 per cent in a subject you never got more than 33 per cent in before, or if you contributed to a discussion for the first time. We feel good when we are praised, recognised or are successful. This means that praising others increases positive self feelings all round and improves personal relationships. In a context of criticism, personal relationships and morale are destroyed. If feedback is positive we will be willing to develop, mature, reach out and grow without worrying about failure, anxiety or embarrassment. Negative feedback inhibits growth, involvement and performance. Many students have received negative messages at school and this negative self-concept about their competence as a learner impedes willingness to re-enter education activities later on.

A well known, true account of the effects of positive feedback on the self-concept is recounted by Guthrie (1938). He had a dull, unattractive female student in one of his classes. As a joke, some of the male students in the class started to treat her as though she was tremendously popular and attractive. Within a year, she developed an easy manner, confidence and popularity, which increased the positive reinforcing reactions from others.

The self-concept is involved in a self-fulfilling prophecy, whereby if a person is made to feel they will not succeed then it is likely they will give up but if they are given the impression by others that they can succeed then they probably will. So a large part of what we do or think is conditioned by the impressions of ourselves we gain subjectively from our interactions with others.

## affirmations

We can easily talk *ourselves* into a negative self-concept with negative internal feedback. But if we can think ourselves into negative beliefs about our competencies and qualities we can equally talk ourselves into positive beliefs. This self-talk or personal affirmation is easy to establish. To start preparing positive affirmations for yourself, write out simple sentences on small cards that you can keep in your pocket. Start them with 'I', be positive and write them in the present, indicating achievement. For example:

- I am a valuable, worthy and capable person.
- I have pride in my performance.
- I am warm and friendly towards all I have contact with.
- I do my job better than most.

Read the affirmations several times each day, particularly when you wake up and just before going to sleep. As you read the affirmations try to visualise yourself experiencing the change you want or the end result you desire. You are displacing negative images with positive images of how you want to feel and act. Very soon these behaviours become part of you as you move easily and naturally to your new performance standards.

Team affirmations can also be written out, such as 'We produce tremendous results from our teamwork' and 'We take great pride in our achievements'.

## self-concept and learning

Of the influences on self-development, education stands out. Self-concept and education performance are strongly linked. The evidence so far (Burns, 1991) shows that educational performance and level of self-concept are closely related with ample evidence of consistent correlations between +0.3 and +0.4. The strongest link is at the low end of performance, so low attainment and low self-regard are more strongly connected than high performance and high self-concept.

Educational institutions are arenas in which learners are traditionally compelled to compete and, in doing so, are forced to reveal personal adequacies and inadequacies in public contests, frequently on unequal terms with others, in events (subjects and exams) not of their own choosing and judged against imposed external standards. Given the heavy emphasis on competition and the pressure brought to bear by teachers, parents and employers on students at all ages to achieve success it is not surprising that people employ academic attainment as a major index of self-worth. A successful student comes to feel competent and significant; a failing student comes to feel incompetent and inferior. There has always been an emphasis on catching learners out in education. With its ubiquity of assessment and competition and the cultural stress on success, it is no wonder that education is a massive influence on self-esteem.

Many research studies attest to the fact that negative self-esteem, which involves the view that the person is incompetent and cannot succeed in school, tends to produce underachievement and in some cases withdrawal from academic activity. What is equally certain is that a person who possess positive self-concepts that include an image of competency in education will produce results in line with their self-perceptions. Most people are relatively good at something but the narrowness of the curriculum at all levels destines many to be relative failures from their own point of view. Freire, in increasing literacy among adults in Brazil, showed how ineffective it was to try to teach reading skills to those who saw little worth in themselves. It was only after a program of self-awareness building that the illiterates saw themselves as capable and began to believe that they could achieve reading skills.

The need for the development of coping skills, flexibility, resourcefulness, human relationship skills and creativity in order to cope with escalating change points to the importance of a positive self-concept for it is this that enables the person to manifest and develop these personal skills. Only a person who is positive about themselves can be positive to others and feel capable of achieving and perceive and grasp opportunities.

Educational institutions have often been like factories, rather than like homes and families. They mass-produce a uniform student product acceptable to the consumer (State, business and industry, taxpayer). Students are obedient, busy with schedules based on arbitrary time intervals and work emphasising skill determined as necessary and assessed by standardised techniques and competency levels. It is reminiscent of Taylorism. Dehumanisation and psychological failure are the built-in features of this model. On the other hand, the family model involves mutual support, concern, warmth, positive expectations and socio-emotional growth as well as cognitive growth. No wonder adults are hesitant about re-entering educational establishments or undertaking further learning activities.

## self-concept and the adult learner

The adult conceives of themselves as an adult and therefore to treat them like a child, imposing education on them in a formal manner, would cause resentment as it is incongruent with their self-concepts. An adult requires consideration of their learning needs, consideration of their experiences, involvement in planning their future development and a learning climate that encourages involvement.

Some adults no longer hold a self-concept of themselves as capable of learning. Even society might view the adult as a non-learner. This failure to internalise the learner role is a major restraint in the adult's realisation of their learning potential. When an adult believes that learning, education and self-development are possible and part of their life they will be much more likely to involve themselves. The potential is there but it requires personal and societal support and expectations to bring it to fruition.

An adult learner who has high self-esteem and a positive conception of themselves is less likely to feel threatened by new learning experiences. However, one who has neither of these will be unnerved by the situation. Clearly, this could be the result of experiences in early school education and it is a sad reflection on school education that it turns people off education involvement later in life. Adult educators must create the conditions Rogers proposed that facilitate the raising of self-esteem and the removal of anxiety (unconditional acceptance, empathy and genuineness) so that adult learners gain the necessary confidence and go on to profit from an educational experience.

Many adults have low self-esteem as learners. They do not realise how much they actually know and what skills they possess, but once they do they experience a great surge of confidence. When workers are underused and no-one takes notice of what they say or do, they get frustrated and less eager to give of their best. If they live with a sense of being undervalued they will come to believe that they are not valuable. People are often concerned with their weaknesses, the things they think they cannot do, rather than with their strengths. Having accomplished something already is the best motivation for taking on something else.

Argyris has demonstrated that a lack of competence feelings leads to lower levels of self–esteem, which in turn lead to even lower job performance and poor health. Kornhauser's (1965) work on the relation between mental health and working conditions indicates that jobs that do not allow the individual to use their own resources tend to bring about passivity and diminished health. Many studies show that self-esteem, well-being and health are strongly related, so that when negative conceptions about human ability and performance lead to detailed supervision and control, the worker emerges as passive, lacking initiative and of low self-esteem and diminished health, in other words a self-fulfilling prophecy.

## teacher self-concept

Much research at all levels of education reveals consistently that effective teachers and trainers as judged by learners:

- are flexible
- are empathic and sensitive to the needs of the learner
- have an appreciative reinforcing attitude
- personalise their teaching

- have a warm, easy, informal, conversational style
- are emotionally well adjusted.

These are major elements of a positive self-concept. These teachers are not afraid of close personal contact or of exposing their knowledge and skills. Self-concept appears to influence teaching style. Those with poor self-concepts tend to avoid active contact and espouse more didactic approaches that impose information. A progressive approach, and the more intense personal relationships that go with it, is threatening to those with low self-esteem. A teacher with positive self-concepts has no need to defend; the individualised context offers no threat. This suggests that to change the method of teaching for some teachers to a more learner-centred approach could be very threatening and such teachers would thwart the attempt. Thus a move towards andragogy (Chapter 7) needs teachers who have positive self-concepts, given the more humanist approach of that methodology. Different levels of self-attitudes function like lenses limiting the perspectives from which the teacher's role is viewed. The teacher with a low evaluation of themselves finds it difficult to undertake another type of role. An informal style is more demanding, both intellectually and emotionally, exposing personal inadequacy and insecurity. A learner-centred approach places more demands on the teacher, who has to be a better type of person in a large variety of ways. Burns (1979) has shown that teachers who prefer student-centred teaching approaches possess more positive feelings about themselves and have more positive attitudes to others. Able to accept themselves, they are able to relate naturally to others.

Hence more needs to be done to prepare teachers who will be sensitive to others and who view teaching as a human process involving human relationships and human meaning. The teacher/trainer must be an inviter, sending invitations through verbal and non-verbal means to students to see themselves as able, valuable and acceptable. Good teachers enable students to see themselves in as positive a way as possible, enabling them to grow and reach their potential. A disinvitation is an interaction that tells students they are incapable, worthless and not acceptable. This is the self-fulfilling prophecy that causes students to behave as they believe themselves to be labelled. Positive thoughts and creative behaviours are killed off by another person's negative comments, physical gestures or other negative behaviour. This is why Rogers emphasises unconditional regard, acceptance, warmth, genuineness and empathy as essential characteristics of good therapists and teachers since these characteristics are most likely to encourage others to perceive themselves as worthy, capable and acceptable.

In order to ensure the development or maintenance in students of a positive self-concept teachers and trainers should:
- provide opportunities for success and ensure that demands made of and tasks given a learner are commensurate with their potential so that a successful outcome is likely

- show interest and unconditional acceptance, for example smile, greet and talk
- never emphasise failings or shortcomings but concentrate on positive aspects and provide encouragement
- prevent fear of trying through fear of failing
- be pleased with a worthwhile attempt and give credit for trying; praise learners realistically
- teach learners to evaluate themselves realistically.

## locus of control

Another personality characteristic that has impact in the workplace and on willingness to involve learning behaviours that lead to advancement is locus of control. Some people believe that they are masters of their own fate. Such people are termed internals. Others see themselves as pawns in the game of life — what happens to them is due to luck and chance. These people are externals. Individuals who rate high on questionnaires as externals are less satisfied with their jobs, more alienated from the work setting, have higher absenteeism rates and are unwilling to undertake further study. This is because they see themselves as having little control over organisational outcomes that are important for them, so feel disinclined to bother.

Internals are more motivated to achieve and try to take control of their environment. They are more interested in improving their skills and knowledge as they recognise that they can deploy extra skills to their advantage and control their careers to a greater extent. Externals are more compliant and willing to take direction. Internals are therefore more suited to jobs that require initiative and independence of action, which includes most managerial jobs. Externals are better on jobs that require routine and are well structured, where success depends heavily on following the directions of others.

Locus of control is also related to managerial strategy. Internal managers perceive constraints as loose and malleable and turn competitors' challenges into opportunities for innovation. External managers see their environment as having too many rigid boundaries that cannot be crossed. Thus internal managers are proactive, risk-embracing and create an innovative, dynamic environment. Externals have a conservative strategy (Miller *et al.*, 1982).

Spector (1986) summarised the literature and found that internals have a stronger belief in their own competence and that they therefore put in greater effort, are more career-effective, record better job satisfaction and prefer participative approaches in leadership styles of superiors. They are more interested in undertaking training as they expect success and advancement of their careers. They also have lower stress levels and absenteeism rates and less illness.

There is a strong correlation between locus of control and self-concept. Since self-concept can be made more positive by providing positive expectations and enabling the person to succeed, it is likely that these sorts of experiences will also help to modify the behaviour and thinking of those with an external locus towards a more internal locus. In the current period of change and in view of the need to develop and enhance skills and knowledge, the possession of external locus is a constraint. Organisations need to ensure that employees at all levels believe that they can have some input in and effect on what is planned, and that structures and processes are set in place to give most employees an opportunity to be involved in deciding their own futures through deciding the future of the organisation. Greater externality of locus among employees will give organisations staff who are more proactive, innovative and risk-friendly. Locus of control is an important human factor in determining work motivation, productivity and involvement.

## SUMMARY

Individual differences in personality, learning style, motivation and self-concept relate to occupational success and to motivation to be involved in further training and education. Selection for training for new skills should relate to individual differences in personality and learning style; however, assessment is no straight-forward task.

Individual differences in learning and training needs owing to personality and motivational and learning styles must be considered by training and education staff so that each employee can gain from involvement in further learning. A major omission in the whole area of training is considering how systematic, individual differences affect preferences for training methods, and the efficacy and transference of training.

Motivation can generally be divided into that which is extrinsic or imposed from outside, involving reinforcement and the satisfaction of basic needs, and that which originates from inside the person or intrinsic motivation, which is concerned with personal growth needs such as self-esteem, self-actualisation and achievement. It is intrinsic motivation that provides the main drive to seek further knowledge and skills, although initially it might be seeded by extrinsic motivation in the form of, say, better pay and conditions.

Personality traits, particularly extroversion and introversion, are related to work and education performance. The self-concept develops out of subjectively evaluated feedback from the environment. Positive self-concepts provide positive expectations of success, while those with less positive self-attitudes expect to fail. These expectations function as a self-fulfilling prophecy. Teachers, peers and friends therefore have a considerable impact on how an adult learner feels about returning to learning or about how well they are doing. The teacher must never do or say anything that could damage a learner's self-concept of themselves as able to achieve. Freud's defence mechanisms provide a useful way to understand learner behaviour as defences are often used to prevent self-knowledge, avoid further educational experiences and justify a person's attitudes to education in an irrational way.

# part three

## educating the adult

**Adult learning theories** are based on the belief that adults are different from children, particularly when it comes to life experience and the ability to reflect on experience and undertake self-directed learning. Since adults are older, have a larger fund of experience and enjoy greater independence of thought and action than children, it is apparent that replicating school education is not appropriate for adults.

Good adult learning programs must be structured to meet the needs, experiences and preferences of learners. In adapting to the needs of adult learning and lifelong education, teachers, trainers, supervisors and managers have to learn new rules, skills and techniques. While training and teaching are delivery systems, education and learning are the ways in which people acquire, interpret and assimilate information, skills and attitudes. This takes place through daily interaction, learning contexts both formal and informal, planned and fortuitous, and in many cases cannot be planned for.

# chapter 7

# theories of adult education

Want of occupation is not rest.
A mind quite vacant is a mind distressed.
(W. Cowper, *Retirement*, 1782)

'.... education should not cease when one leaves school...Education means the enterprise of supplying conditions which ensure growth or adequacy of life, irrespective of age.'
(John Dewey, 1916, p. 51)

Perspectives on adult learning have changed dramatically over the decades. Adult learning has been viewed as a process of being freed from the oppression of being illiterate, a means of gaining knowledge and skills, a way to satisfy learner needs, and a process of critical self-reflection that can lead to transformation. The phenomenon of adult learning is complex and difficult to capture in any one definition.
(P. Cranton,1994, p. 3)

## ■■■ WHAT IS AN ADULT?

There is no single point in time when a person suddenly and unambiguously becomes an adult in modern industrialised society. The biological definition would argue that adulthood commences when the individual can reproduce. The most common way to define adulthood is by chronological age. Age is quantifiable, easy to apply as a classification, but it does not address such factors as maturity or socialisation practices in subcultures. Legal definitions lay down a variety of age criteria, each of which can provide a different chronological age for such activities as marrying without parental consent, obtaining a driving licence, gaining the right to vote and fighting for one's country in times of war.

This leads to another sort of criterion, that of social roles. A social definition suggests that we become adults when we exercise adult roles and behaviour, such as parent, spouse and worker. A person who is married is an adult, regardless of age and social maturation. Many students drop out of school in order to be regarded as adults and no longer as schoolchildren.

Much contemporary research in developmental psychology is based on the assumption that individuals progress sequentially through defined stages of age-related development, adulthood being one. Major theories, such as those by Piaget on cognitive development, Freud on psychosexual development, Kohlberg on moral development and Erikson on psychosocial development, reveal that adulthood isn't a homogeneous period, but is composed of a sequence of developmental phases that suggest that adult life is not a plateau but full of ups and downs. While there might be predictable changes in childhood, adulthood is much longer and involves a changing panoply of roles, events and circumstances that unfold through the period and that are unpredictable in timing for each adult, creating considerable differentiation between the 25-year-old and the 55-year-old. In addition, individual lives take a unique trajectory. Adults do not attain maturity, sit back and cease to learn, then go into decline as biological ageing obtrudes.

Knowles (1980) suggests that the basis for treating people as adults is that they behave like adults and perceive themselves as adults. Behaving like an adult means behaving in a more mature way. This is cultural expectation, even though the person might not be of a chronological age that defines adulthood in a technical sense. Our expectations of adulthood are revealed when we tell children 'to grow up', or tell adults 'to stop acting childishly'. The adulthood of adults therefore becomes an important defining aspect of education for adults.

In educational terms, the definition of adult comes later rather than sooner. Adult education begins where existing, distinct provision in Technical and Higher Education areas ceases. Some institutions distinguish between 'ordinary' and 'mature' students, using the age of 25 as a yardstick.

This question of defining the adult is posed because methods of teaching adults centre on the presumed potential differences in maturity, experience and needs between pre-adults and adults. The extent to which adult education should be different from the process of educating children is a basic issue in the education and training of adults.

## ■■■ SETTINGS AND FORMS OF EDUCATION FOR ADULTS

Just as definitions of 'adult' are not clear, the same is true of 'adult education'. The idea underlying initial compulsory education provision is that by fairly early in the life span the individual has stored away sufficient knowledge and skill to serve them for the remainder of their life so that education is then complete. This is the petrol tank notion of education, which has dominated education mainly through compulsory formal schooling. We fill up our tank at the only garage before the freeway and away we go on life's journey. Unfortunately, some young people don't get the opportunity to fill their tank completely and leave with it half empty at 16. Others might only get two-star petrol and chug their way through life. Then there are the fortunate ones who power away full throttle on four star, equipped for the entire journey. What we need is to establish a variety of service stations that offer a range of facilities along the full length of the life span.

When you read about providers of adult education, you usually only see the kinds of learning that are attached to specific educational institutions, but learning can happen in many kinds of settings. Several educators have attempted to come up with frameworks to include learning in non-traditional settings. There is some overlap here between the settings and the kinds of learning that take place in them. The framework for legitimate sources of adult learning ranges from having external direction to self-direction. It is useful to think of adult education and training being provided under four broad headings:

1. *Formal learning.* Educational institutions that teach adults alongside younger students, such as universities, and a range of post-school colleges mainly in the technical and business fields. Sequences of learning are organised, goal-directed and certified by a diploma or degree that has currency in the public educational system.

2. *Formal learning.* Educational institutions and training organisations set up primarily for adults, including community education, workplace skill learning, university extra-mural/extension/continuing education units and entrepreneurial training companies. Organised and often sequenced, but more commonly one off. Might have some currency and creditworthiness.

3. *Non-formal learning.* Some community education plus other non-educational organisations, which teach adults as a by-product of their main activity such as workplace learning in industrial and business companies, trade unions, churches and the armed services. Sequences of learning that are organised and goal-directed for specified ends but might not be certified with formal education credentials, e.g. health and safety training; community action projects.

4. *Informal learning.* Independent adult learning conducted by individuals interested in particular topics using resources to hand such as the Internet, libraries, museums and bookshops. Ranges from serendipitous learning, resulting from daily experience, to self-directed individual intrinsically-motivated learning.

Merriam and Caffarella (1999) emphasise the role of non-formal settings for community-based learning and indigenous learning. Community-based learning can take many different forms: citizens of a town gathering to overcome an issue in their community, cooperative extension programs, literacy and job skills programs. According to Merriam and Caffarella, 'A common thread to all of these programs is their focus on social action and change for the betterment of some part of the community' (p. 30). This was touched on earlier in Chapter 3 as a valid element of the learning organisation. Indigenous learning refers to processes and structures people within particular societies have used to learn about their culture throughout their history. This kind of learning is often connected to oral traditions and indigenous arts as in Aboriginal society and can be used in other non-formal learning programs to enhance learning.

Thus the scope of lifelong education possibilities and provision for adults is very wide but somewhat ill-defined, uncoordinated and lacking in integration in many respects.

Additionally, a variety of terms and concepts has emerged to describe the education and training offerings available to those seeking or required to expand their knowledge, develop skills or satisfy interests during their working lives. However, each carries different connotations. Even the term 'education' has an overly scholarly ring to it; while 'leisure activities' carries flavours of idleness; 'recreation' has connotations of strenuous activity; and 'cultural activity' is too pious. All these terms have imbued adult education with specific implications of a middle-class leisure-time pursuit motivated by personal desire. It has overtones of basket weaving, of non-vocational, liberal courses not leading to any qualification. Even more academic vocationally related studies are often limited to persons who are already reasonably well qualified and are aware of the need to continually advance their knowledge and skills. Industrial training required of workers has not been seen as education owing to its very specific intent and narrow expediency. Therefore, viewed as mainly a form of self-indulgence, it is hardly surprising that adult education has been regarded as a marginal activity catered for by university extramural and local authority evening classes, and that the term adult education no longer seems appropriate. Lifelong learning with its huge range of contexts, conditions, purposes and 'curricula' is a far more appropriate concept for the twenty-first century as changing environments require all of us to learn continually for integrated work, social, community and personal reasons.

It has also become impossible to define adult education in terms of a curriculum or what is taught as everything is taught. Adult education is not just education for people who happen to be adults, since much of the content is also taught to other age groups. So there appears to be no unique content or purpose, apart from the concept of lifelong learning. Its only uniqueness might lie in the teaching approaches advocated as appropriate for adults, yet even here the methodology is perhaps no more than a progressive teaching methodology that would be equally appropriate at school level (see below *Pedagogy and Andragogy*).

As lifelong education becomes more necessary, given changing technology and the restructured economic base to industry and business, a variety of concepts that arose in the post-Second World War era also fail to encapsulate the concept of education for adults in the workplace. These labels are important as they signify particular emphases in a field that is as much a movement as a service. Some of these are reviewed below.

## continuing education

This implies that the learner is continuing to pursue education beyond the point where they left formal education, thus promoting the concept of education through the life span. Continuing education is often taken as synonymous with lifelong or life-span education and implies all the learning opportunities that can be taken after full-time, compulsory education has ceased. It can be full or part time; vocational or general; it includes in-service, upgrading and updating education; and it might include occupational training or personal development. It can be viewed as further development of human abilities after entrance into employment or voluntary activities. Continuing education is a very acceptable term in many quarters as it is politically neutral, makes no criticism of initial education, nor implies any radical approach to education.

Continuing education claims education needs to be lifelong because life is long, and the issues that challenge us continue to change in complex and bewildering ways. Education in its most imaginative sense is the provision of life-enhancing opportunities. We do not conceive of health services as having a compulsory final medical at age 16, so why should we of education?

Much continuing education is actually not so much continuing as compensating; it is not building on what went before but, for many, making up for what was missed or not achieved in the compulsory years of education.

## critical education

Some writers believe that adult education should be viewed in the context of critical education, that is recognising the potential of adults to influence the direction of society (e.g. see Freire below). Viewed from a critical perspective, education in contemporary Western cultures simply promotes widespread acceptance and perpetuation of the prevailing traditional behaviours and attitudes. One of these, of course, is the emphasis on the economic drive behind education and an instrumental view of education.

Adult education as critical education should enable workers to reconceptualise work with its social and technical dimensions as well as the usual economic one. It should also enable learners to participate through their work in the transformation of society into a more fair and humane social arrangement. Adult education as critical education should enable workers to become aware of where social power and control lie hidden, of discrimination by age, sex and ethnicity, to be able to connect work to a variety of issues such as family and environment, and to consider the impact of work on the organisation of society.

## community education

Community education is often used in a generic sense to denote any kind of educational program or activity designed to serve people in the community at any age. It should not be confused with community development, which is action-oriented community problem solving. Yet its most active proponents have offered it in this latter sense. Freire is the best-known exponent of this view and claims education can never be neutral. He saw community education as education for action and development within the community as a response to social inequality, based on his experience of the context of poverty and illiteracy in South America. However, these ideas are relevant in all parts of the world. He believed that education should make people aware of their social condition and remove their false consciousness. This demythologising would then lead people to create a better society. Community education therefore involves local participation within a humanist framework to enable people to enrich their lives and the quality of human relationships and social living in their neighbourhood, as well as a more general set of education activities to meet public needs.

## lifelong education

This is an ideal adopted by UNESCO and OECD (see Chapter 2). Lifelong education is often used as a reconceptualisation of the whole education process of which education during the adult period is but one essential part. The term lifelong education is perhaps the best inclusive umbrella term we have, as the other terms, above all, have particular and more specific connotations. It refers to all educational or training processes undertaken by adults, whether general or vocational, whether located in the workplace, in an educational institution, by distance education or in a community setting, and whether formal or informal. This term also implies that education is not completed at any stage of the life span and can be part or full time in presentation. Lifelong education is education for life.

As the major part of lifelong learning, adult education must acknowledge that the adult should be encouraged to become engaged as an active learning agent in their own development. Teachers and trainers must transform themselves into facilitators, enabling, encouraging, guiding, coaching and mentoring aspiring learners. In adult education the learner is sovereign, not the teacher.

Lifelong education in the adult years must enable adults to realise what they know and can do, and how this proficiency can be used to advance their own development and further learning. This is often what does not happen. In formal institutions they are treated like adolescents and it is clear that in many respects education is an adolescent society where responsibility is withheld and where learners must fit into the structure. Adults approach formal settings with diffidence, low confidence and feelings of inferiority. They are out of their comfort zone. They doubt they really can study or possess valuable knowledge. We have a way to go to make educational institutions fit for adult society.

**TABLE 7.1** THE FIVE MAJOR PHILOSOPHIES OF ADULT EDUCATION

| ADULT EDUCATION | | | | | |
|---|---|---|---|---|---|
| | LIBERAL (CLASSICAL, TRAD.) | BEHAVIOURIST | PROGRESSIVE | HUMANIST | RADICAL |
| PURPOSE | To develop intellectual powers of the mind; to make a person literate in the broadest sense: intellectually, morally and spiritually. | To bring about behavioural change by deliberate manipulation of environmental contingencies. | To transmit culture and societal structure to promote social change; to give learners practical knowledge and problem-solving skills, to reform society. | To develop people open to change and continued learning; to enhance personal growth and development; to facilitate self-actualisation; to reform society. | To bring about fundamental, social, political and economic change in society through education; to change culture and its structure. |
| LEARNER | A cultured person, always seeking knowledge rather than just information; conceptual; theoretical understanding. | Learner takes an active role in learning, practising new behaviour and receiving feedback; strong environmental influence. | Individual needs, interests, and experiences are key elements in learning; people have unlimited potential to be developed through education. | Learner is highly motivated and self-directed; assumes responsibility for learning and self-development. | Equality with teacher in learning process; personal autonomy; people create history and culture by combining reflection with action. |
| TEACHER | The 'expert'; transmitter of knowledge; authoritative; clearly directs learning process. | Manager, controller; predicts and directs learning outcomes; designs learning environment that elicits desired behaviour. | Organiser; guides learning through experiences that are educative; stimulates, instigates, evaluates learning process | Facilitator, helper, partner; promotes, but does not direct, learning; sets mood for learning; acts as a flexible resource for learners. | Provocateur; suggests but does not determine direction for learning; equality between teacher and learner. |
| METHODS | Lecture; study groups; contemplation; critical reading and discussion. | Programmed instruction; contract learning; teaching machines; computer-assisted instruction; practice and reinforcement. | Problem-solving; scientific method; activity method; experimental method; project method; inductive method. | Experiential; group tasks; group discussion; team teaching; self-directed learning; self-paced learning; discovery method. | Dialogue; problem-posing; maximum interaction; discussion groups. |
| SOURCE OF AUTHOURITY | Western beliefs | The environment | Situations that learner finds themselves in; culture | The self/learner | Socio-economic and socio-political imbalances |

| | | | | | |
|---|---|---|---|---|---|
| **PEOPLE/PRACTICE** | Socrates, Plato, Aristotle, Aquinas, Adler, | Skinner, Thorndike, Watson, Tyler, competency-based education and training; behaviour modification programs | Spencer, Pestalozzi, Dewey, Lindeman, citizenship education; community schools; cooperative extension schools; schools without walls. | Erasmus, Rousseau, Rogers, Maslow, Knowles, May, Tough, encounter groups; group dynamics; self-directed learning projects; human relations training. | Holt, Reich, Neill, Freire; Freedom Schools; Summerhill, Freire's literacy training; free schools. |
| **TIME FRAME** | Oldest philosophy of education in West. Roots in the Classical Period of ancient Greece. | Founded by John B. Watson in 1920s. Extended by Skinner. | Origins can be traced to 16th C. Europe. Based on empiricism and pragmatism. Began as a serious movement in early 1900s with Dewey. | Roots go back to classical China, Greece, and Rome, but became a movement in 1950s–60s through work by Maslow and Rogers. | Origins are found in the 18th C. anarchist tradition, Marxist thought, liberation theology. Left. Modern movement began in early 1960s in Brazil with Freire. |

Lifelong learning in part cannot be separated in time or place from work. Human resources are for many organisations the most valuable resource they possess — an investment rather than a variable cost. Learning is part of work and production. It is now no longer simply a matter of retraining workers, but a process that draws everyone into learning what changes are needed in the firm as a whole, learning how to apply new skills, learning how to continue learning and, perhaps of most importance since all the rest are based on it, learning how to develop as a person. Education is participation in life, not preparation for life.

Workplace education must also be directed in part towards community competence. A competent community is one in which the various parts are able to collaborate effectively. The essential criteria of community are commitment, communication, articulateness, self–other awareness, participation, conflict containment, facilitative interaction and decision making. The workplace is a minisociety.

# ■■■ PHILOSOPHIES OF ADULT EDUCATION

There are numerous philosophies that underlie approaches to adult education. These feed into five major strands: liberal, behaviourist, progressive, humanist and radical. Rather than expound on each at length, it seems preferable to summarise them in tabular form. Table 7.1 opposite is not exhaustive, but it gives a basis for comparing, contrasting and understanding these theorists' ideas.

# ■■■ PEDAGOGY AND ANDRAGOGY

Because of the differences in capabilities, experiences and knowledge, different educational approaches have been promoted for teaching children and adults. Pedagogy with its content-based approach is the core of school education. Andragogy with its process-based approach is presumed to be more appropriate for adults.

## pedagogy

Pedagogy means the art and science of teaching children and is based on assumptions that evolved from teaching boys in monastic schools in Europe in medieval times. Pedagogy assigns full responsibility to the teacher or education authorities to decide what is to be learnt, how it will be learnt and when it will be learnt. The learner is a passive recipient and a dependent personality. The learner has to adjust themselves to an established curriculum and teaching method. As self-direction and self-responsibility are not encouraged, the growing maturity of young people creates a gap between the need and ability to be self-directing and the opportunity to do so. Hence the tension, resentment and even rebellion that is common in secondary schools today. The child's experience is not counted of worth. Learners only learn what is in the syllabus or what they must pass. Learning experiences are organised round the logic of the artificial subject divisions. Motivation is engendered by marks, assessment, parental pressure and teacher approval. As a result, many students leave school having lost interest in learning, disillusioned later in adulthood about the value and enjoyment of returning to learning.

Much of child education is based on behaviourist operant and classical learning approaches. Specific facts and skills litter the curriculum. The school day is filled with assessment, nagging, rejection, criticism, competition, unsuitable standards and punishment, all of which destroy most children's self-esteem, produce negative self-concepts and close off motivation for future growth, since only a few can be at the top and gain positive strokes of reinforcement. There is a strong preoccupation with the correct answer and right answers come only from authority figures. The pupil gets the idea they have no business thinking, and no entitlement to an opinion. An autocratic atmosphere produces conformity, dependence on authority and deceitful behaviour such as deviance and avoidance. Schools are organised to produce standardised individuals in a mechanised process of teaching. CBT follows this pedagogical approach. The failure of conventional pedagogy is expressed by those who say 'I taught them that but they didn't learn it'. This is equivalent to and as nonsensical as a salesman saying 'I sold them that but they didn't buy it'.

Humanist goals of self-fulfilment and self-actualisation are impossible in this context. These goals are possible only where individuality is an asset, where belonging and acceptance are paramount, where there are opportunities to explore and gain self-understanding, where there is trust, dignity and security and where self-confidence, self-reliance, originality, enterprise and independence are encouraged. It is only in this sort of therapeutic learning milieu that a person is open to experience and therefore capable of maximal utilisation of their potentialities and environmental opportunities for self-development, learning how to learn and developing the curiosity, enjoyment and intrinsic satisfaction from learning that will draw them back again and again to lifelong learning.

Differences, if any, between adult learners and young people are extremely relevant to designing and delivering learning activities. If adults do learn and behave differently from traditional school and college students then this affects critical program decisions. Thus the pedagogical model with its teacher-centred, information-based authoritative approach has been regarded as inappropriate for adults. Education and training for skill as well as personal development in the context of a learning organisation or learning community must adopt a more appropriate client-centred emphasis with adults.

## andragogy

There is nothing inherent in the concept of education that links it specifically to childhood and adolescence. But the fact that it is so linked has led adult educators to define the nature of their enterprise in different terms. Some educationalists believe that teaching adults is a unique arena of professional activity, meriting specialised approaches and training so that a theory of andragogy has been developed (Knowles, 1984).

Andragogy is the science of teaching adults. The term was originally formulated by a German, Kapp, in 1833 to describe elements of Plato's education method. Andragogy, coined from two Greek words, means 'man leading', whereas pedagogy means 'child leading'. Andragogy continued to be used in Europe but only came into vogue in the USA when Tough (1968), Houle (1980) and Knowles (1978), influenced by the writings of John Dewey, promoted it. Many educationalists have tried to adapt child learning to adult learning. Ranks of desks in a typical classroom configuration with all students at the same point in an externally derived syllabus, receiving teacher-distilled wisdom, is not appropriate for most adults returning to learning. In particular, the child is a dependent personality and has had limited experience of life. The dependency is reinforced as decisions are made on the child's behalf in the home, school and playground until with increasing age the adolescent starts to make decisions and commence directing their own life. By adulthood, the person is self-directing. This is the concept that lies at the heart of andragogy, as expounded by Knowles. The following account of andragogy is based on Knowles' writings.

Knowles claimed (1978) that there are three main assumptions that differentiate andragogy from pedagogy. These are:

1. A focus on the maturing self-concept. 'As a person grows and matures his self-concept moves from one of total dependency to one of increasing self-directedness.' (1978, p. 55). Thus a teacher-imposed traditional approach creates resentment as the adult feels their adulthood is being questioned or challenged at a fundamental level.

2. A focus on experience. Mature persons have a store of experience which is a rich resource for learning. Adult experience increasingly constitutes who or what the adult is. Teaching should tap adult experience and involve them in analysing their own experience.

3. Adults are more likely to be motivated or ready to learn if they perceive a learning need. Adults actually want to learn in an area that is a problem for them or which they regard as relevant. Therefore, the curriculum should aim at immediate rather than deferred application and be problem- rather than subject-centred. 'The adult comes into the educational activity largely because he is experiencing some inadequacy in coping with current life problems. He wants to apply tomorrow what he learns today.' (1978, p. 58). Adult orientation towards learning is problem-centred rather than subject-centred.

From these assumptions Knowles draws some implications. The planning and evaluation of courses should be a joint act between teachers and students in a climate of mutual respect. There should be minimal emphasis on authority, formality and competition. The curriculum should be structured around problems and sequenced according to the logic of the learner not that of the subject matter. Experiential methods of teaching should predominate. Andragogy is a process model of teaching whereas pedagogy is a content model.

Thus andragogy is based on the belief that the deepest need an adult has is to be treated as an adult, as a self-directing person. Adult education must be student-centred, experience-based, problem-oriented and collaborative — very much in the spirit of the humanist approach to learning and education. It is not student-centred in the simple sense of using methods that allow the student considerable control over their learning but in the profound sense that the whole of the educational activity turns on the student. Unfortunately, andragogy has often been cited as the ways adults learn, but the key assumptions apply equally well to children, particularly as we enter the information age with its capacity to provide unique learning and significant experiences for those whose curiosity and motivation impel them through cyberspace.

Training in work-related activities has often been given by people who have not really learnt how to teach people to learn. In formal institutions of learning, adults are usually placed in classes with 18- and 19-year-olds. Courses of study are watertight compartments, denying the reality of inter- and intradisciplinary learning.

Teachers function according to a right/wrong approach rather than a maybe one. Successful learning attracts marks and vocational certificates rather than self-confidence in being able to apply knowledge as part of living. That is why adults find a return to formal learning in institutions so formidable and discouraging. They must fit in with the institution. No wonder they expect to fail, as indeed many did at school. Some adults protect themselves against more education by demonstrating an indifference to learning. This is why recognition and ownership are so important as organising principles for teachers working with adults. What institutions must do is rework their mission, objectives and methods. Institutions need to discharge their responsibility to increase knowledge, disseminate knowledge and act as the guardians of knowledge — a validating role that ensures quality while, at the same time, recognising that there are so many ways of learning open to individuals and that they do not have a monopoly on knowledge and learning.

A class of children are at approximately the same age, with the same characteristics and levels of knowledge. A group of adults varies tremendously not only in age but also in range of experience, knowledge and reasons for study. Adults' abilities to learn might depend as much on lifestyle, social roles, motivation, interest, attitudes and their teachers' communication and relationship skills as on their ability to learn. Adult education is not preparatory, as with children, but lifelong — education has a mission of helping adults realise their potential and better carry out the roles and duties associated with work, home, recreation and citizenship.

Adults can judge the value of a learning activity and its relevance to their own lives. The teacher of an adult functions best as a resource person who views the learning situation as a cooperative endeavour. That is not to say that the learner possesses knowledge equal to that of the teacher but that the teacher respects and values the experiences of the adult student and uses them as a basis to advance the learning process.

By 1984 Knowles had altered his earlier position on the distinction between pedagogy and andragogy. The child-adult dichotomy became less marked. He even added a fifth assumption: as a person matures the motivation to learn is internal (1984, p. 12). What we describe as adult learning is not of a different kind or order from child learning. Indeed our main point is that humans must be seen as a whole, in lifelong development. The same principles of learning and education will apply to all stages in life. The differences with pedagogy are not really to do with age but with educational philosophy and aims. Children are no less motivated to learn than adults about things that are relevant to them. Children also have experiences that can be used as a resource for education. Andragogy is, in fact, similar to progressive movements in child education (such as Rousseau, Pestalozzi and Freobel), which would see the learner increasingly direct their own learning with the teacher as a resource, formulating education experience around problems rather than set pieces of curriculum that have to be taught. Perhaps Knowles overemphasised his concept of andragogy because adult education had up to then been neglected.

# ■■■ KNOWLES' ANDRAGOGICAL MODEL

Adults need to know why they are required to learn something before being moti-vated to learn it. Adults will invest considerable energy in probing the benefits of studying a topic and then do it wholeheartedly if it will be of benefit. While chil-dren can be persuaded to engage in learning material that apparently lacks relevance to their present lives, adults need to see the relevance and relatively immediate utility of what they are doing. *Teachers and trainers must make a case for the value of the learning for improving the effectiveness of the learner's performance and/or the quality of their lives.* Potent tools are real or simulated exercises from which the learners discover for themselves the gaps between where they are now and where they wish to be.

Adults have a self-concept of being responsible for their own decisions and for their own lives. Therefore they need to be seen by others and treated by others as capable of self-direction. They resent and resist imposition. When they walk into any activity labelled 'education' or 'training', their conditioning from previous school experiences makes them unmotivated and resentful learners or leads them to avoid such contexts. The self-concept of 'I failed before therefore I will fail again', 'I will look a fool', 'I am incompetent' tends to stop adults approaching any learning situation positively. *Therefore, the role of the teacher is to engage in mutual enquiry rather than transmit knowledge and evaluate their conformity to it.*

Adults come into education activities with a greater volume and a different quality of experiences from schoolchildren. This has several consequences. First, in any group of adult learners there will be a greater range of individual differences than among a school group. This means more emphasis must be placed on individualised learning strategies. Second, adults carry within themselves a huge reservoir of learning resources, hence experiential techniques, group discussion, simulation exercises, case methods, problem-solving exercises and peer-helping activities are eminently appropri-ate. Of course, experience is not always positive. Experience can cause the development of biases and habits that close minds to fresh ideas and alternatives. Thus values clar-ification and sensitivity training are required. Another factor is that adults derive their self-concepts mainly from their experiences. So if their experiences are devalued their identity suffers diminution and rejection. To reject adult experiences is to reject the adult. *Therefore a core methodology for adult education is the analysis of experience.* Adults have functioned for much of their lives in an expanded world of work, home and leisure, with formal and informal social relationships all giving them a comprehensive fund of personal meanings, values and skills. It is easy to understand why adults create and define their view of the world in very different terms from children. But because of the range of experiences and varying rates of development adults are more heterogeneous than children and more sensitivity is required by the teacher to locate each person's particular experiential position and make the learning and problem solving relevant.

In contrast with subject-centred learning in childhood, adults are task/problem-centred in their approach, particularly to problems they face in everyday life at work, home and leisure. Young people think of education as the accumulation of knowledge for use in the future; adults tend to conceive of learning as a way to be more effective today. Their orientation to learning is life-centred, *therefore the appropriate unit for organising adult learning are life situations, not subjects.* They are motivated to learn as they experience needs and interests that learning will satisfy. Therefore these are the appropriate starting points for organising adult learning activities.

> Adult education is a process by which the adult learns to become aware of and evaluate their experience. They cannot do this by studying subjects in the hope that one day this information might be of some use to them. An adult actually begins by paying attention to situations in which they find themselves. Facts and information are not accumulated, but used to solve problems.

FIGURE 7.1 SUMMARY OF KNOWLES' ANDRAGOGICAL ASSUMPTIONS

### CONCEPT OF THE LEARNER

During the process of maturation, we move from dependency to increasing self-directedness, but the rate at which and the dimensions in which this happens differ from individual to individual. Teachers have a responsibility to encourage and nurture this progression. Adults have a deep psychological need to be generally self-directing, but they might be dependent in certain temporary situations.

### ROLE OF THE LEARNER'S EXPERIENCE

As people grow and develop they accumulate a reservoir of experience that becomes an increasingly rich resource for learning for themselves and for others. Furthermore, people attach more meaning to learning they gain from experience than to that they acquire passively. Accordingly, the primary techniques in education are experiential ones — laboratory experiments, discussion, problem-solving cases, field experiences, etc.

### READINESS TO LEARN

People become ready to learn something when they experience a need to learn it in order to cope more satisfyingly with real-life tasks and problems. The educator has a responsibility to create conditions and provide tools and procedures for helping learners discover their 'needs to know'. Learning programs should be organised around life-application categories and sequenced according to learners' readiness to learn.

### ORIENTATION TO LEARNING

Learners see education as a process of developing increased competence to achieve full potential in life. They want to be able to apply whatever knowledge and skill they gain today to living more effectively tomorrow. Accordingly, learning experiences should be organised around competency-development categories. People are performance-centred in their orientation to learning.

### MOTIVATION TO LEARN

As a person matures the motivation to learn becomes internal or intrinsic.

Adult motivation seems to be based on intrinsic factors such as quality of life, self-esteem and job satisfaction. Adults seem motivated to keep growing and developing, but this can be blocked by barriers such as a negative self-concept as a student, time constraints and programs that violate principles of adult education. Adult readiness to learn and teachable moments peak at those points where a learning opportunity is coordinated with recognition of a need to know. No questions are stupid; all questions are opportunities for learning. Individual differences increase with age, *therefore adult education must make optimal provision for differences in style, time, place and pace of learning*.

> Andragogy suggests a teacher role that is more responsive and less directive. The model encourages high levels of self-directed learning, with the adult student having input in content, methodology, assessment techniques and even program design.

## criticism of Knowles' concept of andragogy

Knowles conception of andragogy is an attempt to build a comprehensive theory or model of adult education anchored in the characteristics of adult learners (Merriam & Caffarella, 1991, p. 249). It might be better to use such characteristics in a more limited way to offer a framework for thinking about *what* and *how* adults learn. Such approaches might be contrasted with those that focus on changes in consciousness (e.g. Mezirow 1983, 1990; or Freire, 1970 — see below).

Knowles makes extensive use of a model of relationships derived from humanist clinical psychology — and, in particular, the qualities of good facilitation advocated by Carl Rogers (see below). However, Knowles incorporates other elements that owe more to scientific curriculum making and behaviour modification (and are thus somewhat at odds with Rogers). These encourage the learner to identify needs, set objectives, enter learning contracts and so on. In other words, he uses ideas from psychologists working in two quite different and opposing therapeutic traditions (the humanist and behavioural traditions). This means that there is a rather confused human deficit model lurking in the background of his ideas. In terms of Table 7.1, Knowles' version of pedagogy looks more like liberal education transmission; and andragogy, as represented in the chart, like process.

Jarvis (1985) points out that what lies behind these philosophies are competing conceptualisations of education itself. Crucially, these are not directly related to the age or social status of learners. There are various ways of categorising educational thinking and practice — and they are somewhat more complex than Knowles' setting of pedagogy against andragogy.

On the positive side, andragogy has heightened awareness about whether the learning needs of children are really different from those of adults. However, a raft of significant questions has been raised, such as:

- Has Knowles provided us with a theory or
  - a set of guidelines for practice

- assumptions that can be read as descriptions of the adult learner
- prescriptive statements about what the adult learner *should* be like?
- Is andragogy a theory about teaching or learning?
- Is self-actualisation an appropriate or realistic goal?
- Is the ethic of individualism overplayed through a focus on self and ignoring of community?
- Is self-direction as rooted in our constitutional make-up a myth?
- Is self-development a process of change towards higher levels of existence?
- Is learning at adulthood really different from learning during childhood?

There seems to be a failure to set and integrate this range of ideas within a coherent and consistent conceptual framework. As Jarvis (1987b) comments, there is a propensity to list characteristics of a phenomenon without analysing the literature of the area or trying to develop a coherent conceptual system. Undoubtedly, Knowles had a number of important insights, but because they are not tempered by thorough analysis, they can be interpreted and applied in many ways. Focusing on andragogy might obscure real areas of similarity in adult learning with that of younger persons. It is more a description of good practice for all learners than a prescription for one age group.

Scepticism has been voiced, particularly in regard to the assumption that since pedagogy appears to specify a single methodology correct for all young learners, as a corollary, andragogy does so also for adults. Knowles tries to avoid this trap and argues that while *it seems* that pedagogy is for children and andragogy for adults, in fact the latter is more appropriate for *all* learners and at times pedagogy might be appropriate even for an adult. This would be, for example, when entering a new subject area for the first time or to accomplish required skilled performance. The danger is that the teacher and learners then get locked into it, even when there is an opportunity for an andragogical approach. An adult returning to education might not be ready for self-directed learning. They might need to be led gradually into it by reducing the structure bit by bit (a sort of behaviourist shaping, with success increasing confidence) so that the adult does not become confused by too much freedom and too many options initially. Thus the good andragogue will seek movement towards an andragogical approach where possible, making learners feel respected, accepted, raising their self-esteem, giving them some responsibility in choosing methods and resources of learning and involving them in evaluating their learning. A learner might prefer and require different types of learning events, processes and methods at different times, so pedagogy and andragogy are not mutually opposed.

The pedagogy/andragogy division would be more appropriately addressed by using the terms teacher-directed and self-directed rather than focusing simply on the teaching of children versus the teaching of adults.

In summary, adult learners do exhibit some differences from children but these should not be exaggerated. Adult learners are individuals who differ from each other as much as children do. The temptation is to assume that all adult learning should be self-directed. This ignores individual differences in learning, in knowing how to learn, in motivation, in need for support and in type of content or purpose of study. An effective teacher must be able to select appropriate learning experiences and activities in relation to the group, the individual and the content. Teaching is a process based on the uniqueness of a given situation. Figure 7.2 summarises some of the major contrasts between pedagogy and andragogy.

FIGURE 7.2 CONTRASTS BETWEEN PEDAGOGY AND ANDRAGOGY

| | PEDAGOGY | ANDRAGOGY |
|---|---|---|
| DEPENDENCE | Learner is a dependent personality. Teacher therefore determines what, how and when anything is learnt. | Adults are independent. Strive for autonomy and self-direction in learning. |
| RESOURCES FOR LEARNING | Learner has few resources so teacher devises transmission and banking techniques to store knowledge in learner's head. | Adults use own and each others' experience. |
| REASON FOR LEARNING | Learn in order to advance to next stage. | Adults become ready to learn when they experience a need to know or do something to perform more effectively. |
| FOCUS OF LEARNING | Learning is subject-centred, focused on prescribed curriculum and content planned sequences according to the logic of the subject matter. | Adult learning is task- or problem-centred. |
| MOTIVATION | Motivation comes from external sources, usually parents, teachers and a sense of competition. | Motivation stems from internal sources such as the increased self-esteem, self-confidence and recognition that derive from successful performance. These are more powerful motivators than salary increases and promotion. |
| ROLE OF TEACHER | Teacher designs the learning process, imposes the material and is presumed to know best. | Teacher is enabler or facilitator of learning. Establishes climate of mutual respect, collaboration and openness for learners in planning of learning and diagnosing needs. |

# the assumptions explored

With these queries and issues in mind, we can look more critically at the assumptions that Knowles makes about adult learners:

1. *Self-concept.* As a person matures their self-concept moves from one of being a dependent personality toward one of being a self-directed human being.

   According to Knowles, the point at which a person becomes an adult psychologically 'is that point at which he perceives himself to be wholly self-directing. And at that point he also experiences a deep need to be perceived by others as being self-directing' (Knowles, 1983, p. 56). Self-direction becomes the dominant paradigm of what it means to be an adult and is therefore integral to the sort of learning in which adults engage. As Brookfield (1986) points out, there is some confusion as to whether self-direction is meant here by Knowles to be an empirically verifiable indicator of adulthood. He does say explicitly that it is an assumption. However, there are some other immediate problems:

   Both Erikson and Piaget have argued that there are some elements of self-directedness in children's learning (Brookfield, 1986, p. 93). Children are not dependent learners for much of the time, quite the contrary, learning for them is an activity that is natural and spontaneous. It might be that Knowles was using 'self-direction' in a particular way here or needed to ask a further question — 'dependent or independent with respect to what?'

   The concept is culturally bound — it arises out of a particular (humanist) discourse about the 'self', which is largely North American in its expression.

2. *Experience.* As a person matures they accumulate a growing reservoir of experience that becomes an increasing resource for learning.

   The next step is the belief that adults learn more effectively through experiential techniques of education, such as discussion and problem solving. There might be times when experiential learning is not appropriate — such as when substantial amounts of new information are required. We have to ask what is being learnt, before we can make judgments. A second aspect here is whether children's and young people's experiences are any less real or less rich than those of adults. They might not have the accumulation of so many years' experience, but the experiences they have are no less consuming, and still have to be returned to, entertained and made sense of. Does the fact that they have 'less' supposed experience make any significant difference to the process? A reading of Dewey (1933) and the literature on reflection (e.g. Boud *et al.*, 1985) would support the argument that age and amount of experience make no educational difference. If this is correct, then the case for the distinctiveness of adult learning is seriously damaged. Moreover, some adults might have less valid, relevant experience than an older adolescent.

3. *Readiness to learn.* As a person matures their readiness to learn becomes oriented increasingly to the developmental tasks of their social roles.

   As Tennant (1988, pp. 21–22) puts it, 'it is difficult to see how this assumption has any implication at all for the process of learning, let alone how this process should be differentially applied to adults and children'. Children also have to perform social roles.

There are other problems. These appear when Knowles goes on to discuss the implications of the assumption. 'Adult education programs, therefore, should be organised around "life application" categories and sequenced according to learners' readiness to learn' (Knowles, 1980, p. 44). First, these two assumptions can easily lead to a technological interpretation of learning that is highly reductionist, so that it becomes rather instrumental and moves in the direction of competencies.

Second, as Humphries (1988) has suggested, the way Knowles treats social roles — as worker, as mother, as friend and so on — takes as given the legitimacy of existing social relationships. In other words, there is a grave danger of reproducing social inequalities, the very conditions that other adult educators are trying to eradicate through adult and lifelong education.

4. *Orientation to learning.* As a person matures their time perspective changes from one of postponed application of knowledge to immediacy of application, and accordingly their orientation toward learning shifts from one of subject-centredness to one of problem-centredness.

This is not something that Knowles sees as 'natural' but rather as conditioned. It follows from this that if young children were not conditioned to be subject-centred then they would be problem-centred in their approach to learning. This has been very much the concern of progressives such as Dewey. The question here does not relate to age or maturity but to what might make for effective teaching. We should also note here the assumption that adults have a greater wish for immediacy of application. Tennant (1988, p. 22) suggests that a reverse argument can be made for adults being better able to tolerate the postponed application of knowledge.

The focus on competence and on 'problem-centredness' in Assumptions 3 and 4 undervalues the large amount of learning undertaken by adults because of innate fascination. Much of adults' most joyful and personally meaningful learning is undertaken with no specific goal in mind. It is frequently unrelated to life tasks and, instead, represents a means by which adults can define themselves.

5. *Motivation to learn.* As a person matures the motivation to learn is internal (Knowles, 1984, p. 12).

Again, Knowles does not see this as something 'natural' but as conditioned — in particular, through schooling. This assumption sits awkwardly with the view that adults' readiness to learn is the result of the need to perform (externally imposed) social roles and that adults have a problem-centred (utilitarian) approach to learning.

## summary

The search for andragogy might well be pointless. It is an overgeneralised, humanist theory of education that can be applied at any age, based on no research. Knowles tends to ignore the contingencies that impact on the teacher–learner interaction. Individual student characteristics, teacher characteristics and context characteristics all interact to suggest to the experienced teacher ways of operating with a particular class, group or individual. Some adults have an external locus of control and low self-esteem and are far better in a teacher-directed context, certainly until their self-esteem and feelings of competency increase, before embarking on more self-directive endeavours. Some adults need to learn how to cope with independence and it is one of the functions of the educator of adults to lead some of their flock that way. In some subjects, particularly sciences like physics, experience might be of little relevance but it is vitally important in arts and personal development courses. Knowles' theory does not specify aspects of experience that are vital or relevant nor does it generate a learning sequence.

Andragogy can be seen as an idea that gained popularity in at a particular moment — and its popularity probably says more about the ideological times than it does about learning processes. Perhaps its strength lies in the way it forces adult and lifelong educators to re-slant their teaching approach and its humanist thrust towards the recognition of the value of the individual — a direction that is a valuable corrective to the oversold behaviourist man in a machine concept and management by objectives. It is a subjective formulation based on attempts to prevent the perceived limitations of school education, based on the banking concept of knowledge being imposed on adults. Andragogy is therefore a philosophy of education that might provide useful guidelines to a thoughtful teacher of adults.

## ▪▪▪ OTHER ADULT LEARNING THEORISTS

We clarified how people learn in Chapter 4 and highlighted above critical points concerning the concept of andragogy and Knowles' approach. It is appropriate now to consider other major theoretical views on adult learning and see how their views fit in with the previous discussion. The major writers to be considered are Freire, Dewey, Bruner, Rogers and Mezirow. Each has contributed in different ways to the theory of adult learning; all are humanist in orientation, except Bruner who subscribes to the cognitive approach.

### John Dewey

Dewey was one of the first exponents of progressive education and it was his ideas that initially stimulated Knowles. For Dewey the human is born with unlimited potential for growth and development so that education must relate to the whole of life. Dewey recognised that the scientific method should be the major approach in education. That is, the learner needs to start with a problem, develop hypotheses and test them using empirical evidence. Hence problem solving was central to his education methodology. He recognised too that problem solving altered the relationship between teacher and taught so that the teacher facilitates and guides rather than interferes or controls (Dewey, 1933).

Dewey's educational philosophy is organised round a number of key concepts. The major one is experience. He saw the central problem of education as selecting experiences that are fruitful and creative for future experiences and that lead to the need to problem solve. Democracy is another central feature. He believed that democratic social arrangements promote a better quality of human experience that can be more widely enjoyed than life under authoritarianism.

He uses the key concept of continuity to emphasise that every experience takes something from those who have gone before and modifies in some way the quality of those who come after. He considered freedom and experience to be significant in education and maintained that continuity of experience leads to growth and maturity. The teacher's role is to provide the right sort of experience, through which understanding can come. The learner would mature without having a structure of knowledge thrust on them.

> Dewey regards the teacher's role as including:
> - being aware of the capacity, needs and past experience of those under instruction
> - using environment and experiences as a basis for learning
> - taking a guiding and cooperative role
> - ensuring learning experiences are conducive to growth.

Dewey defined curriculum as the study of 'how to have a world'. Education is not what subject we teach or what method to use but how we are to learn from what currently exists in the totality of our environment and bring about potential life enhancement.

Dewey felt that education had a role in social reform and reconstruction. Liberating the learner released potential for improving society and culture. He saw democratic societies as essentially progressive, and aimed at a great variety of mutually shared interests. For Dewey a democratic society is one committed to change. He was also among the first to conceive of lifelong education. All of life becomes the curriculum.

## Jerome Bruner

Bruner has constructed a theory of instruction out of cognitive theory. It is concerned with discovery/self-directed/problem-solving learning. He argues that the will to learn is an intrinsic motivation. It becomes stifled when a pedagogical learning context prevents the operation of spontaneous learning, curiosity, a desire for competence and aspiration.

Discovery has four major benefits for Bruner. It increases intellectual powers, shifts motivation from extrinsic to intrinsic rewards, develops discovery and problem-solving techniques and makes information and concepts more meaningful and therefore more easily remembered and understood.

With discovery, learning becomes a process not a terminal event. Success is measured in the behavioural change of the learner, manifested by the cogency and relevancy of questions they ask, the challenges they pose to the assertions of others, their willingness to suspend judgment when they have insufficient data, their willingness to modify their position when presented with new data and their ability to apply generalisations to novel situations.

## Carl Rogers

Carl Rogers has been the major humanist to expound on humanist learning and teaching.

Rogers focuses on the relationship between the therapist and the client in his psychotherapeutic techniques, and between the teacher and the learner in the education context. He starts from the viewpoint that therapy is a learning process and seeks to apply insights from his technique of therapy to education. This process enabled him to conceptualise student-centred teaching as a parallel to client-centred therapy.

The goal of education is the fully functioning person. This orientation reflects the therapist in Rogers. The distinction between education and therapy is sometimes blurred in his writings. He moves the focus of educational methodology away from the objective intellectual side of man towards the subjective, self-feeling and attitudinal aspect.

He holds that the real challenge of education is to find out what it takes to produce whole communities of learners who maintain their thirst for education without any carrot or stick to motivate them. Education for Rogers must be changed so as to free curiosity, unleash a sense of inquiry, open everything to questioning and exploration and recognise that everything is in a process of change.

Rogers assumes that all persons have a natural inclination to want to learn throughout their lives. But they will really learn and understand only those things that are meaningful to them. The real concern should be with those experiences that make it possible for the student to integrate new information and ideas as part of themselves. Rogers assumes that one should avoid experiences that call for drastic change in one's self-perceptions as such changes can only come about in an emotionally supportive climate when external threats are at a minimum, and the classroom is not necessarily like that. Evaluation too should be student-based so that self-criticism and self-evaluation are primary.

Underlying the whole process of humanist learning is the notion that real learning can be attained only when the learner themselves is involved in the learning process. Learning is not a passive process or one of accumulating bricks of factual knowledge as behaviourist or narrow competency training would suggest. Learning occurs optimally when the student participates responsibly in the learning process and when learning involves 'a continuing openness to experience and incorpora-tion into oneself of the process of change' (Rogers, 1969, p. 163). Rogers claims 'I know that I can't teach anyone anything. I can only provide an environment in which h/she can learn'. He also regards teaching as 'a relatively unimportant and vastly overvalued activity' (1969, p. 103).

Rogers' student-centred approach to education was based on five hypotheses.

1. *We cannot teach another person directly; we can only facilitate his learning.* This stems from his basic phenomenological perspective that each person responds to the environment as they perceive it. Thus in educational terms, there is a shift from what the teacher does to what is happening in the student.

2. *A person learns significantly only those things that he perceives as being involved in the maintenance of or enhancement of the structure of self.* This underlines the importance of making the learning relevant to the learner and calls into question the academic tradition of required courses. It also introduces the self-concept, the picture each person holds of themselves, as central to what is learnt and whether it is in fact learnt. The self-concept was discussed in depth in Chapter 6.

3. *Experience that, if assimilated, would involve a change in the organisation of self tends to be resisted through denial or distortion of symbolisation, and the structure and organisation of self appear to become more rigid under threat.*

4. *Experience that is perceived as inconsistent with the self can be assimilated only if the current organisation of self is relaxed and expanded to include it.* Hypotheses 3 and 4 acknowledge the reality that significant learning is often a threat to individuals and their self-concept, and suggest the importance of providing an accepting and supporting climate in which learning can take place.

5. The fifth hypothesis extends the previous four into educational practice. It states: *The educational situation that most effectively promotes significant learning is one in which threat to the self as learner is reduced to a minimum.* Again, the role of the self-concept as a determiner of learning is expressed. If self-esteem is threatened, the person will avoid the learning situation.

Rogers delineates two types of learning: one he calls *cognitive learning* the other *experiential learning*. By cognitive learning he is referring to all learning approaches derived from traditional psychological theory, including behaviourism and cognitive theory, that requires the student to absorb some body of knowledge. In contrast, Rogers depicts experiential learning as something that is personally and emotionally meaningful as well as cognitively relevant.

This self-directed, experiential learning involves two basic steps. The first is for the teacher to create a climate of trust and openness in which self-direction can occur. The second step is for the individual or group to work out a self-directed plan for learning or development, negotiating its own learning contract. Rogers requires qualities in teachers that are generally facilitative of healthy human relations, notably *genuineness* (the capacity to accept and deal with their own feelings), *empathy* and *positive acceptance of others,* including accepting their right to make decisions.

Rogers proposes eight guidelines for creating such an emotional and intellectual learning ethos.

1. The teacher must communicate their trust in the pupils at the start. This helps to set a facilitative and positive climate for learning.
2. The teacher must help students clarify and articulate their individual and group objectives. The teacher must permit individuals a sense of freedom in stating what they would like to do, which might involve accepting contradictory purposes and conflicting aims. This again aids in the creation of a climate for learning.
3. The teacher must assume that students have intrinsic motivation that will enable them to pursue their studies. The teacher might need to act as a guide initially to activate the intrinsic motivation.
4. The teacher must act as a resource person, making available the widest range of learning experiences possible for the learners' stated objectives and for the fulfilment of their own purposes. The teacher is a flexible resource, available as facilitator, counsellor, lecturer, someone with experience in the field to be used by individuals and the group in the manner that is most meaningful and relevant for them.
5. The teacher should learn to recognise and accept emotional messages expressed within the group and should balance intellectual and emotional components of learning.
6. The teacher should be an active participant in the group, expressing their views as a member of the group and not as an imposed leader.
7. The teacher must be open in expressing their feelings in the group. Just as students are free to express their feelings, so too is the teacher free to express their feelings in giving feedback to them as individuals. It is the sharing of owned attitudes, not judgments or evaluations of others.
8. The teacher must have empathic understanding of group members' feelings. In accepting tensions, they help to bring them into the open for constructive understanding and use by the group.

Rogers also identifies some practical methods that, in his opinion, can facilitate experiential learning.

1. Students should participate in an open, non-threatening and free classroom experience, with control over its nature and direction.
2. The student and the teacher should develop contracts in which they agree what is a meaningful unit of work.
3. Rogers recommends discovery learning with the aim of learning how to learn rather than rote learning.
4. Classroom learning must be made personally relevant by having real-life

experiences simulated in the classroom where possible. Significant learning takes place when the subject matter is relevant to the personal interests of the student.

5. Responsibility for learning must be given to the students. Self-initiated learning is the most lasting and pervasive.
6. Self-evaluation is the principal method of assessing progress or success.

There are distinctions between the self-actualising and problem-solving learning of Dewey and Bruner. These are listed in Figure 7.3.

FIGURE 7.3 SELF-ACTUALISING AND PROBLEM-SOLVING LEARNING COMPARED

| SELF-ACTUALISING APPROACHES | PROBLEM-SOLVING APPROACHES |
| --- | --- |
| emotional focus | intellectual focus |
| learning group develops own curriculum | identification of appropriate subject matter by learner and teacher |
| learners reassess their feelings around a learning experience | learning built round a problem |
| group spontaneity | group discussion with some degree of organisation |
| participatory | some teaching/guidance |
| personal growth | assessable learning gains |
| informal | more formal |

While these differences appear distinct they shade into each other: many cognitive–Gestalt proponents involved in developing problem solving as a valid education technique in educating adults would see their approach as being aimed at the self-actualisation of the learner as well as enabling the development of skill or knowledge. Likewise, Rogers would also acknowledge that his experiential learning contains both affective and knowledge components and that the teacher has a facilitating role in creating growth and a problem-solving milieu. Rogers certainly comes close to Knowles in promoting self-development and self-direction in that Knowles regards maturity as a major goal in education. Both would regard evaluation by the learner as to whether it is meeting their needs as far more important than whether or not it has academic quality or accords with some predesigned syllabus.

Rogers places experiential learning at the other end of the spectrum from memory learning.

Experiential learning is characterised by the following principles:
• Humans have a natural propensity to learn.
• Significant learning occurs when the learner perceives the subject matter to be of relevance.

- Learning involves a change in self-perception.
- Learning occurs when the self is not threatened and changes can be assimilated into the self.
- Significant learning is acquired by doing and through responsible participation in the learning process.

Rogers' humanist psychology offers more a philosophical position or general orientation than a formalised instructional base. There are important guidelines for the teacher of adults but as there is no consideration of the wider socio-cultural milieu or of the role of intellect, his proposals do not present a comprehensive picture. The ideas are admirable but criticised by those who seek more specific indications of methods and objectives. But its strengths are its ability to make educators think more deeply and critically about contrasting behaviourist approaches and the fact that even though a teacher might not want to take all Rogers' ideas on board they are sufficiently eclectic for the selection of those that appeal. Rogers has made educators think about questions of who should determine objectives, who should set goals for individuals and what should be the role and form of assessment.

## Paolo Freire

Freire's writings are well known among educators and reflect a synthesis of Catholicism and Marxism that emerged in South America in the context of liberation theology. His ideas developed from a consideration of the oppression of the masses by an elite in Brazil. At the centre of his educational ideas is a humanist conception of the learner coupled with a realisation that once the learner is involved in the education process they cannot be passive — they must be an active participant in it and in the wider world. Education is not neutral, but will either facilitate freedom or maintain acceptance of the status quo.

Freire claimed that the culture being transmitted in South America (as indeed in other parts of the world) was one of colonialism with its implicit positioning of the indigenous culture as inferior and subordinate. He illustrates this with reference to the fact that colonisers generally regard the cultural productions of the indigenous people as folklore and their language as dialect. Thus education imposes a construction of reality on indigenous people that is false to their own heritage. The masses are incarcerated in this false reality through education, which transmits the imprisoning values.

Freire used literacy education as a way to enable the adult illiterates eventually to reflect on their own understanding of themselves within their socio-cultural milieu. This combination of reflection and action he called praxis. The individual becomes aware of realities other than that into which they have been socialised. Adult education for Freire in his particular situation was a liberating process in which the learner discovers themselves and achieves humanity by acting upon the world to transform it. Freire's approach is often dubbed political rather than educational but it does sensitise educators to the fact that what they transmit is often only that which is acceptable to the ruling group, so that a cultural hegemony exists. We educate, particularly at school level, to preserve the existing culture. While education must obviously transmit knowledge, it can trap learners into particular values, opinions and positions, without the learners (or teachers for that matter) being aware of this subtle, often non-deliberate indoctrination.

Freire speaks of changing the world view and the consciousness of individuals to produce a free and autonomous individual. Each person must become conscious of the social forces working on them, reflect on these forces and acquire their capability to change the world. To be human is to guide one's own destiny. Freire calls oppression *the culture of silence* as it can only exist under controlling and authoritarian education.

In place of the banking concept, Freire offers problem solving and dialogue. This will make the person aware of the situation and the reality they live in and enable them to become aware of possible ways to change society. Participants must be free to create the curriculum with the teacher. The only justifiable content is that which emanates from the student. Insight into the learners' world comes through dialogue with the teacher. Employing mutual trust and reciprocal teaching and learning they are coparticipants in a reflexive activity. Freire marries education with political action so that it becomes an active process in which the teacher neither controls the knowledge learnt nor the learning outcomes.

Freire's pedagogy found ready acceptance among many community-based educators who viewed conventional schooling as part of the problem contributing to the marginalisation of minorities and the poor. He suggested several pedagogical techniques based on the mass literacy campaigns he organised in Brazil and Chile. These techniques were incorporated in many literacy and basic education programs round the world: viz. reflection on the political content of the learner's experiences, the organisation of cultural circles to promote dialogue and peer interaction and the use of peoples' knowledge as the basis for the curriculum. A facet of his approach not easily located in a Western context was the link between learning and action. Opportunities for collective action are required. As a result, consciousness raising might occur among Western adult learners but rarely produces social change.

Despite Freire's model being political in emphasis, there are some similarities with the phenomenological views of Knowles and Rogers in his emphasis on the humanity of the learner, his concern that the learner should be free to reflect on their own experiences and be able to act on their socio-cultural milieu to transform it. However, it can be well argued that while the conditions in developed Western-style countries do not approximate the highly structured Brazilian society, education for adults *should*, as a matter of course, raise their level of consciousness so that they can become aware of the variety of forces — economic, political, social and psychological — that are affecting their lives. It is more than likely that most adults in the developed world are no more aware of the forces that constrain them

than people in underdeveloped countries. Thus Freire's ideas might be more significant for adult education and lifelong education throughout the world than a first
reading would suggest. From a synthesis of Christianity, Marxism and existential-
ism, Freire has produced an approach to teaching that is inspiring and challenging.

There is an assumption that the teacher is on the same side as the learner
(oppressed) and that as they engage in dialogue together they will uncover the
same reality. However, teachers are also determined by gender, age, beliefs, experiences, social class, etc., and will bring these to bear in any teaching relationship as
they give meaning to what is experienced and discussed. In this there is always
implicit power, which can limit the role of the liberational teacher, and Freire fails
to address such issues and the contradictory position of a teacher as concurrently
one of the oppressors and the oppressed.

Freire suggests that the teacher:
- break down the barrier between teacher and taught
- speak the same 'language' as the learners
- be aware of how they construct their universe of meaning
- be aware of their learning needs
- start from where the learners are
- encourage them to learn and explore from their experiences.

## Mezirow and transformative learning

Mezirow's early work (conducted with women returning to higher education)
focused on the idea of perspective transformation, which he understood as the
learning process by which adults come to recognise and reframe their culturally
induced dependency roles and relationships. Later he drew on the work of
Habermas to propose a theory of transformative learning 'that can explain how
adult learners make sense or meaning of their experiences, the nature of the structures that influence the way they construe experience, the dynamics involved in
modifying meanings, and the way the structures of meaning themselves undergo
changes when learners find them to be dysfunctional' (Mezirow, 1991, p. xii).
Transformative learning is basically the kind of learning we do as we make sense
of our lives. This is important because, as adults, the meaning-making process can
change everything about how we look at work, family and the world.
Transformative learning is rooted in the philosophy of constructivism, which
unlike behaviourism with its external reality, argues that reality is constructed by
the observer through interpretation of experience. Cognitive and Gestalt psychologists, as well as humanist-oriented (phenomenological) psychologists fall within
a wide ambit of constructivism in which people respond to the world as they see
it. External phenomena are meaningless except as the person interprets them.

A defining condition of being human is that we have to understand the meaning
of our experience. For some, any uncritically assimilated explanation by an authority figure will suffice. But in contemporary society we must learn to make our own

interpretations rather than act on the purposes, beliefs, judgments and feelings of others. Facilitating such understandings is the cardinal goal of adult education. Transformative learning develops autonomous thinking (Mezirow, 1997, p. 5).

Transformation is something that is usually triggered by a problem, and very often transformative experiences are painful to go through. After identifying their problem or challenge, people seem to enter a phase where they reflect on the matter critically — this is typically a problem that one has never experienced before, so it takes a lot of thinking and talking to others to work through. During the thinking phase, people might find that they can no longer keep their old ways of thinking and being — they are compelled to change. Finally, there is an action phase where people decide to do something. This could mean that you have to break off certain relationships that no longer fit your beliefs; it could mean that you decide to make a career change; action can take many forms.

So, clearly, transformative learning is not just learning, and this is one of the problems people have with this whole theory. For example, what if you go back to school and get a degree — have you transformed yourself? This is a tough question and the answer won't be the same for everybody. What Mezirow says is that learning 'can consist of a change in one of our beliefs or attitudes' (Merriam & Caffarella, 1999, p. 320); this is what he calls a 'meaning scheme'. But this isn't transformational learning in Mezirow's opinion. It's only when we change our entire perspective on something (our meaning perspective) that we really transform.

The meaning schemes that make up meaning structures might change as an individual adds to or integrates ideas within an existing schema and, in fact, this transformation of meaning schemas occurs routinely through learning. This deconstruction is a rational activity that occurs frequently as a result of increasing experience. Perspective transformation leading to transformative learning, however, occurs much less frequently. Mezirow (1995) suggests this happens through a series of phases that begin with the *disorienting dilemma*. A disorienting dilemma is triggered by a life crisis or major life transition, although it might also result from an accumulation of transformations in meaning schemas over a period of time (Mezirow, 1995, p. 50). Other phases include self-examination, critical assessment of assumptions, recognition that others have shared similar transformations, exploration of new roles or actions, development of a plan for action, acquisition of knowledge and skills for implementing the plan, trialling the plan, development of competence and self-confidence in new roles and reintegration into life on the basis of new perspectives.

As described by Mezirow (1997), transformative learning occurs when individuals change their frames of reference by critically reflecting on their assumptions and beliefs and consciously making and implementing plans that bring about new ways of defining their worlds. His theory describes a learning process that is primarily 'rational, analytical, and cognitive' (Grabov, 1997, pp. 90-91). For Mezirow all meaning is based on interpretation and the critical dimension of adult learning is reflection, or the process of validating ideas and assumptions based on prior learning. He defines learning as a process of construing a new or revised interpretation of one's experiences in order to guide future action.

For learners to change their 'meaning schemes (specific beliefs, attitudes, and emotional reactions)', they must engage in critical reflection on their experiences, which in turn leads to a perspective transformation (Mezirow, 1991, p. 167). 'Perspective transformation is the process of becoming critically aware of how and why our assumptions have come to constrain the way we perceive, understand, and feel about our world; changing these structures of habitual expectation to make possible a more inclusive, discriminating, and integrating perspective; and, finally, making choices or otherwise acting upon these new understandings' (op. cit.).

A number of critical responses to Mezirow's theory of transformative learning have emerged (e.g. Cranton, 1994; Taylor, 1998). One major area of contention surrounding Mezirow's theory is its emphasis upon rationality. Although many empirical studies support Mezirow's contention that critical reflection is central to transformative learning, others have concluded that the process is too rational and cognitive, and ignores possibilities of transformative learning as an intuitive, creative and emotional process.

On the surface, the two views of transformative learning presented here are contradictory. One advocates a rational approach that depends primarily on critical reflection, whereas the other relies more on intuition and emotion. The differences between the two views, however, might best be seen as a matter of emphasis. Both use rational processes and incorporate imagination as a part of a creative process. Grabov (1997) suggests that the two views share a number of commonalities, including 'humanism, emancipation, autonomy, critical reflection, equity, self-knowledge, participation, communication and discourse' (p. 90).

Both forms of transformative learning might also occur together in practice. Differences in learning contexts, learners and teachers all affect the cognitive and emotional experiences of transformative learning. Based on findings from empirical studies, Taylor (1998) suggests that not all learners are predisposed to engage in transformative learning. The same can be said for teachers. Not all teachers of adults might feel comfortable with a goal of transformative learning. In addition, many adult learning situations do not necessarily lend themselves to transformative learning.

Additionally, the idea of phases is rather artificial — isn't it possible to transform instantly? Or without critical reflection? Some people also criticise Mezirow's theory for dealing too much with individuals; they believe that transformation involves society and that the individual can never be isolated from society. Other scholars feel that transformative learning has to be put into a context to be really understood as transformation. Basically, what's important to understand is that this issue is still not settled, and although Mezirow is considered by many to be the guru of transformative learning, even he doesn't represent everyone's ideas about this.

There seems to be a gender bias in transformative learning since women are far more comfortable than men with using dialogue to change and examine beliefs

(Manbeck & Bruhl, 1997). Men were more reluctant to examine their past and preferred to look forward to the future. Women enjoyed sharing more, whereas men talked about 'bragging' and had little desire to share experiences with others. As a result male subjects were more removed from the group, while the women found encouragement in groups to take more risks in learning. Manbeck and Bruhl found paradoxically that women dominated the group discussions and actually attacked males whenever they attempted to express their feelings — the very males who were getting the message about understanding their experiences. Thus in efforts to raise the voices of students we might silence the voices of some — the males, as women find transformation and self-reflection more acceptable. Thus the appropriate methods for male and female adult students might be different.

However, when transformative learning is the goal of adult education, how can it best be fostered given the variables of learning contexts, learners and teachers? Whether transformative learning is approached as a consciously rational process or through a more intuitive, imaginative process, any fostering of a learning environment in which it can occur should consider:

- *The role of the teacher.* The teacher's role in establishing an environment that builds trust and care and facilitates the development of sensitive relationships among learners is a fundamental principle of fostering transformative learning. Loughlin (1993) talks about the responsibility of the teacher to create a 'community of knowers', individuals who are 'united in a shared experience of trying to make meaning of their life experience' (pp. 320-321).
- *The role of the learner.* Taylor (1998) believes that too much emphasis has been placed on the role of the teacher at the expense of the role of the participant. Although it is difficult for transformative learning to occur without the teacher playing a key role, participants also have a responsibility for creating the learning environment.
- *The role of the rational and the affective.* Transformative learning has two layers that at times seem to be in conflict: the cognitive, rational and objective and the intuitive, imaginative and subjective. Both the rational and the affective play a role in transformative learning. Although the emphasis has been on transformative learning as a rational process, teachers need to consider how they can help students connect the rational and the affective by using feelings and emotions both in critical reflection and as a means of reflection.

Transformative learning might not always be a goal of adult and lifelong education, but its importance should not be overlooked and all adult educators should strive to understand it, even if they do not choose to foster it. Becoming free from our own distorted ideas of the world — according to proponents of transformative learning is what adult education is all about.

As an educator or trainer, you have to develop your own philosophy about all of this. You might not feel that this is the goal of adult education. However, you also need to be aware of the kinds of learning that you are promoting in your classroom. Of course, our learners are all adults; they have to make their own decisions and it is almost impossible for us, as educators, to know how to cause our learners to think! The point is, there are times when we are in the position to trigger some critical reflection and we have to be careful how we go about doing this. At the same time, we can't force people to reflect critically on anything and we certainly cannot 'schedule in' transformative learning experiences. In other words, we need to engage in some critical reflection of our own when it comes to our own teaching and training practices:

- Why do we teach or train the way we do?
- What are our goals for our learners and for ourselves as professionals?
- Is critical reflection something that needs to be fostered in the context in which we teach or train?

Once we've become a little clearer on these questions, we'll be closer to formulating our own opinions on the whole topic of transformative learning and how it fits into our practice.

## summary of principles derived from adult educators

The principles of teaching that follow from the discussion of the theoretical perspectives of major adult educators are that teachers should:

- help learners identify and clarify the problems that they experience and that they wish to overcome; acknowledge their past experience and assist them to use and understand their own experiences as resources for learning through the use of discussion, role-play, simulation, etc.
- assist learners to apply the new learning to their experiences, to make the new learning more meaningful
- develop a learning environment characterised by mutual trust and respect of learners' feelings/ideas; encourage mutual helpfulness, freedom of expression and acceptance of differences; accept each learner as of worth
- encourage cooperative activities and refrain from creating competitiveness or making judgments
- contribute to learners' resources as a co-learner in a spirit of mutual enquiry, involving them in a collaborative process as they share thinking about the options available in the design and articulation of learning experiences for the group
- help learners organise themselves into groups for independent study etc.
- assist learners to develop procedures for self-evaluation
- acknowledge and promote self-direction in learning and participate actively in the learning experience
- give learners a sense of progress towards their goals.

# ■■■ ASSESSING ADULT LEARNING CONCEPTS

Self-directed learning, critical reflection, experiential learning and learning to learn have all been proposed as constituting unique and exclusive adult learning processes. We are still currently far from a universal understanding of adult learning. A general theory of adult learning might be a chimera anyway, given the multitude of contexts, contents and purposes of adult learning. Moreover, theory development in adult learning is weak, hindered by the persistence of myths that are etched deeply into adult educators' minds (Brookfield, 1992). These myths, which, taken together, comprise something of an academic orthodoxy in adult education, hold that adults are self-directed learners, use experiential learning and critically reflect on this learning and that education must meet the needs articulated by learners themselves.

## the self-directed learner

*'Learning on one's own, being self-directed in one's learning is itself a context in which learning takes place. The key to placing a learning experience within this context is that the learner has the primary responsibility for planning, carrying out and evaluating his or her own learning. Participation in self-directed learning seems almost universal — in fact, an estimated 90 per cent of the population is involved with at least one self-directed learning activity a year...Adults engaging in self-directed learning do not necessarily follow a definite set of steps or linear format. In essence, self-directed learning occurs both by design and chance — depending on the interests, experiences and actions of individual learners and the circumstances in which they find themselves. Self-directed learning does not necessarily mean learning in isolation — assistance is often sought from friends, experts, and acquaintances in both the planning and execution of the learning activity.'*
(Merriam & Caffarella, 1991, 54–55)

Self-directed learning (SDL) is a common element among adult education theories, and research (e.g. Candy, 1991) reveals that most learners do prefer this mode. SDL is related to humanism, especially Maslow's ideas about self-actualisation, and to Rogerian perspectives of a learner being able to make significant personal choices. Knowles makes it a centrepiece of his andragogical theory. SDL implies a democratic commitment to shifting to the learner as much control as possible for conceptualising, designing, conducting and evaluating their learning.

SDL sees the learner as the primary impetus for and initiator of the learning process. Teachers and other educational features are secondary aids in the process. Learner autonomy appeals to fundamental rights — a person should be able to study what and how they please if they wish to advance themselves. The argument has been supported by educators, economists, businesses and politicians of all political hues to support a range of conflicting philosophies and purposes.

- From the right, self-direction and autonomy are attractive as they reduce the individual's dependence on State or business organisations' funding and provision. The more people can manage their own learning at a time when lifelong learning is necessary, the more cost effective it will be. In this perspective self-direction is the permission to choose between course and study options or, even more starkly, between studying or not studying.
- The left argue about empowerment and redistribution of power à la Freire.
- The educational argument is concerned with efficiency as independent learners are more efficient learners, better motivated, have a sense of ownership, are interested in what they are doing and therefore likely to succeed.
- The social argument suggests that democracy cannot flourish without people who are capable of independent thinking.
- The economic case emphasises the arguments that support the greater development of lifelong education, presented in the opening chapters, the shift to the information economy and the need to advance one's skills/knowledge to remain a competitive worker or organisation. Arguments for adult and lifelong learning focus on the 'information explosion', the rapid pace of change, the global economy and workplace transformations. The future belongs to those who are innovative, enterprising, decision makers, able to develop new skills as part of career development and able to plan for the future in a unpredictable world, or rather to those organisations and businesses that understand this.

But while in all these arguments the case for the self-directed person is strong, there are a number of problems with the ideal. Kerka (1999) has offered a critical review of educators' views on self-directed learning (SDL), although the notion of its centrality in adult learning tends to be assumed without question (Rowland & Volet, 1996, p. 90) despite the obvious presence of situational, cultural, learner and teacher variables in every learning context. Thus there are a range of controversies and misconceptions about the definition and dimensions of SDL. The major ones concern the following:
- SDL has been primarily based on individualistic attitudes and values related to individual responsibility and workforce development but this formulation ignores the social construction of knowledge and of the self shaped by social context (family, friends, workplace and society) by focusing on the individual, isolated learner (Long, 1994).
- If SDL is intrinsically about self-determination, it should have emancipatory potential, or does it serve to accommodate learners to prevailing social and political beliefs while providing an illusion of individual control (Maehl, 2000, p. 51)?
- The presence of situational, learner and teacher variables will also determine how much self-direction there can be.

- Although, according to Knowles, by 2020 learning at all ages and levels will be based on the principles of SDL (Hatcher, 1997, p. 37) and as even more learning shifts to electronic media, Gray (1999) thinks it likely that forms of teacher control will still persist and perhaps dominate.
- Research on SDL has tended to focus on middle class subjects and ignore issues of power, control and previous educational experiences affecting learners' assuming responsibility for choices and judgments about what can be learnt and how.

## experiential learning

The emphasis on experience as a major defining feature of adult learning was originally expressed in Lindeman's frequently quoted aphorism that 'experience is the adult learner's living textbook' (1926, p. 7) and that adult education was, therefore, 'a continuing process of evaluating experiences' (p. 85). This emphasis on experience as central to the concept of andragogy has evolved with later writers (e.g. Knowles) to describe adult education practice. The belief that adult teaching should be grounded in adults' experiences, and that these experiences represent a valuable resource, is held to be crucial by adult educators of every conceivable ideological hue. Of all the models of experiential learning that have been developed, Kolb's has probably been the most influential in prompting theoretical work among researchers of adult learning (Jarvis, 1987). Almost every textbook on adult education practice affirms the importance of experiential methods such as games, simulations, case studies, psychodrama, role-play and internships and many universities even grant credit for adults' experiential learning. Not surprisingly, then, the gradual accumulation of experience across the contexts of life is often argued as the chief difference between learning in adulthood and learning at earlier stages in the life span. Yet, an exclusive reliance on accumulated experience as the defining characteristic of adult learning involves two discernible pitfalls.

1. Experience is not an objectively neutral phenomenon, a flow of thoughts, perceptions and sensations into which we decide, occasionally, to dip our toes. It is culturally framed and shaped. How we experience events and the readings we make of these are problematic; they change according to the language and categories of analysis we use, and according to the cultural, moral and ideological vantage points from which they are viewed. In a very important sense we construct our experience: how we sense and interpret what happens to us and to the world around us is a function of structures of understanding and perceptual filters that are so culturally embedded that we are scarcely aware of their existence or operation.
2. Second, the quantity or length of experience is not necessarily connected to its richness or intensity. For example, an adult educator with twenty years' experience might in fact be repeating the same one year's experience twenty times. Because of the habitual ways we draw meaning from our experiences,

these experiences can become evidence for the self-fulfilling prophecies that stand in the way of critical insight. Such 'experience' might lead to uncritical interpretations to 'prove' to oneself that students from certain ethnic groups are lazy or that fear is always the best stimulus to encourage critical thinking. Experience can be misleading in its interpretation through cultural filters. Uncritically affirming adult students' histories, stories and experiences risks idealising and romanticising experiences that are impediments to more open learning.

## critical reflection

Individuals need to reflect on experience in order to learn from it. The essence of learning from experience is to be found in the relationship between the learner and the context. The vital process is noticing, being aware of what has happened and taking action.

Developing critical reflection is for many adult educators the form and process of learning that could be claimed to be distinctively adult. Evidence that adults are capable of this kind of learning can be found in developmental psychology, with constructs such as dialectical thinking, working intelligence, reflective judgment and post-formal reasoning describing how adults come to think contextually and critically (Brookfield, 1991). Critical reflection focuses on three interrelated processes:

1. The process by which adults question and then replace or reframe assumptions that up to that point have been uncritically accepted as representing commonsense wisdom.
2. The process by which adults adopt alternative perspectives on previously taken-for-granted ideas, actions, forms of reasoning and ideologies.
3. The process by which adults come to recognise dominant cultural values and understand how self-evident renderings of the 'natural' state of the world actually bolster the power and self-interest of unrepresentative minorities.

Writers in this area vary on the extent to which critical reflection should have a political edge, or the extent to which it can be observed in such apparently apolitical domains of adult life as personal relationships and workplace actions. Some confusion is caused by the fact that psychoanalytic and critical social theory coexist uneasily.

As we read above, the most important work in this area is that of Mezirow (1991). Applications of Mezirow's ideas have been made with widely varying groups of adult learners, such as displaced homemakers, male spouse abusers and those suffering ill health, though his work has been criticised by educators for focusing too exclusively on individual transformation (e.g. Clark and Wilson, 1991).

Many tasks remain for researchers of critical reflection as a dimension of adult learning. A language needs to be found to describe this process to educators that is more accessible than the psychoanalytic and critical theory terminology currently employed. Greater understanding of how people experience episodes of critical reflection and how they deal with the risks of committing cultural suicide entailed by such episodes would help educators respond to fluctuating rhythms of denial and depression in learners. Much research in this area confirms that critical reflection is context- or domain-specific. How is it that the same people can be highly critical regarding, for example, dominant political ideologies, yet show no critical awareness of the existence of repressive features in their personal relationships? At present, theoretical analyses of critical reflection (frequently drawn from Habermas' work) considerably outweigh the number of ethnographic, phenomenological studies of how this process is experienced. Contextual factors surrounding the decision to forego or pursue action after a period of critical reflection are still unclear, as is the extent to which critical reflection is associated with certain personality characteristics.

## learning to learn

The ability of adults to learn how to learn — to become skilled at learning in a range of different situations and through a range of different styles — has often been proposed as an overarching purpose for those educators who work with adults. Like its sister term 'meta-cognition', learning how to learn suffers for lack of a commonly agreed definition. An important body of related work (focusing mostly on young adults) is that of Kitchener and King (1990). These authors emphasise that learning how to learn involves an awareness deeper than simply knowing how one scores on a cognitive style inventory, or what one's typical or preferred pattern of learning is. Rather, it means that adults possess a self-conscious awareness of how it is they come to know what they know; an awareness of the reasoning, assumptions, evidence and justifications that underlie our beliefs that something is true.

Studies of learning to learn have been conducted with a range of adult groups and in a range of settings such as adult basic education, the workplace and religious communities. Yet, of the four characteristics of adult learning discussed, learning how to learn has been the least successful in capturing the imagination of the adult educational world and in prompting a dynamic program of follow-up research. This might be because in lifelong education the function of helping people learn how to learn is often claimed as being more appropriate to schools than to adult education. Many books on learning to learn restrict themselves to the applicability of this concept to elementary or secondary school learning. Research on learning to learn is also flawed in its emphasis on college students' meta-cognition and by its lack of attention to how this process manifests itself in the diverse contexts of adult life. That learning to learn is a skill that exists far beyond academic boundaries is evident from the research conducted on practical intelligence and everyday cognition in settings and activities as diverse as grocery shopping and betting shops (Brookfield, 1991). The connections between a propensity for learning how to learn and the nature of the learning task or domain also need clarification. Learning how to learn tends to focus on areas of clearly defined skill development or knowledge acquisition, and tends to ignore emotional learning or the development of emotional intelligence.

# ■■■ AIMS OF ADULT EDUCATION

The material in this chapter has demonstrated that adult education can mean all things to all men. Lindeman, one of the earliest writers in the field, saw adult education as definitely social and integral to the democratic struggle and expanded Dewey's notions about school-based education for democratic participation to adults who need to participate in social and economic decisions affecting them. Adult education was initially seen as an essential for the creation of democratic society. Its absence leaves critical decisions in the hands of educated elites, promotes a cult of experts and erodes democratic social order. The later writings of Freire emphasised this approach in a more radical way.

However, the prevailing view is that everyone needs a continuous re-education or lifelong education. This is a radical departure from the Dewey, Lindeman and Freire concepts of the civil rights movement, liberation theology, revolutionary leftist movements of the 1960s, ideas and movements that only occur at unusual historical and transitional times. The present is more in tune with Knowles, who emphasised learning to adapt to change. There is tension therefore between radical educators who are hopeful of transforming the social order and those who promote adult education as routine maintenance for adaptation to changing reality, like tailors taking in a bit in here and letting out a bit there to enhance an individual's fit. Lifelong learning also expresses this tension; the romantic view clashes with managerial responsibility and professionalism. Most educators prefer not to create a maelstrom of social unrest and simply legitimate new knowledge and skills for market-driven organisations.

Most adult education has been adaptive and conformist, bringing learners into the mainstream, compensating for inequality of access and provision, levelling the playing field to ensure equality of opportunity. This has become more potent over the past two decades as human capital theory, although the education–job performance relationship is doubtful, is reflected in the favouring of job-related learning and competency-based learning. Adult educators often talk now about credit transfers, franchising, strategic plans, etc. Instrumental components are obscuring the social vision. However, the 1990's subordination of adult education to the workplace and learning of job-related competencies is not neutral and is an expression of political values as adult education 'empowers' workers to 'keep up' and be consumers of education. Adult education for democratic social change has virtually been driven off stage. A few adult educators (often indigenous leaders, 'activists' and 'organisers'), uncharitably referred to as 'popular educators', continue to promote more liberatory activities but Freirean projects, no matter how well grounded in the local community, are always at risk in competition for funding since accountability and funding-source ownership still constitute controls. The most successful community projects are those that have rejected outside funding and have a broad base of community support. So the question for a dichotomised adult education is quo vadis.

# SUMMARY

This chapter has attempted to clarify some of the terms used to conceptualise adult education. Only the term 'lifelong education' really covers the wide gamut of what occurs in a variety of locations.

The perspectives and educational theories of Knowles, Rogers, Bruner, Freire and Mezirow are presented to provide a conception of an education for adults (andragogy) that contrasts with pedagogy for children. In andragogy, education is a process guided by the teacher as facilitator, enabling students to reflect critically on their experiences in a self-directed and self-paced context.

This theory of adult learning contradicts what happens in childhood education. A strong case can be made for the variables of culture, tradition, personality and political ethos to assume far greater significance in explaining how learning occurs and is experienced by the learner than the variable of chronological age, since the processes and methods within andragogy can be applied to learning at any age. Knowles later acknowledged this and no longer claims that andragogy is exclusive to adulthood. He suggests that andragogical assumptions are appropriate as enlightened teaching for learners at all ages but particularly for adults who are resource-rich in experience, have a problem-centred approach to life and are capable of more intrinsic learning.

Dewey and Bruner emphasise the problem-solving nature of learning that should dominate adult learning. Mezirow focuses on transformative learning, which Freire, working independently, has taken to underpin his political purposes for adult education, that is emancipation from taken-for-granted assumptions. But although the emphasis differs, experiential and self-directed learning are central to all approaches as educators recognise that adults learn most effectively by reflecting on experience and applying it to a problem or need, and the changing perceptions of self and self-potential that all this engenders. Critical issues abound, however, especially whether self-directed learning is individual or collective, emancipatory or oppressive, inevitable or not.

Perhaps the biggest misconception might be in trying to capture the essence of adult and lifelong education in a single definition. It is clearly a multifaceted concept that cannot be approached through one perspective. Practice should in the future start to acknowledge both individual and collective goals for learning, ethical and political considerations, the diverse learning preferences of multicultural populations and the effects of new technologies as the concept of self-directed learning continues to evolve.

Generally speaking, the following characteristics should define a learning environment for adults:

- Mutual responsibility for defining goals and planning and conducting activities that are based on the real needs of the participants.
- Participation of learners in decision making.
- Self-direction for learners.

- The role of the teacher as a resource and facilitator.
- The use of learners' experiences as a basis for learning.
- An open, democratic environment.
- Concern for the worth of the individual and their self-concept.

# chapter 8

# methods in educating adults

**The greatest good we can do for others is not just share our riches with them but to reveal theirs to themselves.**
Anon

**Empowered learners are empowered citizens. Empowered learners are also empowered workers and managers. Empowered learners produce an empowered society which by definition is involved continuously in the creation of its own destiny. Cast in this context adaptive learning systems offer the opportunity for developed and developing nations to transcend boundaries of time, space, competence and social position which historically have limited life chances.**
Morrison (1995), *Int. J. of Lifelong Education*, 14, p. 212

## ■■■ IMPLICATIONS OF LEARNING THEORY

From discussion in Chapters 5 and 6, the following general psychological principles should guide educational practice involving adults as learners.

1. An adult's readiness to learn depends on the amount of previous practice and learning. The more stored knowledge a person has (variously termed schemas, concepts, phase sequences) the better able they are to assimilate new information.
2. Intrinsic motivation produces more pervasive and permanent learning. What is learnt becomes part of the learner. Building an educational activity around an adult's needs, interests, experience and curiosity ensures more permanent learning.
3. Positive reinforcement of learning is more effective than punishment or

ignoring behaviour. Feelings of success that raise self-esteem and confidence are vital for the entry and continuation of adults in education after their negative experiences in earlier schooling.

4. To maximise learning, information must be presented in an organised fashion, proceeding from simple to complex or organised around a concept. The starting point for organising a body of knowledge for adults is related to their past experiences and knowledge.

5. Learning, especially with regard to skill development, is enhanced by systematic repetition over time.

6. Meaningful material and tasks are more easily learnt and remembered longer than non-meaningful material. Any task has potential meaning. The challenge is to find ways to relate it significantly to the experiences and needs of adult learners.

7. Active rather than passive participation in the learning activity enhances learning. Adults who are personally involved discover relationships, concepts and meaning as their own and are intrinsically rewarded. Adult educators who allow active participation help bring about more meaningful and permanent learning.

8. Factors such as fatigue, tension, time pressures, criticism, context of learning, interpersonal relationships with teachers and compulsion all affect learning.

9. Teaching practices that help raise self-esteem and positive expectancies of success must be used.

The conditions under which adult learning is facilitated were discussed in Chapter 7 in examining the concept of andragogy and the perspectives of various theorists who have expounded on teaching adults. The major educational principles suggest that education is a humanist process, with the humanity of the participants primary in the learning process, and these are summarised in Table 8.1 below along with their implications for teaching.

Knowles (1980, pp. 222–247) additionally suggests that teaching adults involves seven stages:

1. Setting a climate for learning that includes both the physical and psychological climate.

2. Establishing a structure for mutual planning.

3. Diagnosing learning needs.

4. Formulating directions for learning.

5. Designing a pattern of learning experiences that includes continuity, sequence and integration.

6. Managing the execution of the learning experiences as resource person and coach.

7. Evaluating and rediagnosing learning needs.

**TABLE 8.1** CONDITIONS OF ADULT LEARNING AND IMPLICATIONS FOR
TEACHERS AND TRAINERS

| CONDITIONS OF ADULT LEARNING | IMPLICATIONS FOR TEACHING ADULTS |
|---|---|
| Learning is a basic human activity and need | Teaching is not essential to learning but may facilitate it |
| Learning is motivated when there is incongruence or lack of harmony betewen an individual's experience and their perception of the world | Teachers and learners need to structure the process of learning together so that it may be relevant to the experience or problem that created the felt need to learn |
| Adult learners need to feel that they are treated as adults | Teachers must not regard themselves as the fount of all knowledge but create a learning engagement between all participants |
| Adults bring their needs to the learning situation | Learning should be individualised if possible and students should be helped to become aware of the relevance of the material to their needs |
| Adults bring their own experiences and meaning systems to the learning situation | Teachers must use these experiences as learning resources and build on the meaning system so that students can integrate new knowledge in old |
| Adults learn best when the self is not threatened | Teachers must create an ethos in which no adult feels inhibited or threatened. Cooperation rather than competition should be encouraged |
| Adults learn at different speeds | Teachers should employ methods that encourage adults to learn at their own pace |
| Adult learners have a variety of learning styles and personal traits | Teachers must recognise these styles and be flexible in their approach |
| Adults have developed a crystallised intelligence | Teachers should not be influenced by previous academic records |
| Adult learners bring their own self-esteem, self-perception and confidence to the learning context | Teachers must be empathetic and sensitive to the humanity of the learner and try to create a successful learning outcome to engender self-confidence and esteem |
| Adults bring some declining physiological features into the learning context | Teachers should ensure material is not presented too quickly for processing, that it is visually and auditorily at a level most adults need |

The principle that emerges is that the teacher's role performance and the methods employed should never undermine the dignity and humanity of the learner but always seek to enhance these.

All this must be done in a rapidly changing context where the developing paradigm is that of lifelong education. This chapter approach is more practical than theoretical: it looks at the ways in which adult learning principles and adult psychology can be put into practice to serve the imperatives of lifelong learning and coping strategies for the twenty-first century. Currently in Australia, 25 per cent of all VET participants are 40 years of age or older, usually already employed and seeking to advance their job skills and/or knowledge (Ball *et al.*, 2001). All parts of the world face similar contexts and demands, which cannot adequately be dealt with by the inherited content model of education. The essentials of the new educational design are now visible. The challenge is to articulate those principles as a basis for a new system of learning and a new way of thinking about learning. The content model of education managed to remain intact even in the face of earlier social and economic change after the Second World War by broadening the base of what was seen as the legitimate curriculum: in a form of curricular licence almost anything was respectable. This allowed for business as usual. But the contemporary dynamics of knowledge creation, its diffusion and creation in a multiplicity of contexts outside education, telecomputing technologies and the rapid redundancy of initial education and training, allied with local and global economic and social change affecting workplace, occupational structures and lifestyle, are not amenable to a purely content solution. The dynamics require a process solution — it is not so much *what* to learn but *how* to access learning, how to manage systems, how to link with technology, how to cope with developing and extant social, economic and ethical issues, how to distribute opportunity, how to develop human potential, etc.

Lifelong learning might now be seen generally as preferable and a 'good' thing, but given the driving forces of economic and social necessity embedding lifelong learning into the fabric of society, lifelong learning is likely to go beyond this and become an expectation, an entitlement with the right to continue learning as important as the right to work. Institutions cannot manage all this. It will be learning networks rather than institutions that will provide the bridge to the future. Nations will have to design education systems in such a way that not only do they have internal coherence but also an open architecture — able to work and network with other educational and learning systems. In the future learning will be part of globalisation rather than an internal affair for each nation State. Thus the new education design must:

- address the issues of a nation's policy agenda
- accommodate autonomous, self-reliant, empowered learners with their increasingly diverse demands
- turn national capability outward towards preparation of its citizens and society to function effectively in a global interdependent world
- improve the life chances and capabilities of individuals, organisations and communities.

Evidence of a movement towards an adaptive system can be found in the emergent development of distance education systems, computer assisted learning, new powerful and portable condensed technologies for storage, processing and transmission, international satellite networks, entry into the education marketplace of private sector training and learning systems and the proliferation of community-based learning network delivery systems. The challenge to be met for a viable future is to integrate all these and other parts in a complete adaptive learning system.

The new educational model for adult and lifelong learning should be:

- self-directed — self-chosen, self-set goals and learning methods, self-paced and flexible
- portable — moves with person
- interruptible — provides option to stop and start study
- non-linear — no fixed sequence
- transferable — moves across educational and national boundaries
- timely — provided when needed
- customised — designed for specific needs
- adaptable — modifiable as circumstances change
- flexible — allowing for a variety of modes/styles of learning
- inclusive — permitting enlarging of educational opportunity
- collaborative — linking people in their learning.

This would produce lifelong learners who have:

- the capacity to set realistic and personal goals
- the ability to apply knowledge and skills effectively
- the ability to evaluate their own learning
- the ability to locate information from different sources
- the capacity to use different learning strategies to best effect in different situations
- a positive self-concept and an increased sense of responsibility towards self and others.

## ■■■ ADULT AND LIFELONG LEARNING METHODS

It is apparent by now that the general approach to adult and lifelong learning should involve active participation in self-paced, self-directed learning in which new material, skills and information can be made meaningful and related to existing knowledge, facilitating successful understanding, raised self-esteem and intrinsic motivation to continue learning.

Unfortunately, the most common approaches in education are teacher-centred. A cursory glance at these will precede a more detailed consideration of methods that are congruent with the principles of andragogy and lifelong education. The term 'teacher' is being used in a generic sense in the material below to refer to any person who is teaching or training.

# ■■■ TEACHER-CENTRED METHODS

The teacher/trainer-centred approach is very common in formal courses and specific industrial skill training and includes a variety of methods such as the lecture, guided discussion, demonstration, simulation and tutorial. However, while these methods can be strongly teacher/trainer-directed, in the hands of a skilled and thoughtful professional most of them can evolve gradually towards more student control/leadership as learners obtain experience and skills in the techniques. Thus teacher-centred need not always be so if the method is skillfully used.

## demonstration

The demonstration is one of the most common methods in skills training. Good demonstration teaching involves breaking down the skill into a number of discrete stages, each demonstrated with an air of confidence but more slowly than normal at the outset so that learners can see every step/movement in the sequence. An extremely skilled performance that appears effortless on the part of the teacher might discourage some students. Therefore, small, easy subroutines should be learnt first and practised at a slow pace, gradually speeding up as skill and confidence increase. This is using the behaviourist approach of shaping with reinforcing feedback of results. Only later, after successful achievement, are appropriate subroutines linked until the whole skill can be integrated and performed. A danger is that an experienced operative/trainer might transmit imperfections and slack habits to learners.

## guided group discussion

Guided discussion is a step-by-step discussion with the teacher using a carefully prepared sequence of questions with a view to drawing from the learners implicit knowledge that they have yet to articulate, crystallise or relate to a wider perspective. Although teacher-directed, the discussion group, like its parallel under student direction, requires that members share their ideas, experiences, knowledge and feelings. A group discussion cannot function on pooled ignorance. If the facts and theories are outside the knowledge of the group members then the teacher should consider some other form of learning.

## lecturing

The lecture is one of the most overused and perhaps ineffective methods in post-secondary education. It is supposed to be a carefully prepared oral presentation of a subject by a qualified person. Unfortunately, not all lectures are well prepared and nor are all lecturers sufficiently expert. Boredom, wandering minds and the imposition of a mass of information generally leads to learners forgetting most of the material expounded. Research on the curve of forgetting (Chapter 6) reveals that most material is forgotten soon after presentation, particularly if it is 'meaningless' to the individual, and this is usually the case with lecture material.

It is a passive one-way communication street with the same material presented in the same way at the same pace to all those present, irrespective of previous experience or familiarity with the subject matter. The material is structured in a way the lecturer chooses, which might not be easy for some to integrate in their existing knowledge to make it meaningful. The lecture cannot consider individual needs or differences, which impedes participation and self-initiated learning.

Where class lecturing has to be done, it should be made as stimulating as possible with visual aids such as overheads, video clips, slides and demonstrations. There should be plenty of interesting examples, and a structure presented at the beginning. With the addition of visual aids, far more material is likely to become more meaningful and therefore better remembered. This method can also be improved by using follow-up, small-group sessions and by including questions and discussion points to be followed up within the body of the talk. With adults the lecture should be used sparingly. It cannot produce effective learning for most.

## the tutorial

The tutorial is a small-group or individual session. The student might meet the teacher after the latter has marked some work or observed some practical activity to discuss the content or performance issues. A group tutorial might involve discussion on some prearranged topic. Practical tutorials based in a laboratory or workplace would practise and discuss practical skill matters. Tutorials can be valuable if the teacher drops into the background and allows the students to present material and discuss and argue, only coming back in to ask awkward questions or help summarise, etc.

## ■■■ STUDENT-CENTRED GROUP METHODS

Although these methods are termed student-centred, there is a grey area of who is in control, with teachers/trainers relinquishing initial control as learners develop the skills necessary for directing their own learning activities. Many of the methods below could be teacher/trainer-directed initially, with students gradually assuming more responsibility as they gain experience.

Group methods describe a range of activities including games, simulations, role-plays, team building and brainstorming. There must be a leader to guide the group towards achievement of its objective, though the leader's style might vary from authoritarian to democratic and participatory. Teachers new to group methods are concerned with getting the task done; those with more experience are more focused on the group process as well as the task.

Active learning in groups promotes learner involvement through experiences and inquiry. Providing experiences for active involvement in the completion of a task might give the subject area far more relevance in the mind of the adult than simply reading about it or discussing it.

As each adult student brings to the learning situation a great wealth of unique life experience, this can be used as a major resource. The teacher facilitates the learning context but does not control the outcome. Group discussions should involve around 10 persons as this enables all to have an input and yet produce a variety of opinion. The leader must remain impartial and facilitate the involvement and development of the group.

## brainstorming

Brainstorming is an intensive discussion session in which the quantity of ideas produced or potential solutions offered to a problem are more important than the quality. All suggestions made are recorded and no group member may criticise any idea or suggested solution during the agreed time period, no matter how strange or ludicrous, as this would create inhibition. At the close of the agreed period the members are free to analyse the points raised and to arrive at a consensus about courses of action or solutions. Formulating a list of possible solutions or ideas is the initial stage in a facilitative teaching and learning cycle. Students can, as a group or individually, explore/reflect/analyse the products of the brainstorming session. This will lead to other ideas and projects.

## buzz groups

Buzz groups are similar to brainstorming sessions but they have a smaller membership and used for a shorter time within the process of a lesson or lecture. The intimacy encourages participation by all members and helps in the process of reflection.

## debate

Debate is a more formal approach to discussion that is rarely used in class but often employed as an enjoyable leisure activity. It is a useful method for presenting students with student-led opposing and challenging viewpoints and demonstrating how these opposing viewpoints can be analysed and assessed. This helps students to reflect on their own and others' views and develop more understanding and empathy. For those taking part it assists their powers of logical reasoning and argument, shows them how to present convincing cases, and how to deal with opposing views. These are valuable skills for the team based workplace where decisions and argument must be settled within an acceptable format.

## case studies

Case studies are widely used as a learning method and as assessment procedures. They are commonly used in legal and business education. What makes a case particularly useful is its reality, its relevance to problems faced by the group, the completeness of available data and the significance of issues/values at issue. A good case study is a record of an issue that has actually been faced by a person or group, together with the surrounding facts, opinions and prejudices upon which decisions often depend. The value of the case is that it enables the group to analyse, identify fact from opinion, weigh and test alternatives and consider values. It is usually a deliberate effort to interpret and apply principles to a real situation. The case method is particularly suited to fields where there are few or no final answers and where sound judgment is the essential quality.

## free group discussion

Group discussion is a common feature in the education process of adults in both institutional learning and community learning. Free discussion is where students decide the topic and direction. It enhances human relations and self-awareness and creates a willingness to consider new ideas. Again it is a useful learning ground for workplace decision making and discussion. Other discussion could be problem-centred. Here the group has a task to perform that is set by the tutor or themselves. The outcome might be enhanced by analytic thinking and the ability to make decisions and evaluate them.

A good discussion topic must interest all participants, be clearly worded, be capable of producing alternative points of view and be able to be discussed meaningfully. These criteria are useful since adults are likely to opt out if the topic is of no interest or relevance or they have nothing they can contribute. Thus topics should be picked in conjunction with students. The discussion encourages group sharing, responsibility for own learning and a sense of teamwork and develops self-confidence. There is always the danger that dominant personalities will try to dominate proceedings.

Andragogy requires teachers of adults to know when to stop talking and start listening. Group activity is not facilitated by a teacher who jumps in with unnecessary intervention, pounds their own agenda or insists their way is the only way. Students must be encouraged to give opinions, feedback, ideas and advice. This, of course, requires a non-threatening environment in which all feel able to contribute. Questions such as 'How do you feel about that?' or 'Can you say more about it?', plus head nodding and smiling should be employed by the group leader to encourage further development.

In a group discussion the teacher is no longer the only source of information. The teacher might engineer a situation to which all members can contribute. Members learn from each other as they ask questions, clarify and argue their case against other views. A discussion must have a clear aim set by the group or teacher and students must come prepared with something useful to contribute. The success of group work depends on the amount and quality of planning and preparation. Generally, participants must have a common interest for it to succeed.

## the panel

The panel is like an interview but uses the experience of visitors or of several members of the group. Panel members discuss a topic, then questions are asked by the audience of students. The panel should present alternative views, create a wider understanding of the topic and generate debate. The difficulties are that class members might not know enough to ask questions or have sufficient confidence if the panel are outsiders.

## project

Individuals and groups can make significant discoveries from projects. They are exciting, motivating and students learn by doing. Adults should become self-directed learners and being involved in a project as a group member is an excellent way to develop individual enquiry skills. A project will provide individual experience, under guidance, of how to plan a project, find resources, carry out a project, write it up and evaluate it. Even traditional teaching can invoke self-directed activity in the form of projects, research papers, interview projects, etc. The most valuable skill a learner can acquire is that of learning how to learn. This opens the doors to all sorts of new learning and skill in the future.

## seminars

Seminars involve larger numbers of people who have a common need. They are invariably led by an expert who tries to improve knowledge, or provide new knowledge. Seminars involve the presentation of a paper by a student or visitor, which forms the basis for a group discussion. The paper should be provocative, topical and interesting. Someone must understand a topic well in order to explain it to others. Thus if adult students are given the task of being responsible for teaching a small topic to the rest of the class they will learn more than from passive listening. It does not have to be a formal presentation; taking the lead in introducing a topic in a seminar could suffice. Students could initially work in pairs with someone more experienced assisting a less experienced student.

A seminar can lead to passive learning by the audience if there is no opportunity to interact and can also prove daunting to students if they have to present and answer argument from their peers or fear asking a foolish question.

## workshops

The number of workshops run has increased dramatically over the past few years although their impact on workplace learning and the work practices and personal development of participants is questionable. Workshops have tended to be one-off and bear little relationship to a broader training strategy in the organisation, that is if one existed. What is apparent is that workshops are no quick fix for effecting rapid, long-lasting and significant change in the workplace or in the personal effectiveness of individuals. In order to be of value workshops must be integrated in the training objectives and framework, be used for specific purposes and be followed up to ensure that the learning outcomes are introduced. Too often a workshop is a day off work for a stand-alone experience that motivates participants temporarily and makes them feel good about themselves and their work. However, the euphoria soon dissipates on returning to the workplace, where the workshop learning starts to appear very remote in view of the disinterest of superiors in the outcomes.

The selection, planning and articulation of workshop activities must be linked back into a workplace context if they are not to be a waste of time and money. Workshops have benefits for three groups of people. First, management often perceives workshops as cost-effective ways of meeting staff training needs as staff are lost to the workplace for a short, manageable period. There is an unfounded belief that the workshop skill can be translated into the workplace. Second, trainers have found workshops allows them scope to devise a wide range of activities for multiskilling the workforce fairly quickly with less effort on their part than would be required by having to devise a lengthy course. Thirdly, workforce members see a gain in developing a range of new skills in a short time without attending lengthy courses, which skills might be useful for presentation later for recognition of prior qualifications and skills if attendance at more formal courses is required. However, a certificate of attendance at the end of the day is no formal recognition of competence.

Workshops might be high in structure for the learning of specific skills, for example advanced Word for Windows. There will be less structure in workshops on communication skills and stress management. The degree of individual control over learning by the adult in the workshop is also related to the topic and the degree of structure needed. A workshop on OH and S dealing with legislation has a structure and content that learners have little control over, whereas a workshop on exploring how different levels of management might relate better to each other would be far more open. However, effective workshops, even in a more structured form, should allow adults to bring their experience to bear, should be sensitive to individual differences among adults (personality, ability and learning style), should include opportunities for enhancing self-esteem, should ensure there is some opportunity for experiential and self-directed learnings, using a variety of teaching methods and changing pace at least every 20 minutes, and should be based on negotiation between the needs and expectations of both the employer and the employee. To achieve this last objective, a needs analysis and a skills audit should be conducted.

Learning outcomes should be monitored to determine to what extent aims were achieved, the success of particular methods and the implementation of learning back in the workplace. Workshops should enable a group of students to apply theory to practice. The end product might be improved skill — a product useful to professional practice — or simply additional learning. It is feasible for learners to design their own workshops and lead them, given a suitable subject or problem that all can involve themselves in.

## games, simulations and role-play

Role-play, simulation and gaming are popular techniques. They allow participants to discover outcomes rather than be told. Many organisations have found these techniques very useful for improving understanding, insight and understanding of the effects of various courses of action.

A game is an activity, exercise or illustration of a point the teacher is attempting to get across. It is normally brief and is usually unthreatening, inexpensive, uncompli-cated and requires all participants to involve themselves. There is usually a predictable general result, which is adaptable across a range of situations. The relevance of the game to the training point must be made apparent to the players or else motivation is lost. Gaming tends to highlight patterns of behaviour in human interaction and reg-ulation in social living. Some business games might involve role-play as well.

A role-play is similar to a simulation, except it doesn't use any props. All that is often required is a script or an idea and some willing actors. Role-play is similar to psychodrama but with an educational rather than therapeutic objective. It can be employed when a teacher wants learners to experience something. It should be used naturally and fit logically into a planned learning sequence.

The role-play might be a brief excerpt from someone's life or a role for which the individual is being prepared. The situations, often problem situations, can be related to the workplace where human relationships and behaviour can be pre-sented, for example the role of supervisor, team leader or employee with a home duties conflict or a counselling situation. Participants could learn how to negoti-ate with employers/unions, negotiate a contract or deal with difficult customers in a face-to-face situation. Role-plays are quite natural in vocational and community education, reflecting as they do situations the players are or will be involved in at work, home or in the community.

The role-play is an opportunity to practise new behaviours and new scripts to see their effect. Other group members can provide a critique, which is used as a basis for further replaying, practise and development. To the extent that the stu-dents are able to identify and involve themselves in what is being enacted, they might be better able to appraise their own behaviour or understand the situa-tion/relationship more empathically. The assumption is that one will be able to deal more calmly, understandingly and effectively with real conflicts when real feel-ings are released. It is a very commendable approach for adults who are socially mature enough to participate seriously and who are willing to reflect on and learn from the experience. Different scenarios and outcomes of the same episode can be tried out in a non-threatening context.

Role-play cannot be predicted precisely, as the development depends on the players. It can be time consuming to prepare. It is hard to evaluate its effectiveness and it might cause trauma for a few sensitive persons to whom the teacher might be unable to respond or counsel competently.

A simulation is usually a more complex problem or situation than a role-play (although role-play is often a constituent part of it) and is usually a mockup of the real thing. It might be a simulation of decision making on the shop floor, or of a work context such as emergency procedures or an in-basket exercise or air traffic control problem. Some simulations can be expensive, as with pilot training. However, interpersonal simulations such as learning how to interview or dealing with an industrial relations dispute are cheap but need lots of trainer preparation time for briefing, scripting, creating the ethos, etc. The simulation permits a learner to practise new behaviour without endangering the real product or suffering dire personal consequences if something goes wrong.

Debriefing must occur at the end of a simulation or role-play to enable members to discuss, evaluate and rethink the issues and solutions and enable them to integrate their experiences with their previous knowledge and practice. A debriefing period also enables students to readjust to their normal roles.

## snowballing

Snowballing starts with each individual learner and then becomes a group process. Initially, individuals are asked to reflect on a task or proposition and come to some conclusions about it. Then they work in pairs to reflect on their conclusions as individuals and come to a joint conclusion. Pairs then form groups of four and the process is repeated. The collective finding of each group of four is reported to the whole group in a plenary session. All members have input at the beginning and the technique encourages the arguing of a case and reaching consensus. These are all useful skills in team work and decision making.

## visits, tours and field trips

Visits, tours and field trips provide effective personal experience and common experience and can help to integrate a group early in a course. The main benefit is to provide knowledge and experiential resources. There is a need for preparation and debriefing so that each learner gets the most out of the trip, sharing and reflecting on experience. They can be time consuming and expensive.

## ■■■ INDIVIDUALISED LEARNING

We noted in the previous chapter that theorists like Knowles and Rogers advocate self-directed learning as the basis for education in the adult years, although the criticisms levelled at the concept should be borne in mind.

## self-directed learning

Such learning stems from the varied life experience of the adult and the need to solve real-life problems, is motivating, assists the person to develop research skills and to learn how to apply new knowledge to real-life situations. People have different learning styles too and, as adults, prefer greater autonomy over what they do. Most humanist educators argue that the only learning of significance is that which has been personally appropriated and assimilated into experience. Many educators see self-direction as an intrinsic personality or cognitive quality of adulthood.

There are three essential elements in self-directed learning:

- In terms of course structure, there is no prescribed content that teachers feel has to be transmitted to students.
- The content and the way the content is learnt is determined by the interests and needs of all participants, including the teacher.
- What the students get out of it is measured by the extent to which they attain their own learning objectives.

Self-directed learning refers to any application that gives the learner responsibility for their learning and grants them autonomy in choosing the material they will learn, how they will learn it and at what pace. Much institution-based, self-directed learning can be accommodated in a learning centre, which can be a room or a larger suite of rooms containing a variety of resources. A facilitator will often be present to assist with queries. The main advantage of a learning centre is its physical presence, somewhere students and employees can go to seek resources and study away from their work station or home. Of course, it can take place in the home with support from communicative technologies (and very understanding close relatives).

It is only in personal learning and courses that extend knowledge that student choice is really available. In many cases, courses and content are prescribed by training bodies or by the job, trade or profession. Thus, in industrial settings self-directed learning might be limited by practical reality that dictates what needs to be learnt, the economics of class teaching over individual instruction and the need to keep everyone up to pace on a fixed-time course. Even here, some of the statements of competence are broad enough to permit some measure of choice of content. It is obvious that genuine self-directed learning is not possible where academic, institutional and/or work-based skill courses are involved. But some degree of movement towards it, even within constraining environments, is possible if the environment can encourage some intellectual freedom, experimentation and creativity, if adult learners feel supported, if their individual needs are acknowledged and their achievements respected, if experience and critical reflection can be involved as learning tools and if they have from time to time some responsibility for their own learning. Self-directed learning is a major educational approach, which needs to be widely and flexibly used for individual improvement beyond the basic skills if any country is ever to be a clever country.

Given the will, self-directed learning in areas of competency skills can actually be done from prepared packages if these involve a variety of combinations of media presentation and assessment methods as well as varying degrees of structure or direction, taken at the learner's pace. Such packages should indicate the learning objectives that are vital since there is no instructor. The material should be chunked into convenient units capable of being studied in a normal span of attention, say 30 to 45 minutes. This allows for a break before repeating the material until it is understood. This method reduces interference with the memory processes and provides for distributed or spaced learning, both of which improve the efficiency of learning (Chapter 5).

Some of the learning packages can be taken to the workstation when learning on the job is necessitated by the material to be learnt. It could even be taken home. Therefore, self-directed learning requires a much less formalised training setting.

The transition from teacher-directed to self-directed learning can be confusing and cause learners to become anxious, lose confidence and even withdraw. While developmentally mature adult students resent formal institutional demands or fixed curricula that interfere with their own interests and needs, there are less mature and more anxious adult learners who still prefer a tightly controlled curriculum and clear directions as to what to study. In fact, many learners who enrol in formal classes do so deliberately to avoid flexibility and learner choice. They want unambiguous direction with clear objectives and routes to get there, particularly if the end qualification will provide status and career advancement. In these situations self-directed learning is more concerned with an internal change of consciousness than with the external management of instruction. The aim of the teaching in this situation is to enable the student to become aware of the interrelated and interdependent nature of knowledge and its relativistic and contextual nature. This process is essential in the development of an active, thinking and independent learner and is more fundamental than simple situational autonomy.

The most important message is that teachers of adults have to cope with as wide a range of learners in terms of ability, interests, learning styles, motivation and personality as primary school teachers do. In the initial stages, the teacher might have to be a little more directing than they would wish to be. But over time they can relinquish more autonomy to students through using operant-conditioning processes to shape and reinforce the necessary behaviours, eventually being able to remove these techniques as intrinsic motivation takes over. This movement should be clearly explained to students who can then accept a planned and structured movement away from teacher direction and are prepared to take on the increasing self-management of their own learning. As part of this movement, students need to be given the skills required for self-direction, such as accessing resources, managing time, practice at making notes, using the library, using the computer and sample assignments.

Thus the transition to self-directed learning is not served well by throwing out all the external structures at once. In fact, it usually takes more careful and detailed planning and structure to support and shape the individual's learning or developmental efforts than are required in more traditional learning operations. Students appear to gain more satisfaction from self-direction than teacher direction, although the outcomes in terms of competency should not be different. Students will certainly gain more in personal terms such as a sense of worth, a feeling of being able to achieve by their own efforts and an affirmation of their sense of autonomy. Learning becomes a personal development process and a personal growth matter, not just an intellectual activity, and this is important in preparing the stage for lifelong learning.

But we must not confuse self-directed education with therapy. This confusion has probably originated from Rogers' emphasis on a non-interventionist facilitator who helps clients to become aware of their feelings. Therefore, a teacher must ensure that content is not neglected, that students do get challenged and extended, albeit within an ethos that lends itself to personal development. The teacher's task is to use a variety of ways, utilising student activity and self-direction methods, to get skills and knowledge across in a non-alienating way to adults and to ensure that they becomes part of their experience. Learning contracts are a vehicle at the heart of this, as a contract provides an adult with considerably more opportunity to direct their own learning than any other approach.

Self-directed learning using contracts is not a cop-out for the teacher, but involves the teacher in more work as intensive one-to-one tutorials occur, resources are negotiated/provided, learning is facilitated in groups and missing perspectives are advocated. It is a broader, more creative function than simply being an information giver and authority figure. Contracts can remove the distaste for learning and the anxiety of class learning with its competitive element for students whose history in the field of education is not strong or pleasant. Students are able to focus on matters of concern to them in the workplace and relate their formal learning to the job. For example, analysing issues and dilemmas arising in a work context can lead to changes in work practices.

A number of attempts within formal educational institutions along the lines of Independent Studies courses have been attempted. For example, at Lancaster University, UK, there is a School of Independent Studies offering an undergraduate degree. While this is possible at university level for students who want to investigate particular topics, issues or problems as part of the advancement of knowledge, within the workplace there is a significant limitation. How can adult employees 'know' what they need to know and make appropriate choices. To what extent can they negotiate their own learning when employers need the development of particular skills and knowledge. For many workers, self-direction is not a consideration as predetermined competency courses provide the gateway to pay increases and promotion. And given the pressures of work, how realistic is it to expect employees to manage their own learning. The major tension in lifelong education for learners and teachers is how to square a more client-centred focus with credentialism, occupational relevancy and cost effectiveness.

## self-paced independent learning and flexible delivery

Self-paced learning is provision in the structure of the learning activity that allows the learner to work through the material at their own pace. Flexible delivery is also generally used as a synonym, exemplified by ANTA's (1996) definition of flexible delivery as 'an approach rather than a system or technique...It gives clients as much control as possible over what and when and where and how they learn' (p. 11). A major source of contention in the delivery of education and training for adults in all educational settings is the extent to which there should be provision for self-paced learning. It has long been argued that self-paced learning is not only desirable but essential in adult education and can be used to teach anything from a small 20-minute remedial skill program to a whole course. Self-pacing develops independence and helps those whose gradually slowing nervous system would impede their performance if they were required to keep to a set time frame. Even the competency system considers the criterion to be not time spent but competency achieved. The full potential of any adult education and training can only be achieved if innovative teaching strategies such as self-pacing, individualised learning and flexible sequencing are tailored to the needs of individuals.

Self-paced learning also permits greater efficiency in the use of time and resources. In industrial contexts self-paced learning can be articulated without too much difficulty since much training is done in small groups or on a one-to-one basis. Many TAFEs are embracing self-paced learning, according to Watson (1993). Some of these TAFE programs employ an open entry, open exit policy as well. Self-paced learning requires a sound support of learning resources. The most common resource is a learning guide that directs learning through a variety of sequenced learning activities, projects, tests and tasks necessary to meet performance criteria. Further resources might include videos, audio tapes, print materials and computer-assisted learning packages.

In self-paced, individualised activity, learners work in learning resource areas or workstations individually or in small teams. Work is progressively checked and teachers/trainers are rostered to work areas to facilitate, act as resources and test students as required. Although learners are working on their own, many institutions/course leaders/teachers require learners to attend for a stipulated number of hours over the course if practical work requiring the use of equipment is part of the course, even though the learner still decides when that attendance will be. But even self-paced courses have to set eventual deadlines, such as the end of the semester or year. Learners begin to realise that with freedom comes responsibility, if they are to succeed.

Self-pacing can be provided for in several ways:
- External study programs in which students receive study materials and work on their own away from campus — there is usually an assessment deadline though.
- Campus-based programs in which students attend at mutually agreed times but work through the material at their own pace — again assessment deadlines are usually set.
- Totally flexible programs on and off campus in which students decide when, where and how they study and when they are assessed.

All these variants in a variety of combinations might be print-based or online.

Some of the reasons given for self-paced learning include:

- Adults learn at different rates and have different preferred learning styles.
- Self-paced learning encourages the development of personal skills and competencies useful for future personal development, such as independence, initiative, time management and problem-solving ability.
- Self-paced learning is congruent with principles required for the recognition of prior learning, multiple entry and exit points and alternative delivery modes.
- Self-paced learning is especially adaptable in industrial settings where learners are not always available at fixed, regular times, for example shift work, emergencies.
- Self-paced learning helps lifelong learners to become more self-directed and proactive.

Self-pacing is not synonymous with self-direction, although the two might seem like twins. Self-determined learning must include self-pacing but self-pacing can be an element on its own. Self-paced courses might require students to follow highly structured resource materials/activities. This often occurs in workplace contexts where very specific skills and knowledge are required and the pacing of learning is tempered by employee availability and ability. Self-pacing can be linked to mastery learning so no student can proceed without meeting criterion-performance levels and is therefore more congruent with CBT than other elements of adult learning.

Self-pacing is quite beneficial for older learners who often need a slower intro-duction and to be allowed to come to terms with new information, ideas, materials and equipment at a pace they dictate. New material is best presented as a solution to a problem already identified by the person. In this way, it integrates with past experience. They do not appreciate being paced or working to a tight timetable. They prefer working at their own pace and attempting to improve on their own previous best performance rather than being evaluated against others or some objective standard.

Programs that employ self-paced individualised and flexible delivery modes also serve to foster wider aspects of competence needed for coping with future change sought by employers, such as independence, self-reliance, research skills, time and resource management and team activity.

However, the method does not suit all students. Some prefer structure and face-to-face teaching and the steady supporting hand of an ever-present teacher. The presumed advantages of increased flexibility for learning and taking responsibility for one's own learning is not to everyone's taste. Even those who do prefer it still need a sense of responsibility and motivation (a good work ethic) to manage their time and plan their studies effectively, and teachers must give wise advice to indi-vidual students about their choice of study mode. No teacher should abandon their duty of care to a student on the grounds of infringing their autonomy, but at the end of the day the student's decision is finally theirs to make after counselling.

Flexible delivery and self-paced learning does not always lead to good completion rates. Misko (2000b) reveals that external study modules had the lowest completion rates related perhaps to students' comments that they had difficulties disciplining themselves to get work done. The most common reason for students choosing this method was lifestyle-related so that they could manage study within a matrix of other commitments in their home, work and social life. Such busy people might in fact require more structure to their studies, prioritising tasks using established time management practices. Students without the learning, literacy and personal skills for self-paced, independent study, whether on or off campus, will damage their progress by indulging in this form of study.

Some students too might rush through learning tasks to finish as quickly as possible, thereby missing the extra incidental knowledge that comes from thoroughly studying something and reading round the topic. They have an instrumental approach, which is exactly what adult education is trying to avoid, and self-pacing allied with independent study can unfortunately come to replicate a 'banking' form of education as learners seek a quick self-managed fix for promotion. Misko (2000a) provides a detailed exposition of the advantages and disadvantages of self-pacing with studies of real examples of self-paced courses that are operating.

Learning materials for self-paced learning have not always been adequate either; written in English of too high a level, not catering for migrants, etc. Some students, unless helped to develop the appropriate study methods, can get lost and fall well behind. Learners also need to be shown how to use resources, such as finding books in a library and operating audio, video and computer equipment. It must always be remembered that just as some students revel in self-paced and self-directed learning, there are others who, because of personality or learning style traits, do prefer and indeed need a conventional teacher-directed approach.

Self-pacing might generate problems with student needs being neglected when there are high teacher-student ratios. In this context, we might find courses presented entirely from written booklets in the absence of other teaching resources; learners waiting for assessment when finished instead of being able to move forward into the next program; difficulties in maintaining student records when students are all at different points; teachers and/or students unused to the system and needing support. Therefore, for any introduction of self-paced learning in the workplace or institution sufficient staff must be able and willing to implement the system and there should be sufficient resources and materials, a variety of methods that allow students to select one consistent with their preferred style of learning and a records and management system geared to asynchronous assessment.

## contract learning

Contract learning is not new and has been espoused both by behaviourists, who see it as a method of control, and by adult educators (like Knowles and Rogers), who promote it because it eliminates passive learning, which adults dislike, and because of its easy integration into experiential, self-paced and self-directed learning. In contract learning, the learner chooses the topic or competency they wish to learn. Contract learning permits learning that is relevant to the learner since personal choice is involved. It can be related to the work requirements of the individual so that the learner can select tasks that have a meaningful work-related outcome.

Another advantage is that the learner can have control of the design of the project and learning if they write their own objectives, determine what work is to be done, what resources are to be used and design the evaluation criteria. The learner owns the learning project, which provides them with the motivation to see it though. The contract allows for differences in time, style and learning speed. The whole process is congruent with the major principles of andragogy and adults appear to learn more deeply and permanently as a result of their involvement.

The contract itself is an agreement with a teacher to undertake a particular, chosen learning project within a time frame at a particular level of competency. It must be negotiated with the teacher as a learner might plan a project that is too easy or too hard or easily go off track without a facilitator to advise them during the formulation and learning stage and during evaluation. If there is no one to check or keep the learner on track then it could become a waste of learning time and resources. As the contract must be negotiated, several meetings might be necessary until both parties agree. To maintain parity between contracts it is useful to develop a model that all teachers use, or have other teachers review a contract to ensure a reasonable standardisation of requirements and assessment.

The contract is usually written and should include the following:

- The initial diagnosis of the learning need. Within a workplace context the competencies required to perform a role or task are a useful starting point.
- The translation of the learning need into a list of specific learning objectives, both personal and skill-based, which describe in non-complex terms what is to be learnt (the outcomes) with a realistic time frame for completion; objectives being what the learner will learn not what the learner will be doing. These must be written in clear and measurable terms.
- A list of the resources and strategies needed to achieve each objective, including human resources such as experts in the field. Other resources include literature, film/video, Internet, techniques, methods, etc.
- Evidence of accomplishment. This might be reports of knowledge acquired as shown in essays, projects, assignments, exams, audio-visual presentations, industrial products, working models, annotated bibliographies and diaries. For skills one could use ratings by assessors of live or videotaped performance. Attitude change could be shown by ratings, feedback and role-plays.
- Specified criteria that will be used to judge the evidence. Criteria for knowledge might be clarity, comprehensiveness, accuracy, etc. For skills, the evidence might include precision, flexibility, speed and safety. All these judgments must be made in a reliable and valid way. The form of assessment

must be included, for example when, how often and what type of assessment.

- A review of the contract with supervisor, teacher, mentor, etc. Are the objectives clear, understandable and realistic? Are there other objectives that could be included? Are the strategies and resources appropriate and available? Is the evidence for assessment relevant or are there other sources available? Are the criteria for judging the evidence appropriate? Can the judgments be made reliably? Finally, a completion date must be agreed.

Modifications can be made as the project progresses or as issues or difficulties come to light. New knowledge and skills can also suggest a redirection of the work. The learner needs to recognise when there is a problem so they can retain ownership. As the learner works at the pace each has decided they can manage the teacher does not need to worry about keeping faster learners occupied or about how to get slower learners to catch up. This method is very useful in areas where the learner has a very narrow focus or specific area of study or for a highly motivated learner who wants to learn a subject independently. A learning contract can give the learner a reason for getting organised and carrying out a learning activity.

Using contract learning to facilitate self-directed and self-paced learning does present a problem. This occurs mainly in the workplace or vocational colleges where contracts are operated in a system that ultimately requires certification for courses that involve formal recognition for trade or professional competency purposes. The support function of staff in contract learning can for a few students become a prop, which they exploit, becoming perversely dependent when the aim is the opposite. Attempts to extend and challenge are then seen as attacks and betrayal. Teaching staff might also feel that they always have to be supportive in the Rogerian unconditional-acceptance sense, overhelpful to students and papering over unsatisfactory performance. This makes it hard for a teacher to confront, challenge or fail a student, even in appropriate circumstances. The result is that some students might pass when they should have failed.

Thus the humanist model on which contract learning is based does not fully meet the needs of students and teachers for self-directed learning when the context is tightly constrained by syllabus demands and time. Totally open-ended support and complete freedom to choose what to investigate or study, even within the framework of a contract, is not part of the reality of gaining valid knowledge, understandings and skills. Therefore, the teacher must ensure that content is not neglected and that students do get challenged and extended. While the aim for adult educators is to enable adult individuals to accept responsibility for and have control over their own lives, this aim is far more complex than many humanist writers claim, as they tend to ignore the fact that life is a complex process and interpersonal, institutional and broader social issues are also involved. A contract does provide a balanced means of allowing self-pacing and self-direction, while explicitly designating and ensuring the required performance.

## Keller Plan or personalised systems of instruction (PSIs)

The Keller Plan is an example of a personalised system of instruction. The main feature of this method is that students work on their own at their own pace but they study prescribed units of text. The student then demonstrates mastery of the unit, usually by successfully taking a multiple-choice test or a short-answer-recall test before they are allowed to proceed to the next unit. Typically, students are expected to score 90 per cent or more. If they fail to meet this criterion they can restudy the unit or receive some remedial help before they do so. This is referred to as mastery learning. Lectures and demonstrations may be included, but they are for motivational purposes, not as sources of critical information. There is stress on the written word. Proctors (or tutors) provide immediate assessment and meet some personal social needs in the learning process. It is essential that each new unit introduces new material in such quantities that ensure the student makes no or few mistakes. The value is that the learner is active, self-paced and assessed when ready. The Keller Plan incorporates many principles of distance learning.

Research demonstrates that this method is remarkably effective in terms of examination results. Many PSI course are now computer-based (Pear & Novak, 1996). The problem is that though effective for the transmission of factual information of a basic kind that every student needs to know in the early days of studying a subject and although it allows for individual differences, there is no encouragement of independent learning and thinking.

Thus it seems on the surface to espouse elements of andragogy, but the underlying theme is essentially behaviourism with its simplistic rote learning and transfer of information common for all learners, followed by regurgitation for assessment. Other disadvantages are that the material is selected and organised by the teacher and the emphasis on the written word can be quite discomforting to many adult learners.

## problem-based learning

While the principles of cognitive learning theory are not as clear-cut as those of behaviourism, problem-based learning does clearly lie in this area. Chapter 4 revealed the approach of such psychologists as Bruner on this topic. In this mode, the instruction is based on problems, with the provision of a wide range of resources to assist students to achieve their objectives. Students are assumed to be responsible and motivated adults, are encouraged to define their own learning goals and often work in groups. The achievement of the goal is often jointly assessed by students and staff. One key idea is that in trying to solve one problem others arise so the notion of sequential learning is abandoned. Problems can be self- or group-chosen within a particular field. Boud and Feletti (1991) report problem-based learning in medical education, mechanical engineering, management and social work, to name a few.

The principle of the method is that the starting point of learning should be a problem or puzzle that the learner wishes to solve. The acquisition of knowledge occurs as a by-product. The method is usually characterised by:

- the use of real-life problems
- problems that cross traditional subject divisions
- providing necessary resources but no instruction on how to solve the problem
- students working in small groups with access to a teacher
- students working on one problem at a time.

## assignments

Assignments are a common feature of most courses and might involve an essay, a case study, a research project or the production of some equipment. The assignment can enable students to work in a medium other than the written word and this is an advantage for adult learners. Persons must be available for consultation at all stages of the assignment and library and other resources must be accessible. Written assignments might prove difficult for adults who have not written a lengthy piece of work before and are not proficient in the use of the written word. The assignment can be tutor-set or chosen by the student. While the latter enables the learner to choose something that is interesting to them or relevant to their needs, there is always the chance they might select something they already know.

Grading assignments is a difficult task as it involves subjective judgment. There is no objective standard against which to judge the work unless it is a piece of working equipment that must do a particular job.

An assignment enables the learner to adopt an analytic approach to a problem, collect data/information, construct an argument in response to the analysis, plan a logical structure and reveal the results of their reflection and evaluations, reach argued conclusions and test them against wider reality. Preparing for, undertaking and writing up an assignment is a method of learning in itself. Tutors must give feedback after marking so that defects can be remedied as this continues the learning process. The teacher should encourage students to reflect on what they have written. Negative comments inhibit the learners from continuing to pursue their ideas and to reflect. A tick or a cross is not helpful and provides mere reinforcement, not extension of thinking and the production of further ideas.

## practicals

Practicals are valuable where skills are being taught. Most students can master skills if they are divided into component parts and each element is mastered separately. Some practical work must be undertaken under supervision in a laboratory. It would be too dangerous in some situations to allow the learner unsupervised free reign as they learn to handle dangerous chemicals, welding metals or carry out medical-biological techniques, etc. Practicals are common in all sciences and even in social sciences, such as psychology, where replications of standard research can aid understanding and stimulate interest.

## personal tutorials

Personal tutorials can be used in on-campus courses and off-campus distance learning via teleconferencing or after the submission and assessment of work when detailed discussion can occur. This discussion should deal with the issues and problems raised by the learner and be a context of interaction between two people seeking greater understanding of a topic rather than one of the teacher simply telling the student where they went wrong or what to do to get it right. The context also permits a counselling role for the teacher and an opportunity for the development of a positive working relationship. Tutorials are important at all stages during a period of study. At the outset, students need help to get going, to understand administrative procedures and they need immediate feedback from early assessment. In midstream, tutorials are centrally focused as an interactive teaching technique, while at the end of a course they perform the vital function of ensuring students are prepared for the final assessment, not only in terms of knowledge and revision but also format and administrative factors.

## critical or reflective thinking

Critical thinking is reflective thinking that is focused on deciding what to do or believe. It involves seeking reasons and valid information, being open-minded, taking into account the total situation, looking for alternatives, changing position when evidence is sufficient, analysing arguments, seeking clarification, identifying and challenging assumptions, making judgments and deciding on action. Critical thinking is not a single capacity that learners have or don't have but a complex of components that they have to a greater or lesser degree. They will become better at critical thinking to the extent that these qualities are developed.

There are many reasons for wanting learners to learn and use critical thinking skills. First, it will be needed to perform effectively in the workplace of the future. Non-routine abstract work, with employees taking more responsibility for decisions operating within system-wide geographic and time horizons, places a premium on broad thinking and problem-solving skills. As stable, well-defined environments in which ready-made solutions to regularly experienced situations and problems could be applied disappear, citizens and employees all need high level and flexible thinking skills. Innovative, high quality and flexible production of goods and services requires a thinking employee. In a more general context, critical thinking is essential for citizenship as there can be no liberty for a community that cannot distinguish lies from truth. This links into the andragogical approach that claims adults learn best in conditions of problem solving and independent inquiry.

Costa and Lowery (1990) suggest specific ways for teaching critical thinking. Teachers should structure classes and content so that active thinking is encouraged. Questions and directions help learners gather information and apply it in novel situations. Direct instruction tends to inhibit critical and creative thinking, which flourish best in a classroom climate where learners are in the decision-making role, decide on strategies to solve problems and evaluate their answers and motivation is derived from the intrinsic reward of satisfying one's intellectual curiosity and one's desire to be responsible, productive and to master challenges. A variety of classroom patterns can be used — from individual learning and groups working collaboratively on problems to discussions involving the total group.

Teachers should facilitate the development of critical thinking by asking questions that require synthesis, analysis, summarisation, drawing cause and effect relationships, comparing and classifying. Other questions can lead learners to apply concepts and principles to novel and hypothetical situations and to make critical judgments, build models, forecast and speculate. Paraphrasing and reflection are useful tools for all this. 'What you are suggesting is...' ; 'Let's work with John's strategy for now'; 'You believe this analogy is helpful'.

Using appropriate words in the classroom can throw out challenges to think. For example, instead of saying 'Let's look at these two examples', why not say 'Let's compare these two examples'; or instead of 'What do you think of this result?' ask 'What hypotheses might explain this?' or again 'How do you know it is true?' translates in thinking terms into 'What evidence do you have to support your hypothesis?'. These are only slight changes, but they convey a greater challenge to think. Other thoughtful speaking that causes learners to define, be specific and use accurate descriptors is for teachers to eliminate universals such as 'never', 'all' and 'everybody'. Unreferenced pronouns like 'they', unspecified groups like 'big business' and 'politicians', ill-defined comparisons like 'more nutritious', 'better' and assumed rules conveyed in words like 'ought' should all be avoided. When teachers hear such phrases as, 'Everyone does it' they should question 'Everyone?'; 'Employers always...?'; 'Governments never respond to community needs?'; 'They won't let us...?'. Ask 'Who are they?', 'Can you give examples', etc. Teachers need to outlaw 'I can't'.

Criticism is a technique that should not be used if critical thinking is to be enhanced. Rather, the use of clarification and further questions will help to redirect thinking. Silence is also a useful technique as it allows time for thinking and reflecting, rather than saying the first thing that comes into one's head. Teachers are unfotunately uncomfortable with silence as there is an assumption that silence means that nothing is going on.

## overview

While this section has attempted crudely to distinguish between teacher-centred and learner-centred approaches in many instances there is a fine line and an effective teacher is able to use flexibly a variety of methods to suit the material and the needs of individual students and groups of students. The answer is not to follow Knowles' assumptions slavishly but to find accommodation between the content/discipline requirements of a course, professional judgments of responsible teachers, the needs and experience of students, the existing student knowledge base and student confidence and motivation, etc. There are a host of variables that make prescription impossible. There will be times when a learner needs some predigested information in an expository style that will facilitate ensuing learner-centred activity/problem solving/self-choice of further study and self-responsibility in learning, etc. The educator has to make deliberate choices about which model(s) of teaching are appropriate for given situations, but this should be done with an overriding concern to show respect, sensitivity and warmth for the learner as an adult person and for the ultimate purpose of facilitating the independence and the interdependence of learners.

## ■■■ MENTORING AS A LEARNING TOOL

Like most things in a world of change, the age-old practice of mentoring is being influenced by new forms of work, technology and learning. Mentoring is typically defined as a relationship between an experienced and a less experienced person in which the mentor provides the protégé with guidance, advice, support, and feedback (Haney, 1997). Mentoring is a way to help new employees learn their jobs and about organisational culture to facilitate personal and career growth and to expand opportunities for those traditionally hampered by organisational barriers, such as women and minorities. The benefits of mentoring are not only work-related; mentoring can provide individuals with opportunities to enhance cultural awareness, aesthetic appreciation and the potential to lead meaningful lives (Galbraith & Cohen, 1995).

Cleminson and Bradford (1996) identify three types of learning: trial and error, 'sitting by Nellie' (simply observing an experienced person) and guided learning. This last, they suggest, is characteristic of the most effective mentoring. The traditional guided-learning mentoring model is an apprentice learning from a master. The Information Age is demanding a wide range of cognitive, interpersonal and technical skills from employees, and mentoring is seen as an adjunct to normal learning systems to ensure these expanded needs are met.

Mentoring is commonly thought of as relating mainly to roles played by management and professional staff but it is also employed on the shop floor where an experienced and reliable older worker can take a new member under their wing. Mentoring can help to bridge gaps in training and education, particularly that conducted in formal institutions that needs to be transferred to the workplace. Important elements of informal learning and application of learning can be addressed more appropriately and validly in the more informal mentor setting in the real context. No matter how detailed an analysis of a job or skill is on which to base a training program, there are always subtle elements of jobs that require interpretation and integration of knowledge and skills. Therefore, mentoring usually not only includes skills but also learning the implicit norms and mores of the workplace.

Mentor choice should be available to both learner and mentor. Supervisors are not always the best people as they might also have to assess the person for work performance, pay or for competency skills, which can lead to role conflict. Potential mentors should have experience and skills directly related to the needs of the learner, be approachable, be given time release, have exemplary attitudes to work, possess sound communication and relationship skills and show patience, genuine care and concern. Those doing coaching or mentoring must be trained and supported and carefully matched with their allocated person, and possess a high level of personal skills as well as relevant work skills. They must have access to appropriate resources such as training aids, curriculum material and space and time. They must be given a specific task and an indication of the time they have in which to perform it.

The mentor acts as a role model for the learner and gives them something to aim at that is tangible. But it takes time for a mentor-learner relationship to grow. Mentors must stress at the outset what they will and will not do for their charges, and establish ground rules and boundaries. The logistics of mentoring are a cost to the organisations. Mentors often experience time constraints and might have to be taken off their normal jobs from time to time if they are to mentor properly. How to implement an effective mentoring program has been detailed by Lacey (2000).

## mentoring and organisational change

Organisational trends, such as downsizing, restructuring, teamwork, increased diversity and individual responsibility for career development, are contributing to the resurgent interest in mentoring. Downsizing has heightened the need to preserve institutional memory and to share the information and experience that remain within an organisation (Jossi, 1997). Mentors represent continuity; as mentors, older, experienced workers can continue contributing to their organisations and professions. The Mentoring Institute (1997) maintains that, in the past, mentoring typically just 'happened' as experienced people recognised and developed new talent or as beginners sought the counsel of knowledgeable elders. Now, a new mentoring paradigm exists: today's protégés might be better educated but still need a mentor's practical know-how and wisdom ('craft knowledge') that can be acquired only experientially. Therefore, many organisations are instituting formal mentoring programs as a cost-effective way to upgrade skills, enhance recruitment and retention and increase job satisfaction (Jossi, 1997).

Mentoring programs can be targeted specifically at women and minorities as a way of helping them break into the 'old boy network' and through the 'glass ceiling'. Gunn (1995) suggests that a more democratic approach to mentoring is emerging — open to more employees at more levels. For example, a high-level new employee hired because of specific expertise might still need the coaching in organisational culture that mentors can provide, a form of partnership that becomes a two-way transfer of skills and experience. Another democratic approach is a trend toward group mentoring in which the mentor is a learning leader of a team or 'learning group' within a learning organisation (Kaye & Jacobson, 1996).

Members of a diverse learning group can learn from each other (peer mentoring) as well as from the learning leader.

## mentoring and technological change

Although the Internet offers a vast and often bewildering array of information resources, there is still no substitute for human relationships. Telementoring is emerging as a way to pair teachers and learners with subject-matter experts who can provide advice, guidance and feedback on learning projects. In the USA, several sites have developed to match online mentors with protégés, e.g. Mentor Center <http://mentorcenter.bbn.com/>, The Electronic Emissary <http://www.tapr.org/emissary/> and Learn Well eMentors <http://www.learnwell.org/>. Technology is also assisting mentoring in organisations as corporations with offices around the nation and the world connect mentors and protégés via electronic mail or video-conferencing (Jossi, 1997). Telementoring is also proving essential in distance learning. The isolation that often contributes to distance learners dropping out can be overcome by pairing learners with faculty telementors (see below).

The combination of digital technologies and organisational changes is making individuals more responsible for their own learning and career development. Freelancing, consulting and 'portfolio work' make it more difficult for people to connect with traditional sources of mentoring in organisations. At the same time, teleworking increases physical distance from the workplace and decreases workers' ability to acquire the tacit or craft knowledge that comes from interaction with experienced workers. For these reasons, mentoring becomes even more important for individuals attempting to develop an array of flexible skills and for organisations seeking to maintain institutional knowledge.

## learning through mentoring

Mentoring supports much of what is currently known about how adults learn, including the socially constructed nature of learning and the importance of experiential, situated learning experiences (Kerka, 1997). Constructivist theory, both cognitive and humanist, emphasises that learning is most effective when situated in a context in which new knowledge and skills will be used and individuals will construct meaning for themselves but within the context of interacting with others. Mentoring can facilitate learning by experts modelling problem-solving strategies, guiding learners in approximating the strategies, while learners articulate their thought processes. Mentors can coach learners with appropriate scaffolds or aids, gradually decreasing assistance as learners internalise the process and construct their own knowledge and understanding. These processes are reflected in the mentor's roles of guide, adviser, coach, motivator, facilitator and role model within a contextual setting (Haney, 1997). Functioning as experts, mentors provide authentic, experiential learning opportunities as well as a supportive interpersonal relationship through which social learning takes place.

## guided experiential learning

Bell (1997) likens the mentor's role in experiential learning to that of birds guiding their young in leaving the nest; they support without rescuing, provide scaffolding (e.g. asking in a problem situation, 'What do think you should do next?'), but have the courage to let learners fail. Learning from experience, mentees speed past learning basic routines and get on to the job, linking up what was learnt in the classroom and what is needed in the workplace. With trust as the foundation of the relationship, mentors give protégés a safe place to try out ideas, skills and roles with minimal risk (Kaye & Jacobson, 1996). Acquired knowledge is thus constantly reinterpreted and developed through practice as the authenticity of practice is located within real-world activities.

## learning through relationships

Although learning is a matter of individual interpretation of experiences, it takes place within the social context (Kerka, 1997). Therefore, the interpersonal relationship of mentor and mentee is recognised as essential. The idea of learning as a transaction — an interactive and evolving process between mentors and their adult learners — is considered a fundamental component of the adult mentoring relationship. Mentoring performs two primary functions: career/instrumental and psychosocial. The instrumental function is the external value of the relationship: mentees benefit from their mentors' knowledge, skill, feedback, contacts, support and guidance. The psychosocial function is the internal value of the ongoing interpersonal dialogue, collaborative critical thinking, planning, reflection, role modelling, friendship, integration in a work group and informal counselling.

The psychosocial function of mentoring is a form of relational learning, the value of which is being recognised increasingly in a less hierarchical team environment. Women especially have been found to enjoy relational learning. For the executive women in Bierema's (1996) study, relationships informed them about their company's culture and helped them process both cognitive and experiential learning experiences. Mentoring is a personalised and systematic way to be socialised in an organisation's culture and to become culturally competent.

However, a critical issue is that such socialisation can also be constraining if the novice is exposed to a limited or biased repertoire of practices, views and expectations. The question arises whether mentoring could become a base for assimilation and exclusion. The personal relationship at the heart of mentoring can become problematic when mentor and mentee are of different genders, races or cultural backgrounds. There is disagreement about the advantages and disadvantages of matching characteristics in mentoring relationships. Ensher and Murphy (1997) found that perceived and actual similarity affected the amount of instrumental and psychosocial support mentors provided, as well as protégé satisfaction. Some argue that race and gender should not play a role in mentor selection (Jossi, 1997), but mentors still need to be sensitive to different cultural perspectives or mentoring will merely perpetuate homogeneous, exclusionary values and culture.

If developing learning organisations in a learning society is a desirable social goal, mentoring can perform an important function in helping people develop their full potential. If everyone is capable of being a teacher (mentor) and a learner (mentee) individuals should strive to develop their capacity to learn from and support the learning of others.

## ■■■ ONLINE LEARNING

On average people only remember about 20 per cent of what they hear, but between 50 per cent and 80 per cent of what they both see and hear. Striking visual presentation is very powerful in reinforcing information that is delivered simultaneously through hearing. Now we can link the two in novel ways through the rapidly expanding use of computerised information and communication technology in teaching and learning, which has caused transformations in the ways in which knowledge is produced, stored, disseminated and used. Information technologies can be employed at three levels: as a tool in the learning process (word processing), as an aid (data analysis, Internet search) and as a medium by which teaching and learning are conducted. Multimedia technology that uses a combination of text, still images, animations and sound and video to present information in an interactive environment can improve the education process, but issues of production cost and scalability have prevented education from using this technology in any but limited applications.

Recent Y2K issues, for example, provide evidence of the dependency of modern life on computer technology. Web site addresses now appear regularly in the media with the assumption that they will be consulted for further information. In work settings, employees are expected to use computers for such tasks as communication, information management, problem-solving and information seeking. So most of the population, including adults, are now used to the idea of computers at work or around the house. The mode is not new in a sense and most people can readily adapt to it. One primary advantage is that most people are now more 'visual' learners than ever before and thrive on interacting with computers from early childhood right up to the old age, where oldsters are using Internet and email in retirement homes to maintain contact with relatives and friends and learn new things (Cody *et al.*, 1999). Introduced to computers gradually and in a nonthreatening way, older persons coped well if given longer to learn, more pauses, more time for questions and plenty of self-paced hands-on practice (Cody *et al.*, op. cit.). Games, Internet and email are the best elements to introduce to adults who have previously had little or no contact with computer technology, as well as working in pairs. However, there might be some adults who are still anxious about using a computer, particularly middle-aged women who went to school when technical things were for male students only.

In the beginning was the word — the printed word. Sherron and Boettcher (1997) contend that distance education has been in existence since the nineteenth century in the form of correspondence schools. In its earliest form, the first generation of distance education was the 'correspondence model', which presented a passive subject with the to-be-learnt material, usually transmitted by 'snail mail'. The 1960s to 1980s saw this replaced by the 'multimedia model', the second generation of distance education incorporating other forms of media such as radio, television, audiocassettes and videocassettes in distance education programs. It has been in this context that distance learning has become very popular throughout the world, with the Open University in the UK showing the way. The current development is towards a third generation 'telelearning model', based on electronic information technologies, as microcomputers, the Internet and the World Wide Web shape the current generation of online learning and distance learning.

Open Learning Australia (OLA) now offers over 200 course units and they are not TV-based in the main. They are all print-based, supplemented with TV-, radio- or computer-aided learning. Other institutions that offer off-campus courses include Open Learning Institute in Queensland, the Open Learning and Technology Network (OTEN) in NSW and many universities and TAFE colleges. Many of these existing external courses are not based on online delivery as yet, but it is likely over the next few years that more will be so. In the UK, the Open University is a prime example of a dedicated distance learning institution that is embracing online teaching and learning to achieve its mission of providing accessible education. Similarly, City University, Washington USA, is providing online courses that are attracting students from round the world. Most institutions of learning are now starting to enter this field, leading to the prospect of the 'virtual university', which will challenge the dominant paradigm of on-campus, face-to-face teaching.

The terms 'online learning', 'online education', 'virtual learning', 'virtual campus (classroom)', 'web-based learning', 'online delivery', 'computer-mediated learning' and 'flexible delivery' tend to be used interchangeably to represent the use of computerised information and communications technology to enhance delivery of courses and allow interaction in both real and asynchronous time modes. Distance learning is a major element of online learning. Some use the term 'distance education' to refer to the use of print or electronic communications media to deliver instruction when teachers and learners are separated in place and/or time (Eastmond, 1995). However, others emphasise distance learning over education, defining it as a system and process that connects learners with distributed resources, implying learner-centredness and control.

The literature is also replete with definitions of 'multimedia', but basically it is a catchall phrase used to describe the new wave of computer software that deals primarily with the provision of information in an interactive form. The multimedia component is characterised by the presence of text, pictures, sound, animation and video, some or all of which are organised into some coherent program. The interactive component refers to the process of empowering the user to control the environment, usually using a computer (Phillips, 1996, p. 3), and removes the one-way communication flow from teacher to student character of earlier distance education information transfer. The merging of technologies in the communications and the computer and information technology fields also opened up new opportunities for two-way communications using online technologies such as electronic mail, chat sessions and bulletin boards. The distinguishing characteristic of currently developing technologies is their increasing use of high-band-width technologies, enabling students to participate in live interactive video learning experiences (Sherron & Boettcher, 1997) and highly specialised authoring tools (e.g. Asymetrix Toolbook, Macromedia Director and Dazzler) that require the services of highly skilled production staff to create them.

But whatever we choose to name these developments there is now a real opportunity to customise learning environments to meet the diverse needs of students in various blendings of campus-based, distance and open learning systems. What must be remembered is that all possibilities and combinations of course delivery are available in a potentially very flexible system that can transcend regional and even national boundaries. For example, the course might be entirely online, or there might be an on-campus face-to-face version as well or only some parts might be online for on-campus students (e.g. TAFE Virtual Campus in Victoria). Online students might be a considerable distance away or just around the corner from the campus but prefer to study in their own time because of various personal constraints or a preference for the mode.

This convergence of multimedia and Internet technologies provides educators with a powerful new medium for the delivery of teaching and learning materials, which can be developed in ways that fundamentally improve upon traditional resource production techniques. The use of these technologies impacts on knowledge in fundamental ways, breaking traditional knowledge linkages, developing new knowledge management practices and creating new teaching and learning cultures. The major paradigm shift has been in the development and use of flexible online education delivery in distance education and in vocational education and training. In general, these communication and information technologies' new methods support adult learning principles such as the following:

- Constructivist principles of teaching and learning, which are based on the belief that individuals construct their own understanding of the world as they acquire knowledge and reflect on experiences, can replace traditional instruction. Dede (1996) describes how carefully designed online learning can assist the construction of knowledge by showing learners the links between pieces of information and supporting individual learning styles.
- Students become more responsible for specifying and managing their own learning activities, in other words learner-centred, self-paced.
- Teaching and learning resources can be accessed globally, which improves access and equity, including access to current and archival information.

- Time and distance barriers to learning are reduced. Dispersed communities of learners can be supported and networks built between them, encouraging the sharing of knowledge, experience and understanding among dispersed group members.
- Reflective interaction is encouraged.
- Learning experiences are provided that are not always available in classrooms, with a variety of presentation methods.
- A learning community is created between students, teachers and experts, using chat/email and bulletin boards.
- Teacher–learner roles are broken down so the former becomes a mentor and facilitator.

A Commonwealth of Learning report (Farrell, 1999) claims that online delivery will rapidly increase owing to:
- the increasing capacity and flexibility of communications technology for educational applications
- the decreasing cost of technology
- the rapid growth of knowledge and its increasing rate of obsolescence
- the increasing demand by people seeking opportunities for lifelong learning and flexibility in how they learn
- opportunities to enhance learning experiences
- opportunities to overcome the tyranny of distance
- easy updating of content, as well as archival capabilities.

But impediments noted in the report included:
- high start-up costs for institution and learner although unit costs reduce over time
- limited access to technology and networks by some learners
- copyright restrictions
- inability of teachers and learners to cope with the innovations or use them appropriately — it can take valuable student time away from actual study to learn how to use the system
- reduced learner support systems — some students still value occasional direct contact with teachers and peers at induction and pre-examination times
- the need for improved teacher support systems — teachers feel overwhelmed if faced with learning web design, being software troubleshooters or CD makers as well as teachers.

The current emphasis on the educational applications of new computerised delivery methods differentiates this wave of technological innovation from those of the past (Merriam & Brockett, 1997) in that it is now both an educational delivery method and an instructional tool applied across the education spectrum in school, post-school, vocational and personal development learning. However, a survey by Harper *et al.* (2000) suggests that while there is significant online activity in Australia and most other developed countries, it has yet to become the mainstream activity, and there is no universally accepted wisdom on the best methods for implementing online learning. Robinson *et al.* (1997) identify online learning as the future driver of flexible learning as it can greatly increase access, provide flexibility and increase the possibilities of self-directed learning, and it will make State and national boundaries obsolete. The Commonwealth Government (1998) has linked the principles of lifelong learning and online skills. Educators of all age groups and in all sectors are attracted by the possibilities of any-time, any-place access of students to learning as it provides a real opportunity for lifelong education at all ages and for all groups in society everywhere.

However, it is often introduced without much thought, and currently rapid technological advances in the field can make current decisions about infrastructure quickly redundant. Nor is it a simple conversion process for teachers, students and administrators to move to the online mode. It requires a reconceptualisation of teaching and learning, with the development of new skills by both teacher and learner, and an understanding of student needs and motivations. For example:

- The online student not only needs familiarity with the mechanics of the technology but also to be socialised to the online environment. This points to thorough and sensitive orientation workshops etc., as well as access to technical and academic help.
- The online teacher requires an understanding of instructional design so that technology is integrated into the way they work rather than being an add-on.
- The impact on resources, structures and practices of educational organisations and systems is rarely assessed at the outset and only becomes salient as the project develops.
- Online students paradoxically might need more help than face-to-face ones. Lack of interaction between student, teachers and peers, particularly for those who have low literacy and ability levels, makes it difficult to pick potential failures and drop outs until too late at assessment time. Thus a sensitive support/help-desk-type of system is also required, or occasional individual tutorials/weekend schools. Some students might be reluctant to ask for help when in difficulty. Most students do appreciate contact with other students and staff to discuss common problems and issues. Thus some personal contact should be built into every course, if possible, at times convenient to all parties. Structured activities throughout a course also enable teachers to pick up problems early. The learning environment should also involve emailing, bulletin boards and chat rooms to overcome problems of isolation and facilitate one-to-one teaching as required.

There is also the fear that the flexibility derived from online learning, both on and off campus, is geared less to the needs of learners than to the needs of providers and enterprises who can get delivery value for money (Evans & Smith, 1999), which is leading to a greater focus on the technology than the learner (ANTA Learnscope project http://www.learnscope.anta.gov.au). Adult learners, in particular, must be given baseline skills to use the systems flexibly and fully, if they are to benefit. The unprecedented mass of information on the Web and learners' ability to manage it has led to the development of sites that index online education and learners' resources, for example EdNA (http://www.edna.edu.au/Edna); ERIC; and http://www.accesseric.com:http://www.tafe.sa.edu.as/Isrsc/learn/springboards/main. html. However, it has the potential to become mainstream in post-compulsory education and training.

The extra costs for students of studying online are an issue. Internet access costs for urban students are often lower than for rural students. One issue still to be solved is who should pay for access. In ethical and equity terms it is unjustifiable for students, mainly those at a distance, to have to bear an additional cost because they are studying online rather than face to face or being posted, at the institution's cost, print-based distance education.

Students without facilities, particularly in rural areas, might not have local alternative access sites like Internet cafes or public libraries. In advancing lifelong learning opportunities through the new media, we might be providing another fateful basis for social division, amplifying that which already exists when it comes to gaining access to learning. To limit this effect, there will have to be in many rural areas and inner cities access to technology in such places as learning centres and public libraries, or else the information-poor will become even poorer. Affordability becomes a major problem, particularly with the need to upgrade regularly to be able to receive communications from new diffusion systems. The developments in information and communications online delivery must be placed within the context of a clear commitment to widening and deepening participation and achievement in learning by substantially enlarging the community of lifelong learners in workplace, community and home, making these key settings for learning in addition to the accepted institutions of learning.

However, this must be seen against a global backdrop of more user-pays philosophy entering education provision. Thus while information and computer communications technology has the potential to expand learning opportunities in the lifelong ethos, its actual operation could reduce access and affordability for some groups if the mode becomes the one of preference for providers (Bates, 1997; http://www.cstudies.ubc.ca/brisbane.html). Most TAFE systems and private providers are offering courses online now and a comprehensive listing of online courses is to be found at http://cleo.murdoch.edu.au/gen/trdev-aus/trdev_courses.html. A case study of online delivery may be consulted at http://www.westone. wa.gov.au/about/online.html.

## the case for online delivery

Online delivery technology also has a role to play in the instructional process for it can serve as a means of supporting and enhancing instruction. Based on an analysis of the literature, Hopey (1998) noted that online delivery technology can accomplish the following:

- Improve educational attainment and skill acquisition.
- Reduce the educational disparities created by race, income and region.
- Improve the relationship between learning, assessment and effectiveness.
- Provide a relevant context for learning.
- Accommodate differences in learning.
- Motivate and sustain learning — shifting from passive to active learning.
- Provide a wider range of learning opportunities, particularly for older persons.
- Empower learners.
- Change role of teacher from giving information to facilitating learning.
- Shift from whole-class instruction to individual and small-group learning.
- Remove tyranny of distance and isolation characteristic of traditional distance education, for example contact with other students, decreased turnaround of assessments and access to staff.
- Allow those training on the job to study at the workplace. The flexibility permits the lowering of barriers to participation in lifelong education for adults who are usually constrained by the inflexibilities of the conventional system.
- Enhance through carefully designed Internet courses interactivity between instructors and learners and among learners.
- Through the relative anonymity of computer communication, give voice to those reluctant to speak in face-to-face situations and to allow learner contributions to be judged on their own merits, unaffected by 'any obvious visual cultural "markers"' (Bates, 1997, p. 209). The medium also supports self-directed learning — computer conferencing requires learner motivation, self-discipline and responsibility.
- Through the additional use of Internet and CD ROMS, provide access to teaching and information resources worldwide.

There are some noteworthy disadvantages:

- Limited bandwidth (the capacity of the communications links) and slow modems hamper the delivery of sound, video and graphics, although the technology is improving all the time. Reliance on learner initiative can be a drawback for learners who prefer a more structured learning context.
- Learner success also depends on technical skills in computer operation and Internet navigation, as well as the ability to cope with technical difficulties.
- Information overload is an issue; the volume of email messages to read, reflect on and respond to can be overwhelming and the proliferation of databases and web sites demands information management skills.

- Access to the Internet is still a problem for some rural areas and people with disabilities. Social isolation can be a drawback, and the lack of non-verbal cues can hinder communication.
- Although the Internet can promote active learning, like television, it can breed passivity (Filipczak, 1995), with students simply reading, memorising and regurgitating.

The positive effects will come about only if the technology is used appropriately. Like any other instructional tool, it can serve to perpetuate poor educational practice or it can become a means for transforming learning. Good online teaching is not just an academic exercise, it must meet the human needs of students, such as building community, caring and being responsive. It must be infused in the instructional process (Sulla, 1999), accorded a presence in its own right and used in ways that maximise the different strengths that it has to offer. For example, let's take flexible access technologies that can be used at a time and place chosen by an adult student who is studying mainly part time. Such a student may study at home, while travelling to work, at work in the learning centre or in time granted for study/instruction/learning during work time. Learning disabled, homebound and handicapped persons can benefit from this technology, with visually impaired adults able to choose larger font sizes and use computer programs that print material in Braille. Different keyboards (e.g. Braille), and voice-activated programs, among other developments, all permit greater access to learning.

## online delivery in adult and distance learning

When these online technologies are used appropriately, their advantages far outweigh their disadvantages. The ability to support new ways of teaching and learning is one of the most frequently cited reasons for using them in adult education. For example, they provide opportunities for more learner-centred instruction; they permit instruction to be contextualised; they allow adult students to explore, make mistakes and learn from their errors; they lead to more active and interactive modes of instruction; and they result naturally in greater collaboration, cooperation and small group work (Gillespie, 1998; Kearsley and Shneiderman, 1998; Petraglia, 1998). These characteristics of teaching and learning are particularly attractive to adult educators as they are frequently associated with good educational practice in this field.

- *Learning outcomes should drive the process of technology choice.* It is easy to get caught up in all the hype and to want to be acknowledged as someone who is using the latest IT innovation. But it should not wag the dog. It is only a tool and decisions to use any technology must be made as a part of an overall instructional plan. Technology does not determine learning outcomes, and it does not teach students. Teachers and learners make the choices that determine learning outcomes and manage the teaching and learning process. The role of the new electronic information technology is to expand these choices (Ehrmann, 1998). These technologies are not neutral tools, however. The choices made about which to use, as well as how to use them, will reflect values the educator holds — consciously or subconsciously — about their teaching objectives and relationships with learners. Questions to consider include 'What am I trying to accomplish?' and 'Will it help me achieve that goal?'

- *Infuse and/or integrate online technology in the instruction.* Technology should be integral to the teaching and learning process. Ginsburg (1998) presents a helpful way to think about integrating technology in adult learning by proposing four basic approaches: technology as curriculum, delivery mechanism, complement to instruction and instructional tool. Each approach has its benefits and limitations but the last — technology as an instructional tool — is superior to the other approaches. In this approach, the primary instructional goals remain the same, with technology being used to enrich and extend them. The approach moves technology beyond being seen as an end in itself to being a tool that is integral to learning (Sulla, 1999). It is also useful to provide instruction about the technology itself and the skills needed to use it, that is technology as curriculum.

- *Use technology to shift the emphasis in teaching and learning.* Traditionally, the emphasis in teaching and learning has been on the instructor, as both the subject matter expert and as the primary deliverer of instruction. Chapter 7 suggests that the theories that undergird much of adult and lifelong education call for a different emphasis, one that is more learner-centred and that depends on contextualised learning opportunities. Under the more traditional teaching–learning paradigm, such goals have not always been easily achieved. The emergence of online access, the Internet and the World Wide Web supports the use of these more collaborative, contextualised approaches. Learners can take a more active role in the learning process, use a greater variety of learning styles, use self-pacing, have more choice of content and method, have access to a wider range of resources and engage in collaborative learning through increased interaction with other students (Gillespie, 1998).

- *Be prepared to modify the teacher role.* When the emphasis in teaching and learning shifts to be more learner-centred, the role of the teacher changes. IT can assume some of the tasks formerly performed by the teacher, freeing the teacher to facilitate the process of discovery for the students. The teacher can become a facilitator of learning as well as a planner, guide and mentor. With access to information and knowledge outside the classroom, the teacher no longer has the primary role of subject matter expert for the student (Koehler, 1998; Whitesel, 1998). For those adult learners who prefer a less directive style of instruction and a less hierarchical relationship, this change is particularly welcome.

- *Use technology to shift the focus away from low-level cognitive tasks to higher-order thinking skills.* The traditional model of systematic instructional design (for example basic schooling and CBT) requires the specification of precise levels of content and learning objectives and is based on the teacher as content expert and controller of student learning. New technologies, however, can be used to move away from a focus on these low-level cognitive tasks to the development of higher-order thinking skills. To develop synthesis and integration skills, for example, students can be given an assignment to use the Internet to find material that represents a variety of perspectives and then asked to develop an interpretation of it.

Used appropriately, technology can support many of the goals of adult and vocational education. The path to wise use begins by asking, 'What do I want to accomplish?' and then considering how technology can play a role in achieving those goals.

## implementing online delivery

A number of models have been proposed for the implementation of online delivery in post-school education (Bates, 1995, 1997; Yetton, 1997). Bates (1997), in arguing that 'The new technologies will be exploited best by those that lend themselves to the new post-Fordist environment', signals a rethinking in the methods by which educational systems and institutions manage their most precious resource — the knowledge they deliver. Models proposed to address this issue seem to be driven by pressures exerted on institutions, such as market competition, virtualisation and internationalisation, but they need to be flexible enough for institutions to be able to respond to them in dynamic and flexible ways. The solutions within any proposed framework will change rapidly, depending on the changing economic, social and technical exigencies, or need to be reviewed on at least an annual basis (Reid, 1999a). This then gives rise to a dynamic strategy for knowledge management. Such an approach considers the production, storage, dissemination and authorisation of knowledge no longer to be the private domain of an individual academic. Instead, the management of knowledge becomes a fundamental concern of an entire institution. This requires that it must employ its knowledge resources in ways that maximise market advantage, utilise the pedagogical potential provided by technological mediation and improve the national and even international reach of its teaching and learning activity. Cross-functional teams are needed to design and develop online delivery, but the teacher and trainer should become familiar with the basics of instructional design so that they can relate what they are teaching to other members of the course team.

Critics argue that interactivity with a teacher is far more limited than in traditional teaching. However, developing interactive features can provide meaningful interaction with teachers, fellow students and with the material. It is a bit of a myth in any case to assume that students attending courses actually engage in face-to-face interaction with teachers and fellow students in lengthy and meaningful ways. Most adult students have not the time and for both conventional and distance learning most students spend most of their time interacting with text books or other information-presentation devices.

While physical and temporal barriers might be broken down with online, flexible learning, new barriers might arise. Computer malfunctions, difficulties in accessing ISPs, overloaded sites, connections dropping out, dialling up costs, capacity of institutions' servers, bandwidth limitations, etc., are annoyances that detract from study. These are not intractable problems but they do undermine motivation and confidence in the mode and create frustration for both student and teacher. Another problem of flexible online delivery is ready access to teachers at the time that learning problems arise and need resolution. Students need to be made well aware at initial briefings that unless they are strongly self-disciplined, the flexible online approach is not the best mode for them. Supportive instructional activities, clear instructional materials, availability of teacher and peer support, timely feedback and time and willingness to meet requirements all are necessary for successful study in this mode. A personal tutor system might also be necessary so that there is someone to discuss difficulties with who is not the person who is going to assess performance. The personal tutor in league with the academic tutor can assist in organising study groups of distance students who live or work reasonably close to each other. This stops a learner feeling too isolated or experiencing the loneliness of the long-distance student.

In planning to use online delivery, you must decide:
• what are your learning objectives for the course
• what types of instructional strategies and assessment will be used to achieve these objectives
• what media or combination of media will work best for meeting your objectives
• how much online learning will there be — part or whole of course
• if in part, which part
• how much interactivity do you want and in what form — just email or chat rooms etc.
• are resources available — experts who can create web pages etc., technology/network on campus, computer workstations on campus, help with upgrading, funding, etc.
• do the learners have the requisite skills, hardware and software.

As online delivery is complex and costly, it must be used because it is the best way to achieve the kind of learning we want our students to do.

A simple model of online and distance learning usually involves a combination of the following elements:

- Print materials (lecture notes, handouts, assignment details, journal articles, etc.) converted to HTML and graphics.
- Integration of the Web with its offering of up-to-date worldwide information, ideas and discussion points, presented in a motivating format with teacher-produced material leading to more informed understanding, analysis of different viewpoints and synthesis.
- Electronic mail (delivery of course materials, submission of assignments, getting/giving feedback, using a course listserv, that is electronic discussion group).
- Discussion groups set up for interaction between teacher and students and between students, using email, chat rooms, bulletin boards/newsgroups, video conferencing, etc.; real-time interactive tutorials/conferencing using MOO (Multi-user Object Oriented) systems or Internet Relay Chat.
- 'Intranets' or organisation web sites protected from outside access that distribute online learning for students and/or employees.
- Informatics, the use of online databases, library catalogues, and gopher and web sites to acquire information and pursue research related to study.
- Computer course management to track the learner's progress by testing learning and maintaining records.

This model can be used for whole, or parts of, courses.

There are many different systems available and it would be wise for those entering the field for the first time to access http://multimedia.marshall.edu/cit/webct/compare/comparisopn.html and peruse the comparison of five benchmarked products. But don't let the hype about these new interactive technologies allow learners' real needs to be obscured. It is essential that educators distinguish between the medium and the message. Educational technologies are only vehicles that deliver instruction. Unless standards are high the quality of the product will be poor and fail to achieve the objectives.

## some issues and problems

Resourcing, professional development and administration tend to be ad hoc in most cases and the real costs are rarely examined before a system is introduced. The major concern of providers is that with the constant evolution of technology (e.g. the current changeover to digital transmission and live video input and the introduction of broadband services), they are constantly having to revamp, upgrade and relearn, with all the attendant costs and disruption to services. In addition to the constant technical innovations, the limited scope to evaluate effectiveness of online learning makes administrators loath to make confident decisions about large-scale deployment of the mode. The extra costs for equipment, maintenance, buying in expertise and staff training might not be justified. There is a lot of hype about potential, but apart from improving the quality of distance learning and meeting the access needs of learners who, because of time and space constraints, would normally be disadvantaged, most students could be accommodated with more flexibility built into on-campus and workplace learning. Even meeting adult learning needs can be greatly improved by more student-centred approaches in conventional course modes. In any case, most skill-learning practical courses do not lend themselves to online learning when students need to undertake practicals or learning activities with new equipment or in laboratory settings, etc. Competency assessment of workplace skills is rarely possible using online learning. Additionally, where the establishment of relationships and mentoring has a strong role to play, online delivery is again not the method of choice.

Some educators actually doubt whether improved learning will stem from these new developments. The debate arises from research on educational media over 30 years, as new media (e.g. TV, videos) have arrived on the educational scene, showing that no significant effects have been noted. It is argued that improvements in learning actually derive from the instructional design not the medium that delivers it (e.g. Clark, 1994). However, current developments are not using flexible online delivery with interactive technology only as a medium, but also as a tool that enhances the potential of adult learning principles and the potential for lifelong learning that transcends national boundaries. Of course, sound instructional design remains vital, but it is now intertwined with the medium in providing the learning experiences. The key lies in how effectively the academic and technical teams can work together to get the best out of the linkage to create learning experiences of higher quality than basic class teaching ever could.

The confidence of providers is also undermined by the distance crunching effects of online delivery and by start up costs that lead to tension between cooperation and competition in the marketplace. Local, regional and national boundaries are nonexistent in cyberspace. New forms of cooperation are needed to generate more sustainable funding and mutually beneficial relationships between institutions, private providers and community, prevent oversupply and duplication, and generate excellence in production, content and delivery through collaboration between expert professionals drawn from a group of organisations. The disadvantage of a large-scale decrease in cost and competition with an increase in quality is that it flies in the face of greater customisation, just-in-time training, more focused modules, local adaptation and increased training in the workplace geared to each workplace's needs. These tensions are still to be resolved.

For a successful online delivery course, providers must ensure the following:
- Well-considered instructional, graphic and interface designs, which are pedagogically sound, interactive and will engage learners. It is useless simply to dump existing notes and handouts onto web pages.
- Content and activities that encourage self-direction and self-pacing.
- Strategies that encourage task-oriented learning activities to apply knowledge and skills. The learner who sits for long periods in front of a

screen that shows only text will soon lose interest. Therefore, it is not only necessary to make the material interesting, the learner must be made active.

- Good student support in terms of technical advice as well as academic content, tutorial provision and counselling — on-campus and distance students all need feedback, support advice and information.
- Effective partnership between teacher and technical and design experts — a committed and enthusiastic team approach.
- Clearance for copyrighted material and protection of individual and in-house intellectual property.
- A 24-hour, seven-day-a-week technology and maintenance service to resolve students' technical glitches reliably and quickly.

## the social nature of online delivery and distance learning

A common stereotype is 'the loneliness of the long distance learner'. Learning at a distance can be both isolating and highly interactive, but electronic connectedness is a different kind of interaction from what takes place in traditional classrooms, with which some learners are not comfortable. Lack of nonverbal cues can create misunderstanding, but communications protocols can be established and relationships among learners developed. Because humans are involved, social norms do develop in cyberspace, but they require new communications competencies. Online courses often feature consensus-building and group projects, through which learners can develop skills in collaborating with distant colleagues and cooperating with diverse individuals. Such skills are increasingly needed in the global workplace.

Answering charges that online learning environments cannot duplicate the community of the classroom, Cook (1995) argues that the assumption of a sense of community in traditional classrooms might be false. If community is defined as shared interests, not geographic space, electronic communities are possible. Wiesenberg and Hutton (1995) conclude that building a learning community is of critical importance to the creation of a successful virtual classroom. Even shy students can participate in a tutorial or discussion with other students in the less personal chat room and asynchronous communication. As techniques for improving compression of data and very high-speed Internet connections become common there will be an increasing use of synchronous communication with live audio and video, enabling computer conferencing to simulate classroom experience.

## strategies for flexible online delivery and distance learning

Filipczak (1996) notes that online and distance learning can be cheaper, faster and usually more efficient than other learning modes, but not necessarily more effective. Access to data does not automatically expand students' knowledge nor intrinsically create an internal framework of ideas. To help learners make effective use of materials and online distance learning methods, skilled facilitation is essential.

Rohfeld and Hiemstra (1995) suggest ways to overcome the challenges of the electronic classroom:

- Establish the tone early in the course.
- To overcome the text-based nature of online discussion and to build group rapport and cohesion, introduce participants to each other, match them with partners and assign group projects.
- Structure learner-centred activities for both independent and group work that foster interaction.
- Offer training and guidelines to help learners acquire technical competence and manage discussions.
- Provide a variety of activities, such as debates, polling, reflection and critique.
- Use learning contracts to establish goals for participation.
- Plan for technical failures and ensure access to technical support.

What is often forgotten in the rush to use new technology in teaching is a rational argument for the approach proposed. Those eager to get the show on the road need to stop and consider why a particular method is more appropriate than another. The rationale behind the choice on every occasion must be articulated and accepted by the teacher/trainer and management. To what extent will the method be congruent with what is known about adult learning? To what extent will the method be suitable for the particular skills or learnings involved? To what extent will the method be suitable for the numbers of employees to be trained? How does the cost-benefit analysis compare with those of other methods? Education and training methods must meet the varied requirements of individuals and organisations as to what, where, how and when learning will take place.

## evaluation studies of flexible online delivery

There is a dearth of evaluation studies of flexible online delivery although the few that do exist reveal positive feedback from students (e.g. Graham & Scarborough, 1999; Oliver & Omari, 1999). The latter study found that problem-based activities online contributed substantially to student learning and their enjoyment of the course. Students who contribute less in face-to-face tutorials contribute much more in online situations (e.g. Goddard, 1996). Some evaluation studies have demonstrated gains for students with lower levels of language skills (Agostino *et al.*, 1997), students with disabilities (Harasim, 1993) and female students (Ruberg *et al.*, 1996), while high drop-out rates for distance education decrease (Webb, 1999) as more online delivery is structured to support effective learning interactions. However, Wiesenberg and Hutton (1995), conducting a continuing education program using computer conferencing, found it necessitated two to three times more delivery time. Learners appreciated the convenience of asynchronous communication, but many were anxious about putting their written words 'out there'. The course was more democratic but less interactive than expected, and the instructors recommended orienting learners better to the online learning environment, providing technical support and fostering self-directed learning and learning-to-learn skills. Harper *et al.* (2000) noted that many students did not use the facilities of online learning well and when communication tools were used asynchronous communication was the most popular — valued for its flexibility and convenience for both students and teachers.

Eastmond (1995) was able to highlight the ways that computer discussion both required and facilitated learning-how-to-learn skills, such as locating and accessing information resources, organising information, conducting self-assessment and collaborating, among his adult learners. These learners found the following strategies critical to success in electronic learning: becoming comfortable with the technology, determining how often to go online, dealing with textual ambiguity, processing information on or off line, seeking and giving feedback and using one's learning style to personalise the course. In a general sense, using online learning is a learning experience in itself, so that learners of all ages, not necessarily preparing for IT occupations, gain experience in computer use and communication tools that are becoming ubiquitous in most workplaces, daily living activities and leisure pursuits. Now anyone is potentially a distance learner, a concept that has implications for the organisation of educational institutions and for teaching.

Goldman (1996) found that students on a communications studies course in South Australia who studied online believed they benefited from using online technologies and were more satisfied than a control group of face-to-face students on the same course. Aspin also reported positive outcomes for both learners and teachers at a Victorian TAFE, with the mean final mark being 84 per cent, compared with the 72 per cent of the previous year. Students felt they understood the subject better and both teacher and students reported improved computer skills. Students also appreciated completing assessment when they felt they were ready. Freeman (1997) found his students believed a web-based business education program assisted their learning, improved interactivity within the group and improved their computer skills. Misko (2000b) discovered that the external/correspondence mode had a completion rate below the other modes, as it recorded a third of all withdrawn or failed students. However, when judged in terms of module pass rates, nontraditional delivery was as effective as other methods.

## SUMMARY

Although the principles of andragogy and the psychological characteristics of adults are well known, the diversity of learning contexts, differences between individual learners, problems of work and home constraints and of accessibility all preclude a simple approach to the development and operation of learning in adulthood.

There are a large range of specific teaching methods, but most can move from an early emphasis on teacher direction towards being learning-centred as the adult learner develops skills in managing their learning. In summary, adults want to be treated as adults, given a solid body of knowledge or skill linked to prior understanding and experience, unambiguous learning expectations, able to study at a sensible pace, given access to resources, given opportunities for adult-to-adult interaction with teachers and peers, realistic and appropriate feedback and, if problems arise, empathetic counselling. Self-directedness, self-pacing and contractual learning are, in fact, all elements of self-responsibility. Mentoring is seen as a valuable way to provide personal support and guidance in learning new skills, ways of working and in-house norms/culture for adults in a changing workplace.

The escalating use of new communication technology and online learning is changing the face of both on-campus and distance learning, facilitating more possibilities for most adults to involve themselves in a range of lifelong learning experiences, both formal and informal, for occupational and personal reasons. These innovations support the principles of andragogy and are an important way of implementing flexible, interactive, self-directed and self-paced learning for large numbers on a cost-effective basis, minimising the tyranny of distance and access. However, designing quality, interactive computer-based learning systems/programs takes time and experience, the attendant costs for institutions and learners need consideration and strong support systems are required for technical, academic and personal matters, with teachers released from instruction to become resource, support and guidance persons. So despite the diversity of learners, learning contexts and the constraints touched on, there is increasing potential to develop lifelong education for all, based on flexible delivery and permitting adults to enhance their sense of identity, self-determination, autonomy, mastery and self-worth.

# chapter 9

# implications for teaching, training and the organisation

**Your job as an educator is to know that the potential is there and that it will unfold. Your job is to plant good seeds and nurture them until they get big enough to grow up...People have the potential for growth, it's inside, it's inside the seeds.**
Horton, 1990, p. 133

**Increasingly companies will only survive if they meet the needs of individuals who serve in them; not just the question of payment, important as this may be, but people's true inner needs.**
Harvey Jones, 1987, *Making it Happen,* p. 249

## ∎∎∎ MODELS OF ORGANISATIONAL TRAINING

Organisations are generally focused on improving performance. There is considerable evidence that effective learning by employees (e.g. Blandy *et al.*, 2000) improves the effectiveness of organisations. Thus education and training is a competitive tool, part of the strategy that will keep the organisation ahead in times of tight profit margins and foreign competition. A highly skilled workforce is becoming as important as a strong capital base for long-term survival of individual organisations and nations as a whole. Learning is no longer a cost but a benefit that can be quantified. Thus external and internal teachers and trainers are becoming more central to economic development and to the planning and articulation of long- and short-term organisational objectives. Learning must be a central feature of corporate strategy for the future.

Within industry, the old, systematic training model with its rationality and apparent efficiency was a series of sequential steps moving from identification of training needs, through implementation, to evaluation and review of the training. This model focused attention on the need to act in a structured way and to involve evaluation. However, it no longer suffices because it demands a precision of approach that fits uneasily with objectives that derive from continuing change and that require generic as well as specific skills. It ignores changing organisational relationships in which there is a devolution of responsibility to line management. It also defines training objectives narrowly, ignoring the link with general human resource development and benefits that can be enjoyed by adopting a proactive, lifelong learning approach.

A more comprehensive perspective is required. Two other alternatives have been developed: *the consultancy model and the learning organisation*.

## the consultancy model

This model promotes the training function as an internal or external consultancy. The former enables the person in the organisation responsible for the training resources to be fully integrated in the management process. However, it is debatable whether the whole of the training function can be an internal consultancy role, given the wide range of skills and learning to be provided. Outside help is often needed for new specialist skills. The role of the external is becoming more favoured as external training organisations, both private and public, are able to provide specialist training and learning with pre-tested packages and experienced consultants. The problem is that the actual training and learning might not exactly suit each organisation and such consultants do need to work closely with management to determine what the requirements are rather than simply offering 'off the shelf ' packages.

## the learning organisation

As we discussed in Chapter 3, this is an organisation in which training and education have been highly developed, where learning and training are highly accepted and where they are occurring as a matter of course with resource implications understood and endorsed. It takes a great leap in faith for senior managers to embrace this approach, especially a manager who is struggling to achieve short-term targets and who requires a few more operatives with a specific skills level. The learning organisation does have value in firmly embedding learning and training activity in the organisation, linking it to strategic objectives, operating in a corporate context and in articulating learning needs as well as responding to them. The HR manager must develop and manage an appropriate learning culture for the organisation as this culture is the measure of the role accorded learning and training in the life of the organisation, as well as articulate a clear strategy with clear targets, control and accountability and secure agreement for this from senior management to ensure its implementation throughout the organisation. In this way, the learning organisation develops through capturing the wider human resource benefits with its more effective development of people in the organisation. This is a significant and distinctive contribution to the viability of the organisation.

Within the learning organisation, the learning and training function will not necessarily be equated solely with the activities of those who carry the name of trainer. There will be pervasive activity delivered by a variety of people at all levels, including supervisors and peers and occasional external provision. As well as expected delivery skills, trainers need strategic awareness to translate the organisation's business strategy into learning terms, diagnostic skills to offer unique technical expertise in methods of skill enhancement and influencing skills to wield influence and leverage in the organisation.

While many people believe that top management is interested mainly in the short-term benefits of training and staff development, a study by Kane *et al.* (1994) suggests that longer term perspectives are actually employed, which ensures that education and training get a fair share of resources, are a focus of interest for management and that a more positive performance-based climate exists in organisations. However, training and staff development were generally isolated from other management aspects and needs of the organisation, and not factored in in any strategic or purposeful way. The survey in Kane's study identified some organisations that still only resorted to education and training when some major change in equipment or legislation made it essential and some others that made token gestures by circulating lists of courses periodically for staff to express interest in. Kane identified three approaches to training: the individual benefit, the cost-benefit and the human resource planning approach.

## the cost-benefit approach

This approach sees education and training as a cost, only justifiable when there are benefits down the line in terms of savings from reductions in down time, accidents and staffing levels, accompanied by consequent increases in productivity. Training is based on a behavioural assessment of what skills are needed, with measured behavioural objectives and assessment of competencies achieved. This is unfortunately the format in which much competency training will occur. Individual career development is irrelevant unless it fits in with the reskilling and multiskilling needs of the organisation. Staff appraisal programs focus on improved performance linked to rewards. This system might have worked well in the days of mass production of goods and services but it will not provide the basis for innovation, creativity, autonomous action and team building that is needed to compete on an international basis today.

## the individual development approach

This assumes that maximising individual potential will bring long-term benefits to the organisation, including improved motivation, flexibility, creativity and commitment. Employees are seen as assets and it is they who will provide the competitive edge in the future if they can develop specific and generic work and personal skills. There is as much focus on general skills as on specific skills, with employees helped with self-assessment and career-development plans. Staff development becomes the role of every supervisor. This approach has been criticised as non-strategic and based on selfish, individual needs rather than the realities of business. But it is very much in accord with the view that to be successful in the future you require a vision and mission and respect for the development of employees.

## the human resource planning approach

This combines a more structured, centrally controlled process than that envisaged in the individual development approach, with an investment view of training and staff development.

It is an attempt to ensure that suitable changes in staff attitudes, knowledge and skills occur in line with new strategies and needs of business. Job rotations, special placements and broader educational courses might be used. Career development profiles are created and updated to fall into line with projected needs of business. Skills audits might be conducted so that projected skill needs are met in the future, and attitudes and motivation are improved. It is conceivable that such strategic plans might collide with some employees' expectations and aspirations.

## integration of learning and business strategy

Kane's study showed that the individual approach received most support from managers (44%). The cost-benefit approach was next (33%) but was associated with inadequate resources for training and staff development, a negative organisational climate, a lack of goals and low standards of performance.

When education and training is disconnected from the structural and strategic changes in a organisation, a vicious circle of low status, underresourcing and marginal contribution ensues. Instead of becoming a dynamic source of new ideas and a custodian of best practice, training might come to represent only a supermarket of offerings unrelated to future needs of either individuals or the organisation. Such a state of affairs can be likened in some instances to a sheep dip approach, where everyone gets a mandatory day on customer care or safety issues. Even if learners do develop new technical and personal skills, they quickly become unmotivated in an environment where structures, procedures and policies hinder or senior management are uninterested in the application of what they have learnt. They have become 'maladjusted' to their environment. Unfortunately, educators and trainers might in these circumstances be doing their clients a disservice by offering new insights, raising awareness of self and others' potential, and encouraging consideration of new ways of working. If ruthless individualism is rewarded by promotion then why attend or try to operate on a team basis. Teaching junior managers about mentoring and counselling is perceived as a cynical exercise if more senior managers show scant regard for these skills.

A libertarian idea such as being able to seek personal development and fulfilment in what are predominantly authoritarian structures creates all sorts of difficulties — philosophical as well as practical. There is a tension between organisational effectiveness and personal development. Figure 9.1 represents the situation in too many organisations today where training is undertaken inadequately as either a knee-jerk reaction to a sudden need or haphazardly as a token gesture not integrated in the corporate plan. There might be a narrow perception of training focused on the development of specific occupational skills while neglecting broader competencies, or a perception that training is a company gift, like the annual Christmas tie from the manager that is never worn, or an excuse for a few days away from work.

FIGURE 9.1  TOKENIST TRAINING IN THE INEFFECTIVE ORGANISATION

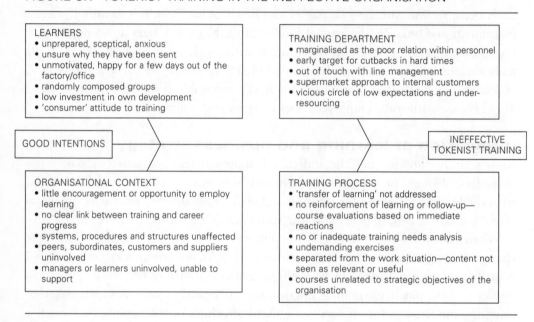

The message is that you cannot change organisational culture by sending people on courses. The vision, structures, strategies, policies and procedures must be developed first and accepted by all levels before learning and training provide the required skills. Developing people and organisations is not just a matter of attending courses, it is concerned with the learning process and the system within which this process occurs.

Therefore, educators and trainers must be involved in the design of learning systems that integrate learning with work activities, with organisational core values and strategic objectives, with management endorsement, with performance improvement initiatives and with career development opportunities. Figure 9.2 provides a model of the learning organisation where the education and training program is part of the corporate plan — an essential part of the health of the organisation.

FIGURE 9.2  INTEGRATED LEARNING IN THE LEARNING ORGANISATION

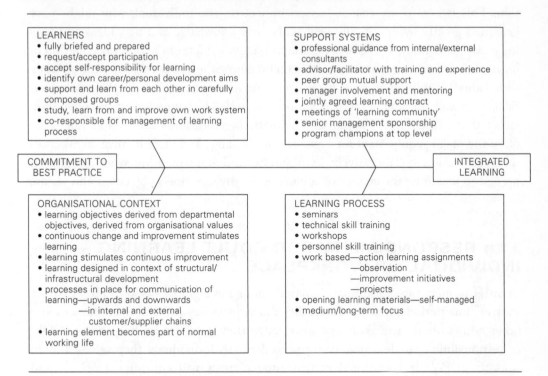

An organisation has got it right when it has an education and training plan linked with a specific program for organisational change, when it maintains a specific budget for this, evaluates training using end-of-course questionnaires and maintains a small inhouse staff of suppliers of training, supplemented by outsourcing to deliver other programs.

Individual education and training programs that are not integrated in an overall organisational improvement effort will have little positive impact on the organisation. As an individually oriented strategy, it tends to assume individual change is the major cause of organisational change. There are three problems with this assumption.

1. There is the problem of transfer of learning. Much individual learning on courses is not used or applied when the person returns to the workplace, often because the situation does not allow for it.
2. There is a critical mass problem. How many people must be trained to achieve the desired effect on the organisation? In a big organisation this question is difficult to answer.
3. Individual behaviour in a group setting is strongly shaped and regulated by the social norms of the group. Individual training necessitates deviance from the group's ways of doing things — from group conformity — and it takes a strong individual to stand out against group norms and established management practices.

Thus for these reasons individual training seldom has much impact on the organisation. This is not to say that it has no impact on the individual, who might have benefited greatly by developing new skills, new knowledge and new ideas and having grown personally. These benefits might be applied later in another occupation or organisation. Some people who have been on courses might become frustrated when they cannot apply what they have learnt on the course back in the workplace. Education and training is often given on the basis of assumed need or convention rather than on real needs appraisal. Changing organisational norms and values are often the major requirement for organisational change and must involve members of the organisation collaboratively in planning and implementing what training is needed to maximise the chance of achieving the organisation's objectives and vision.

## ■■■ RESPONSIBILITY FOR ADULT LEARNING — INDIVIDUAL OR WORKPLACE

In order to meet rapid and unanticipated change in a global world in progressively shorter time periods, inadequate traditional approaches to helping employees and other adults obtain the skills and knowledge they need are leading to the weight of responsibility for learning being passed on to individuals themselves and to workplaces. While traditional institutional courses will continue, teachers and trainers in institutions, workplaces and community settings will need to adapt their skills to this new context of learning for adults and employees who are returning to learning. The growing demand for 'knowledge workers' as opposed to 'hand workers' leads the drive for continuous learning both in and outside the workplace. The need to respond quickly also places the responsibility for learning on the shoulders of individuals, so that informal and self-directed education become essential parts of the education process, irrespective of whether or not one supports the philosophy of andragogy. While andragogical principles do appear to be supported and applied in this context, this is perhaps by chance rather than design. There is an apparent tension between the *real* purpose of andragogy — learners learning naturally and self-directedly in response to felt need and as a joyful, wholly fulfilling experience — and learning whose purposeful mission is a far more pragmatic one — a response to the demands of the hour, governed by externality rather than internality. However, while reasons for learning might differ, the spirit governing the teaching and learning methodology can be the same andragogical drive that appropriately motivates adults to learn better in whatever context for whatever reason.

If the workplace is to become a major location of learning, adults will need to be able to learn there for many reasons, some directly related to immediate work needs, others to future personal goals. For many the workplace might be the only place where they will engage in learning after leaving school, so this calls for the adoption of a broad conception of workplace learning. All stakeholders must recognise the value of learning that does not directly and immediately relate or apply to the current job and support the development of wide-ranging knowledge and skills that will enable individuals and organisations to create opportunities as conditions change.

Learning is, of course, happening all the time although the type, quality and benefits vary tremendously, and some environments are more conducive to learning than others. As the workplace becomes a major site of learning, the attitudes of employers and employees, as well as teacher or trainer approaches, need to be more facilitative. It might even be better to consider replacing the concept of training, with its narrow, structured, pre-determined learning arrangements that are really only a narrow subset of the learning potential of everyday experience at work, with the more generic concept of 'learning' and replacing 'trainer' with something like 'learning facilitator' or 'educational facilitator'. Even the traditional terms of 'teacher' or 'educator' have the ring of imposed learning about them as they revive memories of schooldays. The role of the future teacher and trainer will be much bigger. It will encompass not only the provision of information and skill development, but also establishing a learning environment replete with support and resources, encouragement of critical reflection, autonomy of learning, etc., and raising awareness that much valuable learning can stem from experiences and activities that initially might not have learning as their ostensible purpose.

The shift in learning to the workplace from institutions has been mirrored by a broader conception of learning in the workplace. Learning there is no longer synonymous with skill training, and much can be informal. The working lives of employees, whether lawyers or automobile mechanics, are influenced by considerable experiential and incidental learning as they do their work. What is needed is making more of this tacit learning explicit and building on it so that people and organisations continually learn and reflect on experience as individuals and groups get together to review what they are doing — becoming in the process more effective and productive.

However, the learning culture of the individual workplace still dictates what learning is possible through such variables as the way work is organised, the way information is or is not shared, standard operating procedures, the benefits/rewards given for developing new ideas/skills, individual employees' attitudes to learning and management support. These challenges are compounded by the fact that outside educators tend to be involved for a short period of time and leave as soon as their job is done, preventing a continuing support and developmental role. In-house educators might benefit by being in place but their socialisation to the workplace can numb their sensitivity to what is really happening or lead to a resigned acceptance of reality and the failure of new ideas and ways of working to take off.

Training, learning, personal and professional development in and for the workplace is now divided between external and internal provision, with increasing emphasis on the latter although most higher level professional studies and parts of apprentice training continue to be provided externally. Actual learning might be provided from one site but the learning undertaken at another, given flexible online delivery capabilities and the buying in of packages. Thus there is a gradual split between the provision and the learning site. Larger enterprises are expanding their HR or personnel areas with dedicated trainers or learning coordinators, while smaller ones are using skilled and experienced staff in full- or part-time capacities to train, mentor and develop a learning culture. All these people are playing a vital role in translating the rhetoric of workplace reform, organisational learning and lifelong learning into day-to-day reality. But not only do they need the specific skills they are teaching, they require positive self-concepts and personal relationship and communicative qualities as training and teaching are as much a personal relationship as they are a transference of information, knowledge and skill.

# ■■■ RECONCEPTUALISING WORKPLACE TRAINING

The move to the worksite as the major legitimate learning environment has been one of the most fundamental moves of the Australian training reform process as that reform shifts from a supply- to a demand-driven system of education and training. This is resulting in enterprises large and small feeling more pressure to train in house, taking more responsibility for it and absorbing more of its costs, as both employers and government evaluate training on the job as more cost efficient, relevant and therefore more likely to provide a flexible, skilled workforce than that provided by educational institutions. Additionally, such a shift in the location of training would encourage more involvement and interest in learning and training at organisational level, which could lead to learning culture and learning organisation development in the workplace and to one way to generate, create awareness of and satisfy lifelong learning needs.

In many SMEs there is no dedicated trainer or training manager. Training and learning is therefore haphazard and external experts and providers are used on an ad hoc basis. Consequently, much of this training is needs-driven: not so much just in time but 'just too late'. Large enterprises tend to have some training infrastructure, negotiated training plans as part of industrial agreements and associated visions and goals. However, even these can be disrupted by structural factors like shift work, multisite working, small numbers and unwillingness on the part of workers, often through lack of language skills and confidence and past experience of failing in classroom situations. This is leading to flexible solutions that minimise work disruption, that increase the link between learning and work and that use more adult approaches, particularly self-pacing, mentoring, on-the-job training and, where appropriate, online delivery. With these flexible solutions the workplace trainer has a key role to play in the learning network.

The role of the adult educator in developing the work skills and personal skills of employees is crucial. They must fulfil a range of roles, including that of facilitator, mentor, role model, resource and even friend. They must help adults overcome feelings of inadequacy stemming from previous forays into school education. They must create a spiral of learning for learners. The longer the participants extend involvement, the more they come to understand. The more they understand, the more motivated they are to be proactive and the more they want to further their skills. These original learners can act as resource persons and work alongside other colleagues to aid in their development. This is an empowering process, similar to Freire's conscientisation process.

Training reform in Australia over the past decade has gradually been shifting the balance from a supply- to a demand-driven system of vocational education and training in which 25 per cent of students are currently over 40 years old (Ball *et al.*, 2001). In the move from off-the-job to on-the-job training, the on-site workplace trainer has acquired an increasingly vital role in the provision of training opportunities. 'The critical issue is to what extent workplace trainers (especially in micro and small enterprises) are ready, willing and able to meet this enhanced commitment' (Harris *et al.*, 2000).

This issue, particularly in SMEs, which constitute 90 per cent of Australian workplaces, was the focus of a significant investigation by Harris *et al.* (op. cit.) involving organisations of varying sizes across three States in a range of industries and sampling 350 workplace trainers. This study found that few of the sample had undertaken workplace training. Only one-third even knew about training competency standards; and even fewer reported that their training practices had been changed to any degree by such standards. However, what the sampled trainers 'did' is mediated by more than cost and value considerations, with a plethora of context-specific factors affecting trainer activity such as type of industry, enterprise size, type of business ownership and length of trainer's experience. For example, large enterprises do more training while small ones tend to recruit skills from the labour market as this is more time-effective and immediately applicable than a period of training. As Catt (1996) found, SME's owners and managers were often the instigators of training. But the most common form of training reported by Harris *et al.* (op. cit.), whatever the size and type of business, is informal, on-the-job, generally unstructured and too often crisis-provoked training; it is learning through work rather than learning for work as enterprises are more concerned with survival than with learning and professional growth. Poell and Chivers in a UK study (1999) found similar variations owing to workplace characteristics.

Harris *et al.* (op. cit.) identified five functions as central to the role of the workplace trainer that inextricably linked work and learning, shaping each other in a dynamic interrelationship. The five 'functions' were identified as:

- fostering an environment conducive to learning
- working and learning with co-workers
- structuring and shaping work processes to accommodate learning

- promoting independence and self-direction in learners
- linking external learning experiences with work and learning in the workplace.

'Informal' workplace training and learning were very common, judged from the overall frequency of 'trainer actions' reported by respondents, with a high incidence of 'trainer actions' related to encouraging self-direction in employee learning and structuring and shaping work processes to accommodate learning. The least frequent 'trainer actions' were those relating to the linking of internal and external learning experiences, particularly that of liaising with external providers.

While competency standards have been established for workplace trainers, Harris *et al.* revealed that they are paid relatively little attention. Since the quality of VET provision and building a workplace training culture are two key issues in *Australia's National Strategy for VET 1998–2003*, a greater focus is needed by government and organisations on the role of the workplace trainer and their own training so they can play their designated role in the building of training/learning cultures in workplaces effectively. Competency standards for trainers are contained within the Training Package for Assessment and Workplace Training (1999), which replaces the former Workplace Trainer Category 1 competency standards. In fact, only 13 per cent of trainers surveyed by Harris *et al.* had completed a workplace trainer category 1 course, seven per cent a category 2 course and ten per cent a workplace assessor training program. However, the study reported that three quarters of them said they had a genuine interest in and commitment to helping others learn even though only 8 per cent had the role in their job description. That they tended to encourage independence and self-direction, provided feedback and encouragement, challenged, shared expertise and ideas is somewhat remarkable since these trainers had never been given any instruction in these areas. It would seem that adults who need to share their knowledge and skills are intuitively aware of the most suitable methods, perhaps because they too are adults with prior experience of 'being trained', who now know what they would want themselves in a learning context.

Unfortunately, the Assessment and Workplace Training Package is still based on a skills deficit notion derived from an educational institution approach to training and the training role rather than from contemporary notions of a learning organisation or learning that is embedded in daily work or that can occur in an informal way. The trainer's role is conceptualised in narrow CBT behaviouristic ways with the trainer 'in control', identifying specific training needs and matching objectives to identified competency needs, while the training is structured, delivered, assessed and certified. The trainer is assumed to know best and has legitimate authority. The emphasis is on training that has outcomes determinable in advance in an isolated context rather than on facilitating learning, within a community of others with intermeshing tasks, norms, values and relationships, that incorporates specific and generic skills. The standards are no more than the application of what might be encouraged in TAFE or an on-campus course simply relocated to the workplace with no attempt to incorporate the complexity of supporting learning in a work environment. It is no wonder that these national standards appear to be largely ignored (Gillis *et al.*, 1998; Harris *et al.*, 2000) and that they need revision to take account of the changing reality of workplace training as the majority of the 'trainer actions' did not directly match many of the competencies in the Training Package for Assessment and Workplace Training.

In many respects, aspects of training noted in Harris *et al.* now take on some characteristics of mentoring. This issue underscores the differences between provider-based training (using teachers from institution or enterprise) and the workplace trainer concept that it is replacing. The outsider and insider can never play the same roles. There are obviously advantages and disadvantages to both approaches, but if we are going down the workplace trainer road for a variety of reasons (among other things cost, flexibility, relevancy and authenticity of training), then revised competencies for both trainers and employees are needed that reflect the reality of what is occurring. Certainly for general and professional education outside skill areas the provider model is still valid, but in the workplace this is less effective until the provider becomes strongly familiarised with the 'culture' of the enterprise and understands the structures, processes, values and the relationships uniquely inherent in each.

Interestingly, Harris *et al.* do indicate that their study reveals promise in the development of a training/learning culture in industry.

- First, many of the highest frequencies of 'trainer actions' were those that reflected the trainers' keen interest in employees' concerns, usually by making time for interaction in daily working life.
- Second, there was a high degree of encouraging self-direction in learning among employees, a deeper understanding of how learning of various types occurs within the workplace and a rethinking of the role of workplace trainer.

While the basis of CBT is behaviourism, the trainers seemed to be able to operate it in a more andragogical fashion (perhaps more by intuition than by design). As Lowrey (1999) pointed out, the way teachers use CBT does vary considerably, depending to some extent on their sensitivity to student needs. Smith *et al.* (1995) have shown that such shifts are already taking place. But juggling the twin tasks of working and assisting others to learn is a major problem for many trainers, which they 'solved' in a variety of ways such as working longer hours, planning and prioritising work very carefully, supervising 'at a distance', continual judging of abilities and competence of workers and how these could be matched with requirements of the task at hand, using other workers to supervise and delegating training tasks.

Respondents in the Harris *et al.* study offered a range of extra strategies that they felt would be useful to employ to develop the skills of workplace trainers, such as revision of provider curriculum, less formal training opportunities, materials available in the workplace, experiential opportunities in the actual setting with allowance for discussion with others, and a number of specific ways in which employers could play a role in creating conducive work environments and policies.

Harris *et al.* (op. cit.) deployed learning network theory as a useful framework for rethinking the role of the workplace trainer. This theory conceptualises the workplace as a series of networks two of which are of particular significance in understanding workplace learning.

- Work networks shaped by the nature of the work and the relationships and workplace climate created by the interactions of workers within an enterprise.
- Learning networks shaped by the focus of the learning, along with the climate and relationships within an enterprise.

The work network was predominant. Work shaped the learning, and the learning network shaped the role of the workplace trainer, with trainers in different enterprises developing different ways of working.

To be an effective workplace trainer implies being aware of the impact of the work network on learning in the enterprise and how the work network can be shaped and reshaped by their actions in supporting learning. The workplace trainer has a key role to play in changing the 'shape' of work structures, processes, relationships, content and climate to accommodate learning in the workplace. The use of learning network theory in Harris' study has raised the issue of the tension that exists between the self-initiated, self-directed learning needs of individual workers and the learning needs of the enterprises in which they operate. More research that examines the degree to which certain types of learning and work networks foster self-direction and autonomy in learners within the workplace would be a valuable undertaking, given the need for these skills as a basis for lifelong learning.

The data in Harris' study reveal a relatively low level of liaison between workplace trainers and external providers. To increase liaison with outside providers, ways need to be found to facilitate best working practices between outside and inside to shape effective learning cultures that meet the needs of employers and employees. There is evidence that a considerable amount of informal training, and by implication learning, is occurring in small business although it is largely unrecognised and is not of the structured kind that 'counts' in VET statistics. Some means needs to be found to make the hidden world of 'unstructured' informal training offered copiously at workplace level more visible. A way should also be found for it to be credited, recognised and counted as a legitimate form of educational learning and training through the Australian Recognition Framework and therefore recognised and valued as a legitimate form of educational experience.

The Harris *et al.* study describes important implications for the direction of the national policy of building a training/learning culture within industry. As Harris *et al.* suggest, 'While national initiatives are helpful in setting overall climate, a training/learning culture is likely to evolve distinctively in each workplace according to the interpretations of its inhabitants and the nature of its networks, rather than through government fiat' (p. vii). Change management indicates that policy initiatives are often filtered and re-interpreted at shopfloor levels. Thus the role of workplace trainers in this informal re-interpretation is critical and poses the interesting question of whether the culture of training will be a national VET-driven training culture or an individual training culture evolving within enterprises.

Harris' findings also question generally accepted notions of 'workplace trainer', which are founded on assumptions of formal, structured contexts and large business environments, and based on the premise that 'one size fits all'. Their findings implicitly challenge the relevancy of current national competency standards for workplace trainers, and demonstrate that these standards do not sufficiently accommodate the role of the more informal trainer. There is an urgent need to rethink the role of workplace trainers and policy in this area. Established notions about the workplace trainer as conceptualised in competency standards and best practice were derived from the formal structured context of a few large businesses with dedicated HR departments rather than the SMEs that constitute the overwhelming proportion of business.

Workplace trainers are a critical element in evolving a training culture, which ANTA defines as '…a set of distinctive behaviours, beliefs and values shared by all Australians… which leads them to a lifelong interest in education and training…' (ANTA, 1996, p. 20). What trainers are doing has the potential to move in the direction of a training culture and lifelong learning. Most trainer activity in Harris' study reflected interest in employees' concerns, involving encouragement, support, interaction in daily work life, sharing knowledge and experience, listening to difficulties and helping to solve problems. These behaviours help build confidence, boost self-esteem, increase motivation and communication and generally encourage further learning. There was also considerable encouragement of self-direction.

Moreover, to promote a learning environment, we need to think more about the potency of learning networks that are horizontal, self-initiated or external rather than the traditional vertical one. As Harris concludes, 'To chat benignly about learning organisations being those where learning is co-terminous with work or attempt to implement formal training using a top-down vertical model deficit approach only provides part of the picture. The first lacks reality and might be destined to remain in glossy managerial documents as an attractive philosophy with little hope of actual and effective implementation; the second is somewhat colonial…comforting those who need to justify numbers in formal training programmes…and not feasible for small business…' (p. 57). Only by encouraging this mainstream of workplace training along andragogic lines, as seems to be happening in a loose and unformulated way, can we make the rhetoric of a learning culture a reality and a basis for lifelong learning. Revised competency standards for trainers with workplace trainers involved in their design, advice about styles and methods of training disseminated widely and discussed among trainers and greater understanding of how learning and work networks support each other will do far more to facilitate the national aim.

The Harris study is a reminder to think realistically about what is happening in enterprises regarding power relations, roles and work networks, and about the need to take into account the full context of the enterprise when considering training, since training is often considered in isolation, as if it existed in the same form everywhere.

## ■■■ GENERIC SKILLS

In Chapter 1, the skills required to operate as a worker, learner and citizen were considered and these have in part been catered for in the competencies that have been used as the basis for VET curriculum development and assessment over the past decade (see Chapter 2). However, given the emergence of a knowledge- and IT-based society a raft of issues are starting to emerge relating to the inclusion and teaching of generic skills in addition to specific job skills. It is recognised that Australia must move beyond Mayer competencies. A survey of employer views (NCVER, 2000) found 40 per cent of employers regarded generic skills as more important for the future than specific skills. The recent HDWG report (2000) identified creativity, innovation and lateral thinking as essential future skills. Kearns (2001) has produced a review of generic skills for the NCVER. So far in Australia, as in the UK, a narrowly focused and instrumental set of key skills/competencies has been promulgated, which exclude personal attributes and values. The USA model is broader and more holistic. The requirements for broader generic skills go beyond the limited requirements of specific jobs and employers and reach into the heart of the pressure on individuals, workplaces and societies to manage the new information society and a culture that supports lifelong learning, the maintenance of employability and the fostering of an enterprise culture. A major examination of the conceptual issues, character and role of generic skills and their link to human development and learning through the life cycle are currently being examined by a four-year OECD project entitled DeSeCo.

The sort of generic skills being promoted include (i) learning competences (e.g. learning to learn, creativity, problem solving), and (ii) personal attributes (e.g. autonomy, adaptability, confidence, self-esteem, emotional intelligence and social competence to join and act together in groups). This latter set involve what Senge (1990) termed personal mastery, one of his five disciplines. Thus, in its curriculum development and teaching, VET will need to effect a convergence of general and vocational education with new generic skills taking us into the complex realm of psychological functioning, calling for a greater degree of humanism and less scientific behaviourism. Kearns (2001) offers a framework for integrating the Mayer competencies with generic skills.

The importance of generic skills lies not only in their portability and wide application but in the fact that they also foster learning strategies that are congruent with adult learning approaches, new conceptions of intelligence, intrinsic motivation and active self-directed learning, which were presented in earlier chapters. Thus the introduction of such generic skills in Australia will promote learning approaches that are recommended for adults and fit in with psychological knowledge on learning, intelligence, self-concept and motivation. Additionally, there is evidence (Kearns, 2001) that possession of generic skills by employees also impacts positively on the business performance of the enterprise. The danger is that considerations of equity will not be addressed and some employees and adult learners, depending on occupational culture, will receive more significant generic skill development than others. Studies by Down (2000) and Jasinski (1996) reveal that generic competencies and their importance are little understood by teachers and trainers and any teaching of them is ad hoc and unplanned. The five-year *Framework For National Collaboration in VET 2000-2004*, the Australian strategic approach to building a capability for lifelong learning, needs to align teaching, flexible learning strategies and generic skills to the national promotion of the information economy to enable staff, students of all ages and the workforce to become self-directed, motivated lifelong learners. Coordination of policy with teaching and learning strategies is essential to achieve this and not an attempt to integrate competencies in training packages as happened with the Mayer competencies. The acceptance of generic skills, and the ability to teach and develop such skills in learners, is crucial to lifelong learning and the improved performance of the economy.

## ■■■ RETURNS ON TRAINING INVESTMENT

Human capital theory has provided the major explanation of how training is viewed by enterprises and what might encourage investment in training. This theory claims that training is an investment and therefore it will only occur if the estimated return on that investment justifies the cost. Hence enterprises are most likely to consider training warranted when it makes the employee more 'valuable' to them. In this scenario specific skills are far more valuable than generic skills, which, unfortunately, conflicts with the needs of individuals who seek portability rather than limitation in an age of rapid change. However, the theory appears not to be wholly tenable as Harris' study (2000) reveals that a considerable amount of self-directed and generic learning is encouraged by trainers.

A number of studies have investigated the issue of whether or not training pays. These studies (e.g. Moy and McDonald, 2000; Maylen and Hopkins, 2001; OFTE, 1998; Blandy *et al.*, 2000; Deakin University, 1997) generally indicate that enterprises receive beneficial returns from their investment in training, but they agree that more needs to be done to convince employers that this is so in order to encourage them to invest in training. Moy and McDonald offer a technical approach, ROTI (return on training investment), which provides qualitative and quantitative information on enterprise returns from training. There are over 50 possible training outcome indicators available within ROTI. Otherwise, enterprises have been making judgments about whether or not to engage in training on the basis of faith or prejudice and will continue to do so.

Blandy *et al.* in a study of 90 Australian firms found that Australian firms provide more training for new employees than do firms in USA. The profitability of the firms was directly related to the quantity and quality of training. A comparison of workplace- and TAFE-based training (Homesglen TAFE, 1999) revealed that workplace delivery is less costly, but providing learners with mentor support entails considerable costs. There was little difference in satisfaction levels between the two training settings, although TAFE-based students who had to pay fees were naturally dissatisfied with the costs.

## outcomes of VET

Dumbrell (2000) reviews VET outcome measures and reveals that labour market outcomes for VET students are impressive in terms of accessing employment; however, there are marked differences for some groups of graduates. A major issue is how much responsibility the VET system assumes for employment outcomes and Dumbrell compares measures internal to the system, such as participation rates and module completion rates, with external measures such as unemployment rates.

Women, indigenous people, people with a disability and those from a non-English speaking background (NESB) achieve poorer employment outcomes than other graduates. Much VET research relating to equity has identified a need for more specific outcome measures for equity target groups, such as culturally appropriate measures for indigenous people. Another important point to emerge from the research on equity target groups that is of more general relevance is the need for more specific evaluation studies of courses, rather than reliance on wide-ranging data collections.

Several researchers (Gonczi, 1998; Anderson, 1997) have traced the origins of the greater focus on economic outcomes to the globalisation of the Australian economy and related anxieties over Australia's international competitiveness. A theme arising regularly in the literature is the apparent value conflict between what are seen as economic-outcome measures and those identified as educational. The growth of the competitive training market has been the catalyst for what is probably the central theme of the debate about VET outcomes, that is the balance between educational and economic needs and values, for example unemployment (Burke, 1998). There is a legitimate view that the VET system cannot be held accountable for the decline in youth full-time employment. However, some writers have questioned why the large increase in VET enrolments has been largely in older students rather than in young people.

Considering the central role that the training market policy continues to play, it is surprising that there appear to be no measures to determine how much this policy has actually increased choice and diversity within the VET system. Given also that a key rationale for introducing the competitive market approach to VET funding was to effect a reduction in VET unit costs, it is surprising that the Productivity Commission found government expenditure per module load completion rising between 1996 and 1997 (Industry Commission, 1999).

The training market remains a foundation of VET policy, yet its benefits, both in terms of cost reduction and increased choice and diversity of provision, remain largely unassessed. Some evidence suggests costs have not declined, while the only measure of choice appears to be the number of registered providers. Research into user choice and diversity might embrace both employer and student perspectives.

## ■■■ ORGANISING WORKPLACE LEARNING

Although we have seen the movement of training and learning into enterprises, large elements of it are still taught formally in institutions, with other elements delivered online in part or wholly.

### off-the-job or on-the-job training — or should they be integrated?

There are a number of factors to be considered before an organisation decides on the location and/or combination of venues and methods for its training. These are:
- organisational criteria such as availability of in-house trained personnel, mentors, etc.; availability of physical resources and costs
- quantity and speed-related criteria such as the need to minimise training time and the number of employees that need to be trained
- criteria such as how often the skill will be used, how difficult the task is and how great the need is to transfer it into real-life work situations
- trainee-related criteria such as prior experience, aptitudes and disabilities
- other criteria such as the use of training as a selection device, the intervals between training and use of skill and the type of course.

Organisations are able using criteria like the above to assess whether they should do the training internally with their own staff, bring in an external consultant, have it done in a formal institutional setting, in combination with a formal institution or online.

Because there are time lags between industry using new technology and skills and training for such technology being available at TAFE or other learning centres, on-the-job training is the only way to provide training initially in some technical skills. This must be organised so that the skills that are developed in on-the-job training are recognised, assessed and given formal accreditation. On-the-job training is important as it enables immediate transfer of the learnt skills into the work context. It is also easy to draw on the specific expertise of people within the organisation who can assist with training and post-training monitoring. Agreements are necessary so that management knows that training will occur, that time and venues are set aside and that supervisors are involved in the monitoring, coaching and mentoring. This will reduce conflict between the needs for output, maintenance of systems and on-the-job training. Other general training that all employees need such as relationship skills, team involvement skills and problem-solving skills, to name a few, can also be located in the workplace. This is often convenient for employees, although it might disrupt working schedules somewhat.

In-house and on-the-job training is preferable for firms as it reduces their dependence on the recruitment of skilled workers who have been trained elsewhere and it motivates staff whom it already employs to ensure their own skills are developed rather than be demoralised by trained people being brought in. Small business, however, will have difficulty providing in-house and on-the-job training as it would not be cost effective. To ensure their employees obtain new or enhanced skills they must take advantage of external training/consultants, join or form group apprenticeship/trainee schemes and consider the possibility of joining on-the-job training in large organisations on a fee-for-service basis. There are logistical problems for small enterprises where the cost of training is higher than for larger companies.

Larger organisations need to develop learning resource centres to provide a place for self-directed and self-paced learning, replete with computers, video and audio equipment and access to the Internet, text and other resources. It is away from the shop floor and yet is a far remove from the classroom ethos. Individuals are able to learn in lunch breaks and after work, as well as during scheduled activities during work time. It provides a base for trainer/teachers brought in from outside. Cost-effectiveness is apparent as a large number of employees can use the resources before work, during the work day and after work hours. This facilitates a link between work and education, gives work a learning context and benefits both parties.

As links between industry trainers, TAFE, private providers, workplace trainers and community education become more complex, articulation will have to be improved; multiple entry and exit points will have to be recognised and there will have to be prior recognition of qualifications. The system will have to be a flexible integration of education providers and industry — recognising competencies acquired rather than time spent studying — tailoring learning to the needs of adults and individual companies.

## ■■■ IMPLICATIONS FOR TEACHERS AND TRAINERS

The principles derived from andragogy, the needs of adults requiring a range of learning from compensatory education (such as TESL) and formal upgrading of qualifications to personal and generic skill courses and community endeavours, with the emphasis on flexible and on-the-job learning, are all challenges to teachers and trainers implying a change in role and method. Formal traditional teaching declines as more practical, individualised programming replaces it. Teachers and trainers are taking on board more responsibility for administration and assessment, as well as designing and facilitating learning. They therefore need to be better managers of time and resources and they must learn how to facilitate individual learning. They need to develop skills in writing and designing packages and resource materials, particularly for online learning, and they need to learn counselling skills and develop commitment to the new role of support person. Teaching staff must also feel they have an investment in the courses and have some ownership of them. Teachers must feel at home in providing more individual private consultation for academic and personal matters.

Teachers will need to be adept at a variety of teaching methods and be able to recognise when each can be appropriately employed. There must be an increasing focus on the process rather than on the content. Teachers of adults must provide a more self-directed problem-solving approach to learning in which learners collaborate with teachers in the mutual planning, needs diagnosis, objectives setting and learning planning and evaluation, with learning contracts providing some structure at an individual level. Positive reinforcement must be prevalent and efforts turned to the establishment of a non-threatening learning environment. With adults, personal circumstances are important so teachers need to be aware of work and home commitments, as well as time and money factors, that impact on their education endeavours. Other pressures abound. Teachers and trainers are often faced with championing new ways of working, new plans for staff development, etc., without the necessary authority as a manager. They have to contend with the cynicism of the old guard in response to anything new, and the doubt and hesitancy of other employees as yet unconvinced of the benefits of the new deal. Practicalities of obtaining sufficient time, resources and other personal work pressures add to the difficulties of planning and structuring the learning opportunities employees need.

The role of the TAFE teacher and the in-house trainer is therefore changing rapidly, which means that the teacher as a person, and not just as a fount of information, becomes more salient.

## teacher self-concept

The role of the self-concept in behaviour, or how each of us perceives ourselves, particularly our competencies and incompetencies, was discussed in Chapter 6. An effective adult teacher needs not only a good store of wide-ranging knowledge but also the characteristics seen as valuable in a therapist by Carl Rogers, viz. warmth, empathy, unconditional acceptance of others and genuineness, if they are to be effective in the more open ethos of andragogically inspired learning contexts. The basis for all this is the possession of a positive self-concept, which enables the teacher to establish a context that is non-threatening, warm, accepting, informal and respectful — encouraging open communication and questioning. The class must be seen as individuals and each learner made to feel important and recognised. Teaching might be an overrated activity according to Rogers, but it is still at the heart of the educational process. Teaching is the intention of bringing about learning and understanding, but tradition has led most teachers to believe they must take full responsibility for all that goes on and many are still trapped in a narrow conception of the role.

The more learner-centred approach to adult teaching cannot take effect if the self-concept of the teacher/trainer is low. Some teachers are uneasy about their lack of control in adult, self-directed, self-paced learning situations, with students at different points in the syllabus/unit. Considerable unease can be felt by teachers when learners claim they do better working alone, using libraries and other resources rather than turning up for classes. Teachers feel diminished self-esteem in being rejected in what they see as their professional role. They must learn to accept that this role has changed in emphasis from giving information to giving support, advice, counselling and guidance.

Having a positive self-concept enables a person to interact with others in a more sensitive and empathic way. Research generally shows (e.g. Burns, 1991) that teachers with a positive self-concept allow learners to contribute more in class, encourage more divergent thinking and spend less time in routine activities, that is to say a learner-centred approach. Low self-concept teachers tend to talk more in class, permit learners to participate less, concentrate on convergent-thinking tasks and adopt, in general, a teacher-centred approach. Those with low self-acceptance try to reduce personal relationships by adopting more impersonal and authoritarian approaches, which place the professional in an unambiguous role with regard to status and role. A more person-oriented approach is threatening. Teachers with positive self-esteem create a more invitational ethos in their classes and teaching, which makes learners feel wanted, capable and worthwhile. Learners who have teachers with a positive self-concept are given positive expectations of their performance and, expected to do well, they fulfil that expectation. Only when a teacher has a sufficiently positive sense of self can their own needs for recognition, power, security, etc., be reduced so that service to learners is based on learner needs.

Burns (1989) has shown that teachers who prefer student-centred approaches possess more positive self-concepts about themselves and hold more positive attitudes to others. Able to accept themselves, they are able to relate comfortably to others. Self-concept appears to influence teaching style. Therefore, the model of the teacher, for adult education with its learner-centred approach, is one with a positive self-concept.

Effective teachers as judged by learners are better emotionally adjusted and more flexible in teaching approach, empathic and sensitive to the needs of the learner, personal in their teaching with a warm, easy, informal and conversational style than those judged less effective. These are major elements of a positive self-concept. The effective teacher of adults is one who enables adults to feel positive about their ability to succeed by developing and encouraging their skills for independent study and by enabling them to realise their life experiences are valuable learning resources and generally by developing positive thoughts in adult learners. The teacher needs to respect and value the experience of others, and be open to student input about alternatives.

Leach (1996) found that vocation-technical teachers rated highly by their department heads were better adjusted, more creative, sociable, enthusiastic, tolerant, humorous and caring than others rated lower. They were optimistic and generally made a point of creating an upbeat environment, they modified course material and teaching plans to suit the needs of learners, they provided honest feedback, established rapport, listened and accommodated individual differences and encouraged discussion. In summary, there was a student-centred focus within a humanist orientation, which created a context conducive to adult learning. Imel (1995), taking the adult learner's perspective, identified the creation of a comfortable learning environment, adaptation to diverse needs and use of a variety of teaching techniques as elements they sought as education consumers. Obviously, both perspectives strongly support the contention that teachers and trainers need a positive self-concept to generate these student-centred conditions and contexts.

So more needs to be done to prepare adult educators and trainers to be sensitive to others, to view their role as a human process involving human relationships and to be positive about themselves. Teachers of adults must be equipped with personal skills as well as the technical skills they need to pursue their trade. The self-concept is capable of modification as it is learnt and therefore in-service courses in personal growth would go a long way to helping teachers to feel more positive about themselves and therefore adapt more easily to the demands of being a teacher of adults. Academic training for teachers and train-the-trainer courses often neglect the personal growth needed by the professional teacher to function properly as an educator in the full sense of the term. Such courses have been shown to be effective (e.g. Burns, 1991).

## willingness to consult outside class

A major implication of the principles of teaching adults is that an effective teacher/trainer is willing to provide the extra support and time that might be needed by individual adult learners, particularly in their early days of returning to study. Adults appreciate personal interest. The key is listening without interrupting, being aware of non-verbal cues and drawing the student out by asking for clarification. In other words, counselling skills are necessary as well, and all teachers of adults should be taught some basic skills in this area.

## organised course and lessons

When it comes to class teaching, a good teacher is able to provide well structured and organised content, use class time efficiently, provide timely assessment for immediate feedback, organise a realistic schedule for covering the work and offer relevant objectives that are achievable. Adults make many sacrifices to study and don't want to waste their time or money. Objectives give the learner a specific goal and are particularly important for adult learners who are goal-oriented and want to know precisely what is expected of them. They will respond by investing energy in pursuing the goal.

# ■■■ REFLECTIVE PRACTICE FOR TEACHERS

Increasingly, the term reflective practice is appearing in the vocabulary of adult and lifelong educators. Based on the notion that skills cannot be acquired out of context, the reflective-practice movement has emerged as a reaction to technical and competency-based strategies common in the middle to late twentieth century.

## reflective practice

Reflective practice is a mode that integrates or links thought and action with reflection. It involves thinking about and critically analysing one's actions with the goal of improving one's professional practice. Engaging in reflective practice requires individuals to assume the perspective of an external observer in order to identify the assumptions and feelings underlying their practice and then to speculate on how these assumptions and feelings affect practice.

Kottkamp (1990) uses the terms 'offline' and 'online' to distinguish between reflection on action and reflection in action. Reflection on action takes place after the activity (i.e. offline), when full attention can be given to analysis without the necessity for immediate action and when the professional is able to receive assistance from others in analysing the event. Reflection in action, which occurs during the event, might be more effective in improving practice. It results in online experiments to adjust and improve actions even though it requires attention to be paid simultaneously to the behaviour and the analysis, as if from an external perspective. Schon (1988) states that when reflecting in action, a learner becomes a researcher in the context of practice, freed from established theory and techniques and able to construct a new theory to fit the unique situation.

In reflection, learners can expose their actions to critical assessment to discover the values and assumptions underlying them. Reflection has both advantages and disadvantages. It can positively affect growth and development by leading to greater self-awareness, to the development of new knowledge and to a broader understanding of the problems that confront the learner. However, it is a time-consuming process and it might involve personal risk because questioning requires that learners be open to an examination of beliefs, values and feelings about which there might be great sensitivity.

## reflective practice in adult education

In adult education, the teacher must also engage in reflective practice to develop more effective practice. Adult education programs take place in settings that are characterised by a great deal of ambiguity, complexity, variety and conflicting values that make unique demands on the adult educator's skills and knowledge. As a result, adult educators are constantly making choices about the nature of practice problems and how to solve them.

Cervero (1988) maintains that the essence of effective practice in adult education is the ability to reflect –in action. Adult educators must be able to change ill-defined practice situations into ones in which they are more certain about the most appropriate course of action to pursue. They must engage in reflective practice and use their repertoire of past experiences to make sense of the current situation, conducting spontaneous experiments in order to decide on appropriate courses of action.

Reflective practice in adult education can also be a tool for revealing discrepancies between espoused theories (what we say we do) and theories –in use (what we actually do). For example, the andragogical model and its underlying assumptions have been widely adopted by adult educators with one result being the assumption that teaching adults should differ from teaching children and adolescents. However, although teachers perceive adults as being different, these perceptions do not automatically translate into differences in approaches to teaching.

## strategies for reflective practice

Engaging in reflective practice takes time and effort but the rewards can be great. The following list summarises reflective practice processes for teachers of adult and lifelong education:

- Questioning what, why and how one does things and asking why and how others do things.
- Seeking alternatives.
- Keeping an open mind.
- Comparing and contrasting.
- Seeking the framework, theoretical basis, and/or underlying rationale.
- Viewing from various perspectives.
- Asking 'what if...? and hypothesising.
- Asking for others' ideas and viewpoints.
- Considering consequences.
- Synthesising and testing.
- Seeking, identifying and resolving problems.

Fortunately, there are a number of resources available for those interested in developing habits of reflective practice. For example, Peters (1991, pp. 91-95) describes a process called DATA that consists of four steps: describe, analyse, theorise and act.

1. First, the problem, task or incident representing some critical aspect of practice that the practitioner desires to change is described. For example, a

teacher might wish to become less directive and more collaborative in their instructional processes. In the DATA model, they would identify the context in which instruction takes place, how they feel about the directive approach and reasons for changing it.

2. Next, through analysis, they would identify factors that contribute to their current directive approach. An important part of this stage is to identify the assumptions that support this approach and bring to light underlying beliefs, rules and motives governing teaching and learning. Here, the teacher can uncover the theory behind their directive approach.

3. The third step of the DATA process involves theorising about alternative ways of approaching teaching by taking the theory derived from the previous step and developing it into a new one. In this step, the teacher is developing an espoused theory to govern their new, collaborative approach.

4. Finally, the teacher will act and try out their new theory. The goal of this step will be to minimise any discrepancies between the espoused theory and the theory in use, but this will only occur through further thought and reflection.

Additional sources that contain strategies to help adult educators become more reflective in practice are Brookfield's (1987) work on critical thinking and Mezirow's (1990) on fostering critical reflectivity. These resources can help adult educators approach their practice in a reflective manner and deal more effectively with a field characterised by uncertainty, complexity and variety.

## why do adults enrol in VET?

Maxwell *et al.* (2000) investigated the reasons people choose to enrol in vocational education and training (VET) programs using statistical sampling across fields of study, States, program level and full- versus part-time study. It was found that work experience or employment is substantially influential for more people than any other factor in their choice of VET program. But there was no overwhelming single influence for everyone, rather a combination of influences, each contributory but not conclusive in itself. The central message is that choice of course of study is a personal decision linked to basic human aspirations and that it is important to recognise, understand and satisfy those aspirations.

Immediate employer requirements appeared to be of very low importance and might be given too much attention in national policy since employers determine directly only around 10 per cent of VET enrolments. Most enrolments involve adults seeking a job or a better job or broadening their skills for future job possibilities in a changing job market. Employment opportunities in a given field of study therefore rate highly as a reason for choice of program, although personal interest is more important for some.

It would seem, for a changing job market, education and training needs, to serve both personal and societal needs by developing flexibility, allowing for a range of options and better preparedness for an uncertain future. This is training for 'anticipated' labour market transactions in contrast with 'completed' labour market transactions, as in the case of apprentices. Anticipation of this kind has to be encouraged to enable adults to make more rapid and sensitive adjustments to the needs of the market through enlightened self-interest than is likely by either governments or employers. Of course, this demands that training providers be similarly flexible in their response to an increasing future focus on generic competencies, transferable skills, flexibility and adaptability, enquiry and problem-solving skills and capacity to continue learning.

Imperatives are to reduce inflexibility in the training market, recognise the primary agency of adult interests and needs, emphasise long-term, future-oriented training needs more, and continue to broaden the role of training institutions in assisting personal development. These initiatives would revitalise VET and contribute to an improvement in its status, which is regarded as low among respondents.

The VET sector must be perceived as relevant, worthwhile and engaging or else adult learners will continue to flock to community providers who seem to be getting their act together. The VET sector must demonstrate that its programs lead to rewarding work opportunities with scenarios of work opportunities going beyond immediate employment to pathways of personal advancement.

The encouragement of diversity among training providers is valuable as it permits the value and quality of different approaches to be tested in a competitive environment where the choices made by individual enrollees ultimately favour the programs that are seen to be of greatest benefit and highest quality, supporting a culture of deliberate attention to individual needs, especially attention to future lifelong education and work opportunities. The evidence of Maxwell's *et al.* study is that students in VET programs are generally limited in their vision of where their training program might lead, apart from an the anticipated job. Some see obtaining that job as more important than completing the training program. Helping students to develop a vision of their future is about extending their horizons beyond the end of their training programs.

## the 'greying' of learners

Smith's (1999) report has investigated the training implications of the ageing of the Australian population. As people live longer and healthier lives, assumptions about people retiring from work completely at the age of 60 or younger and living lives unconnected to the world of work are giving way to an environment in which an increasing number of older people prolong their working lives past the conventional age of retirement and into what has been, until now, characterised as 'old age'. As the expectations of people regarding their working lives are changing, the nature of work has also been the subject of significant change in recent years. Fewer people are confident of having a job for life with a single employer. The security of employment that was formerly offered by large enterprises and the public sector has disappeared in the wake of constant downsizing. As a result, many more people are experiencing multiple changes in career and older workers often bear the brunt of these enforced changes in working life. Changes in career and the desire of many to remain active in the workforce longer are two of the most important forces reshaping the training and learning experiences of older Australians.

As Ball *et al.* (2000) show, the Australian population is rapidly ageing in line with international demographic trends. The median age of the Australian population, currently at 34 years, will increase to about 45 years by 2051. By this time over 25 per cent of the population will be aged over 65 years, compared with 10 per cent in 1997. A key contributor to the 'greying' of the population is the increasing health of older people. Advances in medical technology have led to a steady increase in the life expectancy of people, particularly in the developed world. For non-indigenous Australians, life expectancy at birth in 1996 was 81 years for females and 75 years for males. These rates are confidently expected to grow in coming years.

The ageing of the population is being accompanied by a significant demographic 'bust', with the lower birth rates of recent years contributing to a steep decline in the numbers of young people aged 19 to 24 years. The combination of more people living longer and fewer young people in the population will have a significant impact on the age structure of the Australian workforce. As employers compete for a decreasing number of younger workers, they will be compelled to reconsider the role of older workers. As Ball shows, labour force participation rates decline sharply for both men and women after the age of 50 years. In the future, it is unlikely that employers will be quite so willing to let their older employees leave or retire as they find it increasingly difficult to recruit younger people. At the same time, the State will find it more difficult to meet the needs of retirees.

Governments in developing countries are already experimenting with new arrangements to allow older people to continue earning after their official retirement in order to reduce the financial burden on the State. The improving health of older people leads to an increasing psychological need to remain active in society and the workforce longer than previous generations — thus fewer wish to give up employment in their fifties and early sixties. Moreover, employer-sponsored pension plans might not be able to cater for people who could be living into their eighties and beyond. A triple dynamic exists already that will increase the participation of older people in the workforce of the future:
- Employers' requirements driven by demographic change
- The interests of the State in reducing financial outlays on older people
- The needs of older people to remain active longer.

These workforce demographics have considerable significance for the training and learning of older people. As older workers remain in the changing workplace longer, access to training and lifelong learning opportunities will become more important to them. Lifelong learning is currently seen as a means of reformulating the education and training systems for the future but often also in terms of the rhetoric of creating a more inclusive society by providing learning opportunities for all. The demographic imperatives of an ageing population and a reduction in the numbers of younger people entering the workforce are placing a more realistic value on the concept of lifelong learning. As older people remain at work, the necessity for reorienting the education and training systems towards reskilling older workers is recognised.

In Chapter 5, the discussion attempted to destroy the negative stereotypes that abound concerning the abilities of older people. While older people might suffer from the physical effects of ageing — reduced aerobic and muscular capacity and an increasing incidence of ill-health — the intellectual capacity of older people is not affected to the same extent. Although there might be evidence of slight memory loss with ageing, older people often have significantly higher levels of relevant experience (or wisdom), which offsets the effects of memory loss and can lead to higher job performance levels than those of younger people who do not possess the same level of experience. Most psychological evidence indicates that older people do not experience any consistent decrease in intellectual capacity until they enter their eighties or nineties. Thus the ability of older persons to learn new jobs and new ways of working is not diminished with age.

Some employers have chosen to recognise the positive characteristics of older workers and adapt their recruitment policies to favour older people. Ball *et al.* (2000) note the Days Inn hotel chain in the USA, which was experiencing difficulties with the transient nature of its younger workers, started hiring people over the age of 50 years and found that, contrary to the stereotype, these workers learnt to operate the computer reservation systems as quickly as younger workers. The older workers stayed with the company longer and were able to handle more reservations per day than younger workers.

Unfortunately, the negative stereotype that leads to age discrimination in the workplace and job appointments is still commonly subscribed to by younger managers, who fail to realise the 'gold' in the old. As a result many older persons pursue self-employment in their later years (Schueler, 1999).

The principal factor in the ability of older people to retain their learning capacities appears to be the level of skills they already possess. Smith (op. cit.) revealed that those who possessed a wide range of transferable or general skills, such as those acquired in a management position, were able to handle career changes more effectively than those who had fewer skills. Thus the acquisition of skills and qualifications at a younger age is a critical factor in remaining flexible and employable with increasing age.

Smith also discovered in his survey that while most older workers had benefited from formal training, they had learnt important skills from a variety of sources, including on-the-job training, self-study, role models in the workplace and other colleagues. Moreover, their success at finding or retaining employment at a mature age was linked directly to their ability to realise the value of these skills by applying them in a different work context. This was particularly true for those who had learnt management and organisational skills that could be transferred into a range of work environments. The key to the utilisation of skills lay in the ability of the older person to 'let go' of their previous occupational identity and create new career opportunities. Thus, older people tend to be more tactical than younger people in their selection of skills to learn and in how to acquire them. They tend not to value the notion of acquiring a qualification but rather seek opportunities to acquire or enhance specific skills. Schueler's (1999) analysis of the VET statistics bears out this point. Older people are undertaking short, non-award vocational courses in greater numbers than younger people and they are targeting specific fields of study to acquire business skills, develop or update computing skills and undertake training for employment purposes.

When asked why they are undertaking a vocational training course, older people overwhelmingly indicate that they wish to gain more skills to apply to employment or owning a business. This reinforces the notion that *skills* are what older people wish to acquire and they will be highly selective about identifying these skills and how they will acquire them. However, whether this tactical approach to skill acquisition translates into successful labour market outcomes for older people is less clear.

As people get older, qualifications appear to become less important when making decisions about training and learning. Older people take a more tactical view of their training and learning needs and are focused on acquiring skills or on updating existing skills rather than on gaining qualifications. As human capital theory suggests, qualifications are of more use to the younger worker as employers will tend to screen applicants on the basis of their academic achievements using this as a proxy for their potential in the organisation. For the older worker, experience and skills assume more importance for the potential employer.

Training and learning experiences need to fit the tactical approaches of older people. The training and education system needs increasingly to offer its programs on a modularised basis so that people at all ages can focus on putting together packages of skills and qualifications that suit their particular needs and circumstances. As part of this tactical approach, older people are also assuming increasing responsibility for their training and learning. As Ball (2000) notes, the incidence of employer-sponsored training declines with age as does their participation in VET. In contrast with this, increasing numbers of older people are undertaking VET programs, with the emphasis on short, non-award courses rather than AQF programs (Schueler, op. cit.). They are picking their experiences selectively from a number of potential sources of learning. As well as being tactical, this is a response to employers backing away from responsibility for training. Smith and Hayton (1999) showed in their study of training practices in 42 Australian enterprises that employers expected individuals to take responsibility for identifying and sourcing their own training needs at work. The enterprise increasingly acted as a broker to individuals rather than providing direct training. For those who have undergone separation from their employers, setting up their own business is an increasingly attractive option. For those who are seeking employment, enhancing their adaptability by transferring their skills to new environments or learning new skills in order to change career is critical to success. In either case, the responsibility for identifying and sourcing training and learning rests squarely with the individual.

Individualisation means that the clients of the training system are as much individuals as industries, professions and enterprises. Along with the need to modularise the offerings of the training and education systems, training providers need to become more conscious of the needs of individuals as their key clientele. The era of standardisation in training needs to be followed by an new era of customisation to the increasingly fragmented needs of an individualised training market, particularly the older adult with their different learning needs as outlined in Chapter 7.

Schueler (op. cit.) reports that older people are flocking to both vocational and personal enrichment programs in greater and greater numbers. While the numbers undertaking VET programs in Australia has grown for all ages by 60 per cent since 1990, the numbers of people in their forties undertaking training has doubled and the numbers of people in their fifties has trebled. As a result, the proportion of people undertaking training through the VET system aged over 40 years increased from 18 per cent in 1990 to 27 per cent in 1998.

Older people are far more highly represented in personal enrichment programs, where people over 45 years of age represent almost 40 per cent of the total. Many of these personal enrichment programs are provided by the non-TAFE sector, in particular by community-based training providers. Community training providers also supply vocational training programs. Schueler's analysis reveals that as people grow older they turn increasingly to community-training providers for both their vocational and personal enrichment training. This suggests the ethos of the typical TAFE college is not well suited to older members of the community, who might find the more relaxed and informal atmosphere of a community-training provider more andragogical and attuned to their training and learning requirements, both in terms of content and method. The problem is that initially most training providers were set up to service primarily younger students. They must now examine the attractiveness of their operations for other groups. Student services on TAFE campuses, for example, are often based on the presumption that students are young.

Ball's (2001) study reveals the relationship between the possession of post-school qualifications and the incidence of training for older workers. Whilst nearly 63 per cent of workers with a post-school qualification aged 50 to 54 years undertook some study or formal training course in 1997, only 36 per cent of those without a post-school qualification undertook a course of study or formal training. Over 85 per cent of those with a post-school qualification aged 50 to 54 years undertook some form of training in 1997 whereas only just over 60 per cent of those in this age group without a post-school qualification undertook some training.

In examining the training and learning experiences of older people and older workers and the factors that influence those experiences, Smith's summary is very pertinent: 'It can be noted that older people are adapting to the changes in society and the workplace by taking up opportunities for training and learning in ever greater numbers but doing so in a tactical way that will enhance their adaptability and flexibility. The old stereotype that you cannot teach an old dog new tricks is demonstrably untrue. Not only do older people retain the ability to learn and adapt to change, they take a very considered view about their own training and learning needs and the ways in which they might best source those needs. Far from acquiescing in the face of change and uncertainty, older people are creating their own futures and are making sure that their training and learning are making their futures productive and sustainable' (Smith, 1999, p. 7).

## ■■■ ASSESSMENT ISSUES

The success or failure of education and training for adults in the workplace depends ultimately on the quality of the assessment methods employed and on the system of monitoring and of recording progress. Assessment essentially drives what people study and learn in that there is a tendency among students to focus only on what is to be assessed (Boud, 1995).

Assessment is a multipurpose activity, with some of its aims being in conflict with each other. The major aims are the following:

- Checking and certifying that specific levels of knowledge and/or skill have been achieved.
- Selection, where there are too many applicants for the places available. In the workplace, promotion and performance bonuses might be involved.
- Monitoring, maintaining and improving standards.
- Motivating learners: the assumption is that learners will not learn unless there is an assessment at the end. Is this controlling what they do rather than motivating them?
- Feedback to learners: knowledge of results enables learners to identify strengths and weaknesses and modify subsequent behaviour.
- Feedback to teachers, which provides teachers with knowledge about the effectiveness of their teaching and enables teachers to identify and remedy weak areas of student performance.

The above list is not finite but most assessment procedures and systems are aimed at one or more of the above aims.

There is a large body of literature on the concepts of reliability and validity of assessment, and readers are advised to consult texts on these topics if they wish to know more. However, some issues bearing on reliability and validity of assessment include the following:

- While standardised and agreed-on criteria that provide a consistent framework for assessment by different assessors at different sites considerably increase the reliability and validity of assessment, they can place unnecessary restrictions on individuals being assessed if they are too specific. Alternatively, assessors can vary tremendously in their assessment of the same performance if criteria are not clear or adhered to, leading to low reliability and validity of assessment. A sense of balance is needed here.

- The assessor can influence performance. The 'man in the white coat', or an assessor from a different ethnic group can lower performance standards.
- Personal coping skills, particularly those for dealing with stress in assessment contexts, and familiarity with undergoing assessment can produce a range of individual differences in performance that are not true reflections of real differences in performance between people. In other words, both nerves and experience play a part, but to what extent is unmeasurable.

The assessment criteria used by educators and workplace assessors can vary considerably. In vocational learning, there can be tension between educators who assess classroom-based theoretical knowledge (often normative-referenced assessment) and workplace personnel who focus on job performance (criterion-referenced assessment) because their objectives and teaching reflect these two areas. This can lead, in its extremes, to ludicrous situations where an employee is defined as incompetent in the classroom but more than satisfactory in applying learnt practical skills on the job (and, of course, the other way around). Assessments for writing about and for demonstrating that are incongruent are inevitable outcomes for many learners as the skills required for each are different and serve different purposes. Sometimes the linguistic skills needed to perform in a written test are beyond many speakers of English as a second language who are beginning to form a significant proportion of employees at lower trades levels.

Appropriate assessment processes are best developed by groups of workplace personnel experienced in that particular area of work, rather than by committees of educators who are remote from the workplace. Assessment criteria might then be expressed in user-friendly terms, with practical assessment instruments and within the language and literacy expectations of the target group. The assessment should also be integrated with daily work activities so that it represents naturally occurring evidence using formative (staged) assessment as well as summative (end point) assessment, as this allows feedback on progress, rather than a once-and-for-all assessment at the end. Any evidence gaps can be filled in by developing specific assessment tasks. Observation and results can be used for more holistic areas like teamwork or problem solving. A learning contract can demonstrate competence in a range of aspects at the same time. There is no reason why learners cannot choose to be assessed by the method they feel most comfortable with. In terms of adult learning principles, continuous assessment should be employed and at times when the learner is ready for it. These issues need detailed consideration when there are implications for assessments being related to promotion, increased pay and/or job security. Workplace assessors are supposed to have completed a training program, but few have.

If a primary learning objective is for the learner to become more autonomous then it is important that they take a large share in the evaluation. In many workplace competency areas, participation by the learner in their own evaluation is difficult. And in more formal academic subjects the teacher prepares the learner for the examination. But when academic credit is not an issue, self-assessment combined with other forms of assessment is recommended. It is not someone's mark, as compared with the marks of others, that should be the criterion but whether the student has shown any growth. That is, the individual's performance should be compared with their previous best rather than with the group, and some self-evaluation or critical reflection is a realistic expectation in many work activities and roles. For self-evaluation some events might be taped, reviewed and reflected on by the learner, sometimes in company with their mentor, trainer or teacher.

## criterion-referenced assessment

Competency and personal skills should be assessed by criterion-referenced tests, not norm-referenced tests. That is, performance is compared against a fixed set of criteria not against the performance of other individuals. A mark obtained in a test, say 82 per cent, does not indicate the learner's level of competence; they might have come top or even bottom! Criterion measures are necessary so that the employer knows that the employee is able to deploy the skill in a specific context at a particular level of competency and the educator knows what aspects of competency the learner needs remediation in.

The basic requirements of a criterion-referenced assessment system are:
- clearly defined criteria (objectives) that indicate the intent of the instruction
- assessment methods that are congruent with the objectives and that provide reliable and valid information about the achievement
- record-keeping methods that clearly indicate achievement
- clearly defined rules for determining whether competency has been achieved or courses passed; minimum standards for a pass must be stated.

## samples of performance

The major approach to the assessment of competence is the use of samples of performance, such as specially set up events like practical tests, simulations and exercises. These can be supported by orals, multiple-choice tests and written papers. Rating scales can even be used for assessing attitudes, such as persistence and willingness to use safety procedures. Criteria are worked out for each element assessed, with assessments made on a pass–fail basis. Complex records of achievement are needed as individuals retry assessment events until successful. Learners are assessed individually when ready.

Assessment records are often computer-managed and available to students.

Reliability of the assessment depends on the usual range of elements such as objectivity of marking, training of assessors, consistency of assessment and standardisation of assessment processes, conditions and situation.

The problem with this approach is the fragmenting of competences, with an atomised assessment of many elements rather than a holistic assessment. This can be reduced by integrating elements already tested in a major task, which is then assessed. Keeping records is also a time-consuming and complex task, particularly if maintained manually. A bigger problem is the assumption that ability to perform in a simulated situation can generalise to performance in the cut and thrust of the workplace with its range of interacting factors such as noise, disturbance and subtle variations in the quality of equipment and materials. This is another argument for cooperative arrangements between providers and organisations to allow authentic assessment over a period of time in the reality of the workplace as additional evidence.

## observation

Observation is the second major source of evidence for assessing competence in the workplace. Most workplace skills should be assessed in the reality of the work situation. This is easier to do when the training is on the job with mentors, trainers and supervisors available to make random and staged assessments of on-the-job performance during normal, daily job routines. Again, a complex recording procedure is required to cover all aspects using a variety of assessors with record cards or computer maintained records. The reliability of assessment is low unless assessors have been trained and are all agreed on performance standards. Assessors need to be consistent in the way they rate elements. The workplace must be able to offer a suitable range of workplace experiences for adequate assessment and sensible decisions need to be made on the number of observations of performance required to make a reliable judgment of performance.

A senior person must verify that the assessment took place and the student must be given feedback. Because each activity might differ slightly each time it has to be performed, the assessment must be done in point form, with points allocated to a variety of criteria. When a preset number of points has been achieved the student can be judged as having demonstrated the competence successfully on a number of occasions and be judged competent in that area. This system has great face validity as it is realistic performance under real conditions and requires integration of skills, knowledge and attitudes. It takes account of the problem that off-course assessment does not pick up: the fact that some instances of the same task might be more complex, time consuming and critical than others. Observation assessment is less straightforward when dealing with personal psychological skills, such as relationship formation, or processes, with the focus on the way the task was done, for example attitude to work.

## written formats

While performance is the main form of assessment in many work skill areas, the standard written test can also be used as a means of assessing understanding. The major problems with written tests is their dependence on language skills, which might discriminate against migrants with non-English speaking backgrounds.

Multiple-choice examinations are popular with adults as they reduce dependence on English language skills. However, it is possible to guess answers and obtain a correct answer by chance on a number of occasions. With five alternative answers to each question it is possible to get 20 per cent correct by guessing. However, when they are well written they can go well beyond simple assessment of factual knowledge to assess higher order skills such as selecting an appropriate principle or procedure, applying it to a problem and evaluating evidence. They do not require learners to generate new responses but are efficient in that they can cover the whole course rather than sample parts of a course as essays tend to. Reliability of marking is high as there is only one correct answer per question and no assessment of the quality of the answer is required. Multiple-choice tests are useful in competence areas to assess mastery of important knowledge and procedures.

The most traditional method of assessment is the essay-type examination, but it is totally unreliable. Student day-to-day variability is not taken into account. A host of research reveals that different examiners will allocate different marks to the same script, while the same examiner will give the same script a different mark, when marking it again after an interval of time (e.g. Newstead, 1996).

Quality of handwriting, length of response, gender of examinee, marker fatigue and position in a series of scripts can all affect the mark given. Written examination essay papers are poor as assessments yet continue to be used, although many professional courses are now steering away from them. They are completely unsuitable for most skill areas and for assessment of personal development. Multiple-choice tests might be more technically reliable but lead to rote learning and results that might be distorted by guessing. Coursework, like projects, presentations and learning contracts, avoids poor performance on a 'bad' day, is less concentrated at the end of a course and leads to deeper learning. However, opportunities for cheating and plagiarism abound and marking can still be unreliable. Adults prefer coursework assessment.

A balance between multiple-choice and essay formats is the short answer and structured response question, which provides an opportunity to assess ability to produce a relevant response, not just identify the correct alternative. It can test factual knowledge and comprehension in a way that requires the learner to produce ideas and solutions. The longer the written response the more difficult to mark in a reliable way as assessors have to make informed judgments on the quality of the response.

## oral assessment

Oral assessments not only assess knowledge and understanding but interpersonal ability and communication skills. While it might pressure the learner, these pressures are similar to those the worker might encounter in their daily activities with customers, with problem solving and fault detecting. But while orals might provide insight in these other aspects of work competence, assessments might be biased by irrelevant personal aspects and the bias that plagues interview procedures.

## self-assessment

One of the new contenders in assessment that leads to deeper learning and higher motivation is self-assessment. Here the learner identifies the standards or criteria that they will apply and makes judgments about the extent to which they have met those standards. It helps learners develop their own learning skills, engage with criteria of good performance and make complex judgments. These skills are congruent with adult learning. Studies reveal that student self-assessment correlates highly with teacher assessment of the same work (Boud and Falchikov, 1995).

## other forms of assessment

Peer assessment, presentations and the portfolio are other popular forms of assessment.

- Peer assessment is characterised by learners rating other students as well as themselves. Peer assessment has long been a practice in the Keller Plan and PSI (Chapter 8). Student marks correlate highly with teacher assessments (Freeman, 1995).

- Presentations are increasingly common as they focus on oral rather than written communication and enable learners to analyse, collate and demonstrate using tabular and graphical techniques. Presentations lead to deeper learning and develop skills of searching, summarising and understanding. However, they are difficult to mark as they cannot be repeated and criteria might be vague. However, both peers and teachers can assess presentations and the final report can be handed in for assessment too.

- The portfolio is also becoming an en vogue approach. A portfolio is useful in areas where learners can assemble a collection of work they have done and include reflections on their products, achievements and methods. It not only suits the collections of models and the like in practical courses, but also case studies in personnel work and management.

This has not been intended as a definitive treatment of assessment, simply a taste of what techniques are available and of some of the issues involved in assessment.

## ■■■ MANAGERIAL TRAINING

Managers are coming to realise that they, as well as their employees, need training — and managerial skills courses are developing rapidly. A managerial skill is the ability to accomplish a managerial goal through personal action. For example, the goal might be that of facilitating a meeting, which is accomplished through direct action. The group might then arrive at a quality decision, an indirect result of the manager's action and skill. Bigelow (1994) identifies 31 managerial skills, such as delegation, team management, conflict management, risk management, proactivity and negotiation.

These are skills needed for both domestic and international activity. Given the need for the export of goods and services and the internationalisation of markets and trade, additional international skills are necessary, such as cross-cultural understanding, adaptability, multiple-perspective thinking and language skills.

It is possible to collate all the managerial skills delineated by various authors into six classes.

- Interpersonal skills in which external relationship goals and changes in others are emphasised.
- Intrapersonal skills in which self-goals such as stress management, delegation and assertiveness are emphasised.
- Learning skills, which facilitate the development of other skills, for example creativity.
- Personal attributes, which are not skills in themselves but are related to skills development, such as self-esteem.
- Entry skills, which are used to assess and understand an organisational setting and establish effective working relationships.
- Administrative skills such as decision making, which are used to carry out administrative functions.

As an organisation moves from a relatively stable unchanging environment into a changing, vibrant market that includes external activity the emphasis for managers moves to adaptive skills that enable a person to learn about and adjust quickly to different managerial situations found across a range of cultural and political settings. In particular, interpersonal skills become very salient.

## ▩▩■ DEVELOPING A LEARNING CULTURE

In Chapter 3, the learning organisation/community was introduced as a means of enabling organisations to enhance their functions and become centres of learning, embodying a learning culture. It is easy to eulogise about learning organisations, learning culture and lifelong learning, but it is far more difficult to bring them about, embedding learning and personal development as a natural pervasive activity.

The following is a brief account of a practical sequential process that might assist an organisation to tread the road to salvation. It is a model and therefore should be modified as required to suit particular contexts and learners.

## stage 1: seek support and develop a team

You cannot hope to change an organisation's learning/training practices yourself. You might not be in a position to influence those who initially have to make decisions and judgments on these matters. It is a case of positioning yourself, gaining allies and influencing the decision makers at least to listen. The allies and support you can enlist might already be on deck but not functioning well.

Pedler *at al.* (1991) suggest a number of possible starting points for developing a learning organisation strategy in an organisation. They suggest that the board of directors in a business or the executive committee in a community organisation is a good starting point as they will have to be involved at some time if the proposal is to be spread throughout the organisation and be supported. Support is also needed from middle management/organisers so find out who is sympathetic.

The human resources department in a business is another starting point as they might be keen to help, particularly if it enables them to operate in a more proactive way rather than responding to directives from management all the time. Their strength is enhanced if you and they can demonstrate the support of most employees for particular policies and practices. There is expertise there and performance review systems might be located there too. But they might be negative and block the ideas if there is any possibility of threat to the existence of the HR department or a reduction in their activities, say through moves towards outsourcing expertise and bringing in local TAFE teachers/trainers for in-house learning.

A joint management-union initiative is also a sound starting point as this links the two groups that are most concerned with challenging and transforming existing work practices and most concerned with the productivity and wellbeing of the organisation and the employees. Such partnerships can transform old positions and thinking, and lead to productive alliances and a win-win situation for all.

In communities also seek support from local politicians (who are always after glory!) and from a wide range of associations and committees, particularly those who will have a part to play or whose involvement would help to convince the waverers or bring pressure to bear on key decision makers.

Many organisations already have a training committee. Try to get on it and influence it from inside. Influence it from outside by proposing well-considered and cogently argued reasons for change that are supported by fellow employees. If this support can be gained from a range of levels and groups, the force of any submission is improved. Do not criticise what has been done before.

Establish a group from this network, who can jointly develop goals, terms of reference and time frames, or establish task forces to pursue particular issues within a set time span. These are temporary groups that do not threaten established structures but that can mobilise much energy and produce creative ideas. But whatever the starting-up method is it must eventually involve as many employees/people as possible across all levels to generate commitment and interest.

## stage 2: assessing the present

The second stage is to identify the ways in which you, the group and/or the task force would like to see the business, organisation or community improve its learning/education/personal development/training endeavours. To do this a complete picture is required of structure, policies, procedures, what training/learning is currently done and how it is done.

Different members of the group/task force can collect information on specific elements. This information provides a basis from which recommendations can be made for future activity and priorities can be established. The essential information should cover what the organisation does and how it is structured to do it, any current education/training program and where it takes place, who has access, who determines access and how it is recognised. Other questions include:

- What is the policy on education/training?
- Has the organisation a vision statement?
- How are staff/members encouraged to show commitment to that vision?
- Is there an education/training goal for the organisation in the vision statement?
- Are education/training goals derived from a detailed analysis of skills, knowledge and attitudes required in the organisation by members/employees?
- Are individuals encouraged to have their own personal development plans?
- Who develops education/training policy?
- Who determines the budget?
- Who has entitlement – the individual, group or department?

## stage 3: building a shared vision

Prior to any changes being made or even suggested, there must be agreement on the need for change and the direction in which it should proceed. The shared vision can include one, some or all of the following:

- Improving the quality of the products or services to clients and/or members
- Redesigning jobs, office/factory layout, equipment to make work/membership more efficient and pleasant
- Producing greater profit/benefits for members
- Increasing the satisfaction and challenge in employees' jobs or in the community
- Providing training and learning for new skills within and outside the organisation/community — a resource for all
- Deploying skills more flexibly
- Recognising employees'/members' skills, knowledge and experience
- Involving employees/members in decision making
- Improving the information flow in the organisation/community.

A shared vision must benefit all or most employees or members and cannot be imposed as it involves commitment from all or else it is of no value. It cannot be created by a small group of senior executives or committee members spending a weekend up on Mount Sinai and descending with the vision statement inscribed on a rock tablet. Nor can it come from a small, unrepresentative group over drinks in the local hotel attempting to impose their own agenda. If open discussion can enable full participation then a shared vision can become a driving force for the organisation and the community. It certainly needs some committed person(s) to drive it but not to impose it, so it is shaped through the consensus of interested parties.

## stage 4: getting going — developing an ethos

Having identified needs in relation to the vision and objectives of the organisation, the next step is to prioritise those needs and establish how they can be met with a detailed discussion and evaluation of education and training options. Concurrently, other assessments must be fed into the scheme, such as an assessment of internal resources, potential teachers/trainers/facilitators/consultants, internal or external or joint delivery systems and collaboration with other groups.

Many competent people are so used to carrying out tasks in their jobs and in their daily lives that they find it difficult to analyse the skills they have, that they can offer or that they need. If they are going to be involved in mentoring or coaching, they must be able to identify skills and how they should be used. Using a core skills list as a checklist helps to identify the skills being used. Finally, individual or group learning plans should be drawn up. An organisation could draw up a skills register that will allow the identification of employees/members who can assist in the learning process by training, coaching or mentoring.

Developing a learning culture for lifelong learning involves changes in attitudes, practices and structures, but change always creates stress. Encouragement should be given to notions that risks can be taken, that mistakes are allowed and that innovation is supported. Misdirected activity, temporary setbacks and false starts are all learning processes. Many innovative ideas simply need more time and support to develop into workable forms, resources for a trial or time for the exploration of possibilities. Failures are inevitable with new ideas but they might well act as a springboard for further modifications and extensions of ideas and lead to something quite different and entirely successful. Risk-taking behaviour is essential in a context of change, provided lessons are learnt from both successes and failures that are incorporated into future activities and structures. In a business context, risk taking might include exchanging jobs, secondments, practising new skills, widening job roles, establishing new work teams, setting up new relationships between teams, managers and internal and external clients. Calculated risk taking can lead to skill enhancement and improvement in the organisational structure.

The learning organisation gives employees/members the opportunity to develop an enhanced sense of purpose and community. It is the organisation's responsibility to provide the resources, the open environment and the opportunities for human development. The result is a group of self-reliant employees or community citizens who can survive and thrive in an era of escalating change. A resilient workforce or citizenry are not only dedicated to the idea of continuous learning but also stand ready to reinvent themselves and take responsibility for their own life management. Innovation, flexibility and awareness are everyone's responsibility.

## SUMMARY

Training and education must be a central feature of individual, corporate and national strategy for the future. Workplace training rather than educational institutional training and education is becoming the norm. This imposes greater responsibility and more costs on enterprises and individuals, as well as giving workplace educators a very significant role in developing the learning culture needed to facilitate lifelong learning for employment and personal development. Workplace training and trainers are the catalysts for this, particularly in the small business workplace, which represent 90 per cent of enterprises in Australia.

Research suggests that what trainers 'do' is mediated by a plethora of context-specific factors affecting trainer activity, such as type of industry, enterprise size, type of ownership of business and length of trainer's experience rather than cost and value considerations. A substantial amount of training occurring in the workplace is of the 'unstructured', informal kind, particularly in SMEs, and the impact of training competency standards upon training practices is minimal as they are minimally relevant.

There is also a need for an exploration of ways in which informal training/learning in the workplace might be more fully recognised and valued so learners are able to receive recognition for their learning

To heed more andragogical, learner-centred principles teachers and trainers need positive self-concepts as these provide the basis for an accepting, sensitive personality, an ability to build positive relationships with others and freedom from feeling threatened in a more flexible and open system. A positive atmosphere produced by a teacher with a positive self-concept engenders growth and learning. The essential part of andragogical teaching is treating the adult as an adult, respecting life experience, problem-solving ability and self-directing ability.

The greying of the adult population is leading to an increase in numbers of older learners whose skills and knowledge need updating. This group will form a significant proportion of the learning community in the future.

The assessment process must become less of a test and more a process of collecting information and evidence from a variety of sources about an individual's skills, whether trade, professional or managerial, in order to make an informed judgment. The sources should not include only obvious ones like demonstrating the skill but also reports from supervisors and work colleagues, portfolios, self-assessment, interpretation of documents, tables and flowcharts, etc., simulations and small projects (such as investigative reports, preparation of models and class presentations). Emphasis should be given to criterion-based assessment rather than normative assessment in workplace and adult learning.

A simple model of how to develop a learning organisation/community is provided.

## CONCLUDING OVERVIEW

As this book draws to a close, it is worthwhile to look back and pull together in brief some of the major themes and issues. Two major themes are dominant:

- As a result of current and future changes in the workplace and society stemming from technological innovation, interactive communication and economic, social and competitive globalism, lifelong learning must become a fundamental activity throughout life. Lifelong learning is the major means by which communities, organisations and societies will survive, generally by developing themselves into learning communities or learning organisations.
- Education for adults needs to be different in method, scope and approach from that of the earlier years if adults are to be enticed back into lifelong learning to continually rehone employment and personal skills. Our knowledge of the psychology of the adult and the philosophy of andragogy suggests that more emphasis needs be placed on self-direction, self-pacing, experience and critical reflection than is possible with children. The intellectual, motivational and personality characteristics of adults demand this emphasis.

These two themes are closely related since any organisation, community or society is only as productive, capable and responsive to change as its human resources permit it to be. These themes raise a number of important points. Among them are:

- A workplace reform agenda with CBT as a central feature is not an appropriate form of educational development as it is too strongly located within a narrowly focused, behaviourist, skills-oriented training context to meet the needs of lifelong education and the emergence of a culture of learning within the workplace and beyond.
- Skill training is only one aspect of the learning that ought to be promoted as part of a total educative process. Portable personal skills and knowledge are equally important in decentralised work structures and more democratic forms of society.
- Education and training must become a more collaborative effort between many stakeholders and be integrated with the needs of individuals, groups, workplace, and nation.
- Lifelong education and self-development must be promoted, not only for

economic reasons but also for social and political reasons concerned with facilitating more access and equity.

- Adults are disinclined to return to learning. Andragogy with its process approach appears to be more suited to the needs of adults and will encourage more adult participation in both workplace and personal learning, as it meets the psychological and learning characteristics of adults.
- Andragogy has lost most of its libertarian thrust but the selfishness associated with self-directed learning might be a drawback in community settings.
- Adult and lifelong education, irrespective of setting, must take advantage of new approaches determined mainly by the characteristics of andragogy integrated with innovative multimedia communication and information devices. These new approaches will pose many challenges for educators, trainers and students as old ways of teaching and learning and even the context of learning alter. Teachers and trainers must be helped to develop positive self-concepts to deal with professional and personal role change threats.

All these points raise a significant question: can we meet this challenge to create lifelong learning and learning communities at work, home and in society in which people of all ages, particularly those of post-compulsory school years, can join in self-development and learning in flexible ways for occupational and personal reasons? The future focus is LEARNING if a nation is to maintain and enhance its social, economic and political performance and quality of life for all its citizens.

# BIBLIOGRAPHY

ABS (1998) *Career Experience*, Catalogue No. 6254.0, Canberra.

ABS (1999) *Labour Force Projections 1999–2016*, Catalogue No. 6260.0, Canberra.

ABS (1999) *Estimated Resident Population*, Catalogue No. 3201.0, Canberra.

ABS (2000) *Australia Now: Adult and Community Education*, AGPS, Canberra.

ABS (2000a) *Survey of Household Expenditure*, AGPS, Canberra.

ABS (2000b) *Australia Now—Employment*, AGPS, Canberra.

Ackerman, P. (1996) 'A Theory of Adult Intellectual Development', *Intelligence*, 22, pp. 229–59.

Agostino, S., Lefoe, G. and Hedberg, J. (1997) 'Online Collaboration for Learning', Paper to 3rd Australian WWW Conference, Lismore.

Alpaugh, P. and Birren, J. (1977) 'Variables Affecting Creative Contributions Across the Adult Life Span', *Human Development*, 20, pp. 240–8.

ANTA (1996) *Participation and Attainment of Client Groups in VET*, Brisbane.

Argyris, C. (1972) *Existence, Relatedness and Growth*, Free Press, New York.

Ashford, S. (1988) 'Individual Strategies for Coping with Stress during Organisational Transitions', *Journal of Applied Behavioural Sciences*, 24, pp. 19–36.

Ashton, D. (1998) 'Skill Formation: Redirecting the Research Agenda', in Coffield, F. (ed.) *Learning at Work*, Policy Press, Bristol, pp. 61–69.

Aspin, R. (1998) *Collaboration in a Virtual World: Support for Conceptual Learning?* Technical Report 98/13, Computer-Based Learning Unit, University of Leeds.

Atkinson, R. and Shiffrin, R. M. (1968) *Human Memory*, Academic Press, New York.

Australian Mission on Management Skills (1991) *Report Vol. 1*, AGPS, Canberra.

Ausubel, D. (1963) *The Psychology of Meaningful Verbal Learning*, Grune and Stratton, New York.

Ball, K. (1999) 'Training and Labour Market Issues', in Smith, A. (ed.) *Creating a Future*, NCVER, Adelaide.

Ball, K., Misko, J. and Smith, A. (2000) 'Training Needs of Older Workers', Paper to AVETRA Conference, Canberra.

Ball, K., Young, H. and Huang, S. (2001) *Adult Retraining and Reskilling in Australia and South Korea*, Project No. cp9909, NCVER, Adelaide.

Baltes, P. and Lindenberger, U. (1997) 'A New Window to the Study of Cognitive Ageing', *Psychology and Aging*, 12, pp. 12–21.

Bandura, A. (1977) *Social Learning Theory*, Prentice Hall, New Jersey.

Barham, K., Fraser, J. and Heath, L. (1988) *Management for the Future*, Ashridge Management College, Berkhamsted.

Barnett, R. and Cavanah, J. (1994) *Global Dreams*, Simon and Schuster, New York.

BarOn, www.greensystems.com.au

Bartlett, F. (1932) *Remembering*, CUP, Cambridge.

Bass, B. (1990) 'From Transactional to Transformational Leadership', *Organisation Dynamics*, 18, pp. 19–31.

Bates, A. W. (1995) *Technology, Open Learning and Distance Education*, Routledge, London.

Bates, A.W. (1997) 'The Impact of Technological Change on Open and Distance Learning', *Distance Education*, 18, pp. 3–10.

Belanger, P. (1998) *Trends in Adult Education Policy*, UNESCO, Paris.

Bell, C. R. (1997) 'The Bluebirds: Secret: Mentoring with Bravery and Balance', *Training and Development*, 51, pp. 30–33.

Bendig, A. (1963) 'The Relationship of Temperamental Traits of Social Extraversion and Emotionality to Vocational Interests', *Journal of General Psychology*, 69, pp. 311–18.

Berliner, D. C. (1996) 'Uninvited Comments from an Uninvited Guest', *Educational Researcher*, 25 (8), pp. 47–50.

Bernstein, B. (1996) *Pedagogy, Symbolic Control and Identity*, Taylor and Francis, London.

Bexton, W., Heron, W. and Scott, T. H. (1954) 'Effects of Decreased Variations in the Sensory Environment', *Canadian Journal of Psychology*, 8, pp. 70–6.

Bierema, L. L. (1996) 'How Executive Women Learn Corporate Culture', *Human Resource Development Quarterly*, 7, No. 2, pp. 145–64.

Bigelow, J. (1994) 'International Skills for Managers', *Asia Pacific Journal of Human Resources*, 32, pp. 1–12.

Billett, S. (1999) *The CBT Decade: Teaching for Flexibility and Adaptability*, Project No. 7029 NCVER, Adelaide.

Billings, A. and Moos, R. (1984) 'Coping, Stress and Social Resources Among Adults with Unipolar Depression', *Journal of Personality and Social Psychology*, 46, pp. 877–91.

Blandy, R., Dockery, M., Hawke, A. and Webster, E. (2000) *Does Training Pay?*, NCVER, Adelaide.

Bolwijn, P. and Kumpe, T. (1990) 'Manufacturing in the 1990s', *Long Range Planning*, 23, pp. 44–57.

Boring, E. (1923) Public Debate with Walter Lippman reported in *The New Republic*, 6 June.

Boud, D. (ed.) (1995) *Enhancing Learning Through Self Assessment*, Kogan Page, London.

Boud, D. and Falchikov, N. (1995) 'What Does Research Tell Us About Self Assessment?', in Boud, D. (ed.) Enhancing Learning Through Self Assessment, Kogan Page, London.

Boud, D. and Feletti, G. (1991) *The Challenge of Problem-Based Learning*, Kogan Page, Sydney.

Boud, D. et al. (1985) *Reflection. Turning Experience into Learning*, Kogan Page, London.

Boyd, R., Myers, D. and Gordon, J. (Oct.–Dec. 1988) 'Transformative Education', *International Journal Of Lifelong Education* 7, No. 4, pp. 261–84.

Braman, O. R. (1998) 'The Cultural Dimension of Individualism and Collectivism as a Factor in Adult Self-Directed Learning Readiness', Ph.D. dissertation, University of Southern Mississippi.

Brockett, R. G. and Hiemstra, R. (1991) *Self-direction in Adult Learning: Perspectives on Theory, Research, and Practice*, Routledge, New York

Bromley, D. B. (1974) *The Psychology of Human Ageing*, Penguin, Harmondsworth.

Brookfield, S. D. (1986) *Understanding and Facilitating Adult Learning*, Jossey-Bass, San Francisco.

Brookfield, S. D. (1987) *Developing Critical Thinkers*, Jossey-Bass, San Francisco.

Brookfield, S. D. (1990) *The Skillful Teacher*, Jossey-Bass, San Francisco.

Brookfield, S. D. (1991) 'The Development of Critical Reflection in Adulthood', *New Education*, 13(1), pp. 39–48.

Brookfield, S. D. (1992) 'Developing Criteria for Formal Theory Building in Adult Education', *Adult Education Quarterly*, 42(2), pp.79–93.

Brookfield, S. D. (1993) 'Self-Directed Learning, Political Clarity and the Critical Practice of Adult Education', *Adult Education Quarterly*, 43, pp. 227–42.

Brookfield, S. D. (1995) *Adult Learning: An Overview*, Tuinjman, A. (ed.) *International Encyclopedia of Education*, Pergamon Press, Oxford.

Bruner, J. (1966) *Towards a Theory of Instruction*, Harvard University Press, Cambridge.

Burke, J. (1998) 'The Real World On A Short Leash: The (Mis)Application Of Constructivism to the Design of Educational Technology', *Educational Technology Research And Development* 46, pp. 53–65.

Burns, J., Clift, J.and Duncan, J. (1990) 'Understanding of Understanding: Implications for Learning and Teaching', *British Journal of Educational Psychology*, 61, pp. 276–89.

Burns, R. (1966) 'Age and Mental Ability', *British Journal of Educational Psychology*, 36, pp. 58–60.

Burns, R. (1979) *The Self Concept: In Theory, Development, Measurement and Behaviour*, Longmans, London.

Burns, R. (1982) *The Self Concept: Development and Education*, Cassel, London.

Burns, R. (1989) 'Self Concept and Teacher Education', *South Pacific Journal of Education*, 17, pp. 27–37.

Burns, R. (1991) 'Teacher Education and Personal Development', *Australian Educational Researcher*, 18, pp. 97–109.

Burns, R. (1992) *10 Skills for Working With Stress*, Business and Professional Publishing Ltd, Sydney.

Burns, R. (1993) *Managing People in Changing Times*, Allen and Unwin, Sydney.

Callan, V. and Dickson, C. (1993) 'Managerial Coping Strategies during Organisational Change', *Asia Pacific Journal of Human Resources*, 30, pp. 17–59.

Candy, P. C. (1991) *Self-direction for Lifelong Learning: A Comprehensive Guide to Theory and Practice*. Jossey-Bass, San Francisco.

Carpenter, P., Just, M. and Shell, P. (1990) 'What One Intelligence Test Measures', *Psychological Review*, 97, pp. 424–31.

Carroll, J. B. (1993) *Human Cognitive Abilities*, CUP, New York.

Cassara, B. (ed.) (1990) *Adult Education in a Multicultural Society*. Routledge, New York.

Cattell, R. (1976) *The Scientific Analysis of Personality*, Penguin, Harmondsworth.

Catts, R. (1996) *Validating Training Benefits in the Workplace*, Centre for Further Education and Training, USQ, Toowoomba, Queensland.

Ceci, S. and Bruck, M. (1994) 'The Bio-Ecological Theory of Intelligence', in Detterman, D. (ed.) *Current Topics in Human Intelligence*, Ablex, New Jersey.

Ceci, S. and Liker, J. (1986) 'Academic and Non-Academic Intelligence', in Sternberg, R.J. and Wagner, R. (eds) *Practical Intelligence*, CUP, Cambridge.

Central Statistical Office (1992) *Social Trends* 22, HMSO, London.

Cervero, R. M. (1988) *Effective Continuing Education For Professionals*, Jossey-Bass, San Francisco.

Chappell, C. (1996) 'Quality and Competency-Based Education', in *The Literacy Equation*, Queensland Council for Adult Literacy, Red Hill.

Clark, M. C. and Wilson, A. L. (1991) 'Context and Rationality in Mezirow's Theory of Transformational Learning', *Adult Education Quarterly*, 41 (2), pp. 75–91.

Cleminson, A. and Bradford, S. (1996) 'Professional Education', *Journal of Vocational Education and Training*, 48, No. 3, pp. 249–59.

Cleverly, J. (1972) *Australian Education in the Twentieth Century*, Longman, Australia.

Clift, J. and Chambers, M. (1994) 'Educational Considerations in the Development of a Generic Degree Program', Report to the NZ Qualifications Authority.

Cody, M., Dunn, D. and Hoppin, S. (1999) 'Training and Evaluating Internet Use Among Older Learners', *Communication Education*, October, pp. 269–86.

Coffield, F. (1999) 'Breaking the Consensus: Lifelong Learning as Social Control', *British Educational Research Journal*, 25, pp. 479–99.

Coffield, F. (ed.) (1997) 'The Concept of the Learning Society Explored', *Journal of Education Policy*, Special Edition, 12 (6), pp. 449–558.

Cohen, G. (1981) 'Inferential Reasoning in Old Age', *Cognition*, 9, pp. 59–72.

Collard, S. and Law, M. (1989) 'The Limits of Perspective Transformation: A Critique of Mezirow's Theory', *Adult Education Quarterly*, 39 (2), pp. 99–107.

Collins, C. (1993) 'Introduction', in Collins, C. (ed.) *Competencies*, Australian College of Education, National Capital Printing, Canberra.

Collins, M. (1988) 'Self-Directed Learning or an Emancipatory Practice of Adult Education: Re-thinking the Role of the Adult Educator', *Proceedings of the 29th Annual Adult Education Research Conference*, Faculty of Continuing Education, University of Calgary.

Commission of the European Communities (1997) 'Towards a Europe of Knowledge', COM (97) 563, Final, Luxembourg.

Confessore, G. J. an Barron, D. L. (1997) 'Learner Orientations among Baby Boomers', in *Expanding Horizons in Self-Directed Learning*, Long, H.B. et al., pp. 39–51, University of Oklahoma, Norman.

Cook, D. L. (1995) 'Community and Computer-Generated Learning Environments', *New Directions for Adult and Continuing Education*, No. 67, pp. 33–9.

Cornford, I. and Athanasou, J. (1995) 'Developing Expertise through Practical Training', *Industrial and Commercial Training*, 27 (2), pp. 10–18.

Cornford, I. (1993) 'Theories of Skill Learning and Research into the Development of Expertise: Some Implications for Competency-based Training', Conference Papers, *After Competence: The Future of Post-Compulsory Education and Training Conference*, Vol. 1, Centre for Skill Formation, Research and Development, Griffith University.

Cornford, I. (1996) 'Experienced Teachers' Views of Competency-based Training in NSW TAFE', Conference Papers, *Learning & Work: The Challenges*, Vol. 4, pp. 105–15, Centre for Learning and Work Research, Griffith University.

Cornford, I. (1997) 'Competency-based Training: An Assessment of its Strengths and Weaknesses by NSW Vocational Teachers', *Australian and New Zealand Journal of Vocational Education Research*, 5 (1), pp. 53–76.

Costa, A. and Lowery, L. F. (1990) *Techniques for Teaching Thinking*, Brownlow, Melbourne.

Cranton, P. (1994) *Understanding and Promoting Transformative Learning: A Guide For Educators Of Adults*, Jossey-Bass, San Francisco.

Cranton, P. (ed.) (1997) 'Transformative Learning in Action: Insights from Practice', *New Directions for Adult and Continuing Education*, 74.

Cross, K. P. (1981) *Adults as Learners. Increasing Participation and Facilitating Learning* (1992 ed.), Jossey-Bass, San Francisco.

Darmon, I. et al. (1999) 'The Comparative Dimension in Continuous Vocational Training: A Preliminary Framework', in Coffield, F. (ed.) *Why's the Beer up North Always Stronger? Studies of Lifelong Learning in Europe*, Policy Press, Bristol.

Davenport, I. (1993) 'Is There Any Way Out of the Andragogy Mess?' in Thorpe, M., Edwards, R. and Davies, P. (1999) 'A New Learning Culture? Possibilities and Contradictions in Accreditation', *Studies in the Education of Adults*, 31 (1), pp. 10–20.

Davies, P. (1999) 'A New Learning Culture? Possibilities and Contradictions in Accreditation', *Studies in the Education of Adults*, 31, 1, pp. 10–20.

Davies, P. and Bynner, J. (1997) *The Impact of Credit-Based Systems of Learning on Learning Cultures*, Economic and Social Research Council Report, London.

Deakin University (1997) *Training Culture in Australia*, Employment Services Unit, Deakin University, Melbourne.

Dearing, R. (Chair) (1997) *Higher Education in a Learning Society*. HMSO, London.

Deary, I. (1997) 'Intelligence and Information Processing', in Nyborg, H. (ed.) *The Scientific Study of Human Nature*, Pergamon, Oxford.

Deary, I. (2001) Report in *The Psychologist* 14, No. 2, p. 87.

Dede, C. (1996) 'Emerging Technologies in Distance Education for Business', *Journal of Education for Business*, 71, No. 4, pp. 197–204.

DEET (1987) *Skills for Australia*, Circulated by the Minister for Employment, Education and Training, J.S Dawkins, Minister for Employment Services and Youth Affairs, AGPS, Canberra.

DEET (1988) 'Industry Training in Australia: The Need for Change', Discussion paper issued by Minister Dawkins, AGPS, Canberra.

DEET (1989) 'Improving Australia's Training System', Policy statement by Minister Dawkins, AGPS, Canberra.

DEET (1995) *Australia's Workforce 2005: Jobs for the Future*, AGPS, Canberra.

Delors Report (1996) *Education in the 21st Century: The Treasure Within*, UNESCO, Paris.

Department for Education and Employment (1997) *The Learning Age: a Renaissance for a New Britain*, Stationery Office, Cm 3790, London.

Department of Trade and Industry (1998) *Our Competitive Future: Building the Knowledge Driven Economy*, Stationery Office, Cm 4176, London.

Dewey, J. (1933) *How We Think*, D. C. Heath, New York.

Diamond, M. (1978) 'Aging and Cell Loss', *Psychology Today*, September.

Dickie, M. (1999) 'National Strategy for Skills and Lifelong Learning', Paper to update seminar, ANTA, November.

Dixon, N. (1994) *The Organizational Learning Cycle*, McGraw-Hill, New York.

Dixon, R., Simon, E., Novak, C. A. and Hultsch, D. F. (1982) 'Text Recall in Adulthood', *Journal of Gerontology*, 37, pp. 358–64.

Dockery, A., Koshy, P. and Stromback, T. (1997) 'The Cost of Training Apprentices in Australian Firms', *Australian Bulletin of Labour*, 23, pp. 255–74.

Donnell, D. (1999) 'Habermas, Critical Theory and Selves-Directed Learning', *Journal of European Industrial Training*, 23, pp. 251–61.

Down, C. (2000) 'Key Competencies in Training Packages', Paper to 9th Annual VET Conference, Coffs Harbour, 4–7 July.

Dumbrell, T. (2000) *Measuring the Outcomes of Vocational Education and Training: Review of Research*, Project NR8015, NCVER, Adelaide.

Eastmond, D. V. (1995) *Alone but Together: Adult Distance Study through Computer Conferencing*, Hampton Press, Cresskill, NJ.

Edgar, D. (1991) *Work and Family: An Important Business*, Australian Institute of Family Studies, Melbourne.

Edwards, R., Hanson, A. and Raggatt, P. (1996) *Boundaries of Adult Learning*, Routledge, London.

Ehrmann, S. C. (1998) 'The Flashlight Project: Tools for Monitoring the Progress of our Hopes and Fears about Technology in Education', *The Technology Source: Case Studies*.

Eisdorfer, C. (1963) 'The WAIS Performance of the Aged: A Retest Evaluation', *Journal of Gerontology*, 18, pp. 169–72.

Eisner, E. (1993) 'Reshaping Assessment in Education: Criteria in Search of Practice', in *Journal of Curriculum Studies*, 25 (3), pp. 219–33.

Ellyard, P. (2000) 'Preparing for Thrival in a Planetist Future', Paper to Community Services and Health Industry Conference, Melbourne.

Engestrom, Y. (1998) 'Transfer of Knowledge', Conference Paper at COST A11 Conference, Newcastle University.

Ensher, E. A. and Murphy, S. E. (1997) 'Effects of Race, Gender, Perceived Similarity and Contact on Mentor Relationships', *Journal of Vocational Behavior*, 50, No. 3, pp. 460–81.

Eraut, M., Alderton, J., Cole, G. and Senker, P. (1998) 'Learning from Other People at Work', in Coffield, F. (ed.) *Learning at Work*, Policy Press, Bristol, pp. 37–48.

Erber, F. and Fiske, S. (1980) 'Outcome Dependency and Attention to Inconsistent Information', *Journal of Personality and Social Psychology*, 47, pp. 709–26.

Erikson, E. (1982) *The Life Cycle Completed*, Norton, New York.

Evans, J. (2000). *Workers in the New Economy*, Trades Union Advisory Committee, OECD.

Evans, T. and Smith, P. (1999) Research on Flexible Learning/Delivery: Understanding Terms.

Eysenck, H. (1967) *The Biological Basis of Personality*, Thomas Press, Springfield.

Farrell, G. (1999) *The Development of Virtual Education: A Global Perspective*, Commonwealth of Learning, Vancouver.

Faure, E. (1972) *Learning to Be: The World of Education Today and Tomorrow*, UNESCO, Paris.

Field, L. (1991) 'Guglielmino's Self-directed Learning Readiness Scale: Should it Continue to be Used?', *Adult Education Quarterly*, 41, pp. 100–103.

Field, L. (1996) 'Is there Room for CBT in the Learning Organisation?', *Australian Training Review*, 18 (March-May), pp. 24–5.

Filipczak, B. (1995) 'Putting the Learning into Distance Learning', *Training 32*, No. 10, pp. 111–18.

Fitzgerald, V. (1994) *Successful Reform*, Report to the Australian National Training Authority from the Allen Consulting Group Pty. Ltd., The Allen Consulting Group, Melbourne.

Fodor, J. (1983) *The Modularity of the Mind*, MIT Press, Cambridge.

Ford, B. (1991) The 'Learning Enterprise Paper' given to the TQMI 2nd National Conference, Melbourne.

Foyster, J. (1997) 'Do We Still Need CBT?' *Australian Training Review*, 22 (March-May), p. 32.

Freeman, M. (1995) 'Peer Assessment by Groups of Group Work', *Assessment and Evaluation in Higher Education*, 20, pp. 289–300.

Freeman, M. (1997) 'Flexibility in Access, Interaction and Assessment', *Australian Journal of Educational Technology*, 13, pp. 21–39.

Freire, P. (1970) *The Pedagogy of the Oppressed*, Herdon & Herdon, New York.

Freyer, R. (Chair) (1997) 'Learning for the 21st Century', National Advisory Group for Continuing Education and Lifelong Learning, London.

Galbraith, M. W. and Cohen, N. H. (eds) (1995) 'Mentoring: New Strategies and Challenges', *New Directions for Adult and Continuing Education*, No. 66, Jossey-Bass, San Francisco.

Gardner, H. (1993) *Frames of Mind*, Harper Collins, London.

Garnaut, R. (1991) 'Australia in the 1990s', *Australian Quarterly*, Autumn.

Garratt, R. (1994) *The Learning Organisation*, Harper-Collins, London.

Gibson, C. C. (1992) 'Distance Education: On Focus and Future', *Adult Education Quarterly*, 42 (3), pp.167–79.

Gillespie, F. (1998) 'Instructional Design for the New Technologies', in Gillespie, K. H. (ed.) *The Impact of Technology on Faculty Development, Life and Work, New Directions for Teaching and Learning No. 76*, pp. 39–52, Jossey-Bass, San Francisco.

Ginsburg, L. (1998) 'Integrating Technology into Adult Learning', in Technology, Basic Skills, and *Adult Education: Getting Ready and Moving Forward, Information Series No. 372*.

Gittens, A.(1999) 'Better Than Warmed-Over Porridge', *New Statesman*, 12 February, pp. 25–6.

Glaser, R. (1991) 'Intelligence as an Expression of Acquired Knowledge', in Rowe, H. (ed.) *Intelligence*, Erlbaum, Hillsdale.

Goddard, J. (1996) 'E for Engagement; E for Email', Paper presented at ASCILTE Conference, Queensland.

Goldman, S. (1996) *Evaluating Online Delivery*, Adelaide Institute of TAFE, Adelaide.

Goleman, D. (1995) *Emotional Intelligence: Why It Can Matter More Than IQ*, Bantam Books, New York

Gonczi, A. (1997) 'Future Directions of Vocational Education in Australian Secondary Schools', *Australian and New Zealand Journal of Vocational Education Research*, 5, pp. 77–108.

Gonczi, A. (1998) 'The Potential Destruction of the VET System', in Andersen, F. and Ferrier, D. (eds) *Different Drums One Beat*, NCVER, Adelaide.

Gonczi, A., Hager, P. and Oliver, L. (1990) *Establishing Competency Standards in the Professions*, National Office of Overseas Skills Recognition Research Paper No. 1, DEET, AGPS, Canberra.

Gould, S. (1983) The Mismeasure of Man, Norton, New York.

Grabov, V. (1997) 'The Many Facets Of Transformative Learning Theory And Practice', in Cranton, P. (ed.) Transformative Learning In Action: Insights From Practice. New Directions For Adult And Continuing Education, No. 74, pp. 89–96, Jossey-Bass, San Francisco.

Graham, M. and Scarborough, H. (1999) 'Computer Mediated Communication and Collaborative Learning', Australian Journal of Educational Technology, 151, pp. 20–46.

Gray, D. E. (1999) 'The Internet in Lifelong Learning', International Journal of Lifelong Education, 18, pp. 119–26.

Greider, W. (1997) One World — Ready or Not, Simon and Schuster, New York.

Guilford, J. P. (1957) The Nature of Human Intelligence, McGraw-Hill, New York.

Gundy, B. (1989) Techniques for Structured Problem Solving, Van Nostrand, Rheinhold.

Guthrie, E. R. (1938) Psychology of Human Conflict, Harper Row, New York.

Haddon, F. and Lytton, H. (1968) 'Teaching Approaches and the Development of Divergent Thinking', British Journal of Educational Psychology, 38, pp. 171–80.

Hager, P. and Gonczi, A. (1993) 'Attributes and Competence', Australian and New Zealand Journal of Vocational Education Research, 1, pp. 36–45.

Hager, P. (1994) 'Is there a Cogent Philosophical Argument against Competency Standards?', Australian Journal of Education, 38, pp. 3–18.

Hager, P. (1995) 'Competency Standards — A Help or a Hindrance? An Australian Perspective', Journal of Vocational Education and Training, 47, pp. 141–51.

Hall, C. (1992) 'Questions about Quality: Focussing on Course Design and the Teaching, Learning Environment', Paper at the New Zealand Vice Chancellors Committee Workshop on Quality Assurance in NZ Universities.

Hammond M. and Collins, R. (1991) Self-Directed Learning: Critical Practice, Kogan Page, London.

Haney, A. (1997) 'The Role of Mentorship in the Workplace', in Taylor, M.C. (ed.) Workplace Education, pp. 211–28, Culture Concepts, Ontario.

Hanson, A. (1989) 'Expectations and Realisations', CNAA unpublished Ph.D. dissertation.

Hanson, A. (1996) 'The Search for Separate Theories of Adult Learning: Does Anyone Really Need Andragogy?', in Edwards, R., Hanson, A. and Raggatt, P. (eds.) Boundaries of Adult Learning. Adult Learners, Education and Training, Vol. 1, Routledge, London.

Harasim, L. (1993) 'Networlds: Networks as Social Space', in Harasim, L. (ed.) Global Networks, MIT, Cambridge, Mass.

Harlow, H. (1949) 'Formation of Learning Sets', Psychology Review, 56, p. 51.

Harper, B., Hedberg, J., Bennett, S. and Lockyer, L. (2000) Review of Research: The Online Experience, NCVER, Adelaide.

Harris, R., Guthrie, H., Hobart, B. and Lundberg, D. (1995) Competency-Based Education and Training, Macmillan Education, Melbourne.

Harris, R., Simons, M. and Bone, J. (2000) Rethinking the Role of the Workplace Trainer, NCVER, Adelaide.

Hartley, J. (1997) 'Academic Performance of Mature and Traditional Entry Students', Journal of Access Studies, 12, pp. 98–112.

Hatcher, T. G. (1996) 'The Ins and Outs of Self-Directed Learning', Training and Development, 51, pp. 34–9.

HDWG (Human Dimension Working Group) (2000) Report, DISR, Canberra.

Hebb, D. (1949) The Organisation of Behaviour, Chapman and Hall, London.

Heinz, W. (1999) 'Lifelong Learning — Learning for Life? Some Cross-National Observations', in Coffield, F. (ed.) Why's the Beer up North Always Stronger? Studies of Lifelong Learning in Europe, Policy Press, Bristol.

Hernnstein, R. and Murray, C. (1994) The Bell Curve, Free Press, New York.

Herzberg, F. (1959) The Motivation to Work, Wiley, New York.

Heywood, L., Gonczi, A. and Hager, P. (1992) A Guide to Development of Competency for Professions, National Office of Overseas Skills Recognition Research Paper No. 7, DEET, AGPS, Canberra.

Hilbert, R. (1982) 'Competency-Based Teacher Education Versus the Real World', Urban Education, 16, pp. 379–98.

Hobart, B. (1999) Globalisation and Its Impact on VET, NCVER, Adelaide.

Hodkinson, P. and Issitt, M. (1995) The Challenge of Competence, Cassell, New York.

Homesglen TAFE (1999) A Comparative Analysis of the Costs of Workplace and TAFE Based Accredited Training and of Student Satisfaction, Project No. 96129, NCVER, Adelaide.

Hopey, C. (ed.) (1998) 'Making Technology Happen In Adult Education', in Technology, Basic Skills and Adult Education: Getting Ready And Moving Forward, Information Series No. 372, pp. 3–9, ERIC Clearinghouse On Adult, Career and Vocational Education, Ohio State University, Columbus.

Horn, J. and Noll, J. (1994) 'A System for Understanding Cognitive Capabilities', in Dettermen, D. (ed.) Current Topics in Human Intelligence, Ablex, New Jersey.

Houle, C. (1980) Continuing Learning in the Professions, Jossey-Bass, San Francisco.

Howe, M. J. (1997) IQ in Question, Sage, London.

Howells, K. (1997) 'Paper to 5th International Conference on Adult Education', UNESCO, Hamburg, July.

Hugonnier, B. (1999) 'Regional Development Tendencies in OECD Countries', Paper to Regional Australia Summit, Parliament House, Canberra.

Humphries, B. (1988) 'Adult Learning in Social Work Education: Towards Liberation or Domestication', Critical Social Policy, No. 23, pp. 4–21.

Hunt, J. M. (1961) Intelligence and Experience, Ronald Press, New York.

Hyland, T. (1994) Competence, Education and NVQs, Cassell, London.

Illich, I. and Verne, E. (1976) Imprisoned in the Global Classroom, Writers and Readers Publishing Cooperative, London.

Imel, S. (1995) 'Reflective Practice in Adult Education', ERIC Digest No. 122, Eric Clearinghouse on Adult, Career and Vocational Education, Columbus, OH.

Imel, S. (1998) *Transformative Learning in Adulthood*, ERIC Clearinghouse on Adult, Career and Vocational Education, Columbus, OH.

Jackson, N. (1993) 'Competence: A Game of Smoke and Mirrors?', in Collins, C. (ed.) *Competencies, Australian College of Education*, National Capital Printing, Canberra.

James (1997) *Business Review Weekly*, 6 April, p. 68.

Jarvis, P. (1985) *The Sociology of Adult and Continuing Education*, Croom Helm, Beckenham.

Jarvis, P. (1987) *Adult Learning in the Social Context*, Croom Helm, London.

Jarvis, P. (1987b) 'Malcolm Knowles' in Jarvis, P. (ed.) *Twentieth Century Thinkers in Adult Education*, Croom Helm, London.

Jasinski, M. (1996) *Teaching and Learning the Key Competencies in Vocational Education*, W. Adelaide TAFE, Adelaide.

Jean, M. (1999) 'MI, the GED and Me', *Focus on Basics*, 3, pp. 3–5.

Jensen, A.R. (1969) 'How Much Can We Boost IQ and Scholastic Achievement?', *Harvard Educational Review*, 39, pp. 1–123.

Jones, B. (Chair) (1995) *Report of the Inquiry into the Workforce of the Future by the House of Representatives Standing Committee for Long-Term Strategies*, AGPS, Canberra.

Jossi, F. (1997) 'Mentoring in Changing Times', *Training & Development*, 51, No. 8, pp. 50–4.

Gunn, E. (1995) 'Mentoring: The Democratic Version', *Training*, 32, No. 8, pp. 64–7.

Kaye, B. and Jacobson, B. (1996) 'Reframing Mentoring', *Training & Development*, 50, No. 8, pp. 44–7.

Judd, C. (1908) 'The Relation of Special Training to General Intelligence', *Education Review*, 36, pp. 28–42.

Kane, R. L., Morris, A. and Crawford, J. (1994) 'Training and Staff Development', *Asia Pacific Journal of Human Resources*, 32, pp. 112–32.

Kanfer, R. (1995) 'Personality and Intelligence', in Saklofske, D. and Zeidner, M. (eds), *International Handbook of Personality and Intelligence*, Plenum, New York.

Kangan, M. (Chairman) (1974) *Report on Technical and Further Education in Australia*, AGPS, Canberra.

Karpin, D. (Chair) (1995) *Enterprising Nation*. Report of the Industry Task Force on Leadership and Management Skills, AGPS, Canberra.

Kearns, P. and Papadopoulos, G. (2000) *Building a Learning and Training Culture*, NCVER, Adelaide.

Kearns, P. (1999) *Lifelong Learning and VET: A Discussion Paper*, NCVER, Adelaide.

Kearns, P. (1999) *Lifelong Learning : Implications for VET*, NCVER, Adelaide.

Kearns, P. (1999) *VET in the Learning Age: The Challenge of Lifelong Learning for All*, NCVER, Adelaide.

Kearns, P. (2001) *Review of Research. Generic Skills for the New Economy*, NCVER, Adelaide.

Kearsley, G. and Shneiderman, B. (1998) 'Engagement Theory: A Framework For Technology-Based Teaching And Learning', *Educational Technology 38*, No. 5, pp. 20–3.

Kerka, S. (1997) 'Constructivism, Workplace Learning and Vocational Education', ERIC Digest, No. 181, ERIC Clearinghouse on Adult, Career and Vocational Education, Columbus.

Kerka, S. (1998) *Learning Styles and Electronic Information. Trends and Issues Alert*, ERIC Clearinghouse on Adult, Career and Vocational Education (ED 420 788), Columbus, OH.

Kerka, S. (1999) *Self-Directed Learning. Myths and Realities 3*, ERIC Clearinghouse on Adult, Career and Vocational Education (ED 99 CO 0013), Columbus, OH.

Kidd, J. R. (1978) *How Adults Learn* (3rd ed.), N.J. Prentice Hall Regents, Englewood Cliffs.

Kilpatrick, S. (2000) *Community Learning and Sustainability*, Paper to 1st National Conference on the Future of Australia's Country Towns, Bendigo, Victoria.

Kim, J. (1980) 'Relationship of Personality to Perceptual and Behavioural Responses', *Academy of Management Journal*, 23, pp. 307–19.

Kirby, P. E. F. (1985) 'Report of the Committee of Inquiry into Labour Market Programs', AGPS, Canberra.

Kitchener, K. S. and King, P. M. (1990) 'The Reflective Judgment Model: Transforming Assumptions About Knowing', in Mezirow, J. (ed.) *Fostering Critical Reflection in Adulthood*, Jossey-Bass, San Francisco.

Kliebart, H. M. (1987) *The Struggle for the American Curriculum 1893-1958*, Routledge, New York.

Knowles, M. (1978) *The Adult Learner: A Neglected Species*, Gulf Publishing, Houston.

Knowles, M. (1980) *The Modern Practice of Adult Education. From Pedagogy to Andragogy* (2nd ed.), Prentice Hall, Englewood Cliffs.

Knowles, M. (1984) *Andragogy in Action*, Jossey-Bass, San Fransisco.

Kohn, A. (1993) *Punished by Rewards*, Houghton Mifflin, New York

Kornhauser, A. (1965) *Mental Health of the Industrial Worker*, Wiley, New York.

Kottkamp, R. B. (1990) 'Means For Facilitating Reflection', *Education And Urban Society* 22, pp. 182–203.

Lacey, K. (2000) *Making Mentoring Happen*, Woodslane, Sydney.

Lasch, C. (1995) *The Revolt of the Elites and the Betrayal of Democracy, Norton*, New York.

Leach, J. (1996) 'Distinguishing Characteristics Among Exemplary Trainers in Business and Industry', *Journal of Vocational and Technical Education*, 12.

Lidbury, R. (1995) 'Level of Awareness of Competency-based Training in the Fabrication and Welding (Heavy) Industry in the Hunter Institute of Technology Region', Unpublished research project submitted for the Bachelor of Education (Technical), University of Technology, Sydney.

Lindeman, E.C.L. (1926) *The Meaning of Adult Education*, New Republic, New York

Long, H.B. (1994) 'Challenging Some Myths about Self-Directed Learning', in *New Ideas about Self-Directed Learning*, Long, H.B. et al., pp. 1–14. Norman, University of Oklahoma.

Loughlin, K.A. (1993) *Women's Perceptions Of Transformative Learning Experiences Within Consciousness-Raising*, Mellen Research University Press, San Francisco, CA.

Lowrie, T. (1999) 'Policy Innovations in the VET Sector', Paper to AARE/NZARE Conference: Global Issues and Effects, December, Melbourne.

Lowrie, T. (1999) *Competency-Based Training*, NCVER, Adelaide.

Lowrie, T. (1999) 'Competency-based Training. A Staff Development Perspective, Project No. 7021, NCVER, Adelaide.

Maehl, W.H. (2000) *Lifelong Learning at Its Best*, Jossey-Bass, San Francisco.

Mahony, C. and Moss, W. (1996) 'Self-directed Learning: Liberating or Oppressive? Developing Autonomy in Open Learning', in Fitzpatrick, S. and Mace, J. (eds) *Lifelong Literacies*, pp. 28–33, Gatehouse Books, Manchester.

Manbeck, N. & Bruhl, R. (1997) 'He Said, She Said', Paper presented at Midwest Conference in Adult, Continuing and Community Education, Michigan State University, October.

Manz, J. and Sims, P. (1991) 'Superleadership', *Organisation Dynamics*, 19, pp. 18–35.

Marginson, S. (2000) *The Changing Nature and Organisation of Work: Implications for VET*, NCVER, Adelaide.

Marshman, B. and Associates (1996) *The Employment of Apprentices*, ANTA Report, Brisbane.

Maslow, A. H. (1970) 'A Theory of Human Motivation', *Psychological Review*, 50, 370–396.

Matuszowicz, P. F. (1996) 'Self-Directed Learning Readiness and Homelessness. Learning in Selected Small Groups in Michigan', Ph.D. dissertation, Michigan State University.

Mawer, G. (1999) *Language and Literacy in Workplace Education*, Addison Wesley Longman, London.

Maxwell, G., Cooper, M. and Biggs, N. (2000) *How People Choose Vocational Education and Training Programs: Social, Educational and Personal Influences on Aspiration*, NCVER, Adelaide.

Mayer Report (1992) *Putting General Education to Work*, Key Competencies Report to AEC and MOVEET.

Maylen, L., Hopkins, S. and Burke, G. (2001) *Training for Productivity*, Project No. 8011, NCVER, Adelaide.

McBeath, C. (1995) 'Overcoming Barriers to Effective Curriculum Change: A Case Study in Dissemination Practice', in *Conference Papers*, Vol. 2, 3rd International Conference on Post-Compulsory Education and Training, Centre for Learning and Work Research, Griffith University, 21–3 November.

McClelland, D. (1961) *The Achieving Society*, Van Nostrand, Princeton.

McGaw, B. (1993) *Competency-based Assessment, National Assessment Research Forum*, NSW TAFE Commission, Sydney.

McGregor, D. (1964) 'The Human Side of Enterprise', in Leavitt, H. (ed.) *Readings in Managerial Psychology*, University of Chicago Press, Chicago.

McKenzie, P. (1998) 'Lifelong Learning as a Policy Response', in *Rapid Economic Change and Lifelong Learning*, ACER-Monash University Centre for the Economics of Education and Training, Melbourne.

Mentoring Institute, The (1998) *The NEW Mentoring Paradigm©*, The Mentoring Institute, Sydney, BC.

Merriam, S. and Caffarella, R. (1999) *Learning in Adulthood: A Comprehensive Guide*, 2nd ed., Jossey-Bass, San Francisco.

Merriam, S. and Brockett, R. (1997) *The Profession and Practice Of Adult Education*, Jossey-Bass, San Francisco.

Mezirow, J. (1978) 'Perspective Transformation', *Adult Education*, 28, pp. 100–110.

Mezirow, J. (1990) *Fostering Critical Reflection In Adulthood*, Jossey-Bass, San Francisco.

Mezirow, J. (1991) *Transformative Dimensions of Adult Learning*, Jossey-Bass, San Francisco.

Mezirow, J. (1995) 'Transformation Theory Of Adult Learning', in *In Defense Of The Lifeworld*, Welton, M.R. (ed.) pp. 39–70, SUNY Press, New York.

Mezirow, J. (1997) 'Transformative Learning: Theory To Practice', in *Transformative Learning In Action: Insights From Practice. New Directions For Adult And Continuing Education*, No. 74, Cranton, P. (ed.) pp. 5–12, Jossey-Bass, San Francisco.

Miller, D., De Vries, M. and Toulouse, J. (1982) 'Top Executive Locus of Control', *Academy of Management Journal*, 25, pp. 237–53.

Misko, J. (2000a) *Getting to Grips With Self Paced Learning*, NCVER, Adelaide.

Misko, J. (2000b) *The Effects of Flexible Modes of Delivery*, NCVER, Adelaide.

Modra, H. (1989) 'Using Journals to Encourage Critical Thinking at a Distance', in Evans, T. and Nation, D. (eds) *Critical Reflections on Distance Education*, Falmer Press, London.

Morgan, G. (1986) *Images of Organisation*, Sage Publications, Beverley Hills.

Moy, J. and McDonald, R. (2000) *Analysing Enterprise Returns on Training*, NCVER, Adelaide.

Moy, J. (1999) *The Impact of Generic Competencies on Workplace Performance*, NCVER, Adelaide.

Mulcahy, D. (1996) 'Performing Competencies', *Australian and New Zealand Journal of Vocational Education Research*, 4, pp. 35–67.

Mulcahy, D. (2000) *Evaluating the Contribution of Competency Based Training*, Project No. 7030, NCVER, Adelaide.

NBEET (1996) *Lifelong Learning – Key Issues*, AGPS, Canberra.

NCVER (2000) *Survey of Employers' Views on Vocational Education and Training*, NCVER, Adelaide.

Newstead, S. (1996) 'The Psychology of Student Assessment', *The Psychologist*, 9, pp. 543–47.

Nottingham Andragogy Group (1983) *Towards a Developmental Theory of Andragogy*, Department of Adult Education, University of Nottingham.

NTUC (1996) Singapore National Trade Unions Congress, *Straight Times*, 14 Sept.

O'Connor, C. (1993) *The Handbook for Organisational Change*, McGraw Hill, New York.

OECD (1973) *Recurrent Education*, OECD, Paris.

OFTE (Office of Training and Further Education) (1998) *Benefits to Employers from an Investment in Training*, OFTE, Melbourne.

Ogilvie, E. (1974) 'Creativity and the Curriculum Structure', *Education Research*, 16, p. 2.

Oliver, R. and Omari, A. (1999) 'Using Online Technologies to Support Problem-Based Learning', *Australian Journal of Educational Technology*, 151, pp. 8–79.

Owens, W. (1953) 'Age and Mental Abilities: A Longitudinal Study', *Genetic Psychology Monograph*, 48, pp. 3–54.

Paine, N. (2000) 'Anywhere–Anytime Computing', Paper given at ANTA National Congress, Melbourne, July.

Pear, J. and Novak, M. (1996) 'Computer-Aided Personalised System of Instruction', *Teaching of Psychology*, 23, pp. 119–23.

Pedler, M., Burgoyne, J. and Boydell, T. (1991) *The Learning Company*, McGraw Hill, London.

Peters, J. (1991) 'Strategies For Reflective Practice', in Petraglia, R. (ed.) *Professional Development for Educators of Adults, New Directions for Adult and Continuing Education*, No. 51.

Petraglia, R. (ed.) (1998) 'Professional Development for Educators of Adults', *New Directions for Adult and Continuing Education*, No. 51.

Phillips, R. (1996) *Developers' Guide to Interactive Multimedia*, Curtin University, Perth.

Pickersgill, R. (1996) *Who is Using the Competency Standards for Assessment?* Survey of the Purchasers of the Competency Standards For Assessment, Clovelly, NSW: CSB — Assessors and Workplace Trainers (ISBN 0 646 291 262).

Podeschi, R. (1990) 'Teaching their Own: Minority Challenges to Mainstream Institutions', in Ross-Gordon, J. M., Martin, L. G. and Briscoe, D. (eds) *Serving Culturally Diverse Populations*, Jossey-Bass, San Francisco.

Poell, R. and Chivers, G. (1999) 'Consultant Roles in Different Types of Organisation', Paper to European Conference on Education Research, Lahti, Finland.

Porter, P., Rizv, F., Knight, J. and Lingard, R. (1992) 'Competencies for a Clever Country', *Unicorn*, 18, pp. 50–8.

Pratt, D. D. (1992) 'Chinese Conceptions of Learning and Teaching: A Westerner's Attempt at Understanding', *International Journal of Lifelong Education*, 11 (4), pp. 301–20.

Rees, T. and Bartlett, W. (1999) 'Models of Guidance Services in the Learning Society: The Case of the Netherlands', in Coffield, F. (ed.) *Why's the Beer up North Always Stronger? Studies of Lifelong Learning in Europe*, Policy Press, Bristol.

Reid, I. C. (1999) 'Beyond Models', *Journal of Asynchronous Learning Networks*, 3, 1–10.

Richardson, J. T. and King, E. (1997) 'Adult Students in Higher Education', *Teaching of Psychology*, 16, pp. 23–30.

Robinson, C. (1999) *New Directions in Australia's Skill Formation: Lifelong Learning is the Key*, NCVER, Adelaide.

Robinson, C. (1999b) 'Promoting a Training Culture in Industry', in *Lifelong Learning: Developing a Training Culture*, Robinson, C. and Arthy, K. (eds), NCVER, Adelaide.

Robinson, P., Calvert, J. and Peoples, K. (1997) *From Desk to Disc*, ANTA, Brisbane.

Rogers, C. (1951) *Client-Centred Therapy*, Houghton Mifflin, Boston.

Rogers, C. (1969) *Freedom to Learn*, Merrill, Columbus.

Rohfeld, R. W. and Hiemstra, R. (1995) 'Moderating Discussions in the Electronic Classroom', in Berge, Z. L. and Collins, M. P. (eds) *Computer Mediated Communication and the Online Classroom*, Vol. 3, pp. 91–104, Hampton Press, Cresskill, NJ.

Ross-Gordon, J. M. (1991) 'Needed: A Multicultural Perspective for Adult Education Research', *Adult Education Quarterly*, 42 (1), 1–16.

Roux-Salembien, D., McDowell, D. and Cornford, I. (1996) 'Teachers' Perceptions of the Introduction of Competency-based Training in NSW TAFE Commercial Cookery', in *Conference Papers, Learning & Work: The Challenges*, Vol. 3, pp. 95–105, Centre for Learning and Work Research, Griffith University.

Rowland, F., and Volet, S. (1996) 'Self-direction in Community Learning: A Case Study', *Australian Journal of Adult and Community Education*, 36, pp. 89–102.

Ruberg, L., Taylor, C. and Moore, D. (1996) 'Student Participation and Interaction Online', *International Journal of Educational Telecommunications*, 21, pp. 69–92.

Ryan, R. (1997) 'Does Australia need CBT?', *Australian Training Review*, 23 (June-August), pp. 21–5.

Ryan, R. (1999) 'From Recurrent Education to Lifelong Learning', Paper at Delors Report Seminar, Finders University, Adelaide.

Salovey, P. and Mayer, J. (1997) *Emotional Development and Emotional Intelligence*, Jossey Bass, San Fransisco.

Salthouse, T. and Somberg, B. (1982) 'Skilled Performance', *Journal of Experimental Psychology*, 111, pp. 176–207.

Savicevic, D. M. (1991) 'Modern Conceptions of Andragogy: A European Framework', *Studies in the Education of Adults*, 23 (2), pp. 179–201.

Schon, D. (1988) *Educating The Reflective Practitioner*, Jossey-Bass, San Francisco.

Schueler, J. (1999) 'Older People in VET', in Smith, A. (ed.) *Creating a Future*, NCVER, Adelaide.

Schweiger, D. and De Nisi, A. (1991) 'Communication with Employees Following a Merger', *Academy of Management Journal*, 34 , pp. 110–35.

Scott, S. M. (1997) 'The Grieving Soul in the Transformation Process', in *Transformative Learning in Action: Insights from Practice. New Directions for Adult and Continuing Education*, No. 74, Cranton, P. (ed.), pp. 41–50, Jossey-Bass, San Francisco.

Senge, P, (1990) *The Fifth discipline: The Art and Practice of the Learning Organisation*, Doubleday, New York.

Senge, P., Roberts, C., Ross, R. B., Smith, B. J., Kleiner, A.and Brierley, N. (1994) *The Learning Company: a Strategy for Sustainable Development, The Fifth Discipline Fieldbook: Strategies and Tools for Building a Learning Organization*, Doubleday, New York.

Sennett, R. (1998) *The Corrosion of Character: The Personal Consequences of Work in the New Capitalism*, W. W. Norton, New York.

Sherron, G. T. and Boettcher, J. V. (1997) 'Distance Learning', CAUSE Professional Series Papers, No. 17.

Simons, M. (1996) 'Something Old, Something New: TAFE Teachers' Ways of Working with CBT', in *Conference Papers, Learning & Work: The Challenges*, Vol. 3, pp. 23–31, Centre for Learning and Work Research: Griffith University.

Singh, P. B. (1994) *The Relationship between Group Empowerment and Self-Directed Learning in Small Groups in Michigan*, Unpublished Ph.D. thesis, Michigan State University.

Skinner, B. (1968) *Science and Human Behaviour*, Macmillan, New York.

Skinner, B. (1971) *Beyond Freedom and Dignity*, Knopf, New York.

Slaski, M. (2001) 'Emotional Intelligence in Organisations', *Autumn News*, 4, pp. 10–18.

Smith, A. (ed.) (1999) *Creating a Future*, NCVER, Adelaide.

Smith, A. and Hayton, G. (1999) 'What Drives Enterprise Training?' *International Journal of Human Resource Management*, 2, pp. 251–72.

Smith, E., Hill, D., Smith, A., Perry, P., Roberts, P., and Bush, T. (1995) *The Availability of Competency-based Training in TAFE and Non-TAFE Settings in 1994*, DEET, AGPS, Canberra.

Smith, J. E., Castle, J. (1992) 'Experiential Learning for Critical Thinking: A Viable Prospect for South Africa?', *International Journal of Lifelong Education*, 11 (3), 191–8.

Smith, R. M. (ed.) (1990) *Learning to Learn Across the Lifespan*, Jossey-Bass, San Francisco.

Snow, R.E. (1980) 'Intelligence for the Year 2001', *Intelligence*, 4, pp. 198–9.

Spearman, C. (1927) *The Abilities of Man*, Macmillan, New York.

Spector, P. (1986) 'Perceived Control by Employees', *Human Relations*, 11, pp. 1005–16.

Standards for Professions, National Office of Overseas Skills Recognition Research Paper No. 7, DEET, AGPS, Canberra.

Stasz, C. (1996) 'Workplace Skills in Practice: Understanding the New Basic Skills', Keynote address at the 4th Annual International Conference on Post-Compulsory Education and Training: Learning & Work: The Challenges, Centre for Learning and Work Research, Griffith University.

Steedman, H. (1994) 'Assessment, Certification and Recognition of Occupational Skills and Competences', *European Journal of Vocational Training*, 1, pp. 36–42.

Sternberg, R. and Lubert, T. (1995) *Defying the Crowd*, Free Press, New York.

Sternberg, R. (1997) *Successful Intelligence*, Plume, New York.

Sternberg, R. J. (1985) *Beyond IQ*, Cambridge University Press, Cambridge.

Stevenson, J. (1995) 'The Political Colonisation of the Cognitive Construction of Competence', *Journal of Vocational Education and Training*, 47, pp. 353–64.

Stevenson, J. (ed.) (1994) *Cognition at Work: The Development of Vocational Expertise*, NCVER, Adelaide.

Sulla, N. (1999) 'Technology: To Use Or Infuse', *The Technology Source: Commentary*, February.

Taylor, E. W. (1998) 'The Theory And Practice Of Transformative Learning: A Critical Review', *Information Series No. 374*, ERIC Clearinghouse On Adult, Career and Vocational Education, Center On Education And Training For Employment, College Of Education, Ohio State University, Columbus.

Tegart, G., Johnston, R and Sheehan, P. (1998) 'Academic Study — Interim Report', in Sheehan, P. and Tegart, G. (eds) *Working For the Future*, Victoria University Press, Melbourne.

Tennant, M. (1988) *Psychology and Adult Learning*, Routledge, London.

Terkel, S. (1975) *Working*, Penguin, Harmondsworth.

Terman, L. and Oden, M. (1959) *The Gifted Group at Mid Life*, Stanford University Press, Stanford.

Thorndike, E. (1928) *Adult Learning*, Macmillan, New York.

Thurston, L. L. (1938) 'Primary Mental Abilities', *Psychometric Monographs*, 1.

Tight, M. (1998) 'Lifelong Learning: Opportunity or Compulsion?', *British Journal of Educational Studies*, 46, 3, pp. 251–63.

Toffler, A. (1980) *The Third Wave*, Collins, London.

Tough, A. (1968) *The Adults Learning Projects*, Ontario Institute for Studies in Education, Toronto.

Towers, John (1996) 'European Foreword', in Longworth, N. and Davies, W. K., *Lifelong Learning*, Kogan Page, London.

Tuijnman, A. and van der Kamp, M. (eds) (1992) *Learning Across the Lifespan: Theories, Research, Policies*, Pergamon, Oxford.

UNESCO (1998) *Providing Lifelong Skill Training through an Integrated Education and Training System: The Australian Experience*, ANTA, Brisbane, Queensland.

Usher, R. S. and Bryant, I. (1989) *Adult Education as Theory, Practice and Research: The Captive Triangle*, Routledge, New York

Van Berkel, C. (1997) 'Does Australia need CBT?', *Australian Training Review*, 23 (June–August), pp. 21–5 & 35.

Van den Heuvel, A. and Wooden, M. (1999) *Casualisation and Outsourcing*, NCVER, Adelaide.

Vernon, P. (1979) *Intelligence: Heredity and Environment*, Freeman, New York.

Vetstats (1999) *Highlights for 1999*, NCVER, Adelaide.

Volkoff, V. (1999) 'The Vocational Essence of ACE', Project No. 7023, NCVER, Adelaide.

Vooglaid, Y.and Marja, T. (1992) 'Andragogical Problems of Building a Democratic Society', *International Journal of Lifelong Education*, 11 (4), pp. 321–28.

Waterhouse, P. (1998) *Review of Research: The Changing Nature and Patterns of Work and Implications for VET*. Project No. 7013, NCVER, Adelaide.

Waterhouse, P., Wilson, B. and Ewer, P. (1999) *The Changing Nature and Pattern of Work and Implications for VET*, NCVER, Adelaide.

Watson, A. (1993) 'Competency-based Vocational Education and Training in Australia: Some Unresolved Issues', *Australian and New Zealand Journal of Vocational Education Research*, 1, pp. 93–125.

Watson, A. (1994) 'Competency-based Education in Australia', *Australian and New Zealand Journal of Vocational Education Research*, 30, pp. 93–123.

Watson, L. (1999) 'Lifelong Learning for All', Paper presented to the 8th VET Training Research Conference, Toowoomba, Queensland.

Webb, G. (1999) 'The Economics of Online Delivery', Paper to Networking '99 Conference, Melbourne.

Wechsler, D. (1958) *The Measurement and Appraisal of Adult Intelligence*, William Wilkens, Baltimore.

Wertheimer, M. (1954) *Productive Thinking*, Harper, New York.

Wesnes, K. and Semple, J. (2001) Report in *The Psychologist*, 14 , 2, p.87.

Whitesel, C. (1998) 'Reframing our Classrooms, Reframing Ourselves: Perspectives from a Virtual Paladin', *The Technology Source: Vision*, April.

Wiesenberg, F. and Hutton, S. (1995) 'Teaching a Graduate Program using Computer Mediated Conferencing Software', Paper presented at the Annual Meeting of the American Association for Adult and Continuing Education, MO, Kansas City.

Wigdor, A. and Green, B. F. (1991) *Performance Assessment in the Workplace*, National Academy Press, Washington.

Winograd, E., Smith, A. D. and Simon, E. W. (1982) 'Aging and the Picture Superiority Effect in Recall', *Journal of Gerontology*, 37, pp. 70–5.

Wittrock, M. C. (1977) 'The Generative Processes of Memory', in Wittrock, M. C. (ed) *The Human Brain*, Prentice Hall, Englewood Cliffs.

Woodrow, H. (1927) 'The Effect of Type of Training Upon Transference', *Journal of Educational Psychology*, 18, pp. 159–72.

*Workforce 2000* (1999) Federal Labour Party Document, Prepared by Centre for Policy Studies, Monash University.

*Workforce 2010* (1999) Federal Labour Party Document, Prepared by Centre for Policy Studies, Monash University.

Yetton, P. and Forster, A. (1997) *Managing the Introduction of Technology in the Delivery and Administration of Higher Education*, Evaluations and Investigations Program, Higher Education Division, AGPS, Canberra.

Young, M., Spours, K., Howieson, C. and Raffe, D. (1997) 'Unifying Academic and Vocational Learning and the Idea of a Learning Society', *Journal of Education Policy*, 12, 6, pp. 527–37.

Zwahr, M. (1998) 'Cognitive Processes Used in Making Decisions about Medical Treatment', in Park, D. and Shifren, K. (eds) *Processing Medical Information in Ageing Patients*, Erlbaum, New Jersey.

## FURTHER READING/RESOURCES

Belsky, J. (1999) *The Psychology of Ageing*, Brooks Cole, Pacific Heights.

Booker, D. (2000) *Getting to Grips with Online Delivery*, NCVER, Adelaide.

Brody, N. (1992) *Intelligence*, Academic Press, London.

Carnoy, M. (1994) Technological Change and Education, *New Education*, 16, pp. 3–12.

Curtain, R. and Ormonde, H. (1994) 'Implementing Competency Based Training', *Asia Pacific Journal Of Human Resources*, 32, pp. 133–43.

Davison, T. (1994) 'Competency Based Training and Competence Based Assessment; Two Criticisms from a Practitioner', *Australian TAFE Teacher*, 28, pp. 33–43.

Easterby–Smith, M. (1990) 'Creating a Learning Organisation', *Personnel Review*, 19, pp. 24–8.

Evans, K. et al. (1990) 'The Changing Role of the In-company Trainer', *Comparative Education*, 26, pp. 142–58.

Field, L. (1990) *Skilling Australia*, Longman Cheshire, Melbourne.

Furnham, A. (1994) *Personality at Work*, Routledge, London.

Garland, M. (1994) 'The Adult Need for Personal Control Provides a Cogent Guiding Concept for Distance Education', *Journal of Distance Education*, 9, pp. 45–59.

Garrett, B. (1990) *Creating a Learning Environment*, Director Books, Cambridge.

Geiger, A. (1992) 'Measures for Mentoring', *Training and Development*, Feb.

Geiger, A. and Boyle, S. (1995) 'Mentoring: A Practitioner's Guide', *Training and Development*, 49, pp. 51–4.

Gonczi, A. (ed.) (1992) *Developing a Competent Workforce*, NCVER, Adelaide.

Hall, W. (1995) 'Understanding the Training Reform Agenda in 2500 Words', *Australian Training Review*, 14, pp. 6–9.

Hammond, M. and Collins, R. (1991) *Self Directed Learning: Critical Practice*, Nichols, New York.

Harper, B., Hedberg, J., Bennett, S. and Lockyer, L. (2000) *Review of Research: The Online Experience*, NCVER, Adelaide.

Houlden, J. and Houlden, W. (1999) *Best Practice in Online Delivery*, TAFE NSW Sydney.

International Council for Adult Education. (1994) 'Adult Education and Lifelong Learning', *Adult Education and Development*, 42, pp. 175–84.

Jensen, A. R. (1998) *The g Factor*, Prager, New York.

Kram, K. (1985) *Mentoring At Work*, Scott, Foresman and Co., Illinois.

Latchem, C. and Pritchard, T. (1994) 'Open Learning: The Unique Australian Option', *Open Learning*, 9, pp. 18–26.

Lemme, B. (1999) *Development in Adulthood*, Allyn and Bacon, Boston.

Lessem (1991) *Total Quality Learning*, Basil Blackwell, Oxford.

Levy, M. (1992) *Work Based Learning Project*, The Staff College, Bristol.

Masters, G. and McCurry, D. (1990) *Research Paper 2: Competency Based Assessment in the Professions*, AGPS, Canberra.

Morgan, A. (1993) *Improve Your Students' Learning*, Kogan Page, London.

Murray, M. and Owens, M. (1991) *Beyond the Myths and Magic of Mentoring*, Jossey Bass, San Fransisco.

Parker, L. and Parker, G. (1995) 'Leading your Organisation Through Strategic Change Management', *Australian Institute of Management Magazine*, April, pp. 9–11.

Piskurich, G. (1993) *Self Directed Learning*, Jossey Bass, San Fransisco.

Smith, A. (1992) *Training and Development in Australia*, Butterworths, Sydney.

Smith, R. (1983) 'Helping Adults Learn How to Learn', *New Directions For Contemporary Education*, 19, Jossey Bass, San Fransisco.

Sweet, R. (1994) 'Forging New Connections in the Workplace', *Australian TAFE Teacher*, 28, pp. 49–51.

*The Workplace in Education. First Yearbook of the Australian Council for Educational*

Watkins, K. (1991) *Facilitating Learning in the Workplace*, Deakin University Press, Geelong.

www.anta.gov.au/lifelong
www.ncver.edu.au
www. mentoring-resources.com/
http://avoca.vicnet.net.au/~cute/
http://www.jansol.com.au/products/research/default.asp
www.learnscope.anta.gov.au
www.ncver.edu.au.research/listdoc.html
www.ou.edu/ap/grad5990/pathfinders/self-directed_learning.html
http://nlu.nl.edu/ace/Resources/Documents/Freireissues.html
http://Ericacve.Org/Docs/Hopey/04.pdf

# INDEX

snowballing, 272
social learning theory, 133-135
Spearman, 150, 152, 162
S-R theory *see* behaviourist theory
Sternberg, 153-155, 164
student-centred group learning, 266-272

TAFE, 50
  competency-based training, 59, 60, 61, 63, 76
  employment outcomes after training, 322
  lifelong education policy, 39
  online learning, 290, 291, 294
  on-the-job training, 323, 324
  Open Learning programs, 36, 290
  self-paced learning, 276
Taylorism, 7, 199, 212
teacher-centred learning methods, 265-266
teachers/trainers, 324-328
  andragogical model, 232, 236
  competency standards, 58, 316
  consultation outside class, 327
  online education, 297
  organisation of course, 327-328
  pedagogical model, 236
  reflective practice, 328-336
  role, 226, 236, 240, 250, 315-316, 325
  self-concept, 213-215, 325-327
  TAFE teacher, 325
  transformative learning, 250
  workplace trainer, 315-316, 319, 325
technological change, 6-9, 73
  education, effect on, 8
  mentoring, 287
  online learning, 289-304
  organisational structure, impact on, 11-16
  work patterns, impact on, 7-8, 11-16, 34, 73
  work-related education, 22-29
telementoring, 287
thrivability, 20
training and learning compared, 95-96
training packages
  Assessment and Workplace Training
  Package, 316, 317
  competency standards for trainers, 316
  nationally endorsed, 47, 51
transfer of training, 130-132
transformative learning, 247-251
tutorials, 266

UNESCO
  International Commission on Development
  of Education, 38
  lifelong learning ideal, 41, 44, 45, 76, 225

virtual learning *see* online learning
virtual office, 14
Vocational Education and Training (VET)
  ACE involvement, 107
  employment outcomes after training, 322
  equity and funding issues, 64-67
  Framework for National Collaboration, 321
  lifelong learning approach, 37, 40, 47, 52, 107
  outcomes, 322-323
  participant statistics, 263, 318, 334, 335
  reasons for enrolling, 330-331
  training culture, 319

Wertheimer, 127
work-home balance, 18, 19
workplace changes, 9, 11-16, 24, 32
  globalisation, 3-4, 34, 73
  learning needs, change in, 15, 24
  management, 19, 32
  role of workers, 12-13
workplace-relevant education, 22-29
workplace training
  assessment methods, 336-341
  community competence as goal, 227
  competency-based *see* competency-based
  training
  competency standards for trainers, 58, 316
  generic skills, 24-28, 320-321
  informal training, 316
  in-house, 323-324
  learning organisation *see* learning organisation
  managerial training, 341-342
  mentoring, 285-289, 317
  on-the-job, 323-324
  organisational training models, 306-312
  organising, 323-324
  reconceptualising, 314-320
  responsibility for, 312-314
  returns on investment, 321-323
  role of trainer, 315-316, 319, 325
  small business, 318
  VET outcomes, 322-323
workshops, 269-270